The genesis of the French Revolution

A global-historical interpretation

BAILEY STONE

University of Houston

CAMBRIDGE
UNIVERSITY PRESS

Published by the Press Syndicate of the University of Cambridge
The Pitt Building, Trumpington Street, Cambridge CB2 1RP
40 West 20th Street, New York, NY 10011-4211, USA
10 Stamford Road, Oakleigh, Melbourne 3166, Australia

© Cambridge University Press 1994

First published 1994

Printed in the United States of America

Library of Congress Cataloging-in-Publication Data
Stone, Bailey, 1946–
The genesis of the French Revolution : global-historical
interpretation / Bailey Stone.
p. cm.
Includes index.
ISBN 0-521-44556-6. – ISBN 0-521-44570-1 (pbk.)
1. France – History – Revolution, 1789–1799 – Causes. 2. France –
History – Revolution, 1789–1799 – Influence. 3. Enlightenment.
4. World politics – To 1900.
DC138.S76   1993
944.04 – dc20   93–1002
CIP

A catalog record for this book is available from the British Library.

ISBN 0-521-44556-6 hardback
ISBN 0-521-44570-1 paperback

This book offers a unique synthesis of the long- and short-term causes of the French Revolution. Instead of focusing exclusively on developments within France, it places the country, and its revolution, within an international setting from the start. This book argues that the French Revolution stemmed from the prerevolutionary state's converging failures in international and domestic affairs; the monarchy failed not only to remain in touch with changing social, intellectual, and political realities at home but also to harness its citizens' ambitions and talents to the purpose of maintaining France's international power and prestige. This analysis also provides a key to comprehending the course of events in revolutionary and postrevolutionary France – and an insight into why revolutionary movements broke out in the former USSR and surrounding countries.

The genesis of the French Revolution

Contents

Acknowledgments

My gratitude must first be directed toward all those in the field of old regime and French revolutionary studies whose assiduous labors have made it possible for me to construct this massive synthesis. Whether they can or cannot endorse my arguments, I hope that they will see in my custom of quoting extensively from their writings one arresting indication of my indebtedness to their inquiries into the French past.

I should also acknowledge, in a more specific fashion, the encouragement I have received from certain colleagues in the profession since embarking on this project seven years ago. Thanks go in particular to Professors Robert Darnton, Albert N. Hamscher, Patrice Higonnet, A. Lloyd Moote, Robert R. Palmer, Harold T. Parker, and Dale Van Kley in the United States, and to Mme Jean Egret in France.

Recognition is due as well to the administration of the University of Houston and to my associates in the university's Department of History. A Faculty Development Leave Grant from the university administration made it possible for me to spend the 1988–89 academic year reading and writing (and making the belated acquaintance of word processing). My colleagues in the History Department's research colloquium have offered critical and therefore valuable reactions to many of the ideas taken up in this book.

I am grateful as well to Frank Smith, Executive Editor for Social Sciences at Cambridge University Press in New York City; to his editorial colleagues; and to the anonymous readers of my manuscript for their roles in its acceptance and preparation for publication.

Finally – but by no means of smallest account – much is also owed to several special individuals in the private corridors of my life. They know who they are.

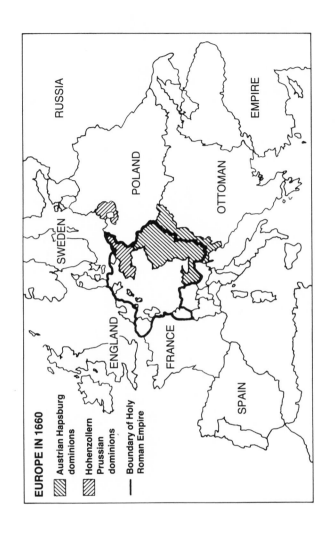

EUROPE IN 1660

Austrian Hapsburg dominions

Hohenzollern Prussian dominions

Boundary of Holy Roman Empire

RUSSIA

SWEDEN

POLAND

ENGLAND

OTTOMAN

EMPIRE

FRANCE

SPAIN

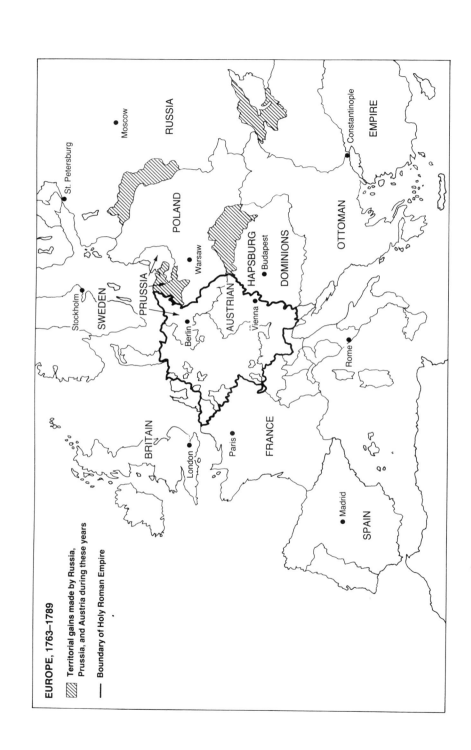

EUROPE, 1763–1789

▨ Territorial gains made by Russia,
   Prussia, and Austria during these years

— Boundary of Holy Roman Empire

RUSSIA

Moscow

St. Petersburg

POLAND

Warsaw

SWEDEN

Stockholm

PRUSSIA

Berlin

HAPSBURG

Budapest

AUSTRIAN

Vienna

DOMINIONS

OTTOMAN

EMPIRE

Constantinople

Rome

BRITAIN

London

Paris

FRANCE

SPAIN

Madrid

Introduction

~~~~~~

Two hundred years have passed since the French fell into their momentous revolution. Over the intervening period the origins of that upheaval have given rise to a contentious and rich historiography. This book, drawing upon that historiography as well as other scholarship, will develop an interpretation of the French Revolution's genesis that political sociologists might see as a species of "modified structuralism" but which historians might be likelier to describe as "global-historical." However it may be characterized, this interpretation will focus primarily upon the state rather than the society of old regime France and in particular on that state's converging failures in foreign (or geopolitical) and domestic (or socio-political) affairs.

Because, however, this study relies heavily on the writings of historians (and, to a lesser degree, of political sociologists), we need first of all to situate it within its proper scholarly context. To do so can help us to define various issues whose consideration will be central to a fully de-veloped global-historical perspective of the Revolution's causes. We can then elaborate on the organization and substance of the argument to follow and explicate the philosophical assumptions underlying that argument.

The American political sociologist Theda Skocpol has grouped explana-tions of major sociopolitical revolutions under the headings "voluntar-ism" and "structuralism." By citing under these rubrics the chief explanations advanced for the onset of revolution in France, we can establish a frame of historiographical reference and define the core ele-ments of a global-historical perspective.

Skocpol has outlined the archetypical voluntarist rendering of revo-lutionary causation as follows:

First, changes in social systems or societies give rise to grievances, social dis-orientation, or new class or group interests and potentials for collective mobili-

1

zation. Then there develops a purposive, mass-based movement – coalescing with the aid of ideology and organization – that consciously undertakes to overthrow the existing government and perhaps the entire social order. Finally, the revolutionary movement fights it out with the authorities or dominant class and, if it wins, undertakes to establish its own ... program.[1]

This kind of interpretation, then, assumes the presence, in the "old regime" in question, of a potentially revolutionary "movement informed or guided by purpose," the existence of "a deliberate effort – an effort tying together leaders and followers that is aimed at overthrowing the existing political or social order."[2]

And what of the structuralist approach to the causes of revolution? Here, according to Skocpol, the prerevolutionary state, in its relations with competing states as well as with groups in its own domestic society, is the key actor, rather than any "purposive movement" arising out of old regime society.

The state properly conceived is no mere arena in which socioeconomic struggles are fought out. It is, rather, a set of administrative, policing, and military organizations headed, and more or less well coordinated by, an executive authority. Any state first and fundamentally extracts resources from society and deploys these to create and support coercive and administrative organizations.[3]

Thus, the prerevolutionary state (like its revolutionary and postrevolutionary successors) is "potentially autonomous from (though of course conditioned by) socioeconomic interests and structures." Rather than being an instrument of "economically-dominant groups to pursue world-market oriented development at home and international economic advantages abroad," the archetypical old regime state is at bottom "geared to maintain control of home territories and populations and to undertake actual or potential military competition with other states in the international system."[4] Consequently a structuralist explanation of the gestation of revolution pivots on the prerevolutionary state's growing inability to compete successfully with other "potentially autonomous" states in the contemporaneous international state system and to harmonize its relations with prominent elements in its "home" society. The resultant collapse of that state paves the way for an unprecedented transformation of the political and social ancien régime.

Theory and terminology aside, the historian of revolution here is confronting one of the most challenging philosophical issues imaginable: the question of whether unempowered persons can and do "make" their own

1 Theda Skocpol, *States and Social Revolutions: A Comparative Analysis of France, Russia, and China* (Cambridge: Cambridge University Press, 1979), p. 14.
2 Ibid., pp. 14–15.
3 Ibid., p. 29.
4 Ibid., pp. 14, 22.

revolutions or whether, in the final analysis, it is bureaucratic "states," pursuing their own impersonal goals, that make revolutions possible. This is an issue to which we shall return before concluding our inquiry into the genesis of the Revolution of 1789. At this particular juncture, however, a few words are in order concerning major voluntarist and structuralist exegeses of the coming of revolution to Bourbon France – and concerning major criticisms leveled against those perspectives.

It stands to reason that voluntarist renderings of revolutionary causation, with their stress on the roles of groups and individuals outside the secretive chambers of power, would have arisen primarily in the realms of social and intellectual history – and this has indeed been the case. Among the social theorists of revolution, for example, we should cite those of a Marxian (or, as some French revisionists would say, a Jacobin) persuasion, as well as several social historians of an anti-Marxian bent. Marxian-Jacobin scholars of illustrious reputation from Jean Jaurès, Albert Mathiez, and Georges Lefebvre to Albert Soboul and Claude Mazauric, over the years have identified as initiators and protagonists of revolution in late eighteenth-century France economically progressive or "capitalist" bourgeois. These individuals, coveting both a greater measure of social recognition and a more influential role in public affairs, and profiting from the support of humble cityfolk and peasantry, supposedly won out in the Revolution over their age-old antagonists in the economically retrograde, or feudal, nobility *and* over an absolutist monarchy bankrupt in its finances, inefficient in its bureaucratic procedures, and antiquated in its vision of society.[5]

Other specialists in the field, rejecting a Marxian approach but not a voluntarist and social orientation, have included Alfred Cobban, Denis Richet, and Colin Lucas. British historian Alfred Cobban, essentially turning the Marxian-Jacobin paradigm on its head by emphasizing the anticapitalist aspects of the Revolution, held that "the revolutionary bourgeoisie was primarily the declining class of *officiers* and the lawyers and other professional men, and not the businessmen of commerce and industry."[6] French revisionist Denis Richet maintained that a vanguard of "notables" issuing from clergy, nobility, and Third Estate and displaying education, talent, landed wealth, and political ambition in abundance, seized power in 1789 and subsequent years. Theirs was a *révolution des lumières*, a "revolution of enlightened notables," helped along, ad-

---

5 The classic statement of this thesis remains Georges Lefebvre, *The Coming of the French Revolution*, trans. Robert R. Palmer (Princeton, N.J.: Princeton University Press, 1947).
6 Alfred Cobban, *The Social Interpretation of the French Revolution* (Oxford: Oxford University Press, 1964), p. 67.

mittedly, by terrible short-term economic conditions that provided these respectable Frenchmen with formidable allies from the laboring masses.[7] Finally, Alfred Cobban's fellow Briton Colin Lucas accepted the revisionist notion of a prerevolutionary elite drawing its propertied luminaries from all three estates, but pointed also to "stress zones" within that elite characterized by rising tensions over a variety of divisive social issues, and in particular the issue of competition for advancement in elite French society. When, in 1788–89, a specific series of events threatened to split the increasingly homogeneous elite of noble and bourgeois proprietors permanently along anachronistic lines, the result, according to Lucas, was "a revolt against a loss of status by the central and lower sections of the elite with the approval of those elements of the trading groups which were on the threshold of the elite. It was this social group that became the 'revolutionary bourgeoisie.' "[8]

What all of these analyses, Marxian and non-Marxian, reveal in common is a voluntarist stress on the role played by unenfranchised groups and individuals at the onset of revolution. Indeed, the very language they employ sometimes indicates this explicitly. Thus, Richet's *lumières* in 1789 displayed an "awareness, first, of their autonomy vis-à-vis the political order and, second, of the inevitability of their seizure of state power."[9] And Lucas strikingly attested his voluntarist faith by speaking of social friction within elite society "eventually sparking off a revolutionary conflagration," and of "a contraction [in the channels of] social promotion leading to social conflict."[10] Nor would it be very difficult to adduce examples of Lefebvre and Soboul exalting an entrepreneurial bourgeoisie carrying all (or at least much) before it in revolutionary France, and of Cobban doting in similar fashion upon his alternative vanguard of languishing *officiers* and "lawyers and other professional men."

But the question for us has to be: Do any of these interpretations satisfactorily explain why France fell into revolution in 1789? No fairminded person would deny that the long-regnant explanatory paradigm associated with Lefebvre, Soboul, and their successors has made an enormous contribution to our understanding of the upheaval in France. Similarly, no fair-minded individual could fail to see much of value in Cobban's assault on the orthodox school's misuse of such terms as feu-

7 Denis Richet, "Autour des origines idéologiques lointaines de la Révolution française: Elites et despotisme," *Annales: E.S.C.* 24 (1969), pp. 1–23. See also his earlier book coauthored with François Furet, *La Révolution française*, 2 vols. (Paris: Hachette, 1965).
8 Colin Lucas, "Nobles, Bourgeois, and the Origins of the French Revolution," *Past and Present* 60 (1973), esp. pp. 86, 103, and 124–25.
9 Richet, "Autour des origines idéologiques," p. 23.
10 Lucas, "Nobles, Bourgeois, and the Origins of the French Revolution," p. 103.

dalism and capitalism as applied to prerevolutionary France. Again, there would seem to be a growing scholarly consensus that revisionists like Richet and Lucas have furnished us with the most impressive conceptualization to date of social dynamics in eighteenth-century France and with an unprecedentedly sophisticated portrayal of the men who emerged in the crisis of the late 1780s as full-blown revolutionaries. Nonetheless, the last thirty years or so have brought telling criticisms of all attempts by voluntarists laboring in the vineyards of social history to account for the maelstrom of 1789 in France.

Of course, many revisionists cut their teeth upon the troubling aspects of the Marxian-Jacobin thesis.[11] They have pointed out that there was no automatic correlation between economic and social roles in the ancien régime: There were more noncapitalist than capitalist bourgeois, and there were businessminded as well as nonentrepreneurial nobles. They have also demonstrated the oversimplicity of the notion of sequential class insurgencies inaugurating revolutionary change in France in the late 1780s. The so-called aristocratic revolution of 1787–88 involved opposition to the government in *all* ranks of society, and in 1788–89 the "revolutionary bourgeoisie" found some of its most articulate tribunes among the progressive clergy and nobility. Revisionists have shown, furthermore, that the assemblies and committees of the revolutionary era drew their members primarily from the economically conservative worlds of bureaucracy and the law rather than from the dynamic marches of capitalism. (Indeed, those circles in France that were profit oriented were actually decimated by the proscriptions of the sanguinary 1790s.) Finally, and perhaps most devastatingly, economic historians like Britain's Roger Price and P. M. Jones have argued convincingly that the economic old regime in France actually outlasted the sociopolitical old regime by a half century or more.[12] There could be, in other words, no cogent demonstration in the French case of systemic sociopolitical change grounded in transformative *economic* change.

But if revisionism has shattered the edifice of the old socioeconomic theory of revolutionary causation, it has yet to raise a durable structure in its place. Thus, British historian William Doyle, by carefully documenting the appreciation in market value of the majority of judicial, administrative, and fiscal offices during the years leading up to the explosion of 1789, has invalidated Cobban's hypothesis regarding "declin-

---

11 For the most thorough review of the critical literature on the Marxist school of thought, consult the initial, historiographical section of William Doyle, *Origins of the French Revolution* (Oxford: Oxford University Press, 1980).

12 See Roger Price, *The Economic Modernisation of France (1730–1880)* (London: C. Helm, 1975); and P. M. Jones, *The Peasantry in the French Revolution* (Cambridge: Cambridge University Press, 1988).

ing" *officiers* as protagonists of revolution in France.[13] Again, Richet, for
all his postulation of an elite of propertied, ambitious *lumières* leading
France into revolution in 1789, had to allow that in the crucible of events
of that year the members of that elite abruptly fell out over what he called
the "problem of privilege" – that is, what economic and social prerogatives to preserve, curtail, or abolish altogether.[14] And in the very year
(1973) that Lucas's rendering of the Revolution's social origins appeared,
three prominent American sociologists published findings inimical to *his*
thesis. They reported that, on the basis of a quantitative study of a huge
number of Third Estate *cahiers de doléances*, or grievance lists, drawn
up prior to the convening of the Estates General in 1789, they could
dismiss the "common claim that the bourgeoisie in eighteenth-century
France was led to revolutionary action by the frustration of being denied
access to noble status."

Indeed, insofar as there was any correlation between the denial of elite
status to bourgeois in the old regime and bourgeois radicalism in the
bailliages (electoral districts) of 1789, it was negative rather than positive:
Regardless of the gauge of "radicalism" employed, these scholars concluded, "the Third Estate in those *bailliages* with any ennoblement opportunities was *more* radical than the Third Estate in *bailliages* with no
such opportunities."[15] Moreover, as we noted, it appears that the majority
of venal offices – purchased or inherited by bourgeois for the most part
– were actually increasing rather than decreasing in value before the Revolution. Hence, the stress zones within the prerevolutionary elite so
significant in Lucas's scenario for their generation of revolutionary social
discontents may not have been so very stressful after all.

Thus for the accomplishments – and limitations – of voluntarist social
history. But what of the voluntarist practitioners of intellectual history?
Have they been able to argue, more persuasively, that the philosophes,
striving in the eighteenth century to disseminate the gospel of Enlightenment, induced cataclysmic change in France?

To do them justice, they have not as a rule tried to forge such a direct
link between a great movement of ideas whose influence is for all ages
and the specific events that convulsed France during 1789–99. Certainly
this was the judicious message of Daniel Mornet sixty years ago. Mornet
was careful not to go beyond the assertion that, in the course of the
eighteenth century, the deductive reasoning that underpinned the old
regime, the willingness to accept what was old for antiquity's sake, to

13 William Doyle, "The Price of Offices in Pre-Revolutionary France," *Historical Journal*
27 (1984), pp. 831–60.
14 Richet, "Autour des origines idéologiques," p. 23.
15 Gilbert Shapiro, John Markoff, and Sasha R. Weitman, "Quantitative Studies of the
French Revolution," *History and Theory* 12 (1973), pp. 186–87.

internalize unquestioningly the dictates of church, aristocracy, and state, was slowly replaced by a new spirit of inquiry, by an inductive way of thinking that tended to judge social and political institutions according to utilitarian criteria. The Revolution, he conceded, broke out for political reasons that only indirectly reflected intellectual change.[16]

In more recent times, Mornet's legatees have attempted to demonstrate significant intellectual or ideological antecedents to the Revolution while still observing his canons of caution. American scholar Robert Darnton, for example, has accentuated the role played by Grub Street publicists and would-be philosophes in preparing the way for sociopolitical upheaval in France.[17] Countryman Keith Baker has posited the need "to reconstitute the political culture within which the creation of the revolutionary language of 1789 became possible."[18] Yet another specialist in the United States, Patrice Higonnet, has maintained that the Revolution "was in large part the political consequence" of a cleavage in prerevolutionary France between a "communitarian" or corporate ethos and the "new rationalistic, optimistic, individuating message of the Enlightenment."[19] Meanwhile, in France, Roger Chartier has been assiduously seeking out the Revolution's "cultural origins."[20] And various bicentennial symposia staged over the past few years have revealed that Chartier has impressive company in his continuing attempt to explain revolutionary causation from an ideological or cultural point of view.[21]

Still, however heroic and insightful these efforts to deal with the intellectual roots of the French Revolution, they have been paralleled by an historiography that has stressed the breach rather than the continuity between the old regime's elegant *soirées* and the Revolution's elemental *journées*. American scholars have led the way in this respect. George V. Taylor's analysis of bourgeois *cahiers de doléances* of 1789 yielded little indication of an Enlightenment ideology motivating commoners to anticipate and work for radical change. True, the men who drafted grievance

---

16 Daniel Mornet, *Les Origines intellectuelles de la Révolution française 1715–1787* (Paris: Colin, 1933).

17 See especially the collected essays in Robert Darnton, *The Literary Underground of the Old Regime* (Cambridge, Mass.: Harvard University Press, 1982).

18 Keith Baker, "On the Problem of the Ideological Origins of the French Revolution," in Dominick LaCapra and Steven L. Kaplan, eds., *Modern European Intellectual History* (Ithaca, N.Y.: Cornell University Press, 1982).

19 Patrice Higonnet, *Sister Republics: The Origins of French and American Republicanism* (Cambridge, Mass.: Harvard University Press, 1988), p. 121.

20 Roger Chartier, *The Cultural Origins of the French Revolution*, trans. Lydia G. Cochrane (Durham, N.C.: Duke University Press, 1991).

21 For the scholarship presented at one of the most notable of these symposia, see Keith M. Baker, ed., *The French Revolution and the Creation of Modern Political Culture*, Vol. 1: *The Political Culture of the Old Regime* (Oxford: Pergamon, 1987).

lists and voted for (or ran as) candidates for seats in the upcoming Estates
General "were ready for a general constitutional overhaul," but "few of
them needed the ideas of the Enlightenment to tell them why that overhaul
was desirable, for the doctrine of a historic constitution, the fundamental
laws that were to be rediscovered and restored, met the needs of those
who called for serious political change."[22] Carolyn Lougee's review of
several books treating aspects of eighteenth-century and revolutionary
France led her to ruminate about "an Enlightenment which was more
reformist (and even religious) than radical, accommodating rather than
subverting the existing order, and a Revolution which discarded rather
than embodied the intellectual compromises of the Enlightenment."[23]

William H. Sewell, Jr., in a stimulating critique of Theda Skocpol's
structuralist exegesis of revolutionary causation, contended at one point
that "ideology plays a crucial role in revolutions, both as cause and as
outcome" – yet, strikingly, he conceded at another point that there was
"no reason to believe" that the "ideological contradiction" he perceived
at the heart of the old regime French state "weakened the state or hastened
its fall." The Bourbon government, after all, "was thrown into crisis by
impending bankruptcy, not by its split ideological personality."[24] And
Thomas E. Kaiser, in a lengthy historiographical essay upon the subject,
has divined no fewer than three problems in one. First, he has observed,
the sociopolitical conservatism of the preponderant majority of philosophes is undeniable; second, there remains no consensus among experts
on "the extent and the nature of the impact of the Enlightenment" on
government and society in the ancien régime; and third, there is not even
fundamental agreement on "how to define the Enlightenment" itself![25]

The fact that skepticism about the linkage between the Enlightenment
and the maelstrom of 1789–99 in France is hardly limited to American
specialists – it is shared, for example, by a number of scholars in Germany
– only underscores the problematic nature of the literature on the Revolution's intellectual origins.[26]

If, then, analysts employing a voluntarist approach have encountered
difficulties in postulating various social "vanguards" – and have never

22 George V. Taylor, "Revolutionary and Nonrevolutionary Content in the *Cahiers* of
   1789: An Interim Report," *French Historical Studies* 7 (1972), p. 501.
23 Carolyn Lougee, "The Enlightenment and the French Revolution: Some Recent Perspectives," *Eighteenth-Century Studies* 11 (1977), p. 102.
24 William H. Sewell, Jr., "Ideologies and Social Revolutions: Reflections on the French
   Case," *Journal of Modern History* 57 (1985), pp. 84, 66, 66–67.
25 Thomas E. Kaiser, "This Strange Offspring of *Philosophie*: Recent Historiographical
   Problems in Relating the Enlightenment to the French Revolution," *French Historical
   Studies* 15 (1988), pp. 560–61.
26 See Jeremy Popkin, "Recent West German Work on the French Revolution," *Journal
   of Modern History* 59 (1987), pp. 737–50.

quite posited alienated philosophes – as purposive instigators of revolution
in late eighteenth-century France, have structuralists enjoyed any greater
success by focusing (more or less) on the prerevolutionary state itself, in
its international and domestic contexts? We can address this question very
briefly by touching on the chief arguments in this genre as well as on the
interpretive problems they raise. We place special emphasis here on Theda
Skocpol's work, both because we have derived from it our distinction
between voluntarism and structuralism and because, as a political sociologist, Skocpol has not invariably attracted the notice of historians re-
viewing the literature on the Revolution's origins.[27]

A number of authorities on the period have employed at least some
elements of what we have defined here as a structuralist perspective. As
far back as the late 1950s and early 1960s, the American Robert R. Palmer
and the French scholar Jacques Godechot broke some important ground
in this direction by placing the Revolution (and to some extent its origins
as well) in an international, "trans-Atlantic" setting.[28] Soon thereafter,
George Taylor, concentrating on domestic rather than international politics, declared roundly that France had experienced "a political revolution
with social consequences and not a social revolution with political consequences." For Taylor, the drama of 1789 stemmed from a fateful but
largely fortuitous conjuncture of short-term factors: state bankruptcy,
the "apprehensions of the taxable groups and creditors of the state," the
"hopes and ambitions of the professional classes," and the "slogans,
myths, and images generated by the struggle" against the now-paralyzed
crown.[29]

At about the same time, the British historian C. B. A. Behrens was
returning to the geopolitical theme. She reexamined the patterns of
chronic Anglo-French conflict that loomed so large in the international
affairs of Europe after 1689 (the so-called Second Hundred Years' War)
and suggested that this Great Power competition more than any other
single factor crippled the French government and made the 1789 Revolution possible.[30] In the course of the 1970s, French revisionist François

27 For instance, William Doyle does not even allude to her work in his otherwise thorough
    review of the relevant historiography in his *Origins of the French Revolution*. Nor does
    he refer to her in his even more recent *Oxford History of the French Revolution*. Other
    examples of this oversight in the current literature could be cited.

28 Robert R. Palmer, *The Age of the Democratic Revolution: A Political History of Europe
    and America, 1760–1800*, 2 vols. (Princeton, N.J.: Princeton University Press, 1959–
    64); and Jacques Godechot, *Les Révolutions 1770–1799* (Paris: Presses Universitaires
    de France, 1963).

29 George V. Taylor, "Noncapitalist Wealth and the Origins of the French Revolution,"
    American Historical Review 72 (1967), esp. pp. 491–92.

30 C. B. A. Behrens, *The Ancien Régime* (London: Harcourt, Brace & World, 1967), esp.
    pp. 138–62.

Furet, following Taylor's rather than Behrens's lead, stressed domestic political antecedents to the Revolution. Holding that the "fundamental crisis of the eighteenth century" involved the dynamic but increasingly dissynchronous relationship between the "modernizing" state and the evolving elite of noble and bourgeois "notables," Furet found that neither monarch nor notables could come forward "with a policy or a set of institutions that might have integrated the State and the ruling society around a minimum of consensus." In fact, the "two antagonistic poles" of eighteenth-century France, "the State and society," had by the late 1780s become "increasingly incompatible."[31] Finally, British specialist William Doyle, in the bicentennial decade of the 1980s developed an interpretation of revolutionary causation that pivoted on political factors both long term and immediate, both domestic and international. These factors (or "origins") included endemic royal indebtedness reflecting a surfeit of Continental and maritime warfare, irresolute royal leadership, bureaucratic infighting and confusion, the unrelenting opposition of the parlements and other vested interests to ministerial reforms, a more "enlightened" and politically sophisticated public, and critical ministerial miscalculations in the "prerevolution" of 1787–88.[32]

It would be difficult to deny that these arguments, especially when taken together, contribute signally to our understanding of the Revolution's genesis. They all appropriate the revisionist school's reconceptualization of social change in the old regime, and they make substantial strides toward a structuralist explanation of the Revolution's genesis that can comprehend both political and social developments and satisfactorily describe their interaction. Yet their shortcomings are also apparent. For example, Taylor's abandonment of long-term causation may be refreshing to those who, like Canadian historian J. F. Bosher, stoutly condemn any "inclination to assume that what happened was meant to happen" and see in the Revolution "a series of events that do not seem inevitable."[33] Others, however, may not be won over by the argument that the Revolution was a phenomenon without long-term analyzable origins, was little more, in other words, than a political emergency that abruptly and unexpectedly became a full-fledged sociopolitical upheaval in the precise context of the year 1789. Again, it is arguable that Behrens's reappraisal of the old regime's geopolitical dynamics was incomplete insofar as it did not say very much about French aspirations in Europe, and, furthermore,

31 François Furet, "Le Catéchisme révolutionnaire," *Annales: E.S.C.* 26 (1971), pp. 255–89; and *Penser la Révolution française* (Paris: Gallimard, 1978), esp. pp. 148–51. The latter translated into English by Elborg Forster as *Interpreting the French Revolution* (Cambridge: Cambridge University Press, 1981).
32 Doyle, *Origins of the French Revolution*, esp. pp. 41–114.
33 J. F. Bosher, *The French Revolution* (New York: Norton, 1988), p. ix.

that Behrens could have defined more sharply the pivotal relationship between foreign and domestic challenges to Bourbon absolutism in the eighteenth century. We may also feel that Furet's postulation of a dysfunctional relationship between the government and the elite among the governed did not enable him to bridge convincingly the formidable gap between eighteenth-century politics-and-society-as-usual and the novel revolutionary process of 1789 and beyond. Had Furet not followed in the footsteps of his admired nineteenth-century predecessor Alexis de Tocqueville by drastically underrating the significance for the ancien régime of statist warfare, he might have seen in the war-induced bankruptcy of August 1788 an explanatory key to the transition from the old regime to the Revolution. Finally, though Doyle exhibited a greater sensitivity than had François Furet to the importance of exogenous geopolitical pressures on the French crown in the years leading up to 1789, he did not really furnish a satisfactory analysis of the international forces making for sociopolitical change within Bourbon France.

This brings us to the self-proclaimed structuralism of Theda Skocpol's comparative study of the French, Russian, and Chinese revolutions. Skocpol's approach entailed a focus on both the international and the domestic roles of (in this particular case) the Bourbon absolutist state. On the one hand, she contended that the Bourbons and their ministers were inveigled by their country's "amphibious geography" into striving simultaneously to achieve ascendancy over the other Continental powers *and* to prevail over the English in the ever-widening competition for overseas colonies and commerce. Over the long term the implications of such an ambitious foreign policy for the finances and, consequently, the basic viability of the monarchy were catastrophic. The cardinal point, Skocpol alleged, was not that the recurrent waging of war left Louis XVI's advisers burdened with enormous annual deficits and an astronomical permanent debt. The ministers of Louis XIV and Louis XV, after all, had grappled with the same problem, yet had been able (at least in the short run) to extricate the French state from its difficulties. But the policy makers of the 1770s and 1780s, unlike their predecessors, could not resort to extorting funds from the "accountants, tax farmers, and other financiers" in *chambres de justice* (extraordinary judicial proceedings). Nor could they trim the fat from the administration of these increasingly parasitical fiscal operatives. Such individuals were by now untouchable – primarily because they had, in the course of the century, bought their way in large numbers into the nobility, into elite society.[34]

On the other hand, Skocpol remarked in light of this last development, there was the question of the ambivalent relationship between the gov-

34 Skocpol, *States and Social Revolutions*, pp. 51–67.

ernment and the elite during these years. The "dominant class," she argued, was "dependent upon the absolutist state and implicated in its international mission." Landlords "no longer controlled significant means of coercion at local levels" and hence "depended upon the absolutist administration as their protector of last resort" against the peasantry. Moreover, the social elite profited handsomely from "the various seigneurial, corporate, and provincial institutions that were preserved under the umbrella of absolutism." Such institutions "expressed and reinforced the advantages of the richer propertied against the poorer," because they conferred upon members of the elite "state-enforced tax advantages and opportunities for income." Again, the absolute monarchy's capacity to "promote the military success and to tax the economic expansion of the country" guaranteed employment at arms and/or additional economic security for nobles – and most assuredly guaranteed the latter for bourgeois. For all these reasons, then, the members of the "dominant class" – and most fatefully the ennobled financiers – would have been well advised to remain faithful to the absolutist French state. Unfortunately, however, this elite (including its strategically situated financiers) was also "interested in minimizing royal taxation of its wealth and capable of exerting political leverage against the absolutist monarchy through its institutional footholds within the state apparatus." Thus, Skocpol concluded, when the eighteenth-century crown's "unquenchable penchant for war" dragged it into "an acute financial crisis, it faced a socially consolidated dominant class" that was impervious to ministerial arguments invoking patriotic *raison d'état*.[35]

Here, then, was Skocpol's explication of the climactic confrontation of 1787–88 between the belligerent absolutist state and the "socially consolidated dominant class" which French historians know more conventionally as the "prerevolution" or "prerevolutionary crisis." In the end, the reformist avatars of the absolutist tradition (Calonne, Loménie de Brienne, and Lamoignon) could not persuade the entrenched elite that a reduction of its privileges was unavoidable under the circumstances. The nobility and the parlements rejected the state's modernizing legislation; the clergy and certain provincial Estates refused the crown critical moneys; army officers, unwilling or reluctant to suppress insurrection effectively, denied the state exclusive control over the crucial means of physical coercion; the equivocal attitude of many financiers toward the authorities powerfully contributed to the sudden collapse of state credit in August 1788; and certain bourgeois notables, in polemical tracts and speeches, began to make the social elite's antigovernment cause that of the entire nation. Once the dominant class started to splinter over the issue of how,

35 Ibid., pp. 59–60, 64.

precisely, power was to be apportioned among social groups in postabsolutist France, the "old-regime administrative system" crumbled, and massive insurrection could well up from below. France was experiencing an unprecedented "societal political crisis" by early 1789; the unanticipated peasant revolt in the summer of that year would then make a veritable "social-revolutionary transformation" of the kingdom possible.[36]

Skocpol's structuralist approach to the causes of revolution, as applied specifically to France, probably yields the most persuasive interpretation to date of 1789. By stressing the "international mission" of the Bourbon state and by describing that bellicose state's interaction with a prerevolutionary social elite conceived in revisionist rather than in orthodox terms, Skocpol has gone a long way toward adequately characterizing the dynamic relationship between state and notables in eighteenth-century France. In addition, her analysis offers much of what is needed for a convincing explanation of the transition from old regime to revolutionary politics in the late 1780s. It does so, first, by presenting the crisis of 1787–88 as a showdown between government and elite society that in some ways was quite conventional but that gradually got out of control; and second, by acknowledging the central role played by the peasantry in transforming the "societal political crisis" of 1789 into a genuine social revolution.

This having been said, there are, nonetheless, two substantial objections concerning Skocpol's argument. The first criticism can be accommodated within the framework of her proclaimed structuralism; the second, however, questions that structuralist approach as such.

In the first place, Skocpol fails to explore all the dimensions of the eighteenth-century Bourbon state's geopolitical "dilemma." The French were not only striving to achieve hegemony or at least to maintain competitive parity on both land and sea; they were endeavoring to do so at a time when power within each of these geostrategic realms was migrating steadily away from the historic Gallic kingdom. This means that the analyst, in reassessing Continental affairs, must stress the tremendous impact on those affairs – and, in particular, on France's Continental standing – of the rise of Russia (overshadowing that of Prussia) to greatness in the 1700s. It also requires that the analyst, in reappraising maritime competition, underscore the extent to which Britain increasingly outdistanced its cross-Channel rival by developing internal resources the French could neither understand nor match and helped to establish an equally mysterious and potentially even more formidable polity on the western rim of the North Atlantic. The "international mission" of Louis XIV and his two successors was, in other words, problematic indeed.

36 Ibid., pp. 64–67.

In the second place, and this is a more basic criticism, Skocpol's approach to revolutionary causation may be too exclusively structuralist in that it too rigorously eschews consideration of cultural and ideological factors such as the emergence of Enlightenment, of new elitist values, and of "public opinion" in the old regime. This is to say that a structuralism modified by a voluntarist stress on sociocultural change is required here. Such a prescription calls to mind François Furet, who, however neglectful of geopolitics, correctly accentuated the gradual development of ideological incompatibility between government and elite in ancien régime France. It also calls to mind William Sewell's insistence on the importance of ideological contradictions at the core of government,[37] and leaves some room as well for American historian Lynn Hunt's hypothesis that the weaknesses and eventual breakdown of the old regime political culture created the opening for the revolutionary process in France in the late 1780s.[38] Moreover, the structuralist postulation of a dominant class insurgency against the crown in 1787–88 may not turn out to be altogether accurate. We may discover instead that Louis XVI's ministers had to reckon with a nationwide uprising that, reflecting altruistic as well as selfish sentiments in *all* social classes, emboldened growing numbers of people entertaining those sentiments to take matters into their own hands. To understand the genesis of a revolutionary situation in France, then, is to accommodate some of the concerns of voluntarist history within a framework of structuralism – in other words, to evaluate sociocultural change within a matrix of power relationships in (and between) governments and societies.

This recapitulation of the historiography on the Revolution's origins has enabled us to do two things. First, it has allowed us to situate our study, synthetic in nature as it must be, within the proper context of debate over the germane historical issues. Second, by constraining us to define and differentiate between voluntarist and structuralist explanations of revolutionary causation, it has helped us to pave the way for an analysis that will be social and ideological even as it plays up international and domestic statist concerns. We can now proceed to an exposition of the argument that is to follow.

This book will present the upheaval of 1789 as stemming from a convergence of long-term, intermediate, and immediate historical factors.

---

37 Consult once again Sewell, "Ideologies and Social Revolutions," p. 66. But refer also to Skocpol, "Cultural Idioms and Political Ideologies in the Revolutionary Reconstruction of State Power: A Rejoinder to Sewell," *Journal of Modern History* 57 (1985), pp. 86–96.
38 Lynn A. Hunt, *Politics, Culture, and Class in the French Revolution* (Berkeley: University of California Press, 1984), esp. pp. 221–24.

The long-term and intermediate factors, analyzed in Chapters 1 through 4 and covering, respectively, the years leading up to 1774 and the years from 1774 to 1788, were in both periods essentially the same. One of these long-term and intermediate factors was geopolitical: namely, the impossible attempt of the Bourbon state to achieve hegemony or at least maintain an acknowledged greatness in two very dissimilar geostrategic domains at a time when power in both of those domains was already moving away from France. The other long-term and intermediate factor was sociopolitical: to wit, the failure of that same Bourbon polity to accommodate the values and aspirations and thereby appropriate the financial and moral support of a domestic "elite of notables" whose very existence derived in considerable measure from the crown's own belligerent policies. The long-term geopolitical and sociopolitical factors combined to produce the crisis that marred Louis XV's final years, 1770–74. The intermediate geopolitical and sociopolitical factors came together even more explosively in Louis XVI's governmental bankruptcy of August 1788. By this time, systemic (although not necessarily violent) change in politics and society had become all but unavoidable in France.

The immediate historical factors, the precipitants of genuine revolution in France, appear in Chapter 5 and cover the dramatic months, weeks, and days from August 1788 to October 1789. They were four in number: (1) the unrelenting pressure of international politics on a paralyzed France; (2) the failure of Louis XVI to strike a sociopolitical compromise with France's aroused "progressive" notables; (3) the polarization within the elite ranks of "respectability" between the progressive notables and their reactionary opposites; and (4) the uprising of the urban and rural masses against the sociopolitical ancien régime.

A concluding section speculates briefly upon how the historical forces that brought revolution to France in 1789 also may have helped to mold the subsequent revolutionary process and, for that matter, much of post-revolutionary French history. It then compares the 1789–99 upheaval to other sociopolitical cataclysms in early modern and modern times, and offers as well an explanatory analogy between certain uprisings in post-revolutionary France and the major changes of the past few years in the socialist East.

To organize our argument in this fashion is to invite the query: Why treat geopolitical and sociopolitical matters (at least for the time prior to August 1788) in separate chapters? Is this not a bit unorthodox? To which the reply must be made: This *is* a somewhat unorthodox manner of proceeding, but it is only in this way that we can give adequate attention to the tremendously significant factor of French competitiveness (or lack thereof) in the world's affairs. No more than the Russians and the Chinese in the early twentieth century could the French in the eighteenth century ignore or escape the incessant pressures engendered by international developments. As British historian T. C. W. Blanning has somberly commented:

To be predator or prey: that was the choice. It was a lesson taught first and foremost by the extraordinary frequency of war. Between 1700 and 1790 no fewer than sixteen wars had been fought between the various combinations of the major powers of Europe.... [O]nly the 1720s were mainly peaceful.... If ever there was a time when war was the normal means of intercourse between states, then this was surely it.[39]

Or, as Blanning's fellow Briton, biographer Rohan Butler, has put it even more succinctly: "In the eighteenth century it was war upon war."[40]

Hence, to organize our presentation in this manner – to speak, that is, of geopolitical factors converging with the somewhat more familiar sociopolitical factors to induce transformative change in France – is to grant international forces the attention they merit, but do not always receive, in scholarly accounts of the coming of revolution to France. But it is equally clear that such an approach imposes a special challenge: to demonstrate wherever possible the linkage between foreign and internal developments in prerevolutionary France, and the ways in which that linkage furthered the gestation of a potentially revolutionary situation within the kingdom.

And there were, after all, so many ways in which France's international role and its internal evolution acted and reacted on each other! The primary, if not the exclusive, stress here must be on how geopolitical tendencies influenced domestic realities. The Gallic "mission" of war and diplomacy helped determine the very structure of Bourbon absolutism. Through the establishment and growth of a massive army and navy, it helped to round out the contours of modern France and generate a patriotic consciousness among many of its inhabitants. It put a premium on the domestic law and order without which cultivation of the land, primitive commercialization and industrialization, and intellectual and artistic endeavors would have been infinitely more difficult, and in myriad ways it drew ongoing sustenance from those economic and cultural activities. But the country's "international mission" also helped over the years to drain the very ancien régime to whose formation and customs it had so signally contributed. Of course it did so most obviously by imposing on absolutist institutions a monstrous financial burden that in the end overwhelmed them. But it did so in other ways as well. It aided in keeping alive the specter of the old Estates General and therefore the

39 T. C. W. Blanning, *The Origins of the French Revolutionary Wars* (London: Longman, 1986), pp. 37–38.
40 Rohan Butler, *Choiseul: Father and Son.* vol. 1: *1719–1754* (Oxford: Clarendon, 1980), p. 247.

idea of consultative and accountable governance. It encouraged the wide-spread vending of public offices of every imaginable description, and in so doing subverted the venerable world of social privilege and inequality. And by bringing the French state up against rival Powers that increasingly outperformed France in strategic and economic affairs, the Bourbons' international mission discredited these monarchs in the eyes of the very Frenchmen whose upward mobility and rising expectations derived largely from the crown's own office-selling (and other) policies.

Naturally, forces within France had a way of influencing and reacting back upon the monarchs' foreign policies. To a certain extent, the Bourbons and their ministers may have pursued intrigue and aggression abroad as a means of sociopolitical stabilization at home – satisfying, for instance, the nobility's yen for military glory and distracting a public opinion critical at times of royal incompetence in home affairs with news of martial campaigns on land and sea. It is equally incontrovertible that domestic society could "take its revenge" upon a crown given too much to pursuit of greatness beyond France's borders: the war-making abilities of even the most bellicose of sovereigns could be, and at times were, severely circumscribed by the demographic disasters, economic tribulations, and social dislocations afflicting their subjects. Nonetheless, the chapters that follow emphasize primarily the former process, the process by which successive Bourbon administrations, driven by what they regarded as the security needs and "manifest destiny" of France, profoundly affected the country's internal evolution – including the fundamental viability of ab-solute monarchy itself.

It remains for us to spell out the four cardinal assumptions upon which this entire edifice is raised.

1. This essay assumes, to begin with, that what needs to be explained above all is the unraveling of governmental authority in France that made violent and thoroughgoing change in state and society possible by the late months of 1789. It follows Georges Lefebvre in adopting the notion that the October Days (5–6 October 1789) made up the crucial watershed between the onset of revolution and the revolutionary process itself, and acknowledges that a detailed account of how the Revolution evolved over the period from the October insurrection of 1789 to the Bonapartist coup d'état of November 1799 lies beyond its scope.

2. The essay also assumes (as, in fact, does most of the historiography recapitulated here) that "great events" such as major social and political revolutions arise from great as well as from immediate and even fortuitous causes. It would be much too simple to view the revolutions convulsing states and societies from late eighteenth-century France to twentieth-century Russia and China, Mexico and Iran, Vietnam and Cuba, and

Turkey and Nicaragua as mere historical accidents touched off suddenly by conjunctures of short-term circumstances. (For that matter, even an "incomplete" revolution like that in seventeenth-century England is often assigned long-term causes.) The cataclysm in France, like great upheavals in other countries, had origins deeply rooted in the past. To deny those origins would be to oversimplify history unpardonably. At the same time, however, we need to be acutely aware that the vexing issue of determinism inheres in such a perspective. There is no need to apologize for this, but there *is* a need to restrain the determinism inherent in this kind of interpretation by accentuating the immediate prerequisites of revolution in 1788–89 after having depicted more broadly the systemic forces operating throughout the preceding century and a half of French history.

3. Embedded in the second assumption is a third supposition: It can be enlightening – and at times even necessary – to view the French Revolution and its causes in a comparative context. To utilize this mode of analysis too frequently would, admittedly, result in obscuring the unique aspects of the French case of political and social transformation; still, judicious use of historical comparisons is essential for a truly penetrating comprehension of this very complex subject.

4. Finally, our argument, laid out in the abstract, assumes as its constituent parts the following sequential propositions. The prerevolutionary state (in the French instance, and in many other cases as well) pursues foreign policy goals that respond primarily to the dynamics of the contemporary international state system but also, if secondarily, to domestic pressures. Such a state will collapse when and *only* when its failure to maintain its wonted credibility in the eyes of its foreign strategic and economic rivals coincides fully with its failure to maintain its traditional credibility in the eyes of its domestic elitist subjects. Only at such a rare juncture does a violent transformation of both state and society become possible. In this theoretical formulation, subjective historical realities – states of mind, social and cultural values, and ideologies – must be considered alongside objectively determinable realities of an administrative, military, and socioeconomic nature.

It should be abundantly clear by now what, precisely, this inquiry's global-historical approach to the genesis of the 1789 Revolution entails. It entails a readiness to conceive of fundamental as well as of immediate causes of the Revolution. It challenges the analyst to place French policy makers in an increasingly global-geopolitical context as well as to view them against the backdrop of sociopolitical developments at home. And it requires that the historian be willing, when he or she finds it useful, to note the similarities between the origins of revolution in France and the roots of upheaval in other countries in other eras.

Moreover, this global-historical perspective undeniably has implications, some of which are already apparent, for a certain philosophical issue raised earlier in this introduction. Such an approach, it is already clear, leaves unempowered subjects in any prerevolutionary society incapable of making their own revolution. They cannot, like Beethoven, "seize Fate by the throat." They must wait for their government to turn to them in desperation for a new source of strength, of legitimacy – and the government will do this only when it has bankrupted itself in the unceasing and amoral pursuit of international security, status, and power. Of course, "revolution" in its fullest modern sense was not even conceivable as an objective to the unenfranchised person in prerevolutionary France, for it had not yet occurred in the real world. But all this was very soon to change – and for reasons that we may be able in some small measure to elucidate.

1

∽◟◞◠◟◞◠◟◞◠◟◞◠◟◞◠◟◞◠◟◞◠◟◞◠◟◞◠◟◞◠◟◞◠◟◞◠◟◞∽

The legacy of French history:
the geopolitical challenge

Most eighteenth-century writers and politicians rendered a cynical verdict on the behavior of the states making up their contemporary Europe. "Each nation in its natural state," averred one widely read author in the 1740s, "must be considered as the enemy of all others; or as disposed to be such." "We cannot rely on virtue," conceded another sadly, some decades later; "it is weak or equivocal, or hidden and unknown; . . . we must thus take as our starting-point only the possible and even probable abuse of power." Prussia's Frederick the Great, reacting in 1742 to concerns invoked by the specter of his fearsome army "living off the land" in neighboring Moravia, commented harshly that "it is the kingdom of heaven which is won by gentleness; those of this world belong to force."[1] And, more tellingly perhaps, even an individual like France's René-Louis de Voyer, Marquis d'Argenson, touted by his friends as a "philosopher" in public office, could pragmatically remark in 1739: "A state should always be at the ready, like a gentleman living among swashbucklers and quarrellers. Such are the nations of Europe, today more than ever; negotiations are only a continual struggle between men without principles, impudently aggressive and ever greedy."[2]

Thus was the endless competition for security and power and prestige among the European states, great and small, of that age. If this was not yet the twentieth century's global system of geopolitics, influencing the lives of all human beings for better or for worse, matters were nonetheless heading in that direction. For it was precisely during the late seventeenth and eighteenth centuries that an international state system rooted by then in two hundred years of European history began to acquire its first truly

---

1 Quoted in M. S. Anderson, *Europe in the Eighteenth Century 1713–1783* (New York: Holt, Rinehart & Winston, Inc., 1961), p. 166; and Butler, *Choiseul*, p. 310.
2 Quoted in Derek McKay and H. M. Scott, *The Rise of the Great Powers 1648–1815* (London: Longman, 1983), p. 214.

20

global characteristics. And no state and society were shaped more profoundly by this process, with major implications for the entire world, than the state and society of France. The pages that follow briefly retrace up to 1774 the old France's drive for geostrategic security and greatness, situate that powerful national tradition in its European and global context, and show how its unsuccessful pursuit produced deep patriotic frustration for many French citizens by the later years of Louis XV's rule.

THE DRIVE FOR FRENCH GREATNESS UP TO 1774

More than one historian of power politics in early modern Europe has seen French foreign policy under Louis XIV (1643–1715) and Louis XV (1715–74) as profoundly conditioned by an earlier French defensiveness against the strategic threat posed by the Austro-Spanish Hapsburgs. Yet, just as we shall see the France of Louis le Grand and his successor driven in international affairs by both aggressive and defensive considerations, so we can see this to have been equally true under France's earlier sovereigns.

The Valois monarchs had scarcely liberated Gallic soil from the English in the Hundred Years' War when they led their troops over the Alps into the fertile plains of Italy. Indeed, Charles VIII's invasion of Italy in 1494 was one of the initiatives of those years that helped to inaugurate modern international politics by forcibly extending the diplomatic relations worked out among the Renaissance states in the Italian peninsula to western and central Europe as a whole. And invasion succeeded invasion over the ensuing thirty years, as first Charles VIII, then Louis XII, and then Francis I obeyed the siren call to glory in the heartland of the ancient Romans. It is possible that only the fortuitous convergence of titles, lands, and powers in the person of Holy Roman Emperor Charles V prevented the French from achieving under Francis I a temporary preponderance in west European affairs foreshadowing the somewhat more durable French preponderance (or, at least, potential preponderance) of the late seventeenth and eighteenth centuries.

Moreover, even though it was the Hapsburgs of Madrid and Vienna rather than the Valois and early Bourbons of Paris who could most realistically aspire to greatness during the 1525–1648 period, the French polity was sustained in its largely defensive struggle of that era by memories of a "French" grandeur long antedating modern times. When Francis I forged alliances with (and among) the petty states of Germany and Italy in the 1520s and 1530s, and when the first Bourbon ruler, Henry IV, did essentially the same thing seventy years later, recollections of Charlemagne's medieval Frankish empire were, apparently, not altogether absent from their minds. For Cardinal Richelieu, too, endeavoring to stave off a Hapsburg strategic encirclement of France during the Thirty Years' War (1618–48), more than purely defensive calculations were in play. British historian Richard Bonney has reminded us that, on 20 September 1641, the redoubtable cardinal "ordered the Chancellor to investigate the claims of . . . France to Milan, Naples, Sicily, Piedmont, and the county of Burgundy." Richelieu, that is, may have "come near to accepting Le Bret's maxim on the inalienability of the royal domain, and the applicability of this concept to areas of the former Carolingian empire which were no longer part of France."[3] Thus, even in the midst of his efforts to hold off the still formidable armies of the Hapsburgs, Richelieu could not help but think (and encourage those around him to think) in terms of a greater French role on the Continent.

It is important to emphasize this point, for recently Peter Sahlins has revived the debate over the role of the "natural frontiers" concept in the formulation and rationalization of French foreign policy. Insofar as that concept harkened back to ancient Gaul, and thereby projected now a France bounded by the Atlantic, Rhine, Alps, and Pyrenees, it described poorly indeed a Gallic foreign policy that, in the ancien régime and beyond, became increasingly opportunistic and ambitious. Sahlins himself has conceded that natural frontiers "were important to the French crown not as boundaries but as passages" or (in Richelieu's words, which he has cited) as "open doors to be able to enter into the neighboring states."[4] The future would belong to geopoliticians at Paris (and, for a hundred years, at Versailles) whose vistas would leave the limits of Julius Caesar's Gaul far, far behind.

For that matter, French ambitions under Richelieu's successor, Cardinal Mazarin, started almost immediately to take on larger dimensions. By the 1640s, armies under the generalship of Harcourt, Condé, and Turenne had turned the tide against the Spanish imperial forces; before very long Gallic troops were promenading up and down the Rhine and striking deep into Bavaria in the Germanic east. The Peace of Westphalia (1648), which terminated the destructive Thirty Years' War, ceded to France nearly all of Alsace and strategic territories in Lorraine; hence the Hapsburg "lines of encirclement and communication" were sundered forever. But this was only a prelude to much greater things. In 1657, on the death of Holy Roman Emperor Ferdinand III, the indefatigable Mazarin attempted through bribery and other means to acquire the imperial title for his young master Louis XIV. This bold stroke failed, but France

3 Richard Bonney, *Political Change in France Under Richelieu and Mazarin 1624–1661* (Oxford: Oxford University Press, 1978), pp. 401–3.
4 Peter Sahlins, "Natural Frontiers Revisited: France's Boundaries since the Seventeenth Century," *American Historical Review* 95 (1990), esp. p. 1433.

resumed its role as protector of a league of medium-sized and petty German states, and Mazarin bequeathed to his royal charge tantalizing aspirations to the Imperial throne. What might not happen if the new emperor, Leopold I, were to die while the arrogant and aggrandizing Louis XIV remained yet empowered in France?

Even more portentous was Cardinal Mazarin's stewardship of Franco-Spanish relations. His German diplomacy had been actuated in part by the desire to keep Hapsburg Austria and all other German states out of the continuing post-Westphalia struggle between Paris and Madrid. In this, Mazarin was unqualifiedly successful. In brief alliance with the English protectorate of Oliver Cromwell, France triumphed over isolated and exhausted Hapsburg Spain. And the Treaty of the Pyrenees, which ended the latest chapter in the secular conflict between the Gallic and Iberian powers in 1659 did far more than expand French power along the Pyrenees to the south and in Luxembourg, Artois, and the Netherlands to the north and east. It also joined Louis XIV in matrimony with Marie-Thérèse, only child at that time of the Spanish king Philip IV and consequently heiress to the global empire of Hapsburg Spain. As British specialist David Maland has observed, Mazarin's astute diplomacy "paved the way for a dramatic extension of the policies of his predecessors. France was content no longer to think in terms . . . of limiting the power of Spain but rather [thought] of absorbing it altogether within a new French empire which would bestride the world."[5] It is true that Philip IV, divining these breath-taking ambitions, insisted that his daughter relinquish all claims to the Spanish succession. But the French made Marie-Thérèse's renunciation contingent upon a marriage dowry that Spain, straitened in its finances, might never be able to pay.

And so it was that, with Mazarin's death in 1661, the handsome and prideful Louis XIV could not only enjoy in full measure a throne rejuvenated in the ashes of the domestic rebellion known as the Fronde but also savor prospects of aggrandizement in the world at large. It is very true that, as British historian Jeremy Black has noted, the Sun King's foreign policy "neither conformed to any master plan nor consistently centred on one issue," and that Louis is too simplistically summed up as "a machiavellian schemer after universal monarchy." Yet Black himself has conceded this prince's "insensitivity, obsession with *gloire* and failure to comprehend the views of other powers," and these were assuredly the attributes assigned to him by many of his contemporaries.[6] Indeed, why

5 David Maland, *Europe in the Seventeenth Century* (New York: St. Martin's, 1966), p. 180.
6 Jeremy Black, *The Rise of the European Powers 1679–1793* (London: Arnold, 1990), pp. 28–30. For another careful reassessment of the "aggressive" aspects of Louis XIV's

should this monarch not have looked upon Europe confidently, at least in the radiant dawn of his personal rule? Who was there to oppose whatever schemes he might devise? Within France, his countrymen had had their fill of political cardinals, weak kingship, and aristocratic and popular sedition. Charismatic and militarily expansionist rule might seem to answer to a domestic craving for *la gloire*. Beyond the country's borders, the situation seemed scarcely less promising. Spain was an attenuated power, Austria had to keep an eye on the resurgent Ottoman Turkish Empire to the southeast, England after Cromwell's death subordinated its interests for nearly three decades to those of France, the Dutch unaided could not hope to frustrate the Sun King's purposes, Sweden was preoccupied by events in the Baltic region of the far north, and the shadows of Russia and Prussia did not yet fall across the political landscape of Europe.

And, as it turned out, events in central Europe and the Iberian Peninsula for many years enticed Louis XIV and his advisers down a primrose path of great expectations. Who could have prophesied in the 1660s and 1670s that the Hapsburg Holy Roman Emperor (and Archduke of Austria) Leopold I would survive a great Turkish siege of Vienna, throw the Turks back into the depths of the Balkan Peninsula, intervene militarily against the French in the west, and live into the eighteenth century? Admittedly, not even Louis XIV was brazen enough to defy Christian Europe by supporting the Turkish thrust up the Danube and climactic siege of Vienna in 1682–83. Nonetheless, on occasions less immediately perilous for European Christendom, he was more than willing to revive the traditional Franco-Turkish alliance in order to menace the Austrian adversary on its southeastern flank. In addition, Louis XIV knew as well as anyone else that an Ottoman conquest of Austria – not altogether out of the question in the early 1680s – would likely create a power vacuum in the rest of central Europe that only the French could fill. Failing such a spectacular development, the Sun King would use every conceivable means to fortify his realm's eastern defenses and, if possible, extend French power into central Europe.

In Spain, events long seemed equally tailored to at least some measure of French expansionism. There was, first of all, bankrupt Spain's failure to pay Marie-Thérèse's marriage dowry, which invalidated her renunciation of her claim to the Spanish succession. (It was, in any case, unclear as to whether Spanish custom could recognize such a renunciation.) Of vastly greater significance, however, was the fact that Philip IV's successor, Charles II, was to be a perpetually frail prince whose ailments

foreign policy, see Ragnhild Hatton, "Louis et l'Europe, éléments d'une révision historiographique," *XVIIe Siècle* 123 (1979), pp. 109–35.

would for the last forty years of the century nourish the Sun King's hopes regarding eventual French acquisition of all (or, depending on specific partition negotiations, part) of the far-flung dominions of Spain. Not for nothing did King Louis observe in his memoirs that "the state of the two crowns of France and of Spain is such today and has been such for a long time in the world that it is impossible to raise one without humbling the other." Not for nothing did he hold that there existed between the two countries an "essential jealousy," a "permanent enmity." And this rivalry can only have been sharpened for Louis and his advisers by the fact that a close kinsman of the Spanish prince, ruling to the east, in Austria, was another aspirant to the European and global Spanish inheritance.[7] Is it any wonder that practitioners of Gallic realpolitik, like their counterparts elsewhere, had a bewildering variety of issues to ponder during these years?

In all of this, Louis himself drew a certain distinction between what was European and what was extra-European. Until the very end, he thought more in terms of precedence, prestige, and power on land, of sieges and battles in the Netherlands and the Rhineland, in Bavaria and northern Italy, than of the stupendous potential for wealth and geopolitical glory that lay in control of the world beyond his little corner of west Eurasia. Thus it is not at all surprising that, as a parochial continental prince, he should have failed to grasp the full significance of Jean-Baptiste Colbert's interest in French acquisition of Spain's global empire and his imaginative reorganization of the French economy. This tireless minister to Louis XIV built up a magnificent navy, chartered merchant companies for overseas trade, fostered exchanges of goods for gold between the entrepreneurs of France and those of the Levant, the East Indies, the Baltic, and other areas within Europe, and encouraged reconnaissance and settlement in the West Indies and the vast wilderness of North America. Whatever the Sun King's personal predilections, his state was assuredly moving in the direction of a global foreign policy, one that in the last twenty-five years of his reign would bring down upon the French the enmity of the maritime as well as the west-central Continental powers.

The extremely long reign of Louis XIV, then, was pivotal in a global as well as in a French and European context. French foreign policy, it is not too much to say, had come a long way from the days when kings of the house of Valois sought martial glory in the Italian peninsula. True,

---

7 Citations from Paul Sonnino, "The Sun King's Anti-Machiavel," in John C. Rule, ed., *Louis XIV and the Craft of Kingship* (Columbus: Ohio State University Press, 1969), pp. 356–57. Sonnino's recent work on the origins of the Dutch War seems to reconfirm the traditional picture of the Sun King's aggressiveness, at least in the early stages of his reign. See Sonnino, *Louis XIV and the Origins of the Dutch War* (Cambridge: Cambridge University Press, 1988).

the Hapsburgs had led the way in carving out a geopolitical sphere of influence embracing both European and extra-European territories; but only with Louis XIV – and, even more, with his successor – did a Continental power regularly engage competing powers in transoceanic wars in which control of overseas colonies and markets (and control of the oceans themselves) began to loom almost as large as did hegemony within Europe itself.

From our perspective in the twilight of the twentieth century, this might appear to be one milestone along a road leading, eventually, to a fully global system of competing states. Quite obviously the men who directed French foreign policy in the years after Louis XIV's demise could have had nothing resembling this slant upon affairs. Nonetheless, the legacy with which they had to deal was an intimidating one. The Sun King, building on the policies of his own forebears, had, in collaboration with great ministers and dauntless men of war, developed over many years a strategic national tradition appropriating a number of interrelated statist ambitions of a continental and extracontinental nature. Furthermore, he had stamped this tradition with the imprimatur of his charismatic kingship, with the imprimatur of his glittering court at Versailles. If petty princelings all over Europe scrambled to imitate the Grand Roi by constructing châteaux and assembling entourages and leading lives styled after his, is it any wonder that French statesmen (and, perhaps, some ordinary French citizens as well) found it difficult in the eighteenth century to measure their country's glory in terms less grand than those bequeathed to them by Louis XIV?

Not that the Gallic state could immediately upon the death in 1715 of its most splendid master plunge into bold new adventures. In the first place, the Sun King's incessant wars had, at least temporarily, exhausted his resourceful people and their still largely rural-peasant economy; more than ever before, time was needed to bind up the country's wounds and regenerate its sources of wealth and power. In the second place, the French (like their rivals the Austrians and the English, for that matter) had a royal succession to secure: Louis XV was but a five-year-old at the time of his regal great-grandfather's death, and some years would have to pass before the survival of the Bourbon line in France could be regarded as assured.

Yet it was not really that long before the French were once again on the move. The accession of a Bourbon prince to the Spanish throne upon the death of the childless Charles II in 1700 (as confirmed by the powers in 1713–14) boded well for Franco-Spanish relations in the new century; and, indeed, intermittently close ties between Versailles and Madrid were to represent something of a bonus for the French in the worldly affairs of the next several generations. Moreover, although French involvement in the War of the Polish Succession in the mid-1730s could not save the Polish throne for the father-in-law of Louis XV, it did afford Cardinal Fleury, Louis' preceptor and principal minister, the opportunity through skilled diplomacy to fill out French territory eastward toward the Rhine by acquiring the ancient duchy of Lorraine from the Austrian imperial Hapsburgs.

Yet improving relations with the former Spanish foe and joining Lorraine to metropolitan France were not actions calculated in themselves to alter the European balance of power in any fundamental fashion. Waging maritime war successfully against the British, however, or helping other powers to dismember Emperor Charles VI's Hapsburg territories would be actions of an altogether different order.

Jeremy Black, in revising the standard view on the first of these options,[8] has suggested, plausibly enough, that Cardinal Fleury was not as determined upon war with London over mercantile and colonial matters as some of his biographers have made him out to be. This may indeed be the case; nonetheless, as Black and all other specialists on the period well know, there was an enormous amount of wealth to be garnered in the West Indies from production and exportation of sugar, tobacco, indigo, and cotton, in the East Indies from spices and silks, and (to a lesser extent) in North America from furs and timber. This was, moreover, true at a time when the huge overseas Spanish Empire was becoming increasingly vulnerable to commercial interlopers of every imaginable stripe. And then, naturally, there was a critical nexus between European and colonial affairs that could not help but occupy ministerial and other politically attuned minds in England and France: namely, the fact that overseas wealth could in so many ways be parlayed into strength in the Continental arena of competition.

It is not surprising that London drifted into war with Madrid in 1739 over tensions in the West Indies. Nor is it surprising that many in British circles feared that France, unencumbered on this occasion by any commitment to fight on the Continent, would ally with Spain and bring all of its rejuvenated strength to bear against its long-standing rival across the Channel.

But the British were rescued from the prospect of sustaining major defeats in the vast world beyond Europe by French insistence in the 1740s on keeping the "precolonial" tradition of continental expansionism uppermost in mind. The end result was that Louis XIV's ghost – the specter of his long adherence to a foreign policy implying simultaneous warfare

---

8 Jeremy Black, "French Foreign Policy in the Age of Fleury Reassessed," *English Historical Review* 103 (1988), pp. 359–84. But contrast against this view Richard Pares, *War and Trade in the West Indies* (Oxford: Oxford University Press, 1936), passim.

on land and sea – continued to haunt Versailles. Even in the mid-1730s, well before his government became involved in yet another struggle in central Europe, Fleury had been hard put to resist calls from his foreign minister Germain-Louis de Chauvelin and from other aristocratic hotspurs for a resumption of hostilities against Austria. The cardinal had prevailed at that time, ousting Chauvelin from his position in the ministry; but several years later, even Fleury had to yield before a tidal wave of sentiment at Versailles in favor of marching once again toward the east.

The events that triggered renewed French intervention in central Europe were, first, the death in 1740 of Holy Roman Emperor Charles VI and, second, the lightning occupation toward the end of that year of Austrian Silesia by Prussia's Frederick the Great. Fleury, aware that France might have to join Spain in warfare against Britain in order to prevent London from achieving hegemony in maritime affairs, wanted to avoid an all-out Gallic commitment to the Continental struggle over the Austrian Succession. Yet he himself had helped to unleash the dogs of European war, not only by secretly encouraging Bavarian demands on the Hapsburgs in the late 1730s but also by appointing the youthful and bellicose comte de Belle-Isle as French ambassador-at-large to the German states of the empire. Belle-Isle's charge originally was limited to securing the election of the French candidate to the vacant imperial throne; but the count, taking up the martial standard of the cashiered Chauvelin, put together in central Europe a coalition of states that aimed at nothing less than the dismemberment of the Hapsburg possessions.

The aging cardinal warned that Belle-Isle's initiative might result in France once again having to duel simultaneously with Britain on the seas and with subsidized allies of London on the Continent; but he was preaching in the desert. Walter Dorn has effectively recapitulated the situation:

It was in vain that Fleury explained to a nobility which for the past two centuries had won honor and fame in wars against the House of Austria that this power was no longer a menace to France. When he gave out that he intended to support the Pragmatic Sanction [guaranteeing Austria's territorial integrity], he was denounced as a pusillanimous and senile dotard. A large part of the ministry and the court were opposed to this sharp breach with the ancient policy of France. Public opinion thought Fleury hesitant and contrasted his conduct with the decisive political action of the Prussian monarch.[9]

Essentially, Fleury's judicious biographer Arthur Wilson has concluded, the cardinal "was carried along a course which he did not care to pursue, simply because his favorite methods of seeking for expedients and adaptations were overwhelmed by the positive and enthusiastic schemes of

9 Walter L. Dorn, *Competition for Empire, 1740–1763* (New York: Harper & Row, 1963), p. 141.

a man [Belle-Isle] who knew that he spoke with the authority of public approval."[10] Most crucially of all, of course, the avatars of the "ancient policy" had the ear of the king. A wiser and stronger sovereign than Louis XV might well have found it difficult to withstand the exhortation of a French diplomat named Chavigny: "Let us unite to save [!!!] the empire with the protestants of Germany; it is by this way, Sire, that your ancestors have marched and they have been fortunate therein."[11]

How to resist this talk of ancestors' glory? And so within mere months French soldiers were campaigning in Bohemia, farther to the east, one historian has contended, than any Gallic troops since the age of Charlemagne. Ludwig Dehio commented of France: "Two souls dwelt in her breast, and even now the real ambitions of the nation lay in the sphere of Continental warfare."[12] But the "two souls" meant that France under Louis XV, as under his great-grandfather, would try to have it both ways simultaneously, defeating the British on the seas and humbling the Hapsburgs on the Continent. Although the attempt to divide up the Hapsburg dominions miscarried, the conquest of the Austrian Netherlands by a brilliant general in the French camp, the Maréchal de Saxe, in combination with the French seizure of Madras in India, meant that Versailles on this occasion could effectively neutralize several victories scored by the British in the maritime theater of combat.

But many French statesmen viewed the geostrategic stalemate that Louis XV extracted from his kingdom's participation in the War of the Austrian Succession as woefully inadequate. That the French and the British switched partners in the so-called Diplomatic Revolution of 1756, with France embracing the traditional Continental antagonist Austria and Britain establishing ties with Prussia, was probably less significant than the fact that French foreign policy (unlike that of any other power) continued to portend major aggression in both the overseas and the Continental arenas. In the midst of the Seven Years' War (1756–63), one diplomatic servant of Louis XV was to articulate to a colleague the philosophy underpinning this policy. "The object of the politics of this crown," wrote François-Joachim de Pierre, cardinal de Bernis to Etienne-François, duc de Choiseul, in 1759, "has been and always will be to play in Europe the superior role which suits its seniority, its dignity, and its grandeur; to reduce every power which attempts to force itself above her, whether by trying to take away her possessions, or by arrogating to itself

---

10 Arthur M. Wilson, *French Foreign Policy during the Administration of Cardinal Fleury, 1726–1743* (Cambridge, Mass.: Harvard University Press, 1936), p. 331.
11 Butler, *Choiseul*, p. 525.
12 Ludwig Dehio, *The Precarious Balance: Four Centuries of the European Power Struggle*, trans. Charles Fullman (New York: Knopf, 1962), pp. 110–11.

an unjust pre-eminence, or, finally, by seeking to take away from her
... her influence and credit in the general affairs [of Europe]."[13]

Inspired by such a canon, the French in the 1750s once again made
war on both sea and land. In North America, Louis XV's forces attempted
to establish a permanent choke on westward British expansion by
strengthening the fortresses that already described a vast arc from the St.
Lawrence and Great Lakes down the Ohio and Mississippi to New Or-
leans and the Gulf of Mexico. On the other side of the world, French
forces endeavored to drive the British out of India. And at many points
in between, French corsairs pounced on British shipping and raided British colonies. In the meantime, Louis XV allowed himself to be ensnared
by Count Wenzel Anton von Kaunitz, Austrian foreign minister, in
Austria's war of revenge against Frederick the Great. Actually, Kaunitz
would have been satisfied with less than a full-scale French role in the
conflict. But the French, motivated as always by the desire to play what
Bernis in 1759 called their "superior role ... in the general affairs [of
Europe]," and therefore taking excessive umbrage at the diplomatic and
military initiatives of their erstwhile ally Frederick, rounded upon him
with such a will as not even Kaunitz could have realistically augured. By
1757, France, already engaged in global combat against Great Britain,
was sending over 100,000 troops into Germany, purchasing the services
of 10,000 German mercenaries, and subsidizing the Austrians into the
bargain. This was following in the imposing footsteps of Louis XIV, and
with a vengeance.

As in the last stages of the War of the Austrian Succession, so in the
early stages of the Seven Years' War, Versailles saw the Austrian Netherlands as a point of intersection between its overseas and Continental
campaigns. Austria's effort to retake Silesia from Prussia, if successful,
would entitle its French ally to gains in the Netherlands; and those gains,
in the eyes of France, would "strengthen her Atlantic position vis-à-vis
Britain."[14] But alas, it was not enough to posit an analogy between the
strategic role undeniably played by the Austrian Netherlands in the war
of 1740–48 and that wistfully envisioned for those Low Country provinces
in the subsequent struggle. For, as early as 1758, Louis XV and his advisers
needed a Continental conquest in hand immediately, and not merely the
elusive prospect of a few territorial acquisitions in the Netherlands contingent on Austrian victory over Prussia. That the duc de Choiseul, who
assumed control of French foreign policy in the midst of the Seven Years'

---

13 Cited in Orville T. Murphy, *Charles Gravier, Comte de Vergennes: French Diplomacy
    in the Age of Revolution, 1719–1787* (Albany: State University of New York Press,
    1982), p. 213.
14 Dehio, *Precarious Balance*, pp. 114–15.

War, should have devised a spectacular scheme to end the conflict to France's advantage by invading the British Isles testified as eloquently to the current discomfiture of the French as it did to the resilience of Gallic ambitions. How often during the "Second Hundred Years' War" of 1689–1815 did the French, overextended strategically, dream of retrieving their sagging fortunes by the deceptively simple means of a thrust across the Channel!

To conjure up the name Choiseul is to underscore the persistence of the French state's attempt to maintain a competitive status in the waning years of Louis XV's reign. The ink was scarcely dry upon the Peace of Paris, documenting the disastrous French reverses in the war of 1756–63, before the untiring Choiseul was once more at work weaving ambitious geopolitical designs – designs aimed for the most part against the hated islanders on the other side of the Channel. In a memorandum of 1765 to his sovereign, the duke left no doubt concerning his conception of Franco-British relations:

England is the declared enemy of your power and of your state; she always will be. Her avidity in commerce, the haughty tone she takes in the world's affairs, her jealousy of your power, the intrigues which she has made against you, make us foresee that centuries will pass before you can make a durable peace with that country which aims at supremacy in the four quarters of the globe.[15]

In Choiseul's eyes, then, France had little choice but to fashion a foreign policy that would, at least for the time being, subordinate Continental affairs to those of the extra-European world. The duke was not indifferent to developments in central and eastern Europe that seemed inimical to French interests in those regions, but his highest priority was with evening the score against the contumacious and all-too-successful British.

In memoranda and correspondence of those years, the imaginative Choiseul advanced various plans for humbling those rivals.[16] Renewed war with London, he thought, was likely sooner or later, and especially likely if William Pitt the Elder, the architect of British triumph in the Seven Years' War, should return to power. Let the French, then, in closer alliance than ever with Bourbon Spain, and with Franco-Austrian collaboration relegated to a back burner, be prepared for yet another struggle with the "modern Carthage." If war should come, let France and Spain attempt to divert the British with military thrusts upon the Continent –

15 Quoted in R. John Singh, *French Diplomacy in the Caribbean and the American Revolution* (Hicksville, N.Y.: Exposition Press, 1977), p. 35.
16 Refer to ibid., pp. 10–11, 35–43; Roger Soltau, *The Duc de Choiseul* (Oxford: Blackwell, 1908), pp. 83–90; Bernard Fay, *The Revolutionary Spirit in France and America*, trans. Ramon Guthrie (New York: Cooper Square, 1966), p. 51; and John Fraser Ramsey, *Anglo-French Relations 1763–1770: A Study of Choiseul's Foreign Policy* (Berkeley: University of California Press, 1939), passim.

perhaps against the Dutch and Portuguese? – while France's navy carried out the essential mission of waging war upon British overseas possessions. British colonies, trading posts, and naval bases everywhere would be fair game – in the West Indies and East Indies, in Africa and the Mediterranean and Baltic seas, in North America and the South Atlantic.

North America in particular drew Choiseul's attention, for he was one of the first to see there the potential for colonial revolt against London. And might not the Bostonians, Philadelphians, and Charlestonians come to blows with their mother country over Canada as well as over their own status? In addition to all these possibilities, Spain's navy might mount an assault on Portuguese Brazil, and – here a variation upon one of the most cherished dreams at Versailles – the Spanish might invade Ireland while the French were themselves invading England. Even if a strike across the Channel should not prove realizable, the loss of its commerce and colonies and the sheer weight of its expenditures might bring Britain to bankruptcy and thus to its knees.

There is something breath-taking, and portentous, in all of this. Even more than Mazarin or Colbert or Fleury, Choiseul had, in his devising of strategic plans, a world vision. (In fact, insofar as, after 1766, his concern over Russian power was also rapidly growing, the foreign minister saw a grand interlocking of events in the overseas theater with those in eastern Europe: Hence he exhorted Turkey to make war on the tsarist regime, and did so in part to put pressure on a British state he viewed as far too amicably disposed toward the Russians.) The duke, it is true, urged no immediate resumption of war with the rivals across the Channel, yet he surely continued to prepare for that eventuality.

Thus, Choiseul and his ministerial colleagues carried out sweeping army and naval reforms and urged their Spanish counterparts to do likewise.[17] The French annexed the island of Corsica in 1768, thereby strengthening their strategic position in the western Mediterranean considerably. Choiseul sent secret agents to the increasingly restless British colonists in America, and incited an Indian prince, Hyder-Ali, to rebel against British influence in the Eurasian subcontinent. He concluded a commercial treaty with Madrid that brought the two Bourbon kingdoms, already linked through the Family Pact of 1761, into an even closer relationship. The French also did what they could to strengthen the traditionally pro-Bourbon monarchist party in Sweden. In addition,

---

17 In addition to the sources cited in n. 16, consult Samuel F. Scott, *The Response of the Royal Army to the French Revolution* (Oxford: Oxford University Press, 1978), esp. pp. 26–27; and Thadd Hall, *France and the Eighteenth-Century Corsican Question* (New York: New York University Press, 1971).

Choiseul's ministry fortified several strategic islands in the Indian Ocean, upgraded the defensive forces in the Caribbean colonies, and sponsored settlers in Guyana on the South American mainland. With ample justification the British could have suspected that their historic antagonists on the Continent were girding themselves for yet more colonial and commercial warfare.

A British diplomatic historian has argued that, as early as January 1770, the duc de Choiseul saw only one more year of peace between Louis XV and George III.[18] This may be an oversimplification of the foreign minister's views; nonetheless, the French and British were almost drawn into war in the course of that year over the Falkland question. For some time, Madrid and London had been contesting possession of the Falkland Islands, whose situation in the far South Atlantic made them a strategic gateway to the South Pacific and a vast region hitherto monopolized commercially by the Spanish. Bourbon Spain, not surprisingly, requested support on the issue from its Bourbon French confederate. Although there is much about the resultant diplomatic confrontation between London and Versailles and the associated political crisis within the French government that remains obscure, it seems that whatever Choiseul *may* have done to resolve the dispute peaceably was inadequate in Louis XV's eyes. This, in turn, enabled a cabal of the duke's domestic enemies to bring about his disgrace.[19]

Yet, although the French sovereign wanted to remain at peace in 1770, it is not necessarily correct to assume, as have some historians, that this was also his attitude with regard to the future. As French scholar Lucien Laugier has established, Louis XV, in his private correspondence with Charles III of Spain during and after the Falkland imbroglio, spoke of restraint now and revenge later. Here is the French king, trying to reassure his royal cousin with a message obviously not intended for British eyes:

Your Majesty would fail to profit from the prudence with which he has so far tolerated the unjust behavior and pretensions of the English were he not to restrain himself on these matters until he could address them with certain advantage to himself. It is for us to plan carefully for that resounding and useful revenge in which our true glory lies. . . . The King of England has pledged himself in Parliament to continue with his rearmament even after achieving success in the Falkland negotiations: for our part, we will continue with ours, and the steps I

18 Ramsey, *Anglo-French Relations*, p. 163.
19 The second volume of Rohan Butler's projected three-volume biography of Choiseul should throw valuable new light on this minister's role in the Falkland crisis. See also Doyle, "The Parlements of France and the Breakdown of the Old Regime, 1771–1788," *French Historical Studies* 6 (1970), pp. 415–58.

am taking to reestablish my government's finances will in time make it possible
for me to act all the more vigorously.[20]

In his exchange of letters with the Spanish sovereign during December
1770 and January 1771, Louis XV repeatedly underlined the need for the
two Bourbon governments to continue with naval rearmament as they
looked forward to "making war against England" and retrieving thereby
the "honor" compromised in 1763.

Was this mere rhetoric, designed to fob off Charles indefinitely so
that the French sovereign might live out his reign in peace? It is not
likely. Although their domestic political and financial problems and
their growing preoccupation with east European affairs led Louis's
ministers to scale down naval spending and suspend or soft-pedal Choiseul's reforms, they labored to restore that royal solvency which, in
the future, could enable France to resume its competitive ways. They
endeavored in addition to preserve where they could the erstwhile
foreign minister's diplomatic initiatives, as, for example, in Sweden,
British North America, and the Indian Ocean. Small wonder, then,
that the "general context of Anglo-French relations was still one of
hostility."[21] So much was this the case that the French could not get
the suspicious British to coordinate with them any kind of response to
the crisis precipitated in eastern Europe by the waxing ambitions of
Russia's Catherine the Great. Though London was not unconcerned
about events in imperiled areas of eastern Europe, it was troubled more
by evidence that its age-old enemy directly across the Channel had not
really abandoned its anti-British orientation.

Still, the fact that France could seriously (if quixotically) argue the case
for intervening in the vast Continental region extending from the Baltic
Sea to the Balkan Peninsula, and yet at the same time pursue its commercial and colonial rivalry with Great Britain, certified the degree to
which it had committed itself to a truly global definition of its national
greatness. Never had any European power gone so far – and that, it is
important to point out, includes the insular British, who had long made
a point of abjuring major Continental ambitions.[22] Yet it was one thing
for the French to harbor such grandiose aspirations and quite another to
realize them. In point of fact, they did not realize them – not, in any
case, up to the death of Louis XV in 1774. And this was so chiefly because

20 Lucien Laugier, *Un Ministère réformateur sous Louis XV: Le Triumvirat (1770–1774)*
   (Paris: La Pensée universelle, 1975), pp. 360–61. Letter of 29 January 1771.
21 Jeremy Black, *Natural and Necessary Enemies: Anglo-French Relations in the Eighteenth
   Century* (Athens: University of Georgia Press, 1987), pp. 75–79.
22 Of course, the British did insist on retaining Hanover, and, at the western entrance to
   the Mediterranean, Gibraltar.

of the transformation in the late 1600s and 1700s of the international state system.

THE EVOLUTION OF INTERNATIONAL POLITICS, 1661–1774

Old regime France could boast a relatively large measure of political unity; two consecutive long-lived monarchs and a galaxy of dashing warriors and cunning diplomats; a moderate climate and fertile soils; and industrious merchants, artisans, and peasants in the most numerous population west of Russia. How, therefore, could such a power fail to achieve that sustained success in international politics that for so long seemed France's due? Have we not already noted how propitious the European strategic situation appeared to be for French triumphs at the commencement of the Sun King's exceptionally long personal reign?

Unbeknown to the godlike Louis XIV, however, forces beyond his kingdom's borders were or would soon be at work to reduce the Great Power role that France could hope to play. In brief: As England, Russia, and Prussia emerged as major players in international affairs, power would migrate relentlessly away from Versailles, toward the west and toward the east. No longer would it be sufficient for the French to overawe the Spanish and the Dutch, to rampage through the Rhineland, northern Italy, and Bavaria, to regard imperial Austria as the permanent enemy to the east. Now the gauntlet would have to be thrown down to rivals more difficult to vanquish. And these competitors would achieve great success in the world's affairs for two interrelated reasons: (1) they would learn how to secure support for government policies from their domestic social elites, and (2) they would learn how to tailor their foreign ambitions to their domestic capabilities.

Our thesis requires first that we scrutinize the English under their late Stuart, Orangist, and early Hanoverian monarchs and then examine the growth of power in the Russia and Prussia of the Romanovs and Hohenzollerns. It was these polities against which France would have to prevail were it to justify expectations raised at home and abroad by its ceaseless will to greatness.

England's ability in the eighteenth century to carry out an international mission drawing massive support from its wealthy and articulate elites was rooted in the political revolutions of the preceding century. Those revolutions had beheaded one absolute Stuart monarch and chased another out of the land. The first, or Puritan, revolution had ushered in a new foreign policy that, under Cromwellian auspices, reflected in its colonial-mercantilist aggressiveness the increasingly powerful commercial and protoindustrial interests of that era. Significantly, the Stuart Restoration of

1660, reintroducing into the polity as it did the religious and constitutional controversies of the pre-Cromwellian years, brought back as well the irresolution and contradictions in English strategic policies that Oliver Cromwell had sought to end. The chronic dissatisfaction in the propertied and entrepreneurial classes with Charles II and his brother James II in the 1670s and 1680s stemmed from those monarchs' inconsistencies in foreign policy as well as from their absolutist stance on domestic politico-religious issues. Indeed, there were in England (as in all states at all times) indisputable connections between foreign and domestic matters. For instance, the Stuarts' all-too-obvious admiration for the Sun King's intolerant Catholicism and absolutist style of governance seemed to Charles' and James' detractors to bode ill for the English people in all walks of life.

Thus, the second, or Glorious, revolution, of 1688, so crucial to burning domestic questions, proved critical as well in the realm of foreign policy. The Glorious Revolution placed the profit-oriented agriculturalists of the peerage and gentry in a more secure position of power, in the localities as well as at the center. John Brewer has written that if "the conflicts of the seventeenth century finally legitimized the potent combination of monarch and parliament, they also demonstrated the strength of a national system of provincial governance which relied for its implementation on local dignitaries. National centralized institutions were tolerable provided they were neither military nor administrative but judicial in character; they were not only acceptable but desirable if activated by the approval of the 'natural rulers' (i.e., landed proprietors) of the nation."[23] It is true that the sovereigns of postrevolutionary Britain ruled as well as "reigned in Parliament," and signified to that institution their determination to retain royal initiative in the framing of foreign policy. Yet they had no choice but to accommodate in that sphere the interests of the kingdom's landed elite.

This political reality points again to the meshing of foreign and home concerns in Britain. The English landlords, who wished to produce cereals and other crops for domestic and foreign markets and to purchase various colonial and domestically processed goods (sugar, tobacco, spices, woolens and cottons, and so on), patently had something crucial in common with English merchants whose livelihood consisted in the domestic and international exchange of such raw and finished commodities. For both groups there was an imperative need for a diplomatic policy that put the acquisition and/or defense of colonies, trading posts, and commerce alongside dynastic and other "political" considerations. Beginning in

---

23 John Brewer, *The Sinews of Power: War, Money and the English State, 1688–1783* (Cambridge, Mass.: Harvard University Press, 1990), pp. 21–22.

1689, the gentlemen farmers and their confederates in trade were ideally positioned, through their influence in the central and local organs of government, to urge such a policy upon, first, William and Mary and Queen Anne, and then, the successive Georges of the house of Hanover. King William may have in his own mind accorded a higher priority to humbling his detested foe Louis XIV than to fostering English commerce, and the Georgian monarchs seemed at times to be obsessed by the need to protect their Hanoverian homeland from predators one and all on the Continent; nonetheless, the logic of British politics ensured that the country's foreign policy became almost as much an instrument of upper- and middle-class economic interests as an expression of the general "patriotic" desire for British security and prestige in the world's affairs.

What this meant in terms of statist policies was that, from 1689 on, the British would spare no effort to compete successfully in what was gradually becoming a global system of markets for raw agricultural and exotic goods and finished industrial products. And because it was now the French rather than the Spanish who posed the chief strategic threat to the British Isles as well as the principal challenge to British mercantile capitalism, the great wars of this age (at least in the west) were inescapably dominated by the Anglo-French rivalry.

That the economic aspect of this competition derived essentially from similarities between the commercial, industrial, and agricultural occupations of the two countries seems obvious enough in retrospect. Both France and Britain, for example, held West Indian islands capable of yielding impressive quantities of exotic goods. Again, the manufacturing sector in both countries was characterized by the predominance of textiles. Moreover, the policy makers in both governments, it is probably fair to say, devoted a greater effort to encouraging exports of domestically produced wares (and reexportation of profitable colonial goods) than they did to subsidizing agriculture. This was true despite the fact that in both states a larger proportion of the gross national product was still coming from the historic agricultural sector than from commerce or manufactures. "Foreign trade," one specialist has observed, was "more susceptible to intervention, more politically significant, was run by groups who either desired or were accustomed to state intervention, and produced wealth that could be taxed readily and used to conduct trade with areas, particularly the Orient and the Baltic, of adverse trade balances."[24]

Because neither power was any more capable of consuming all of its colonial goods than it was able to absorb all of the products of its domestic industries, both countries vied as fiercely for control of consumer markets in Europe and the Levant as they did for possession of the colonies and

24 Black, *Natural and Necessary Enemies*, pp. 134–35.

trading entrepôts throughout the world which actually generated the various forms of extra-European wealth. Furthermore, "the reality of significant competition in some fields in turn affected the perception of economic activity in other fields, such as fishing, where in fact competition was often less intense or shared with other states, particularly the United Provinces."[25] Thus, the importance of fundamentally shared economic preoccupations – especially in the dynamic sector of trade – in pitting London and Versailles against each other.

Yet, again, the struggle for colonies and commerce, as momentous as it was for both cross-Channel combatants in economic and domestic political terms, had also for both powers a transcending geostrategic importance. For England and France (like the United States and Soviet Union after 1945) were competing above all for security and prestige, whether measured in quantifiable terms of relative economic advantage or in terms of their constitutional systems, their religious and cultural values, their historical and national identities, or – most immediate determinant of success – their military and diplomatic establishments. Accordingly, both states saw the vast and unprecedented wealth amassed through trade and colonization as ultimately meet for power-political purposes. For the uniquely ambitious French, coveting Continental glory perhaps even more than maritime laurels, such wealth could fuel campaigns of conquest in Europe. For the fundamentally more defensive British, the danger was, as always, that a power such as France, if dominant on the Continent, could destroy them not only by denying them European markets for their trade but also by cutting them off from the naval stores (timber, hemp, and so on) lacking which no more British ships could ply the seas. Hence, mercantile wealth signified for London a precious means whereby France's Continental rivals might be subsidized in wartime, thus contributing to the strategic diffusion – and ultimate frustration – of the Gallic war effort. In the eighteenth century, Jeremy Black has aptly observed, "Britain and France were competing states, rival cultures and antagonistic peoples"[26] – and their "Second Hundred Years' War" represented one of the two overriding geopolitical challenges for the Bourbons at Versailles and for their revolutionary and Napoleonic successors at Paris.

In this great struggle, the British had over the French two interrelated and (as it turned out) formidable advantages. First, they were protected by their insularity from the threat of sudden invasion by land that had long haunted their French antagonists. Consequently, they could afford to let their military defenses down between wars and, more to the point,

25 Ibid.
26 Ibid., p. 211.

perhaps, focus their wartime armament efforts upon their navy. Second, as a result of the constitutional settlement of 1689, the British achieved an integration of domestic elite values and energies and governmental policy making that would elude their Gallic competitors until they experienced their own revolution a full century after 1689. Because the entrepreneurial gentry (and, indirectly, their allies in the merchant community) *were* to a large extent the government in Britain after 1689, an official foreign policy promoting the colonial and trading interests that flourished so readily in an island power naturally enjoyed a high degree of support among the articulate and wealthy subjects who really mattered.

Obviously, that support needed to express itself – and did so – in financial terms. J. F. Bosher has explained how government policy in Britain, foreign and otherwise, could now profit fiscally from the relatively close identification between official and elite interests in the realm:

After the Glorious Revolution of 1688–9, the financial system of the now-limited monarchy rapidly developed into a truly public administration. Public finance ceased to be royal and became parliamentary.... English business and financial interests had come gradually to exercise more influence in Parliament and parliamentary politics and less influence in administration. The meeting of private interests in Parliament... fostered a sense of the general interest which more and more strictly marked off the revenue departments, Exchequer, Treasury, and the rest of the financial administration as out of bounds to the enterprise of those very private interests.... At the same time, the evolving right and responsibility to scrutinize the budget and to find ways and means to implement it... made every parliament face debt and deficit year after year.[27]

Furthermore, with Parliament now established securely at the center of political life in the realm, men with capital proved more than eager to subsidize public policy by investing in the Bank of England, which (significantly) was founded just six years after James II fled British shores. The bank flourished and assumed management of long-term and short-term government debt before the mid-eighteenth century. That interest rates trended downward throughout the century, heading toward 4 percent and even 3 percent, witnessed at least in part to confidence in a regime held consistently to account for its policies and procedures. Needless to say, no controller-general of finances in old regime France, not even a reputed financial wizard like the Swiss Jacques Necker, would ever be able to secure money for the government at anything like those rates of interest – or keep "public" and "private" finances separated in a kingdom whose public policy making had yet to be reserved to an institution like the British Parliament.

The British, then, could manifest a single-mindedness in their pursuit

27 J. F. Bosher, *French Finances, 1770–1795: From Business to Bureaucracy* (Cambridge: Cambridge University Press, 1970), pp. 22, 23–25.

of maritime objectives that their "amphibious" and absolutist adversaries across the Channel could not match. The implications of this for the global mission of Bourbon France could not have been favorable. Many at the time would have agreed with a French pamphleteer's argument that "the power which is strongest at sea must necessarily be the strongest commercially and thus the most formidable."[28]

The immediate factor determining victory in this maritime conflict was, as we earlier noted, the relative strength of naval forces. Whichever fleet could control the seas could control access to naval stores in the Baltic periphery, to markets for exports, to sources of imports in Europe and the Levant, and to colonies and trading entrepôts in North and South America, the Caribbean, Africa, and Asia. Moreover, such control of the seas would feed on itself, for it would deny to the losing side in this confrontation the long hours of experience on the high seas failing which no navy could establish competitive standards of seamanship, gunnery, and tactics.

And it was "Perfidious Albion," rather than its Gallic antagonist increasingly leagued with Bourbon Spain, that triumphed in this pivotal competition. Before 1692, the French navy so painstakingly built up by Colbert had generally carried the day against the combined navies of England and the United Provinces. With the Anglo-Dutch victory that year off La Hogue in Normandy, however, the laurels of success passed permanently to the other side. Moreover, the Anglo-Dutch coalition became an instrument primarily of British policy as the United Provinces slipped from Great Power status. M. S. Anderson has well described the emergence of British naval superiority in the eighteenth century:

Throughout this period Britain had the largest fleet in the world. She emerged from the War of the Grand Alliance in 1697 as the greatest of European naval powers; and this position she never lost. In 1721 she had 124 ships of the line and 105 smaller vessels, of which roughly a quarter had been built since 1714. These figures were virtually unchanged when war broke out with Spain in 1739. . . . By 1762 . . . she had 141 [ships] of the line and 224 smaller vessels.

Over the same time span, French naval growth was "a good deal more erratic."[29]

Statistics offered by another chronicler of Great Power relations, Paul Kennedy, suggest how surely the tide was flowing against the French during this period. In 1689, they could still boast 120 ships of the line as against the 100 of the British; by 1739, however, the numbers had become 124 to 50 in the islanders' favor; and in 1756, the figures were

28 Quotation from Anderson, *Europe*, p. 165.
29 Ibid., p. 144.

105 for Great Britain and 70 for France.[30] Colbert's precious advantage had been frittered away. Now, rather than the English and Dutch striving to equal the French, Bourbon France and Bourbon Spain were vainly endeavoring to counterbalance the forces on the northern side of the Channel.

The nub of the matter was that the French navy could never escape the contradictions inherent in the French attempt to dominate both the Continent and the oceans. Colbert and his successors, for all their industry in building up and maintaining this branch of the country's military forces, kept the land-based naval administration (the so-called *plume*) separate from the seagoing officer corps (the *épée*). In doing so, they created and institutionalized a systemic tension between administrators on the mainland, who had little knowledge of or sympathy for seafaring and officers of the marine, who had no grasp of overall naval strategy or of its intended synchronization with the kingdom's Continental warfare. But the dilemma imposed upon Louis XV's navy by the "amphibious" nature of his foreign policy was most outstandingly a financial dilemma. James Pritchard, most recent authority on the French navy of the mid-eighteenth century, has aptly described the domestic context of this institution's financial problems:

Relying upon an ever-growing mountain of credit, naval strength became dependent more than ever before on private financiers and court bankers caught up in the meshes of factional struggles.... Sources of funds ebbed and flowed according to public confidence, which fell prey to far more than naval operations. Louis XV's navy strove to find its destiny within a vicious circle circumscribed by limited availability of funds, fluctuating credit, and volatile public opinion continually shaken by a decade of domestic political crisis.

As Pritchard has convincingly shown, the sheer lack of funds for the navy impeded organizational and administrative reforms, inhibited construction and repair of battleships and frigates, undermined morale in the arsenals and among the sailors, limited the opportunities for training in seamanship upon the high seas, and, in general, "severely limited long-term aspirations concerning naval power and effectively denied France fulfilment of the dream that she might one day be mistress of the seas."[31] Yet underfunding of the navy, placed in its broadest context, reflected something larger than domestic factional strife, fluctuating credit, and fickle public opinion: It reflected seemingly unlimited strategic ambitions

30 Paul Kennedy, *The Rise and Fall of the Great Powers: Economic Change and Military Conflict from 1500 to 2000* (New York: Random House, 1987), p. 99.
31 James Pritchard, *Louis XV's Navy, 1748–1762: A Study of Organization and Administration* (Kingston, Ont.: McGill-Queen's University Press, 1987), pp. 207, 214. For further discussion of these issues, see also E. H. Jenkins, *A History of the French Navy* (Annapolis, Md.: Naval Institute Press, 1973), pp. 44, 108–9.

whose satisfaction (if attainable at all) required vast expenditures upon that most prestigious of French armed forces, the army, as well as the less venerable navy. To this problem, of course, was added the related one posed by Britain's ability to concentrate almost exclusively on the naval aspects of military strategy. For all these reasons, consequently, the French navy in the eighteenth century was given more to carrying out specific, limited missions than to risking large-scale warfare upon the high seas with the usually superior British fleet.

In light of this state of affairs, France's attempt to defeat Britain in the conflict over commerce and colonies could not have easily succeeded. At the outbreak of war, the islanders' striking forces might be temporarily unready for battle, but before long those forces would once again be in the ascendant, and British seaborne trade, wounded at first by cruisers and privateers on the other side, would rebound. As for the overseas colonies, those all-important founts of wealth, and therefore of prestige and power, the following commentary appropriately sums up:

British superiority at sea . . . had profound repercussions on events in the British and French colonies. It meant above all that France could be prevented from translating her material superiority in Europe into a corresponding superiority overseas. She might possess enormous armies; but unless they, or adequate parts of them, could be transported to Canada, the West Indies or India, their existence could have little direct bearing on the outcome of the colonial struggle. In fact, British seapower made it impossible for them ever to be deployed effectively outside Europe.[32]

By the time of the Seven Years' War (1756–63), in every way the most decisive Franco-British conflict during this period, these realities became starkly apparent. Louis XV's ministers had as many as 330,000 men under arms in Europe, but they were able to send no more than 10,000 soldiers to Canada and India combined. (By way of contrast, George II's ministers had dispatched more than 70,000 soldiers to North America alone by 1757.) In an area like North America, London probably derived some additional benefit from the presence of five to ten times as many settlers as Versailles could claim. But in this theater of action, as in other quarters of the globe, it was the islanders' control of the overseas lines of communication that proved decisive.

Admittedly, the sheer magnitude of British triumph in the Seven Years' War was ascribable in part to the vision and organizational genius of the elder William Pitt (Chatham). Personalities do, after all, count for something in history. Nonetheless, to enumerate the specific provisions in the successive peace treaties of Utrecht (1714), Aix-la-Chapelle (1748), and Paris (1763) is to acknowledge a stage set for the decline of French influence and prestige in global affairs long before Pitt's accession to power.

32 Anderson, *Europe*, pp. 260–61.

Utrecht qualified as "a very shrewd peace which made ample provision for British commercial expansion." Under its terms, France was forced to cede Acadia, Newfoundland, and the Hudson's Bay region in Canada, as well as its asiento, or monopoly, of the provisioning of slaves to the Spanish American colonies. The British, in addition to securing the lucrative asiento for forty years, acquired "that fruitful source of future contention, the privilege of sending an annual trading ship to Vera Cruz or Portobelo" on the Spanish coast.[33] True, the British at this time did not make further inroads upon the Spanish West Indies; but, much nearer home, the acquisition of Minorca in the western Mediterranean and especially of Gibraltar at the southernmost tip of the Iberian Peninsula proved immensely significant. London's forces could now sever the French and Spanish Atlantic fleets from their Mediterranean counterparts in wartime, control the western Mediterranean if need be, and wield more influence than ever before in Italy and in northern Africa's Barbary States. Finally, the transference of the Spanish Netherlands to Austria left them open to British (much more, henceforth, than to Dutch) commercial exploitation.

The Peace of Aix-la-Chapelle thirty-four years later ended a war (the Austrian Succession) that further underscored London's ability to prevail at sea. During this conflict Britain had intervened in Italian politics more than ever before, had probed points of weakness in the Spanish overseas empire, and had jolted Versailles by seizing the great French bastion of Louisbourg, key to control of the St. Lawrence waterway and to much of Canada. Granted, British superiority upon the seas was not yet as decisive as it would later be – we noted earlier that the French managed to capture Madras in India during this struggle – but perceptive observers were not deceived as to which combatant seemed the likelier claimant of laurels in the future. The outcome of the most recent passage at arms, affirmed Parisian publicist E.-J.-F. Barbier, would "teach the ministers to come that it is not enough that we should be almost sure of conquering on land so long as we have not got a navy which can face at sea the maritime powers who, by reason of trade, will always be allied against us."[34]

Unfortunately for France, however, the "ministers to come" did not learn the proper lesson from the war of 1740–48, or perhaps for reasons already cataloged earlier, they could not really afford to. In any case, the Peace of Paris concluding the Seven Years' War a scant fifteen years later, measured a French disaster that, in some respects at least, had been long foreshadowed. The statesmen at Versailles now had to surrender the

33 Wilson, *French Foreign Policy*, pp. 42–43.
34 Cited in Butler, *Choiseul*, p. 750.

remaining Gallic holdings in Canada, and with them "the vast undeveloped territory of which France had claimed possession to the east of the Mississippi." They also had to relinquish Grenada, St. Vincent, and Tobago in the West Indies; and "perhaps only the unwillingness of British sugar planters to expose themselves to the competition in the home market of the more fertile French islands prevented the loss of Guadeloupe or Martinique as well." In India, France retained its trading stations but was otherwise knocked out of competition with Britain. In West Africa, the French yielded their Senegalese forts to their rivals.[35] Additionally, as if this were not sufficient, in order to placate a Spanish ally stymied by its own failures against the British, the French ceded to Madrid all their lands and claims in that part of Louisiana west of the Mississippi. The global struggle between the cross-Channel opponents, it has been truly said, "had thus changed the political face of much of the world." This proud initial version of a French overseas empire had been reduced "to a few islands – Guadeloupe, Martinique, the western half of San Domingo, Mauritius and the Seychelles – many of which were valuable producers of tropical products, above all of sugar, but none of which offered scope for territorial expansion." At the same time, Britain had been elevated by these conflicts "to the position of a world power."[36]

But statistics of world trade may be the most revealing indicator of the extent to which Britain, rather than France, was grasping the future through competition on the seas. Whereas commerce with America constituted 19 percent (by value) of all British foreign trade in 1715, and 34 percent by 1785, the analogous figures for France were only 13 percent and 28 percent. The disparity between the two countries was even more arresting where their trade with Africa and Asia was concerned. Whereas the proportion of all British foreign commerce represented by trade with those two continents increased spectacularly from 7 percent in 1715 to 19 percent by 1785, the corresponding statistics for France, defeated in the contention for India, were merely 5 percent and 6 percent. Britain, in the course of the eighteenth century, was already pulling ahead of its Gallic rival when it came to the exploitation of the nascent global economy.[37]

Some French merchants were uneasily aware that the tide of affairs was favoring their competitors across the Channel. At La Rochelle, Robert Forster has discovered, the chamber of commerce during the war of 1740–48 complained bitterly about mercantile woes in a letter to the ministry. "The *négociants* and *armateurs* expose with great insistence the deplorable

35 Anderson, *Europe*, p. 250.
36 Ibid.
37 Ibid., pp. 267–68.

state of their maritime commerce, which is totally ruined by continual seizures by English warships. There is no mail which does not bring disastrous news. . . . All expeditions have been stopped because no one in the whole kingdom will insure the ships, nor anyone abroad for that matter."[38] "It is becoming increasingly clear," Forster himself has observed, "that the wars had a permanent debilitating effect upon French overseas trade." And his fellow scholar Jean Tarrade has written: "All local studies of the port-cities show that the great fortunes, the great families dominating the commercial activity . . . ,and the great urban enterprises all date from *before* the Seven Years' War."[39] Prosperity would smile on French traders again, in the late 1780s, for instance, but the sustained good times of the 1720s and 1730s would not return.

"The colonial struggles of the eighteenth century," Anderson has noted, "faced both Britain and France with strategic problems of a hitherto unknown magnitude." Because both states were striving to become "world powers" with embryonic "world strategies," both "had to face the difficulties created by the interaction of events in Europe with those in America or the East."[40] Yet the dilemma here was especially acute for the French, tempted as they were by their geographic situation to pursue Continental and maritime aggrandizement simultaneously. And if the rise of Britain thwarted old regime France in one strategic arena, the addition of Russia and Prussia to the international state system just as certainly complicated its other expansionist mission.

Statesmen of the old France, we have seen, long regarded Hapsburg Austria as their country's principal and permanent antagonist in central Europe. Before the pivotal year 1648, Vienna had been the eastern outpost of a power complex threatening France with strategic encirclement; until the very end of his reign Louis XIV viewed Austria as the most troublesome impediment in central Europe to his Continental designs; and, as late as the 1740s, pursuit of military glory on land seemed in Gallic eyes automatically to entail marching against the Hapsburgs' martial banners. Thus it was only natural for France, in addition to allying with various small German and Italian states, to cultivate close ties with three much larger states in the eastern reaches of Europe: Sweden, Poland, and Turkey. This was, for generations of French geopoliticians, the obvious way to counterbalance and perhaps overwhelm the traditional foe. But in the course of the eighteenth century, this entire strategic calculus was rendered obsolete by the integration of Romanov Russia and Hohen-

---

38 Robert Forster, *Merchants, Landlords, Magistrates: The Depont Family in Eighteenth-Century France* (Baltimore: Johns Hopkins University Press, 1980), p. 12.
39 Quotations from ibid., pp. 12–13.
40 Anderson, *Europe*, p. 257.

zollern Prussia into what now became an infinitely vaster system of European Great Powers. Almost unavoidably, French Continental influence waned in these new circumstances. And just as in the case of Britain, so in the case of Russia and Prussia, the unprecedented ability to project state power abroad derived primarily from the kind of domestic integration of royal political and elite social energies (and judicious limitation of foreign policy objectives) that forever eluded old regime France.

It would be well to start with the Russians. Although they did not directly confront the French in any major conflict of this period, their growing involvement in European affairs sapped the influence of Versailles in eastern Europe and was perhaps the most portentous Continental development of the century.

Until the accession of Peter the Great in the late seventeenth century, the Muscovite state, viewed in the west as semibarbarous at best, had been cut off from most European influences by Sweden, Poland, and Ottoman Turkey. With the arrival on the scene of the amazingly energetic Peter, however, all this was destined to change. The new tsar "imposed on his people European techniques of every kind: the techniques of warfare at sea and on land, economic techniques, the techniques of administration."[41] Substituting for "an organic evolution of society from below," basically lacking in this land, "the highest degree of initiative from above," the indefatigable Peter sought to nullify in a short span of years the western Continental powers' enormous lead in "the development of militarism and bureaucracy."[42] What a stupendous task for this modernizing forerunner of Sergei Witte, Joseph Stalin, Mikhail Gorbachev, and Boris Yeltsin.

Peter, almost single-handedly, had to conjure up a state-service nobility. With essentially nothing of the urbane clergy and educated middle class of the west to call upon, how could he have done otherwise? And, where noble blood did not already flow in the veins of those discharging duties to the omnipotent state, Peter created nobility. Under Peter, Max Beloff has observed, "service began at fifteen and was for life." To counteract the preference of noble or would-be noble families for civilian over military service, the tsar's government stipulated that not more than one-third of each family's members could win promotion in civilian ranks.

The system of service was given form by the famous edict of 1722 by which all the servants of the crown were divided into fourteen orders...rising in two parallel ladders, civil and military, from the registry clerk and ensign at the bottom

41 Dehio, *Precarious Balance*, pp. 94–96.
42 Ibid., pp. 99–100.

to the chancellor and field-marshal at the top. . . . The eight top ranks carried with them hereditary nobility and the last six personal non-hereditary noble rank.[43]

It is true that several of Peter's successors found it politically expedient to mitigate the rigor of state-service requirements. Still, Beloff has insisted, "service to the State in some form continued to be the normal practice among Russian noblemen. . . . The nobility, at the end of the eighteenth century, was no less a subservient element in the Russian State than it had been under the masterful Peter one hundred years before."[44]

Thus did the Romanovs infuse Russian geopolitics with the abilities and energy of the only elite in this raw, rural, and underdeveloped society. And one very tangible measure of their success in this area was the remarkable increase in the Eurasian state's military capacity. The Russian soldiery, Paul Kennedy has estimated, numbered only 170,000 as late as 1690, but 220,000 by 1710, and as many as 330,000 by 1756–60. In addition, 30 ships of the line were in the navy as of 1739, and that figure was to be up to 67 by 1789.[45] Yet the Great Russian state of that era, perhaps more from necessity than from choice, focused primarily upon the possibilities of land warfare. Although the Romanov land forces in this period could not boast the fearsome discipline or the strategic and tactical generalship of Prussia's army, they gradually won repute for their tenacity and bravery. "Experience has proved," one writer would even allege during the Seven Years' War, "that the Russian infantry is by far superior to any in Europe, in so much that I question whether it can be defeated by any other infantry whatever."[46]

As an inevitable consequence of these efforts at modernization, tsarist Russia's shadow began to fall over lands immediately to the west – in what Louis XIV as a child had been encouraged to call "French Europe." As early as the 1680s, the so-called Holy League in central Europe had invited the Muscovite state to collaborate with it in driving the Ottoman Turks out of southeastern Europe. From 1699 on, the tsars concentrated on developing "a network of diplomatic representatives abroad comparable in its extent and efficiency to that of any European State."[47] In the Great Northern War of 1700–21, waged in the far northeastern reaches of the Continent concurrently with the War of the Spanish Succession in the west, Peter the Great's army routed that of Sweden's Charles XII at Poltava. Russia now replaced Sweden on the eastern shores of the

43 Max Beloff, "Russia," in A. N. Goodwin, ed., *The European Nobility in the Eighteenth Century* (New York: Harper Torchbooks, 1967), pp. 175–76.
44 Ibid., pp. 181, 189.
45 Kennedy, *Rise and Fall of the Great Powers*, p. 99.
46 Cited in Anderson, *Europe*, p. 182.
47 Ibid., p. 153.

Baltic, thereby permanently securing its "window on the west." Significantly, in 1716, the year after the Sun King's death, the French *Almanach Royal* for the first time listed the Romanovs as one of Europe's reigning families. The following year, Peter himself visited Versailles in a fruitless quest of a Franco-Russian alliance. Could any of France's gilded courtiers, gawking and laughing at the "barbarian" from the east, have read in this event a premonition of a time when their country's influence in that region would be severely challenged by Peter's successors?

The decades of the 1720s and 1730s witnessed new advances by the Romanov state. In 1726, Russia forged an alliance with Austria that presaged much of what was to come in eastern Europe. The Russian army, stymied under Peter the Great in its drive against the Ottoman Empire, now chalked up impressive victories against this traditional friend of France. And in the War of the Polish Succession, Russia scored at the expense of yet another state long held by Versailles to be one of its clients. St. Petersburg was able to impose on Warsaw its own candidate for the Polish throne; the French candidate (none other than the father-in-law of Louis XV) was banished from Polish soil forever. Henceforward, all of Louis's "secret diplomacy" at Warsaw would be unavailing against an ascendancy of Romanov interests that would in time be translated into the dismemberment of this hapless kingdom. The War of the Polish Succession also occasioned the appearance in western Europe of Russian mercenaries. They were to be used on or near the Rhine as a counter to French troops. The French acquisition in this conflict of eventual rights to Lorraine pales in retrospective comparison with evidence of the continuing integration of the tsarist state into the competitive European state system.

Although Russia could not play a major role in the struggle over the Austrian Succession due to domestic instability, Russo-Swedish tensions, and other factors, its adherence to Vienna's imperiled cause toward the end of that conflict marked a further step in the process by which it inserted itself into the affairs of its neighbors to the west. France may have been able to secure the exclusion of the Romanov state from the negotiations that formally ended this war at Aix-la-Chapelle in 1748. But this rather cheap diplomatic triumph was probably less significant than the fact that, for the second time in less than fifteen years, a contingent of Russian troops in the hire of France's adversaries had appeared on the Rhine to counter Gallic wartime influence in western Europe. Such an intervention would have been unimaginable in the days of Richelieu, Mazarin, and the mature Louis XIV.

The Seven Years' War, so pivotal with regard to the competition between France and England on the high seas, was also revealing (if less decisive) in the matter of the relative Continental strengths of France and

Russia. Contemporaries noted that the French, who so recently had succeeded in shutting St. Petersburg out of central Europe's high diplomacy, were now "found marching shoulder to shoulder" with the Russians (and, of course, with the Hapsburg confederates of Russia). As we have already seen, the statesmen at Versailles were in part actuated to do this by their unending rivalry with the British: Participation in the onslaught upon Frederician Prussia might mean territorial concessions to France in the Austrian Netherlands, concessions that could be of use in neutralizing British successes in the vast world outside Europe. What this meant in Continental affairs, however, was that Gallic influence had to give way somewhat to that of St. Petersburg, which, "following up Peter the Great's Baltic policy," could now "contemplate the conquest of East Prussia – in other words, a drive into German territory past a weakened Poland."[48] Nevertheless, whatever Continental aspirations France might (at least for the present time) be abandoning, it remained concerned about the growth of Russian influence in eastern Europe. Thus, the decision to support the Austro-Russian plan to wage war on Frederick II, whatever logic it may have possessed in the context of the perdurable Franco-British competition, was counterproductive insofar as it helped to realize France's own professed fears regarding the Romanov threat. Russian designs possibly were balked only by the sudden accession in St. Petersburg of Tsar Peter III, an unbalanced admirer of Frederick the Great. And Peter was soon overthrown by his remarkable and utterly ruthless German wife Catherine, who, as true inheritor of the mantle of Peter the Great, would soon raise Russia's international stature to new heights.

Catherine, indeed, wasted no time. Scarcely a year after her bloody elevation to the Russian throne, she took advantage of the death of Polish monarch Augustus III to impose her own ex-lover, Stanislaus Poniatowski, upon Warsaw. France protested; but how could France, already strained to the limit by its endless effort against seafaring and colonizing Britain, hope to retain its wonted prestige in the increasingly perilous marches of eastern Europe? There was, in actuality, nothing that Versailles could do to checkmate Catherine's designs in Poland; Louis XV and Choiseul, however "intensely anti-Russian," had to content themselves with temporarily withholding recognition of Poniatowski's "election" to the Polish throne and refusing diplomatic representation at Warsaw. "Everything that may plunge Russia into chaos and make her return to obscurity," wrote a humiliated and exasperated Louis XV in September 1763, "is favorable to our interests."[49] For the French king, events in

48 Dehio, *Precarious Balance*, pp. 114–15.
49 Anderson, "European Diplomatic Relations, 1763–90," in *The New Cambridge Modern History*, Vol. VIII: *The American and French Revolutions, 1763–93* (Cambridge: Cam-

Poland were personally mortifying: He had, after all, established his notorious *Secret* or secret diplomacy earlier in his reign primarily for the purpose of preserving French influence among the Poles.

This was bad enough; but the French now proceeded to make matters even worse for themselves by seeking to strike at avaricious Russia through their old allies the Ottoman Turks. In the past Constantinople had been useful many times to France against Vienna; against St. Petersburg, however, in the late eighteenth century, the same tactic was less likely to succeed. Though the Russo-Turkish War of 1768–74 may not have arisen directly from French diplomatic activity at Constantinople, Choiseul certainly did all within his power to embroil the Turks with their dynamic neighbor to the north. The war, when it came, brought new humiliation to the French as well as military disaster to their Turkish protégés. Brushing aside protests from Versailles, Britain allowed Catherine the Great to send three squadrons of men-of-war through the Channel and around Gibraltar to the eastern Mediterranean. In those waters they destroyed the Turkish fleet. Brilliant Russian victories on land and sea secured for St. Petersburg by 1774 the Treaty of Kutchuk-Kainardji. A benchmark of Russia's rise to international greatness, this agreement not only extended tsarist influence on the Black Sea and its surrounding territories but also – and ominously – conferred on St. Petersburg the right (behind a façade of concern for Christians at Constantinople) to interest itself in Turkish domestic affairs.

For the French, the outcome of the Russo-Turkish conflict was galling on a number of counts. To begin with, there was the question of whether France's special commercial relationship with the Ottoman Empire would now be jeopardized. Then, again, the government at Versailles had made a special effort to reinvigorate the ailing Turkish army by supplying it with military instructors and technicians; thus, the poor performance of Turkish troops could be seen as an embarrassing reflection upon a French army still reeling from its defeats in the Seven Years' War. Ultimately, there was the reality that French support had not enabled Constantinople to prevail against its foe or to avoid a humiliating peace. In particular, the fact that France had proven utterly unable, "in the face of British hostility, to exclude the Russian fleet from the Mediterranean in 1770," could not help but "shake Turkish faith in her value as an ally."[50] On this last point, of course, the interlocking of the Franco-British and

bridge University Press, 1965), pp. 258–59. On Choiseul's sharply increasing concern over the growth of Russian power in the 1760s, see also H. M. Scott, "The Importance of Bourbon Naval Reconstruction to the Strategy of Choiseul after the Seven Years' War," *International History Review* 1 (1979), pp. 17–35.

50 Anderson, *Europe*, p. 236.

Franco-Russian rivalries had come home to haunt the strategists at Versailles.

And, as if this were not enough bitter fare for the plate of the aging Louis XV, events in the Balkans now rebounded upon his luckless friends in Poland. "The Russo-Turkish war and the Austro-Russian antagonism in the Balkans which sprang from it were not in any fundamental sense the causes of the first partition of Poland," Anderson has observed; "but they undoubtedly did much to accelerate it and perhaps to determine the form it took."[51] It does seem that, from the start of 1771, Prussia, motivated in part by a desire to keep tensions in eastern Europe from boiling over into a conflagration involving all the Great Powers, urged Austria and Russia to join it in a pleasant diversion: that is, carving up Poland. The resultant First Partition (of 1772) robbed the ancient but now helpless Polish kingdom of about 30 percent of its territory. Here, as in the Balkans, developments cast into sharp relief the alteration in the Franco-Russian power equation. Russia, secure in its Eurasian vastness, could receive from the feuding Germanic states of Prussia and Austria propositions regarding Polish territory and turn them to its own advantage even as it continued its assault on Turkey; meanwhile, France, however wounded it might feel in its pride by events in eastern Europe, found once again that its global competition with Britain ruled out in advance any possibility of effective French action in areas menaced by Catherine.

Moreover, the lengthening Russian shadow also fell across that other longtime ally of Versailles in eastern Europe, Sweden. In August 1772, the French-supported Gustavus III, by means of an almost bloodless coup d'état at Stockholm, overthrew a Swedish constitution that since 1720 had deprived the crown of much of its former authority. To diplomatic observers it seemed that here, if nowhere else, Versailles had scored a success. Yet it had done so at the cost of affronting both Britain and Russia. Both had long contended with France for paramount influence at Stockholm. Although Catherine was at the time preoccupied by her state's drive into Poland and the Ottoman Empire, her government threatened to reverse the situation within Sweden by use of force. Furthermore, because the British also looked on the coup of 1772 with a jaundiced eye, Louis XV's government found London unwilling to concert with it a response in the Baltic to Russian threats against Sweden. The scornful comment in British ruling circles that Britain and France could only bring naval pressure to bear against Russia since "as to their [French] troops upon the Rhine they can do nothing for Sweden"[52] pointed to ever more

51 Anderson, "European Diplomatic Relations," p. 262.
52 Black, *Natural and Necessary Enemies*, pp. 75–79.

obvious limitations on Gallic influence in eastern Europe that cannot have altogether displeased London.

By the end of Louis XV's reign, consequently, tsarist Russia had achieved a geopolitical stature curiously similar in some respects to that of Britain. As one historian has put it:

> Russia was the continental flanking power in relation to Europe – indeed, she was a continent on her own. She could as little be outflanked as, for quite different reasons, could Britain, the western flanking power with command of the sea. Just as Britain could retire into splendid isolation on her island, so Russia could withdraw into the oceanlike immensity of the Eurasian lowlands, there to remain secure from assault until she was herself ready to break out and attack.[53]

Catherine the Great and her advisers, to be sure, cannot have regarded matters with quite this aplomb; indeed, the tsarina's celebrated reign witnessed more than one challenge to Russian security from the powers to the west. Still, there is no denying that, as of 1774, the reality of Russian power galled the French in the Continental sphere of politics almost as much as the reality of British power frustrated French designs in the overseas world. Well might Louis XV wish "chaos" on the Romanov domain; well might he wish the Russian state to "return to obscurity." Moreover, Versailles found the waning of French influence in the region extending from the Baltic to the Balkans all the more painful in that it could so easily be associated in Gallic minds with crushing military defeat in Germany at the hands of another rising power, Hohenzollern Prussia.

There were intriguing similarities between Russia and Prussia: In both countries the lack of a strong "middle class" of educated and ambitious entrepreneurs and professionals left elite energies, abilities, and aspirations pretty much in the hands of relatively uncultured aristocratic landowners. In both countries there were few indigenous forces inhibiting the development of autocratic government. In both countries geopolitical ambition and insecurity alike drove remarkable autocratic monarchs to fuse aristocratic energies with the policies of the state. And in both countries, as in Britain, the integration of existing elite abilities and aspirations into the power structure far surpassed anything of its kind in prerevolutionary France.

What Peter the Great and his Romanov successors did for Russia, Frederick William I (1713–40) and his son Frederick II "the Great" (1740–86) of the Hohenzollern family did, over a much smaller area, for Prussia. Under their merciless prodding, Ludwig Dehio has written, a "country on the culturally backward fringes of the Protestant world . . . shot into prominence, from small beginnings, as a power based on a military civ-

53 Dehio, *Precarious Balance*, pp. 100–1

ilization."[54] In his classic study of Prussian institutions, Hans Rosenberg has described concretely how the Hohenzollerns integrated the country's landowning nobles, or Junkers, into the structures of state power:

> By functioning on an increasingly large scale as a bureaucracy in the absolute state, as army officers and administrative dignitaries, the Junkers recovered in new forms and on a different legal foundation many of their old powers. Moreover, they vastly extended their influence by taking possession, under the leadership of the bureaucratic nobility, of the newly built halls of central government. The crux of the matter, then, was that, indirectly, the nobility at large received a most formidable new center of gravity in the professional service elites of the absolute monarchy and that, by the mid-eighteenth century, this bureaucratic hierarchy of political power holders was no longer troubled by a serious confusion of faces at the top. In alliance with the state machine the privileged classes grew stronger than they had been in the days of opposition.[55]

A kind of symbiotic, triangular arrangement developed – the royal autocrat, those of his nobles serving for life or at least for many years in army officer ranks and top-level administrative positions, and those of his nobles dominating social and economic life on the village and county district level. Under Frederick II even more than under his father, the Junkers monopolized officer positions in the army and the more responsible and permanent positions in the civilian bureaucracy, edging out of those seats of power nonnoble professionals. And under Frederick the Great the local squirearchy tightened its grip upon the hapless peasantry and on a bewildering array of fiscal and policing activities.

A British historian, A. N. Goodwin, has noted revealingly that "the most pressing need for the dynasty to offer the aristocracy a 'New Deal' arose from Frederick the Great's determination to conquer Silesia."[56] Indeed, for the Prussians, with their country cut out in morsels of territory extending from the Rhineland in the west to the borders of Russia in the east, sheer survival almost automatically dictated a policy of calculated, preemptive aggression against the other states on the Continent. Hence the devotion lavished by Frederick William I and his more celebrated son on the Prussian army – on its discipline, its fighting morale, its commissariat, its equipment, its strategic and tactical mobility. And as the Hohenzollern monarchs forged their compromises with the Junker squirearchy, impressed Junker sons (and the expendable peasantry) into military service, and toughened the sinews of a war-making capacity, the Prussian army virtually exploded in size, from barely thirty thousand fighting men in 1690 to nearly two hundred thousand by the Seven Years'

---

54 Ibid., pp. 111–13.
55 Hans Rosenberg, *Bureaucracy, Aristocracy and Autocracy: The Prussian Experience, 1680–1815* (Cambridge, Mass.: Harvard University Press, 1958), p. 150.
56 A. N. Goodwin, "Prussia," in Goodwin, ed., *The European Nobility*, p. 89.

War.[57] With its domestic energies thus harnessed to its geopolitical will, Prussia in the course of the eighteenth century became a power to be reckoned with – as the French found to their cost.

The crucial breakthrough to major power status for Berlin was its seizure of the northern Hapsburg province of Silesia in 1740. To retain this conquest, Frederick the Great was willing to wage full-scale war – and, as it turned out, he would have to do so twice, during 1740–48 and 1756–63, since Austria's feisty Maria Theresa bent every effort to recovering the lost province. However, with the signing of the Treaty of Hubertusburg in 1763, concluding Continental hostilities in the Seven Years' War, Vienna had (at least for the foreseeable future) to acquiesce in Prussian control of Silesia.

For Frederick and, indeed, for all of central Europe, this was a development of cardinal importance. "Frederick's acquisition of Silesia," Dorn has gone so far as to say, "was the greatest permanent conquest of territory hitherto made by any power in the history of modern western Europe. It became not merely the largest, but, with its rich linen industry and undeveloped iron ores, the wealthiest province of the Prussian monarchy. Without it Prussia could never have become a great power."[58] Prussia's retention of Silesia, observed Anderson similarly, "appeared to many contemporaries the greatest military achievement of the age; and the leadership of Frederick II seemed sufficient to counterbalance many of her material weaknesses."[59]

But Frederician Prussia's rise to international prominence was almost as humbling to the French as it was to Austria. This was true even in the War of the Austrian Succession, when Berlin and Versailles were confederates in the assault on the Hapsburg state. The unscrupulous Prussian sovereign deserted his French ally on more than one occasion in the course of that conflict as the retention of his precious conquest of Silesia seemed to dictate. Certainly Frederick's adamant refusal to subordinate his personal objectives in the war to the overall strategic conception of the struggle held by Belle-Isle and others at Versailles was one of the factors dooming French efforts to win glory in central Europe by carving up the territories of the ancient Austrian enemy. Subsequent French victories in the Austrian Netherlands did not efface the bitter impression among Gallic strategists that Frederick had played Louis XV for a fool.

This, naturally, made it all the easier for Viennese statesmen to entice Louis XV and his kingdom into their war of revenge against Prussia in the following decade. So, once again, a French army marched east with

---

57 Kennedy, *Rise and Fall of the Great Powers*, p. 99.
58 Dorn, *Competition for Empire*, pp. 174–75.
59 Anderson, "European Diplomatic Relations," p. 252.

the intention of visiting havoc upon a German prince, only to be mortifyingly routed by a Prussian force half its size at Rossbach, on 5 November 1757. "Among the numerous possible points of no return in the history of old regime France," Blanning has asserted, "that day has a strong claim."[60] The angry frustration infecting elite circles in France as a result of military disasters like that at Rossbach was voiced by the comte de Saint-Germain, commander of the French rearguard on 5 November 1757, in a letter to a friend:

No doubt you, like me, were able to predict the Rossbach disaster five months ago. Never has there been such a defective army, and the first cannon-shot determined our rout and humiliation. I am leading a gang of robbers, of murderers fit only for the gallows, who run away at the sound of the first gunshot and who are always ready to mutiny. The King has the worst infantry under the sun, and the worst-disciplined – there is just nothing to be done with troops like these.[61]

And this, in retrospect, from the cardinal de Bernis:

A war levied against the king of Prussia, who was undoubtedly the greatest captain of his century, deserved to be carried on by good generals and by a council composed of enlightened and experienced officers. But neither Austria nor France had any general fit to be opposed to Frederick, and the troops were totally undisciplined. Treachery and incompetence were the orders of the day. Generals and nation were completely demoralised.[62]

Frederick II could have been forgiven if, as reports at the time had it, he made sport of his former Gallic ally for its military impotence.

Modern military historians – André Corvisier, Emile Léonard, Lee Kennett, and others – have generally endorsed this eighteenth-century verdict. To be sure, they have endeavored to be fair in their assessments. Some features of the French military establishment, Kennett has insisted, "were very advanced for their day, and justly excited the admiration of Europe." In many respects, furthermore, "the French war machine very closely resembled those of the other great powers."[63] Still, for this analyst, as for his fellow specialists, it has been all too easy to find reasons why, in Continental as in oceanic warfare, the French forces performed so poorly.

The army was top-heavy, burdened with so many generals that, contemporaries commonly said, they had to exercise their commissions in

---

60 Blanning, *Origins of the French Revolutionary Wars*, p. 41.
61 Quoted in ibid.
62 Soltau, *Duc de Choiseul*, pp. 16–17.
63 Lee Kennett, *The French Armies in the Seven Years' War* (Durham, N.C.: Duke University Press, 1967), pp. 138–39.

rotation.[64] By 1775, the proportion of officers to men would be as high as 1 to 15, with at least 1,100 colonels for 200 regiments and 1,200 general officers. Luxury softened the battle-readiness of generals and officers of inferior rank. No cavalry officer, it was said, could do with fewer than six horses and three valets; colonels and their superiors felt obligated in the midst of war to provide "open table," complete with silver plate, fancy linen, and exorbitant amounts of meat, fowl, and pastry. At the other extreme were those officers of the impecunious provincial nobility whose very survival in the army was jeopardized by the tardy payment (or actual stoppage) of their wages from the government. Quarreling and insubordination among the generals, often favorites themselves of the eternally bickering factions at Versailles, all too frequently found an echo in the pillaging and general nondiscipline of the common soldiers on campaign. The military efforts of the French all too often foundered on their failure to discard the siege mentality of the past, with its reliance on fortresses, cumbersome baggage trains, and inflexible tactics of maneuvering and fighting, in favor of the much more aggressive, mobile warfare of the Prussians. Finally, a social issue that (as we shall see later on) had a much wider resonance in domestic French politics divided army theorists into four camps. Some advocated a fighting force commanded exclusively by old provincial noblesse; others wished to confer offices in the ranks according to strictly defined military criteria; yet others imagined an army commanded by affluent purchasers of office from whatever station in life; and some, finally, envisioned a republican-style institution commingling citizen-officers and citizen-soldiers.

Admittedly, all the other Continental powers (most notably Hapsburg Austria) experienced similar problems in their military establishments to one extent or another. Still, the stunning reverses suffered by French arms in central Europe in the middle decades of the eighteenth century pointed to a complex of especially serious ills afflicting the Gallic war effort.

Yet, in addition to all these factors, there was an even deeper reason for Bourbon France's ignominious thrashing at the hands of a small, agrarian, and poor kingdom situated precariously on the northwest Eurasian coastal plain. Kennett approached this deeper reason when he noted that "the destitute government was financially unable to bear its burdens adequately, and could not lavish on its armies the money that has rightly been called the sinews of war."[65] A similar problem, recall, plagued

64 On the problems in the French army, see, in addition to Kennett's study: Robert Forster, *The House of Saulx-Tavanes: Versailles and Burgundy, 1700–1830* (Baltimore: Johns Hopkins University Press, 1971), pp. 43–44; Emile G. Léonard, *L'Armée et ses problèmes au XVIII siècle* (Paris: Plon, 1958); and André Corvisier, *Armies and Societies in Europe, 1494–1789*, trans. Abigail T. Siddall (Bloomington: Indiana University Press, 1979), esp. pp. 100–3, 162–66.
65 Kennett, *French Armies*, pp. 138–39.

French efforts to compete successfully on the high seas against Britain. Just as its failure to concentrate sufficiently on the requirements of naval warfare handicapped France's campaign against those islanders so expert in matters pertaining to the sea, so its failure to focus single-mindedly on the very different requirements of land warfare crippled France's martial efforts against an indomitable Prussian prince whose very geopolitical vulnerability dictated his expertise in matters germane to Continental warfare. The French, to repeat – and this will be one of two overriding themes throughout this book – tried to have it both ways, tried to achieve supremacy or at least maintain competitive parity in two geostrategic spheres at the same time, and as a result fell short in both theaters of action.

Frederician Prussia, then, flouted France directly at Rossbach and other fields of combat in the Seven Years' War. In the crisis-ridden final years of Louis XV's reign, the Prussians joined Russia and (ironically) France's "ally" Austria in thwarting Versailles less directly – through the assault on Poland. It was Frederick II who, from the early months of 1771, urged upon Vienna and, through Vienna, upon St. Petersburg as well, a partial division of Warsaw's hopelessly exposed territories. Although retrospective analysis indicates the relentless growth of Russian influence to have been the most basic dynamic behind the First Partition of 1772, it suggests as surely that Prussia's resultant annexation of the northwestern corner of Poland critically fortified the Hohenzollern state by linking East Prussia to the heartland of the kingdom.

It is clear that, by 1774, something of the greatest importance was happening in international relations. Power was moving away from the western extremity of Eurasia, or "western Europe" as we would call it more conventionally. It was migrating overseas with Britain's resounding colonial and commercial successes, and it was migrating more deeply into the Eurasian hinterland, into "eastern Europe." Contributing most to this latter process was the rise of Russia and Prussia; playing a secondary role was the geopolitical reassertion of France's supposed ally Austria at the expense of two traditional outposts of French influence toward the east, Poland and Turkey. What is more, "ordinary" French citizens were themselves becoming progressively more aware of and sensitive to these developments, which were reducing their country's power and prestige in the world at large.

THE WINTER OF FRANCE'S DISCONTENT

In her most recent book on the European ancien régime, the British historian C. B. A. Behrens has commented: "It has rarely if ever happened, even in later centuries, that governments which have added significantly to their wealth or territories by military conquest have failed to win the support of their subjects, or that governments which have suffered the opposite fate have managed to keep it."[66] Although it is notoriously difficult to gauge the depth of patriotic sentiment in largely rural and inarticulate societies, especially in historical eras long antedating the application of "scientific" polling techniques, evidence does exist that the French people – humble souls as well as members of the political, social, and intellectual elites – developed some sense of identification with their state's international fortunes. By 1774, such patriotism, it is at least arguable, was becoming a potent component of that elusive but increasingly influential phenomenon known as public opinion and was contributing to the crisis of confidence that marred Louis XV's senescent years.

Intriguing signs of such allegiance to French geopolitical glory punctuate the last century of the old regime. One of the Sun King's enemies grudgingly conceded in 1690 that "whenever the king wins a battle, takes a city or subdues a province, [the French] light bonfires, and every petty person feels elevated and associates the king's grandeur with himself; this compensates him for all his losses and consoles him in all his misery."[67] When, in the bleak days of 1709, Louis XIV's ministers issued a letter appealing for the citizenry's support of the government in the late stages of the conflict over the Spanish Succession, Parisian demand for printed copies of the exhortatory message "was immense... and after the first printing was sold out in a day, new editions were run off that night, while a large crowd waited impatiently outside the printer's door.... Everyone was aroused, and each man resolved to aid the King according to his talents, even to the point of shedding his own blood if it were necessary."[68] But perhaps more significant as testimony to popular patriotism at this painful juncture in the kingdom's affairs was an English agent's report: "We hear from all over France that the people are infuriated at the extraordinary demands we have made and that despite their great misery they are entirely disposed to assist the king with everything remaining to them."[69]

Thirty-five years later, during the War of the Austrian Succession, the baron von Bernstorff, Denmark's perspicacious ambassador to France, alluded to the same phenomenon in a communication to his home government:

[France] is supposed to be drained of men and money, her people discouraged, the court only wishing for peace... Nothing of all that seems to me to be so.

66 C. B. A. Behrens, *Society, Government and the Enlightenment: The Experiences of Eighteenth-Century France and Prussia* (London: Thames & Hudson, 1985), p. 165.
67 Joseph Klaits, *Printed Propaganda under Louis XIV. Absolute Monarchy and Public Opinion* (Princeton, N.J.: Princeton University Press, 1976), p. 18.
68 Ibid., p. 219.
69 Quoted in ibid., p. 220.

... [The people] curses the war whereof it bears the weight, it sighs after peace, but it is its genius that it is not less prompt to sacrifice itself for the glory of the French name so soon as it is urged to or as the least success animates it. It is inconceivable how much irritation the ill-considered attempt of the Austrians to enter France last year has caused, and how much its ill success had raised the spirit of the nation.[70]

In 1743, Parisian publicist E.-J.-F. Barbier noted the reaction in the capital to news of valiant French efforts to recover from a defeat at Dettingen: "People congratulated each other in the streets, people visited each other; some individuals, who had occasionally glimpsed each other but exchanged no words over a period of ten years, now sought each other out and exchanged invitations to dinner."[71] The marquis d'Argenson, after hearing of the Maréchal de Saxe's great victory at Fontenoy, wrote ecstatically to his former *camarade de collège* Voltaire: "The people can find happiness if only they can maintain the hegemony of France, for she is indeed in a position to dictate conditions, fair conditions, to Europe."[72] When, on the evening of 18 March 1746, the Maréchal de Saxe, fresh from his dramatic occupation of Brussels, appeared at the Opéra in Paris, he was crowned with laurels to wild applause, recalling, in one spectator's words, "a Roman triumph."[73] Such effusions of joy, furthermore, were not limited to the presumably sophisticated residents of the capital. At a humble village near the Aube, east-southeast of Paris, for example, the rustic ancestors of military historian Emile Léonard put aside their dislike of taxes, requisitions, and militia duty long enough to celebrate French victories in the war of 1740–48 with Te Deums, festivals, and fireworks.[74]

Popular patriotism continued to manifest itself during and after the Seven Years' War. In 1756, the audience at the Paris Opéra spontaneously acclaimed the comtesse d'Egmont upon learning of the British surrender of Port Mahon (on Minorca) to her father, the duc de Richelieu.[75] Nine years later, the Comédie Française struck gold when it presented Pierre de Belloy's tragedy *Le Siège de Calais*, a drama dealing with the eternal Franco-British rivalry and catering to the chauvinistic instincts of its viewers.

According to all accounts, the success of this play was prodigious, unexceeded, said the contemporary critic La Harpe, in the previous history of the French theater. The company of the Comédie Française gave a free performance for the people of Paris, who came in crowds, applauding and shouting "Vive le roi!" ...

70 Cited in Butler, *Choiseul*, pp. 526–27.
71 Léonard, *L'Armée et ses problèmes*, p. 157.
72 Ibid., p. 217.
73 Ibid., p. 157.
74 Ibid., pp. 157–60.
75 Ibid., p. 157.

Revivals in later years were no less successful than the first run. . . . Baron Grimm, who was neither an ardent devotee of the monarchy nor a French nationalist, remarked: "This piece has really been a state event. . . . Those who have dared . . . to speak of it coldly and without admiration, have been regarded as bad citizens, or, what is worse, as philosophers."[76]

When, in the mid-1760s, Choiseul appealed to the public for funds to be employed in the reconstruction of the decimated navy, "the result must almost have exceeded his hopes." Contributions flowed in from all sides. Ships of the line were given by the provinces of Languedoc, Brittany, Burgundy, Flanders, and Artois, the cities of Paris and Bordeaux, the Marseilles Chamber of Commerce, the Order of the Saint-Esprit, the Parisian merchant guilds, the receivers-general and farmers-general of finances, and an even more numerous group of country gentlemen. Moreover, a patriotic subscription brought in 13 million livres to the ministry's coffers.[77] "Nobody in France believed that the Seven Years' War was definitely closed," one scholar has observed. "A common refrain to resume the war echoed throughout the land."[78]

Even philosophers, allegedly so maligned by admirers of the *Siège de Calais,* and so commonly depicted by specialists of the Enlightenment in our own day as lofty-minded cosmopolites, caught the rising patriotic fever. The abbé Coyer published a pamphlet celebrating the obligations of soldiers, magistrates, priests, and mothers to the *patrie.* His treatise met with widespread "philosophic" approval, and large sections of it were reproduced verbatim in that compendium of Enlightenment knowledge and social criticism the *Encyclopédie.* D'Alembert indignantly refuted Frederick II's charge that the philosophes, as citizens of an international "republic of letters," lacked patriotism. Helvétius allowed that patriotism, however inconsistent with a larger concern for humanity, was "so desirable, so virtuous and so estimable a passion in the citizen." Rousseau, of course, was the eighteenth century's great prophet of modern devotion to fatherland or motherland. But not even Diderot and Voltaire could remain totally immune to such sentiment. Diderot argued that his countrymen, although owing much to the English in the domains of "reason and philosophy," possessed, nevertheless, an "adventurous genius" that had now enabled them to overtake their erstwhile mentors. And Voltaire himself, in a letter to Mme d'Epinay in 1766, declared: "We

76 Frances Acomb, *Anglophobia in France, 1763–1789* (Durham, N.C.: Duke University Press, 1950), pp. 58–59.
77 See Singh, *French Diplomacy,* pp. 56–57, and Jenkins, *History of the French Navy,* pp. 142–45, for information on this patriotic response to Choiseul's appeal.
78 Singh, *French Diplomacy,* p. 201.

are in many things the disciples of the English; we shall end by being the equals of our masters."[79]

In addition, as Frances Acomb and others have pointed out, philosophies of conservative and reformist nationalism claimed numerous adherents in France at this time; and what they held in common was a rejection of much or all that was British. Conservative nationalists warned of England's "imminent material decay." They asserted that war had "disrupted British commerce, injured manufactures, and produced great popular distress. It had entailed a national debt of such proportions that repayment was impossible." Taxation, so they alleged, was crippling the British economy; agriculture was beginning to decline; and the British Empire was becoming administratively cumbersome and unbalanced in its heavy reliance on trade. France, on the other hand, they regarded as balanced in its commerce, industry, and agriculture, as fundamentally healthy, as actuated still by a lively sense of "national honor." "What can Britain do," one of these writers contemptuously queried, "beside a power that can raise a hundred and sixty thousand seamen and two hundred and fifty thousand soldiers? Can she suppose that she will lay down the law to it?"[80] Motivated by its "honor" and rejoicing in its strength, France would defend its own sacred rights and those of other nations against the acts of "injustice" committed or threatened by the haughty imperialists across the Channel. So spoke those Frenchmen who (contradictorily, as it would turn out) combined defiance of the British with opposition to sociopolitical change at home.

As for the reform-minded nationalists, their most prominent spokesmen, at least prior to the American Revolution, were the so-called Physiocrats. For these nationalists, patriotism took root in an agrarian society: Only the citizen with a stake in the soil he laboriously tilled could be consciously loyal to a fatherland. "The Physiocrats," Acomb has noted, "were intensely proud of their own land and people. They preferred French civilization to any other, even in their capacity as reformers. Their 'legal despotism' was a kind of idealization of the historic French monarchy. They vigorously defended the French national character and intelligence against the imputation of inferiority to the national character and intelligence of the English."[81] Even Physiocratic statesmen like Dupont de Nemours and Turgot, noted for their broader humanitarian con-

---

79 For these sentiments of and pronouncements by the philosophes, consult R. R. Palmer, "The National Idea in France before the Revolution," *Journal of the History of Ideas* 1 (1940), pp. 95–111; and Acomb, *Anglophobia in France*, pp. 67–68.
80 Ibid., pp. 59–62.
81 Ibid., pp. 63–65. Refer also to Black, *Natural and Necessary Enemies*, passim, on these themes.

cerns, betrayed an unmistakable pride in country on more than one occasion.

Of course, much of this was but brave talk, defiant braggadocio in the face of French geostrategic failures on land and sea. In the everyday world of international competition, ideas and ideologies are not necessarily anything other than ideas and ideologies; state power and its associated prestige are trump. This was especially obvious, pitilessly so, to elite Frenchmen of that era in and out of government. Their anxious commentaries could be cited ad infinitum. Words penned by the abbé Bernis to Choiseul in 1758 bespoke a widespread regret over Versailles' new alignment with Austria. "The king of Prussia is madly admired, because those who conduct their affairs successfully are always admired. The court of Vienna is detested because it is regarded as a leech on France. . . . Our policy has been absurd and shameful."[82] Ten years later, the same statesman wrote to Choiseul in accents of despair: "We must change our ways, and this task, which would require centuries in another country, might be accomplished in a year in this [country], if there were men capable of it."[83] A one-time secretary of foreign affairs, Gérard de Rayneval, would later expatiate upon the pathetic condition of France in the twilight of Louis XV's reign:

The other nations concluded that France no longer possessed strength or resources. The envy which had hitherto inspired the policies of other courts towards France degenerated into contempt. The government at Versailles lost its prestige and its influence over other governments. Instead of being, as formerly, the hub of European policy, it became a passive spectator, whose approval or disapproval counted for nothing.[84]

And the comte de Ségur would offer an equally bleak assessment in his memoirs:

Thus soon after [the 1756 alliance with Austria had been concluded] the government no longer possessed any dignity, the finances any order, and the conduct of policy any consistency. France lost its influence in Europe; England ruled the seas effortlessly and conquered the Indies unopposed. The powers of the North partitioned Poland. The balance of power established by the Peace of Westphalia was broken. The French monarchy ceased to be a first-rank power.[85]

Was there exaggeration and oversimplification in these commentaries? No doubt. France was not yet reduced to, say, the condition of eighteenth-century Poland. But then, Poland had never deliberately woven

82 Cited in Albert Sorel, *Europe and the French Revolution: The Political Traditions of the Old Regime*, trans. Alfred Cobban and J. W. Hunt (Garden City, N.Y.: Doubleday, 1971), pp. 289–90.
83 Cited in ibid., p. 236.
84 Quoted in ibid., p. 288.
85 Cited in Blanning, *Origins*, p. 42.

into its national traditions the yen to dominate simultaneously both the Continental and the maritime worlds; no ghosts of Louis XIV and Colbert whispered challenging words into the ears of Stanislaus Poniatowski and his counselors and courtiers. Even so, the Poles would soon show themselves capable of rising in defense of their national integrity. Is it any wonder, then, that the mortified French would soon show themselves capable of even huger exploits?

Indignation at Versailles "overflowed," according to Albert Sorel, when in 1772 courtiers there learned about the three eastern powers' initial partition of Poland and fully grasped "to what a point of 'servile dependence' on the house of Austria the king had reduced France."[86] And Ségur recalled somberly: "The illusions of hope had gained for the King in his youth the title of the well-beloved. Having been defeated, he lost it. People change with their fortunes. They love...or hate authority according to the good it does them, and often they bestow without measure their admiration on success and their scorn on failure."[87] Louis XV's embarrassments at the hands of his foreign opponents (even, as in the case of Austria, his presumed allies) thus help to explain why this monarch in death was the butt of so much elite and popular derision.

But if the state that Louis supposedly personified in godlike fashion was losing its credibility in Continental and global affairs, and if it was doing so primarily because of unrealistic strategic aspirations, it was doing so secondarily because of its gradual loss of legitimacy in domestic affairs. It would be well to stress once again in this connection that, of all the Great Powers in the century before the French Revolution, France failed most resoundingly at the task of meshing the values and ambitions – most notably, geopolitical ambitions – of the state with those of elite society. Hence, in order to comprehend all the dimensions of France's national political crisis of 1770–74, we must turn to that sociopolitical challenge to the government that, gradually taking shape over the years, paralleled the government's geopolitical challenge. These two overriding challenges, interrelated to some extent even before the troublous finale of Louis XV's reign, may have come uncomfortably close to explosive convergence during 1770–74. Certainly in hindsight it appears that they came close enough in those years to foreshadow their veritably revolutionary convergence in 1788 and 1789.

86 Sorel, *Europe and the French Revolution*, pp. 289–90.
87 Quoted in Behrens, *Society*, p. 165.

2

The legacy of French history: the
sociopolitical challenge

In 1591, a political theorist named Louis Turquet de Mayerne penned an
eerily prophetic essay entitled *De la monarchie aristodémocratique*. In it,
he "proposed a form of government in which the king was the executive
and the symbol of the state and presided over the Estates General, the
representative body which was the voice of the people, the true seat of
sovereignty, and the legislative power." As the "authentic radical" among
the old regime's political thinkers, Turquet de Mayerne also "proposed
to improve the political system by altering the social structure" – that is,
by replacing the primordial clergy, nobility, and Third Estate with a
novel social elite of industrious and meritorious Frenchmen.[1] The author
of this treatise was a prophet without honor in his own time – indeed,
Marie de Médicis's regency banned the essay immediately after its publication in 1611 – but he nonetheless set the essential sociopolitical agenda
for the entire ancien régime.

If the French Bourbon state wished to compete successfully with its
rivals, it would at the very least have to emulate them in harnessing
domestic elitist energies to the purposes of foreign policy. In itself, this
might not secure the international greatness of the historic Gallic realm,
but it was a prerequisite toward that end. Accordingly, the Bourbon
monarchs would have to discharge at least three interrelated tasks. First,
they would have to admit significant numbers of articulate and ambitious
Frenchmen from all three orders into national and local governance.
Second, they would have to mesh their own vision of society – of its
structure and dominant values – with some prevalent vision emerging
among their enfranchised subjects. Finally, in collaboration with these

1 Quoted and discussed in Elizabeth Adams, "Seventeenth-Century Attitudes Toward
the French Estates General," Ph.D. Dissertation, University of West Virginia, 1976, pp.
170–87.

individuals, they would have to find ways to finance their embryonic global policies.

This, then, was in its crucial dimensions the sociopolitical challenge accompanying and interacting with the geopolitical challenge facing the Bourbons. To review its development is to understand how its gradual convergence with the Bourbons' global mission in the eighteenth century could severely test the social and political world of the old France.

WAR, ABSOLUTISM, AND THE "CONSTITUTIONAL" ISSUE

The monarchs and ministers of the Bourbon dynasty resolved early on to govern France in what we term today an absolutist fashion: to impose a centralized protobureaucracy upon the kingdom and avoid consultation of the citizenry through institutionalized representative assemblies. Yet the national collective memory of consultative governance in crucial earlier periods of French history could not be altogether effaced, and would increasingly dog those wielding power and waging war in the seventeenth and eighteenth centuries. With the growing influence of "public opinion" in the late years of Louis XV's reign would come a genuine national debate over constitutional issues that would begin to expose cracks in the foundations of Bourbon absolutism.

Absolutism in prerevolutionary France, as in old regime England, Russia, and China, pivoted on a sovereign likening his powers to those of God. C. B. A. Behrens has cogently summed up Louis XIV's constitutional canon:

Believing that "we exercise on earth a function wholly divine," and occupy "the place of God," he assumed his relations to his subjects to be comparable to those of God towards humanity. He was the father of his people. He owed them love and protection and the duty to devote himself to their welfare, but they, in their turn, owed tribute to his majesty. He continually referred to the need to maintain "my own splendour of life," my own "magnificence," my own "honor."[2]

And here was Louis XV in 1766, haranguing his most prestigious court of law, the Parlement of Paris, upon *his* godlike authority:

It is in my person alone that sovereign power resides... It is from me alone that my courts of justice derive their existence and their authority. The plenitude of this authority, which they exercise only in my name, remains always with me. I alone possess legislative power without sharing it with, or depending for it on, anyone.... The whole system of public order emanates from me.[3]

2 Behrens, *Society, Government and the Enlightenment*, pp. 33–34.
3 Ibid., p. 25.

Perhaps the crux of the matter, insofar as it concerned domestic politics, was the royal claim to monopolize legislative power. That claim was reflected in the resolution of one Bourbon king after another to rule without consulting the people in the representative body of earlier centuries known as the Estates General.

The desuetude of the Estates General after 1614–15 was surely one of the central realities defining the old regime in France. Whether or not that last convocation of 1614–15 was able "to speak for a united, articulate group and . . . serve the crown as an active instrument of government,"[4] the fact is that no sovereign between 1615 and 1789 convened this assembly. Nor did consultative governance thrive at the provincial level. Only in a few *pays d'états* – most notably, Brittany, Burgundy, and Languedoc – did delegates of the three orders continue to meet at regular intervals to transact public business, and even in those cases, commissioners sent out by the central government, the celebrated intendants, shared with the provincial Estates the management of a host of local issues. In the municipalities of France, too, the tumultuous but relatively free politics of bygone eras gave way to a more orderly disposition of affairs under the paternalistic aegis of administrative absolutism.

Centralized, bureaucratized governance did not develop easily in France. As Robert Harding, William Beik, and Sharon Kettering have shown, the ministers working toward this end had to contend with local institutions and attitudes of mind anchored tenaciously in the past, and had to rely on the cooperation of French people hailing from all walks of professional life.[5] The crown gradually appropriated for its own uses the patron–client relationships that had long bound powerful and dependent nobles together, thus turning patronage in the provinces away from noble and toward statist purposes. Provincial military governorships, traditionally citadels of noble influence, had to be accommodated within the structure of royal authority. And the government could not possibly have functioned, let alone tightened its grip upon this large west Eurasian realm, without the collaboration of clerks in the ministerial bureaux, financiers of various kinds, judges in the hierarchies of law courts, mem-

---

4 See J. Michael Hayden, *France and the Estates General of 1614* (Cambridge: Cambridge University Press, 1974), pp. 215–18, and George Rothrock, "The French Crown and the Estates General of 1614," *French Historical Studies* 1 (Fall 1960), pp. 305–6, for conflicting opinions on this issue.

5 Robert Harding, *Anatomy of a Power Elite: The Provincial Governors of Early Modern France* (New Haven, Conn.: Yale University Press, 1978); William Beik, *Absolutism and Society in Seventeenth-Century France: State Power and Provincial Aristocracy in Languedoc* (Cambridge: Cambridge University Press, 1985); Sharon Kettering, *Patrons, Brokers, and Clients in Seventeenth-Century France* (New York: Oxford University Press, 1986).

bers of provincial Estates, and officeholders in municipalities and villages throughout the land.

By the early decades of the eighteenth century, however, as the magisterial works of Pierre Goubert and Michel Antoine underscore,[6] the architects of the new French absolutism had their task fairly well in hand. Power at the center (and this now meant Versailles) lay in the hands of the sovereign and varying combinations of ministers, "secretaries of state" heading up operative governmental departments, "councillors of state," and "masters of requests" transacting business and setting policy in the "committees" that were specific emanations for specific purposes of the king's Council. Among these high political functionaries, one in particular – the chancellor or keeper of the seals, embodiment after the king of justice in the realm – was losing something of his wonted influence, while another – the controller-general of finances, steward of the moneys that were the sinews of the state's war-making capacity – was becoming increasingly indispensable. Decisions hammered out at Versailles were then transmitted to provincial France, and translated into local policy, by the intendants and their "subdelegates." Maurice Bordes has argued that political initiative and influence in provincial France shifted somewhat back from the crown's agents to the Estates and other local organs in the course of the century.[7] Still, we may easily share Goubert's wonder at how few individuals, relatively speaking, accounted for so much of the actual formulation of state policy.[8] This is, of course, another way of emphasizing the considerable degree to which power became centralized in the old regime.

However, what is especially telling from a global-historical viewpoint is the role played by the crown's war making in the development of this particular kind of absolutism. Again and again, under Richelieu, Mazarin, Louis XIV, and Louis XV, a preference for war over peace that transcended domestic sociopolitical considerations led to a concentration of authority and prestige in the hands of royal ministers, intendants, financiers, and officeholders.

In the 1620s, for example, two of Louis XIII's most powerful counselors, Chief Minister Richelieu himself and Keeper of the Seals Michel de Marillac, clashed over France's prospective role in the Thirty Years' War. As Richard Bonney has noted, Marillac "opposed an aggressive French foreign policy and . . . argued that the war . . . would lead to the

6 Pierre Goubert, *L'Ancien Régime*, 2 vols. (Paris: Colin, 1969–73); and Michel Antoine, *Le Conseil du Roi sous le règne de Louis XV* (Geneva: Droz, 1970).

7 Maurice Bordes, *L'Administration provinciale et municipale en France au XVIIIe siècle* (Paris: Société d'Edition d'Enseignement Supérieur, 1972).

8 Goubert, *Louis XIV and Twenty Million Frenchmen*, trans. Anne Carter (New York: Vintage, 1970), pp. 86, 95–97.

bankruptcy of the crown. . . . A policy of co-existence abroad would permit reform at home. . . . Marillac thus wanted the modification of existing
institutions, not the introduction of new forms of government." Richelieu, on the other hand, although similarly desirous of domestic reform
in his early years as chief minister, also "believed that the demands of
French foreign policy had to take precedence over all domestic considerations." Louis XIII had to choose between these two men and their
respective philosophies; on the so-called Day of Dupes, 10 November
1630, he "declared his intention of retaining Richelieu. Marillac was arrested."[9] As a result, the formidable cardinal was able to pursue a more
aggressive anti-Hapsburg foreign policy, eventually bringing France directly into the war. The domestic concomitants of this critical decision
included the attribution of new tax-collecting powers to the intendants
and their subdelegates in the provinces, an enormous increase in the basic direct tax known as the *taille* and in other imposts, an increasing
recurrence to the vending of judicial, fiscal, and administrative offices,
and an increasing governmental reliance on loans from the financial
community.

Scarcely twenty years after Louis XIII had confronted *his* difficult
choice between war and domestic reform, Cardinal Mazarin and Anne
of Austria, acting on behalf of the youthful Louis XIV during that confused rebellion known as the Fronde, faced a similar dilemma. "Either
they could accept the [Frondeurs'] demands, dismantle the system of war
finances, and recall the intendants permanently, thus risking the prospect
of a humiliating peace; or else the existing foreign policy must be brought
to fruition."[10] The latter course of action would obviously entail a ringing
endorsement of the intendants (and, thus, of the taxes they collected in
the countryside) and a renewed ministerial dependence on financiers'
loans and the selling of new offices. Because Mazarin and Anne were
determined to impose French peace terms on Philip IV of Spain and to
uphold their monarch's glory in domestic as well as in foreign affairs,
their rejection of the Frondeurs' demands and prosecution of the war
against Madrid were foregone conclusions. In quelling the revolt against
the government and achieving victory over Spain, the cardinal-minister
and the mother of the king ensured the continuation of the trend toward
a specific kind of absolutism – fiscal-administrative absolutism – in this
country.

Although scholars have offered different chronologies of absolutist
developments under Louis XIV, generally they have tended to see a
correlation between those developments and international events. J. Rus-

9 Bonney, *Political Change in France Under Richelieu and Mazarin*, pp. 35–38.
10 Ibid., pp. 58–59.

sell Major, for example, has contended that Louis and Colbert initially assigned the intendants "a smaller role in their plans for the reorganization of the kingdom than one might think," seeing them primarily as information gatherers with limited tenures in the various *généralités*, or administrative districts of the realm. "Only with the Dutch war in 1672 when the traditional bureaucracy failed to meet their expanded requirements did Louis and Colbert begin to use the intendants as administrators, a development that the latter at least regretted but had to permit because of the greater efficiency that it brought."[11]

Richard Bonney has posited a somewhat earlier transformation in the role of the intendants. To begin with, he has seen their administrative work in the army as contributing notably to Mazarin's victory over Spain in 1659, patently years before it helped to ensure the military triumphs of the Sun King's personal reign. Furthermore, Bonney has discerned a portentous shift in the way these "commissioners dispatched from the king's Council" viewed their own administrative-fiscal functions:

The intendants of the 1650s and 1660s . . . had quite different political assumptions from their predecessors before the Fronde. They had experienced civil war resulting from a revolt of the office-holders. They had also experienced, and took for granted, twenty years of vast government expenditure. The intendants of the 1630s and 1640s regarded the growth of government expenditure – and as a result, the growth of taxation – as a necessary, but temporary, evil. By the 1650s and 1660s it was apparent that it was not temporary, and for a number of intendants, it was not an evil either.[12]

In this account, then, well before the 1670s the intendants were acquiring a daunting array of responsibilities in civilian and military administration. And power could only continue to accumulate in their hands (as in those of the ministers, councillors of state, and masters of requests at Versailles) as the Great Monarch committed his realm to an ever more expansionist foreign policy.

For Michel Antoine, viewing statist evolution from the lofty perspective of the king's Council, 1661 was an especially crucial year. "Louis XIV and Colbert . . . achieved in 1661 a veritable revolution. In undermining the powers of the chancellor, they had set the monarchy irrevocably upon the path of administrative governance." And this centralization (Antoine could almost call it "bureaucratization") of authority was the great accomplishment of the royal Council, so "marvelously adaptable" in its many forms to the purpose of "facilitating the expansion of the State." Out of the many committees bringing together in varying combinations

---

11 J. Russell Major, *Representative Government in Early Modern France* (New Haven, Conn.: Yale University Press, 1980), p. 668.

12 Bonney, *Political Change in France Under Richelieu and Mazarin*, pp. 282–83 and 131–32.

the Council's administrators arose the preeminence of the fiscal functionaries and of the intendants answerable throughout France, directly
or indirectly, for the collection of taxes. And because "each war demanded
of the Kingdom greater and greater resources, and the last one, that of
the Spanish Succession, called for a genuine policy of national emergency,
. . . fiscal-administrative governance, and therefore statism in general . . .
followed along in a chronology patterned after the chronology of
warfare."[13]

Granted, it would be (in this scholar's words) "premature to talk of a
bureaucracy" in seventeenth-century France, if only because the Sun
King's jealous authoritarianism and assiduous attention to detail in administrative matters ensured him personal (and consequently prebureau-
cratic) fealty in ministerial and even subministerial ranks. But this was
decidedly not to be the case in the years after 1715:

At the death of Louis XIV, the situation was still confused and a bit uncertain.
The next few years sufficed to clarify it . . . definitively. The Regency only increased the stranglehold of financial considerations upon all State activities; it
accelerated and consecrated the rise of the bureaucracy. The system of government
had as of now attained its point of no return. Then, the War of the Austrian
Succession and the Seven Years' War had merely to hasten the decline of the
Royal Council of Finances in order to bring to its apogee the preponderant
authority of the bureau of the controller-general of finance. The reign of Louis
XV thus consolidated the gains of the revolution of 1661.[14]

There were certain humbling implications in all of this for royalty. In
France, as in the other powers competing for security and prestige in
eighteenth-century Europe, the purportedly "absolute" monarch was
coming to play second fiddle to those impersonal administrative procedures that alone afforded him the money, men, and matériel required for
the pursuit of martial glory. As Frederick the Great might have put it,
the French king was becoming little more than the "first servant of the
State." He must, in a real procedural sense, defer to his controller-general
at Versailles, to his intendants and their subdelegates and all the collectors
and dispensers of royal moneys in the field, and to the innumerable,
nameless "bureaucrats" who assisted these agents of his crown at all levels.
Even if we use Vivian Gruder's judicious qualifier "quasi-bureaucratic"
to describe "royal government in the last century of the ancien régime,"[15]
a no less arresting impression remains of war and absolutism – increasingly
global war and impersonal, "administrative" absolutism – having achieved
a highly symbiotic relationship in France.

13 Antoine, *Conseil du Roi*, pp. 76–77, 631.
14 Ibid., p. 631.
15 Vivian R. Gruder, *The Royal Provincial Intendants: A Governing Elite in Eighteenth-
Century France* (Ithaca, N.Y.: Cornell University Press, 1968), p. 208.

Yet this French species of absolutism bore within itself at least a few seeds of decay; and behind absolutism's decline, just as behind its rise, loomed international pressures.

To begin with, the authorities' ability to tax and to foster economic development suffered due to their rejection of consultative governance. Lack of representation in fiscal matters meant lack of legitimization of impositions; and the heavier such imposts became, and the more inquisitorial and oppressive the government's means of extracting revenue from proprietors became, the more serious resistance to taxation would become. By the same token, corporate privileges of every conceivable variety flourished throughout the kingdom in the absence of representative institutions. And the juridical entities coddled by the government included craft guilds and peasant villages, which, in some parts of France at least, seem to have inhibited agricultural and industrial development. The guilds were employed, most notably by Colbert, as "crown agents, supplemented but not supplanted by his Inspectors of Manufactures, for the enforcement of a comprehensive and highly detailed system of industrial regulation."[16] In some regions, as historians like Gail Bossenga and Michael Sonenscher have demonstrated, artisanal workshop production was – and would throughout the old regime remain – fully compatible with emergent commercial and protoindustrial capitalism. In other areas, however, as numerous scholars, including Liana Vardi and Cissie Fairchilds, have pointed out, the system of guilds remained (in Fairchild's words) "restrictive of economic growth."[17] Similar conclusions would seem to hold for the communal rights of the peasantry. In some regions these rural prerogatives coexisted easily enough with a certain degree of agricultural productivity; yet in Burgundy, at least, the crown's defense of communal privileges for short-term administrative and fiscal purposes apparently helped to discourage enterprise upon the land.[18] To do the

16 J. S. Bromley, "The Decline of Absolute Monarchy (1683–1774)," in J. M. Wallace-Hadrill and John McManners, eds., *France: Government and Society* (London: Methuen, 1957), pp. 151–52. On the general issue of the crown's dependence upon a highly "corporate" society, see also David Bien, "Offices, Corps, and a System of State Credit: The Uses of Privilege Under the Ancien Régime," in Baker, ed., *Political Culture of the Old Regime*, pp. 89–114; and Gail Bossenga, "City and State: An Urban Perspective on the Origins of the French Revolution," in ibid., pp. 115–40.

17 See the articles by Gail Bossenga, Liana Vardi, and Cissie Fairchilds in *French Historical Studies* 15 (Fall 1988), pp. 688ff; and Michael Sonenscher, *The Hatters of Eighteenth-Century France* (Berkeley: University of California Press, 1987).

18 On the relatively high productivity of agriculture in northern and western regions of France in the eighteenth century, see Michel Morineau, *Les Faux-Semblants d'un démarrage économique. Agriculture et démographie en France au XVIIIe siècle* (Paris: A. Colin, 1971). On the apparently different situation in Burgundy, consult Hilton Lewis

ministers justice, their patronage of the guilds and of peasant rights responded in part to a frustrating "mentality" of economic conservatism
with which any government in this country, regardless of its ideological
persuasion, would have had to deal sooner or later. The fact still remains
that the crown, committing itself in the end to a particular type of administrative-fiscal absolutism, helped to lay the groundwork for a potentially explosive situation in which the French people, struggling to
make ends meet in a relatively underdeveloped economy, and set upon
by vexatious tax collectors, would refuse to pay – and/or demand a voice
in government.

And the less revenue the ever more globally minded state could expect
to take in from its beleaguered taxpayers, the more it would have to rely
on financiers – bankers, military contractors, and speculators in currencies
and grain – to finance its wars. This produced, as Julian Dent has noted,
a "paradox at the heart of the administrative history of the ancien régime."

The monarchy was simultaneously building two mutually hostile systems. On
the one hand there was the admirable modern administrative machine which
was created largely in the sixteenth and seventeenth centuries and which in the
eighteenth century was to be the envy of the civilised world. And, on the other
hand, there was the deplorable financial system of the state, though system implies a kind of rational organization which was in this instance not readily to be
discerned . . . [19]

Indeed, there was no central treasury into which royal revenues flowed
and from which moneys were paid out to the various creditors of the
state. There were instead a number of treasuries, which were in the hands
of the private financiers who had bought the right to administer their
funds and who were subject to no standardized schedules or accounting
procedures. The financier-accountants in charge of revenues from direct
taxation were variously styled "payers," "receivers," or "treasurers";
their counterparts, who purchased and periodically renewed the lease of
the indirect taxes, were the famous "Farmers-General." The financial
system was indeed in its chaotic complexities a far cry from the ration-
alized administrative machine of ministers, councillors of state, and
intendants.

Ironically, the Farmers-General and the other financiers involved in
the government's "treasury" operations often used the royal funds they
administered to speculate in the government's own short-term and long-
term debt as well as in private ventures on the side. Indeed, the crown,
always living from hand to mouth because of its endless war making,

Root, *Peasants and King in Burgundy: Agrarian Foundations of French Absolutism*
(Berkeley: University of California Press, 1987).
19 Julian Dent, *Crisis in Finance: Crown, Financiers and Society in Seventeenth-Century
France* (New York: St. Martin's, 1973), pp. 234–35.

developed early on a reliance on short-term advances from such men, to whom "anticipated" tax revenue was guaranteed as security for their loans.[20] The crown in its financial straits could not even afford to remove from the Farmers-General's control the internal customs dues, even though abolition of such dues might have done much over the long haul to encourage trade and industry and, indirectly, agriculture.[21] In sum, the same pressures of international competition that made bedrock fiscal reform a long-term imperative for France also made its avoidance a short-term imperative! The geopoliticians at Versailles truly were caught between a rock and a hard place.

What was more, the bellicose Bourbon state had to draw capital from a plethora of venal officers both within and outside the gilded chambers of finance. It had to do this on an especially vast scale during Louis XIV's military campaigns. "At no time under the old regime," J. S. Bromley has commented, "was France afflicted with a greater number of inspectors and controllers, receivers and registrars, accountants and brokers, checkers and weighers, sinecurists of every description."[22] To be sure, just as the government (at least into the early 1700s) could institute so-called chambers of justice to force some of the smaller fry among the financiers to surrender their war profits to the king's agents,[23] so it could coerce officeholders into "augmenting" the original purchase prices of their posts, or into repurchasing those posts altogether. Yet this was, in Bromley's felicitous phrase, "the dry rot of absolutism at its most insidious."[24] To exact what were in effect forced loans from countless *officiers* was to demoralize those venal functionaries who were actually performing useful tasks and to cheapen further the government's already sullied reputation. Moreover, such a practice compounded the original sin of rampant venality of office by diverting capital from economically productive investments, thus in the end depriving the government of the greater tax revenue extractable from a more fully developed economy. (We should note in this connection that among the *officiers* were the most influential guildsmen and peasants, some of whose communities were apparently "restric-

---

20 On this subject, see George T. Matthews, *The Royal General Farms in Eighteenth-Century France* (New York: Columbia University Press, 1958); and J. F. Bosher, *French Finances, 1770–1795: From Business to Bureaucracy* (Cambridge: Cambridge University Press, 1970).

21 As pointed up in Bosher, *The Single Duty Project: A Study of the Movement for a French Customs Union in the Eighteenth Century* (London: Athlone, 1964).

22 Bromley, "Decline of Absolute Monarchy," pp. 138–39. Refer as well on this subject to Bien, "Offices, Corps, and a System of State Credit," pp. 89–114.

23 See Bosher, "*Chambres de justice* in the French Monarchy," in Bosher, ed., *French Government and Society 1500–1850: Essays in Memory of Alfred Cobban* (London: Athlone, 1973), pp. 19–40.

24 Bromley, "Decline of Absolute Monarchy," pp. 138–39.

tive of economic growth" in eighteenth-century France.) In addition, the crown's dependence on loans from purchasers of offices and its reliance on advances of capital from financiers tended to be mutually reinforcing in wartime, as syndicates of financiers would buy up whole categories of posts from the hard-pressed authorities and resell them at a profit.

"These tendencies were not, of course, peculiar to France," Bromley has accurately noted.

Very close links were developed by the moneyed interest of London to the British Treasury. But in Britain public credit was based on a parliamentary guarantee. The absence of any such security under an absolutist system of government was its chief weakness and in the end fatal to it. One consequence was that it was forced back on the credit of institutions which could offer such a guarantee – the Assembly of Clergy and some of the provincial Estates – and which could therefore borrow more cheaply than the state.[25]

Hence, the French government's dependence on ultraprivileged clergy and provincial Estates, as well as gouging financiers of every stripe and *officiers* as powerful as the Parisian parlementaires. It is painfully clear that what ultimately lay behind the government's fiscal woes (at least, among domestic factors) was the crown's lack of credibility, a failing that in the final analysis derived primarily from the Bourbons' practice after 1614–15 of forgoing any attempt at representative governance.

Thus the Estates General, however neglected since the agitated times of Marie de Médicis's regency, never entirely stopped haunting the avatars of absolutism in the ancien régime. "Without a representative body," David Parker has concluded, "French kings had the greatest difficulty in gathering support for their policies throughout the realm. In a sense the administrative apparatus that came slowly into being filled the vacuum which existed. But it was never a complete substitute."[26] Yet it might have been a complete substitute, and served as such far beyond the year 1789, had it not been for the expanding geopolitical mission of the French state. And this is why we find, behind the intriguing partnership between war and absolutism, an equally intriguing *pas de deux* featuring war and one of its other partners in France, the disused but frequently remembered Estates General.

Indeed, scarcely two years after Marie de Médicis dismissed the convocation of 1614–15, Bernard de la Roche Flavin, in his celebrated *Treize livres des Parlemens de France*, was associating the Estates with geostrategic pressures. Though arguing that the parlements rather than the Estates General should inherit the ordinary legislative functions supposedly ex-

25 Ibid., p. 138. On this last point, see also Thomas E. Kaiser, "Money, Despotism, and Public Opinion in Early Eighteenth-Century France: John Law and the Debate on Royal Credit," *Journal of Modern History* 63 (1991), p. 26.
26 David Parker, *The Making of French Absolutism* (New York: St. Martin's, 1983), p. 146.

ercised in the remote past by the Frankish assemblies, this essayist reserved for the convocation of the three estates "the most serious and
important questions, such as peace and war." He also left open the possibility that, even in his day, "such a meeting could be called for weighty
reasons."[27] That the state's pursuit of international greatness might require it some day to institutionalize a representative assembly assuming
the deliberative roles of both parlements and Estates General was not
something that this early seventeenth-century writer could have been
expected to foresee.

Within twenty years, however, that possibility began to be anticipated,
if only faintly, as the French under Richelieu moved toward intervention
in the Thirty Years' War. It is striking that Cardin Le Bret, in an essay
of 1632 that he offered chiefly as an apologia for absolutism, should yet
have advocated a constitutional role for the Estates General:

The Estates General is a useful means of communication between head and members, an institution which should be retained and utilized. . . . The king can learn
from the deputies what abuses and disorders need attention. Afterward, when
he publishes an edict which the Estates have recommended, the people receive it
with all the greater respect and obedience. . . . During the great crises of the realm,
we have always had recourse to the . . . Estates as the sovereign remedy for warding off the evils which menace . . . this flourishing monarchy.[28]

From all that we know of Richelieu, it would have taken a threat to
France even more dangerous than that posed by the Hapsburgs in the
1630s – or the sort of destabilizing convergence of foreign and domestic
crises that would in fact occur late in the next century – to compel his
acquiescence in a meeting of the Estates. Le Bret nonetheless was more
prophetic than he knew on this occasion.

Cardinal Mazarin and Anne of Austria had no more use for consultative
governance than did Louis XIII's great minister. But this did not stop
the Italian cardinal and his royal consort from using promises concerning
the Estates General to battle their way out of the Fronde and impose
their vision of peace upon Spain – in the process suggesting the potential
for linkage between great national issues and the convening of a national
assembly. In immediate political terms, their talk about summoning the
Estates General in January 1649 was designed to neutralize the influence
of the body at that time spearheading the antigovernment rebellion, the
Parlement of Paris. As Elizabeth Adams has explained: "Not only Paris
but also the nation at large might respond to the appeal of the Estates,
the institution which represented all groups and parts of the country and

---

27 Adams, "Seventeenth-Century Attitudes Toward the French Estates General," pp. 143–
   45.
28 Ibid., pp. 140–43.

which, according to theory and tradition, had formerly been the advisor of French kings."[29]

But Mazarin and Anne, almost immediately upon emerging from the "parlementary Fronde" without, indeed, having had to confront the nation's assembled representatives, discovered the perils inherent in even a cynical invocation of this consultative body. For, in the "noble Fronde" which now erupted, an assembly of insurgent noblemen, taking a page from the government's book, "called for a meeting of the Estates General as the traditional body which, with the nobles at the helm, could restore the right functioning of the monarchy and enhance the sovereignty of the monarch while entering into partnership with him."[30] This initiative, moreover, received a theoretical sanction in Claude Joly's *Recueil de maximes véritables et importantes pour l'institution du Roi* of 1652. In this treatise Joly called for "a return to the past when kings were not absolute, the nobles exercised their rightful responsibilities in government, and the Estates General was recognized as the basic political institution."[31]

Had such an assembly somehow materialized in the 1650s, its clerical, noble, and Third Estate delegates might well have found it hard to concur in a program of reform to be imposed upon the crown. In any case, soon after the publication of Joly's essay, the nobles' revolt went the way of the parlementary Fronde. Most French citizens, wearying of civil war and its attendant miseries, were prepared to tolerate Mazarin's and Anne's resumption of power, and would soon be welcoming the personal rule of Louis XIV with jubilation.

But the French state, whose insistence on following up victory over Hapsburg Austria in the 1640s with a comparable triumph over Hapsburg Spain in the 1650s had translated domestically into Mazarin's and Anne's political survival, would approach another conjuncture of foreign and domestic crises in the old age of the Grand Monarque. From 1685 on, a spate of tracts by exiled Huguenots urged Louis XIV's foreign foes to vanquish Bourbon tyranny within France by imposing the Estates General upon the realm once they had defeated Bourbon aggression beyond French borders. More ominously, perhaps, a chorus of voices within France took up the issue of the Estates as the Sun King and his exhausted subjects faced the prospect of calamitous defeat in the War of the Spanish Succession. By 1706, as influential a personage as the duc de Vendôme, general and marshal of the realm, was recommending that the government

29 Ibid., pp. 420–21.
30 Ibid., pp. 422–23.
31 Ibid., pp. 155–69.

convoke the Estates General in order to legitimize yet heavier taxation and win popular support for the king's position in the war.

What was Louis to do? Posterity has been too dazzled by the image of the younger Louis XIV dictating war and peace and receiving at Versailles the deferential advances of princes and ambassadors of a hundred lands; it has not sufficiently recalled the humbled old monarch of the sanguinary conflict over the Spanish Succession. Could Louis convene those Estates that symbolized the antithesis of everything for which he stood as divinely ordained king of France? Unthinkable! – and yet he seems to have come close to doing so. Joseph Klaits has cited a "draft address dating from this period and written in Louis' shaky hand" that "attests to his readiness for unprecedented steps to rally public support." Apparently, the Sun King was thinking seriously of addressing a representative conclave in the following manner:

Up to now I have employed those extraordinary means which have been used on similar occasions to raise sums proportionate to essential expenses. Now that all these sources are nearly exhausted I come to you in order to ask your counsel and your aid in this meeting, which will assure our salvation. By our united efforts our enemies will know that we are not in the state they wish to have believed, and we can by means of the indispensable aid I ask of you oblige them to make a peace at once honorable for us, durable for our tranquility and acceptable to all the princes of Europe.[32]

At some point, this radical gesture envisaged by the exemplar of divine-right absolutism was abandoned. Yet Louis still found it necessary to issue two extraordinary appeals for national support in the form of public letters, one to the French bishops and the other to the royal provincial governors.

"Calls for a meeting of the estates reached a crescendo," Klaits has asserted, in the critical year 1709.[33] Possibly Louis just barely got by without summoning the Estates due to a serendipitous combination of French military valor and allied disunity; we shall never know for sure. As it was, Colbert de Torcy, negotiating for peace on the French side, was morbidly sensitive to allied propaganda on the subject of the Estates. Such touchiness "reflected the crown's real fear that the price of military defeat or a dictated peace might be the destruction of Louis XIV's absolute

---

32 Cited in Joseph Klaits, *Printed Propaganda Under Louis XIV. Absolute Monarchy and Public Opinion* (Princeton, N.J.: Princeton University Press, 1976), pp. 211–13.
33 Ibid., p. 263. See also, on this subject, Lionel Rothkrug, *Opposition to Louis XIV: The Political and Social Origins of the French Enlightenment* (Princeton, N.J.: Princeton University Press, 1965); and Raymond Birn, "La Contrabande et la saisie des livres à l'aube du siècle des lumières," *Revue d'histoire moderne et contemporaine* 28 (1981), pp. 158–73.

monarchy."[34] At home, subversive constitutional commentary did not in fact stop with the "crescendo" of 1709. Fénelon called two years later for the institutionalization of an Estates General armed with legislative powers in fiscal matters and an advisory role in foreign affairs; and Saint-Simon and Boulainvilliers would very soon be penning their own critiques of absolutism.[35]

In the event, France and its adversaries were able to achieve peace at Utrecht and Rastadt. But a generation later, with Gallic statesmen once again waging war on land and sea and scouring the country for new sources of revenue with which to fund such wars, the old constitutional commentary resumed its earlier vigor. (These were the years during which the crown began to exact from noble landowners *vingtième* taxation. Lords who in many cases had already been helping impoverished peasants pay the immemorial *taille*, and who had earlier been assessed for *capitation* and *dixième* taxes, now had to pay permanent imposts assessed at 5 percent upon their own estates.) Toward 1750, Elie Carcassonne has remarked, the marquis d'Argenson "signaled the growing audacity of the criticisms of governmental affairs: the songs, the libels, the popular rumors made him fearfully anticipate . . . a call for the Estates General, and even . . . a revolution." Toward 1758, the prominent essayist Gabriel Bonnot de Mably proclaimed the "very true and incontestable principle" that the "nation" must consent to taxes in its assembled Estates. A few years later, during that decade of the 1760s darkened by the humiliating treaties of Paris and Hubertusburg, Mably could see only one remedy for the ills plaguing the French government: the restoration of the Estates General, "not as it existed in the past, but as it should have existed." Presumably he was alluding here (as Turquet de Mayerne doubtless would have alluded) to the composition and powers of that body. And then Mably prophesied quite remarkably: "It could and indeed must happen at some future point that the kingdom will find itself in such distress, that the government will be forced to have recourse to the forgotten practice of summoning the Estates-General."[36]

Probably more worrying to the authorities, however, were the pronouncements of the parlements, those tribunals of final appeal whose

34 Klaits, *Printed Propaganda Under Louis XIV*, p. 267.

35 Ibid., p. 263. See also Harold A. Ellis, *Boulainvilliers and the French Monarchy: Aristocratic Politics in Early Eighteenth-Century France* (Ithaca, N.Y.: Cornell University Press, 1988).

36 Elie Carcassonne, *Montesquieu et le problème de la constitution française au XVIIIe siècle* (Paris: Presses Universitaires de France, 1927), pp. 380–82, 357–58, 373–74. On Mably, see also Keith M. Baker, "A Script for a French Revolution: The Political Consciousness of the Abbé Mably," *Eighteenth-Century Studies* 14 (1981), pp. 235–63.

acknowledged right to sanction or criticize royal legislation made them lodestones of political controversy throughout the eighteenth century.[37] The judges of these courts were expected to confine their criticisms of royal edicts to protests relayed confidentially to Versailles; but as the parlementaires became increasingly embroiled in religious and fiscal disputes with the crown in the 1750s and 1760s, "private" protests more and more frequently became published pronunciamentos devoured by an alert reading public. The magistrates probably drew some of their resolve to intervene between crown and subjects on public issues from Montesquieu's celebrated *Esprit des Lois* and the works of jurisconsult Louis Adrien Le Paige. Both authors extolled the role of the parlements and other so-called intermediary bodies in preventing the French king from degenerating into a despot, and thereby gave the government's opponents in the ensuing years a handy stick with which to beat "ministerial despots" at Versailles.[38] Although neither Montesquieu nor Le Paige cried up the virtues of the Estates General, with Le Paige, at least, regarding the parlements as the "depositories" of the nation's sovereignty, the judicial *corps* they championed found themselves compelled to invoke the Estates in response to renewed war and its concomitant, heavier taxes.

The Paris Parlement in "remonstrances" of December 1763 advanced an argument whose logical consequence would seem to have been recourse to some national consultative body:

In matters of taxation, Sire, to violate the parlements' sacred right of consent is to injure . . . the rights of the Nation. . . . [To] levy a tax without consent is to do violence to the constitution of the French government.[39]

And what the Parisian magistrates, restrained somewhat by a special working relationship with Versailles, did not precisely spell out, the more vociferous provincial judges did. Here were the high jurists at Rouen, in protests of May 1760:

As long as there were Estates in France, the people through their deputies were familiar with the nature and extent of the government's needs: knowing [also] the nature and extent of their own resources, they could determine and regulate their tax contributions. . . .

Ever since the Estates have fallen into disuse, private interests have ridden roughshod over the public weal. . . . The essence of a law is that it be accepted. The right of consent is the right of the Nation.[40]

37 For an overview of this subject, consult Jean Egret, *Louis XV et l'opposition parlementaire, 1715–1774* (Paris: Armand Colin, 1970).

38 Carcassonne, *Montesquieu*, pp. 271–77. See also Keith Baker, *Inventing the French Revolution* (Cambridge: Cambridge University Press, 1990), esp. pp. 36–37, 41–44, and 231–32.

39 Carcassonne, *Montesquieu*, p. 292.

40 Ibid., pp. 292–93.

And even more forthrightly did the jurists at Rennes articulate the crucial issue in August 1764:

The investiture of St. Louis, the decisions of the Estates-General at the beginning of the thirteenth century, [and] the ordinances of 1355, 1560, and 1576 make it crystal clear that in the common law of France the consent of the three orders of society in the Assembly of the Estates-General is necessary for the establishment ... of taxes.[41]

Not even the mandatories of the three Estates who flocked to Versailles with such heady expectations in the spring of 1789 would put the matter more clearly. As Roger Bickart long ago pointed out, this potentially revolutionary invocation of the rights of the "nation" or "fatherland" was becoming common currency among the parlementaires by the middle of the eighteenth century.[42]

That a call for the Estates General of the realm was echoing through august magisterial chambers all over France testified to two significant developments: first, that geostrategic and constitutional issues were gradually approaching some sort of fusion in the 1750s and 1760s as the bellicose Bourbon state ran up against taxpayers' protests; second, that they were doing so in an ever-expanding arena of public disputation. Thomas Kaiser reminds us that public opinion was already an important phenomenon in the early years of Louis XV's reign, that is, in the time of Abbé Dubos and Finance Minister John Law. Still, as Kaiser has acknowledged, and as Keith Baker and others have emphasized for some time, the transformation of the political culture in France really took hold after midcentury.[43]

The most percipient observers of those years certainly bore witness to such a development. Thus, the marquis d'Argenson:

There is a philosophical wind blowing toward us from England in favor of free, anti-monarchical government; it is entering minds and one knows how opinion governs the world. It could be that this government is already accomplished in people's heads, to be implemented at the first chance; and the revolution might occur with less conflict than one thinks. All the orders of society are discontented together ... a disturbance could turn into a revolt, and revolt into a total revolution.[44]

---

41 Ibid., p. 294.

42 Roger Bickart, *Les Parlements et la notion de souveraineté nationale au XVIIIe siècle* (Paris: Alcan, 1932).

43 See Thomas E. Kaiser, "Money, Despotism, and Public Opinion," pp. 1–28; and "Rhetoric in the Service of the King: The Abbé Dubos and the Concept of Public Judgment," *Eighteenth-Century Studies* 23 (1989–90), pp. 182–99. Also Keith M. Baker, "On the Problem of the Ideological Origins of the French Revolution," in Dominick LaCapra and Steven L. Kaplan, eds., *Modern European Intellectual History* (Ithaca, N.Y.: Cornell University Press, 1982), pp. 216–17.

44 Cited in ibid., pp. 208–9.

Thus, the distinguished jurisconsult Pierre Gilbert de Voisins:

This is a kind of intellectual revolt which, without opposing authority by force, gradually undermines it. . . . There has always been frivolous and inconsequential reasoning in France about the conduct of government: but today the very foundations of the constitution and the order of the State are placed in question. The different degrees of authority and power, the rules and the measure of obedience, the mysteries of the state are indiscreetly debated under the eyes of the vulgar.[45]

It was symptomatic of this situation that Jacob-Nicolas Moreau, a publicist and ardent devotee of royalism, should have exhorted the ministers in a confidential memorandum of 1759 to take the offensive against the parlements, trumpeting the virtues of monarchy as it had developed in France.[46]

Innovative constitutional commentary, then, was acquiring a greater political resonance in the France of the 1750s and 1760s. The economic upturn of much of the century, documented in the massive studies of C. E. Labrousse,[47] and the steady growth in population, reconfirmed methodically by Jacques Dupâquier,[48] probably found their reflection in a growth of the leisured reading public (and in the related rise of public opinion) during these years. That public, in turn, was beginning to encounter in the *Encyclopédie* and a host of less voluminous works the message of the philosophes. On the possible political implications of that message, Daniel Mornet has provided this subtle commentary:

No matter what the diffusion of unbelief and of political unrest, it appears less important . . . than a more general and more certain evolution of opinion. All of France was beginning to think, to reflect. . . .
When one made a habit of "observing" and of "experimenting"; when one expected the sciences to explain everything . . . one started to assume at the same time that politics must not be different from physics, from chemistry, or from the growing of wheat, that there should be no mysteries, no secrets, no *raisons d'Etat*, [and] that one had the right to observe, to discuss and to insist upon real and practical state reforms, just as if one were analyzing the composition of air or meditating upon the ripening of crops . . .[49]

---

45 Quoted in ibid., p. 213.
46 Ibid., pp. 214–15. See also, on J.-N. Moreau, Baker, *Inventing the French Revolution*, pp. 59–85.
47 C. E. Labrousse, *Esquisse du mouvement des prix et des revenus en France au XVIIIe siècle*, 2 vols. (Paris: Dalloz, 1933); and *La Crise de l'économie française à la fin de l'Ancien Régime et au début de la Révolution* (Paris: Presses Universitaires de France, 1944). But see also on this subject, James C. Riley, *The Seven Years War and the Old Regime in France: The Economic and Financial Toll* (Princeton, N.J.: Princeton University Press, 1987).
48 Jacques Dupâquier, *La Population française aux XVIIe et XVIIIe siècles* (Paris: Presses Universitaires de France, 1979). The country's population seems to have grown from roughly 21 million at the start of the century to about 28 million as of 1789.
49 Daniel Mornet, *Origines intellectuelles*, pp. 473–75.

This, of course, recalls Gilbert de Voisins's anxious remarks concerning indiscreet speculation on matters of government – and it may be the most acute insight we have into the Enlightenment's contribution to the troubled atmosphere of Louis XV's late reign.

Moreover, the Enlightenment was even mining the "establishment" from within, for it was during these years that Chrétien Guillaume de Lamoignon de Malesherbes, head censor of the regime, was making it possible for Denis Diderot to bring out the first edition of the *Encyclopédie*, and was encouraging the literary efforts of other social critics as well.[50] In addition, ministers like Jean Baptiste Machault d'Arnouville, Etienne de Silhouette, and Henri-Léonard-Jean-Baptiste Bertin, wrestling with the king's geopolitically induced financial problems, could not help but espouse "enlightened" values insofar as they were endeavoring to rationalize government procedures and curb the tax exemptions and other privileges of regions, groups, and individuals.[51] Their actions were perforce emulated (and their values endorsed) in the provinces by the intendants and their subdelegates.[52]

It was equally true that, outside the precincts of government, unprecedented numbers of noble and bourgeois Frenchmen were conducting "scientific" experiments, attending meetings of provincial academies and Masonic societies, patronizing reading clubs, and discussing in salons and cafés the latest gossip concerning the policies and peccadilloes of the high and mighty at Versailles.[53] Is it any wonder that, in light of such circumstances, observant individuals such as the marquis d'Argenson, Gilbert de Voisins, and J.-N. Moreau should have divined in educated circles an ideological challenge to the crown's authority?

Moreover, the crown was challenged by men still fighting the battles of the past as well as by those striving to define the issues of the future. During the 1750s, religious disputes pitted the parlements and other sovereign courts against the king and his advisers even more frequently,

---

50 See Pierre Grosclaude, *Malesherbes, témoin et interprète de son temps* (Paris: Fischbacher, 1961).
51 Consult, on the first of these individuals, Marcel Marion, *Machault d'Arnouville* (Paris: Hachette, 1891).
52 See Maurice Bordes, "Les Intendants de Louis XV," *Revue historique* 223 (1960), pp. 45–62; and "Les Intendants éclairés de la fin de l'ancien régime," *Revue d'Histoire Economique et Sociale* 39 (1961), pp. 57–83.
53 See, on these various activities, Daniel Roche, *Le siècle des lumières en province: Académies et académiciens provinciaux, 1680–1789* (Paris: Mouton, 1978); Daniel Gordon, " 'Public Opinion' and the Civilizing Process in France: The Example of Morellet," *Eighteenth-Century Studies* 22 (1989), pp. 302–28; Dena Goodman, "Enlightenment Salons: The Convergence of Female and Philosophic Ambitions," ibid., pp. 329–50; and Alain Le Bihan, *Francs-Maçons et ateliers parisiens de la grande loge de France au XVIIIe siècle* (Paris: Bibliothèque Nationale, 1973).

perhaps, than did secular matters like taxation. As Dale Van Kley and other scholars have shown, the monarch and his judges waxed especially wroth over the issues of Jansenism and Gallicanism. Originally little more than a strain of thought emphasizing predestinarian and other austere tendencies within Catholicism, Jansenism eventually became a focal point of constitutional controversy in the old regime. The effort by both papacy and crown to suppress the Jansenists, whom they viewed as subversive, revived in some Frenchmen's eyes the old bugbear of an ultramontane assault upon France's historic "Gallican liberties." "Political" Jansenists in the Paris Parlement, longtime champions of those liberties, were, by the 1750s, advocating a monarchy "controlled by the parlement and ultimately by the nation exercising almost complete control over a democratically constituted and participatory church," as their ultramontane foes "posited a veritably absolute monarch in relation to his lay subjects, encountering his equal only in relation to a similarly authoritarian and monarchically structured church."[54]

Given such polarization between visions of where power should reside within the French state, within the church, and within the larger state–church relationship, it was predictable that some Gallican-Jansenist lawyers and magistrates would be tempted to appeal to "the nation" and even invoke the Estates General explicitly in their increasingly radical constitutional discourse. As Van Kley has pointed out, it was one of their number, Henri de Revol, who in 1757 expressed the desire that an "estates-general adapted to eighteenth-century conditions... effect some veritable change in the constitution of the monarchy and in the legitimate power of the ruling house."[55]

Yet it is significant that Henri de Revol, whatever his Jansenist concerns, was thinking primarily about royal finances on this occasion. As the 1750s gave way to the 1760s, the minds of the magistrates and of all reflective French people were inexorably drawn away from religious controversies (save, briefly, for that over the Jesuits' status within the kingdom) and toward the intractable problem of finances long inherent in the state's internationalist posture. The crown had been thwarted in its efforts during the preceding decade to curb public discussion of ecclesiastical politics; now it fought an even less successful campaign to limit disputation over fiscal and administrative matters. In 1763, that year of French diplomatic humiliation, the government was reduced to soliciting suggestions for fiscal reform from the parlements and other law courts. When

---

54 Dale Van Kley, *The Damiens Affair and the Unraveling of the Ancien Régime, 1750–1770* (Princeton, N.J.: Princeton University Press, 1984), pp. 172–73.

55 Ibid., p. 192. Consult also, on these and related matters in the reign of Louis XV, Jeffrey W. Merrick, *The Desacralization of the French Monarchy in the Eighteenth Century* (Baton Rouge: Louisiana State University Press, 1990), esp. pp. 49–125.

the ensuing public debate threatened to raise all kinds of incendiary constitutional issues, the alarmed ministers responded with an act condemn-
ing all "memoirs and projects formed by persons without standing, who
take the liberty of making [these works] public instead of submitting them
to those persons destined by their position to judge them." The government banned the printing and sale of any works "concerning the reform
of our finances, or their past, present, or future administration."

But the royal declaration of 1764 proved unsuccessful. Its first consequence, in fact, was to provoke the parlementaires at Dijon in Burgundy
to issue their own statement "denouncing the generality of the prohibi-
tion, insisting on the impossibility of stemming the tide of brochures by
such means, and arguing for the importance of public discussion of administrative questions."[56] And more of this was to follow in a steadily
escalating assault on the crown, leading directly into the political crisis
of the early 1770s. "A majority of the magistrates," D. C. Hudson has
observed, "had made a profound shift in their position toward the rights
and authority of the crown. Gone was the belief . . . that only on matters
of religion did the magistrates have the right to refuse a formal command
by the King to obey his will; . . . a majority of them had adopted a secular
ideology which not only permitted them, but commanded them, to refuse
to bend to the will of the government in many different matters, especially
on the increase of taxes."[57]

It is worth reiterating that invocations of the Estates General, as well
as other forays into subversive constitutional discourse by individuals and
institutions after midcentury, would not have been so alarming to Louis
XV and his advisers had they not sensed the appeal of such language to
that tribunal known as "public opinion." And this court of the citizenry
could hardly be ignored. "Of all empires, that of *gens d'esprit*, without
being visible, is the most extensive," C. P. Duclos wrote confidently in
the 1767 edition of his *Considérations sur les moeurs*. "The powerful
command, but the *gens d'esprit* govern, because in the long run they form
public opinion, which sooner or later subjugates or overthrows every
kind of despotism." "In a nation that thinks and talks," G.-T.-F. Raynal
would maintain similarly three years later, "public opinion is the rule of
government, and government must never act against it without giving
public reasons."[58]

Should the crown have heeded the advice of Moreau to mount an

---

56 This controversy is followed in Keith M. Baker, "Politics and Public Opinion Un-
    der the Old Regime," in J. Censer and J. Popkin, eds., *Press and Politics in Pre-
    Revolutionary France* (Berkeley: University of California Press, 1987), pp. 210–11.
57 D. C. Hudson, "The Parlementary Crisis of 1763 in France and Its Consequences,"
    Canadian Journal of History 7 (1972), p. 105.
58 Citations from Baker, "Politics and Public Opinion," p. 233.

ideological offensive against its detractors, to exalt the eternal virtues of divine-right monarchy in France? William F. Church and John Mackrell, among others, have noted that Jean Domat was the last major jurisconsult in the old regime to formulate a complete ideology of absolutism – and he flourished in the reign of Louis XIV.[59] In the eighteenth century the jurists whose predecessors had labored to glorify royalism in their treatises were not patronized by the crown and so devoted themselves either to the private law of the seigneurial landholding class or to the rational and speculative domain of "natural rights" philosophy usually associated with the Enlightenment. Defense of monarchism in France fell more and more to publicists like Moreau, Simon-Nicolas-Henri Linguet, G.-F. Le Trosne, and the marquis d'Argenson – and the government in its short-sightedness often persecuted these would-be paladins of the crown.[60]

Yet, even assuming that divine-right absolutism in France could have continued to receive an elaborate theoretical underpinning, of what use would this have been if absolutism proved increasingly inadequate in the real world? Assuredly there were signs that Bourbon governance, already smarting from humiliation in the realm of international affairs, was also losing some of its credibility in domestic affairs on the eve of René-Nicolas-Charles Augustin de Maupeou's notorious coup of 1770. There was a real question as to whether the administrative apparatus that had come slowly into being in this kingdom could, after all, fill the vacuum left by the disappearance of the Estates General. But this constitutional issue was only one element in the larger sociopolitical challenge facing the globally oriented French monarchy in the last years of Louis XV's reign.

WAR, ABSOLUTISM, AND THE EVOLVING SOCIAL ELITE

There was a vast double irony in the French kings' incessant striving after international greatness. On the one hand, their pursuit of a grandiose foreign policy was incontestably crucial in prompting them to develop certain absolutist institutions as fully as the conditions of the time would permit; and yet this same embryonic "globalism" also helped, over time, to expose and widen the cracks in the constitutional base of Bourbon absolutism. On the other hand, as we shall now see, the belligerent

---

59 William F. Church, "The Decline of the French Jurists as Political Theorists, 1660–1789," *French Historical Studies* 5 (1967), pp. 39–40; and John Mackrell, "Criticism of Seigniorial Justice in Eighteenth-Century France," in Bosher, ed., *French Government and Society*, pp. 129, 131.

60 Ibid., pp. 143–44. On Linguet, refer also to D. G. Levy, *The Ideas and Careers of Simon Nicolas Henri Linguet* (Urbana: University of Illinois Press, 1980).

policies of the Bourbons (in conjunction, to be sure, with socioeconomic forces) considerably altered the nature of the social elite in France and consequently helped to widen the discrepancy between royalty's vision of elite society and the actual structure and values of that society. Hence, the crown became increasingly out of touch with social as well as constitutional realities – and this at a time when its expanding international mission was compelling it to make unprecedented fiscal demands of its subjects.

If we cast an eye in preliminary fashion over the two centuries of prerevolutionary Bourbon rule, we can immediately discern a process of social change. At the dawn of the seventeenth century, the celebrated political theorist Charles Loyseau was still assuming a society divided into three "estates": the "prayers" (clergy), the "fighters" (nobility), and the "workers" (the Third Estate). About eighty years later, however, the eminent jurist Jean Domat "was dividing society on a functional basis; the first rank, with honor, dignity and authority, he accorded to the prelates, high magistrates and military commanders, and in the second rank, endowed with honor but not dignity, he placed without differentiation . . . the *avocats*, the doctors, the members of the liberal and scientific professions generally and also the 'gentlemen' (*gentilshommes*)."[61] Evidently, even if we allow for oversimplification in the perceptions of such luminaries, social description was becoming a more complicated affair under the Sun King. Still later (i.e., in the 1760s), the government was awarding its coveted letters of ennoblement to administrators, wholesale merchants, industrialists, scientists, and artists on an unheard-of scale, and was lauding these Frenchmen for their "usefulness" to state and society.[62] If the hoary schema of prayers, fighters, and workers had ever remotely mirrored social realities in this land, it obviously did not do so any longer in the twilight of Louis XV's long reign.

Why should this situation have come about? There is patently no easy answer to this question; in fact, there are probably *many* answers to it. But the role of the state would have to loom large in most of them. For, as Behrens has discerningly remarked, "Absolutism brought civil war to an end – thus permitting an increase in trade, manufactures, and the arts of peace generally – and greatly augmented the scope and power of the government."[63] From this fundamental process of statist aggrandizement within France, several consequences followed. For one, a burgeoning governmental apparatus, having achieved (at least for the time being)

61 Lucas, "Nobles, Bourgeois, and the Origins of the French Revolution," pp. 97–98.
62 See Guy Chaussinand-Nogaret, "Aux Origines de la Révolution: Noblesse et Bourgeoisie," *Annales: E.S.C.* 30 (March–June 1975), pp. 265–77; and *La Noblesse au XVIIIe siècle. De la féodalité aux lumières* (Paris: Hachette, 1976), pp. 268–70.
63 Behrens, *Society, Government and the Enlightenment*, pp. 55–56.

sociopolitical stabilization at home, was now able to proceed on to prosecution of an increasingly audacious mission abroad, which in turn meant a skyrocketing statist need for money and for professionals to perform the tasks of modern governance. For another, the very encouragement of "trade, manufactures, and the arts of peace" meant that there would be a growing number of moneyed and ambitious bourgeois who could satisfy these statist requirements (and their own social aspirations) by buying their way into the nobility – hence in the long run changing the character of the social elite in France. Finally, the "arts of peace" included, in the eighteenth century, the elaboration and dissemination of an ideology of "enlightenment" that at the very least promoted utilitarian values congenial to the purposes of policy makers, administrators, and bourgeois who were upwardly mobile. In a nutshell, then, the crown did much to create the preconditions for what we might call "primitive capitalist and intellectual accumulation," and resolved (for its own purposes) to minister to the needs and sensibilities of those who flourished in such circumstances.

Serving its own and its subjects' needs meant above all that the bellicose French state sold off vast numbers of titles of nobility and even huger numbers of offices conferring nobility or at least an enhanced social status. As military and social historian David Bien has noted, vending privileged status

> provided a way for an absolute state with weak credit to borrow cheaply. Short of a revolution to guarantee and protect money investments of the propertied by propertied representatives, there may have been no other solution. Clustering the very rich in highly privileged corporations where membership gave access to noble status, or gathering the vastly more numerous men of modest wealth into guilds with local monopolies over production – these were arrangements that assured that urban wealth would be mobilized for the state at a low price.[64]

It may never be possible to determine how many "bourgeois" – that is, wealthy commoners with urban affiliations – achieved upward mobility through purchase of title or office. Yet fragmentary data suggest that the numbers were staggering by the European standards of the time. Louis XIV sold five hundred noble titles by a single edict in March 1696, "and many hundreds more during the last 15 years of his reign."[65] His successors were less inclined toward this practice but could not abandon it altogether. At the same time, the traffic in offices flourished astoundingly. Colbert estimated the number of venal positions at 45,780 in 1664; a government inquiry arrived at a round figure of 51,000 in 1778. Both

---

64 David D. Bien, "The *Secrétaires du Roi*: Absolutism, Corps, and Privilege Under the Ancien Régime," in E. Hinrichs et al., eds., *Vom Ancien Régime zur Französischen Révolution* (Göttingen: Vandenhoeck und Ruprecht, 1978), pp. 167–68.
65 Behrens, *Society, Government and the Enlightenment*, pp. 49–50.

calculations, William Doyle has conjectured, were "probably under-estimates."[66]

It would appear that, of the more than 50,000 venal posts in the eighteenth century, perhaps 3,700 could in theory ennoble the purchasers or their descendants; possibly two-thirds of them actually did so, going to ambitious Frenchmen who had not yet won their spurs of caste. How many people were actually so ennobled over the century? "One estimate is 6,500, another nearer 10,000. Multiplied by five for the families who inherited noble status from their newly ennobled heads, this gives a minimum total of 32,500 or a maximum of 50,000 new nobles during the eighteenth century – a major proportion of the whole order however it is calculated." In addition, we should take into account the likelihood that two-thirds of all French nobles of the late eighteenth century (meaning, perhaps, 200,000 or more people) had acquired their enviable status through such means as familial purchase of office just since 1600. If we note as well that at least 47,000 bourgeois families (meaning more hundreds of thousands of individuals) progressed up the ladder toward noble status through purchase of non-ennobling offices during the 1700s, we can begin to sense how important a mechanism officeholding was for bourgeois infiltration into noble ranks.[67]

It is fascinating to see how, in its central and provincial administration, its financial apparatus, its judiciary, and its huge standing army, the French government was driven by its geostrategic and derivative financial needs to encourage the assimilation of new civilian officeholding ("robe") nobility to old military ("sword") noblesse, and of wealthy bourgeoisie to new "robe" nobility. In the process, the monarchs began willy-nilly to replace their beloved customary hierarchical world with a new society of meritocracy and vertical mobility.

The French social historian François Bluche has argued this point in connection with the secretaries of state at Versailles. "Even though a distinction still existed between the military and . . . civilian branches of the king's service in Louis XIV's reign," Bluche has admitted, "the monarch himself worked continually to reduce the difference in prestige between the two branches; and at the high level represented by the secretaries of state the division had already disappeared. . . . Representatives chosen from [the robe nobility, recently risen from bourgeois ranks] were permitted to integrate with and become the equal of the highest nobility of the realm; from this time onward their status was so high that they dominated the Second Estate." The eighteenth-century situation – in

66 Doyle, "Price of Offices in Pre-Revolutionary France," p. 857, n. 181.
67 For all these calculations, see Doyle, *Origins of the French Revolution*, pp. 119–20, 129–30.

which even commoners like Cardinal Guillaume Dubois and Jacques Necker could hold portfolios of secretaries of state – was, according to Bluche, "the opposite of that of the seventeenth century."[68]

Vivian Gruder's study of the eighteenth-century provincial intendants makes essentially the same point. At the start of the eighteenth century, Louis XIV's intendants "were of older stock in the nobility, the robe, and the pen, with longer-established high standing in society" than would be true of Louis XVI's intendants seventy and eighty years later. "Service to the king on the Council and in the provinces," Gruder has concluded from this fact, "provided increasing opportunities for social mobility in eighteenth-century France."[69] Moreover, the crown, assuming new domestic responsibilities as well as pursuing an increasingly global foreign policy, needed administrators with technical competence in specific areas, as Shelby T. McCloy has emphasized[70] – hence, an additional reason for recruiting into government the skills of those still engaged in the process of consolidating their status in society. Inevitably, administrative nobility in France became more rather than less open to "infiltration from below" as the eighteenth century wore on.

In the ranks of the ever more influential financiers, too, the logical correlation between state service and social promotion manifested itself throughout the last century of the ancien régime. The Farmers-General, managers of the crown's indirect taxes, illustrated this correlation particularly well. As late as 1726, G. T. Matthews has observed, the membership of the "Company of General Farmers" was "a motley of financial speculators, stock jobbers, court favorites, and newly rich bureaucrats drawn from the upper echelons of the General Farms." Before Louis XV's reign was out, however, the Farmers-General were "usually men not only of wealth but of assured and cultivated manner," and their families now "interlaced at every level with the high nobility, the magistracy, and the clans which supplied the state with its chief administrators, such as the intendants."[71] In other words, the Farmers-General, like other state financiers and, more generally, like other servants of the belligerent crown, had "arrived" socially. Yet for this the French government would pay dearly. As J. F. Bosher has pointed out, its fiscal

---

68 J. François Bluche, "The Social Origins of the Secretaries of State Under Louis XIV, 1661–1715," in Ragnhild Hatton, ed., *Louis XIV and Absolutism* (London: Macmillan, 1976), pp. 90, 95–96.

69 Gruder, *Royal Provincial Intendants*, pp. 205–206.

70 Shelby T. McCloy, *Government Assistance in Eighteenth-Century France* (Durham, N.C.: Duke University Press, 1946).

71 Matthews, *Royal General Farms*, pp. 238–41. For corroborative evidence on this point, see: Yves Durand, *Finance et mécénat: Les Fermiers-Généraux au XVIIIe siècle* (Paris: Hachette, 1976), passim.

problems were aggravated in the course of the eighteenth century by the fact that state authorities could not institute against socially "untouchable" financiers the sort of extrajudicial proceedings that their predecessors had used to squeeze profits from less securely ensconced financiers of various types.[72]

The impact of state service was evident in the law courts as well. To be sure, the Bourbon monarchs had never really exercised a tight control over the personnel in the hierarchy of tribunals. The so-called sovereign courts at the apex of the judicial system – parlements, chambers of accounts, courts of *aides*, and so on – had long been self-recruiting bodies, and the ordinary workings of venality and heredity in office ensured that a similar situation prevailed also in the middle- and lower-echelon tribunals. Nonetheless, as careful studies of the Parisian and provincial parlements have shown, the highly educated and technically skilled "robe" nobles, men who were often of fairly recent bourgeois derivation, achieved the same ascendancy in the higher courts as did their counterparts in the central and provincial administration. In these hugely influential tribunals, just as in the king's Council and the provincial intendancies, what the eighteenth century witnessed was not so much an "aristocratic reaction" as the professionalization of elite Frenchmen.[73] In addition, the recruitment of literally thousands of ambitious and intelligent bourgeois into the "presidial," *bailliage*, and *sénéchaussée* courts at the intermediate level and into the provost and seigneurial tribunals at the lowest level served to diffuse professional and civic values – and expectations of social promotion – among even greater numbers in middle-class society.[74] In magisterial as in administrative (and financiers') ranks, then, service to the state was contributing to what we would call today the gradual modernization of elite French society.

Yet state service may have had its most dramatic (and divisive) impact in the army, that most immediate instrument of Bourbon Continental geopolitics. As late as 1629, the Michau Code still apotheosized the vocation of a chivalric warrior nobility whose preeminent role on European battlefields implicitly argued for a similar ascendancy in domestic French politics and society. But here as in so many other areas, the commitment of the Bourbon state to an expansionist foreign policy entailing the waging of war on a massive scale was a turning point.

---

72 Bosher, "*Chambres de justice*," pp. 19–40.
73 The literature on this subject is summarized in Bailey Stone, *The French Parlements and the Crisis of the Old Regime* (Chapel Hill: University of North Carolina Press, 1986), pp. 16–74.
74 A point made by, among others, Ralph Giesey, in "State-Building in Early Modern France: The Role of Royal Officialdom," *Journal of Modern History* 55 (1983), 191–207.

Under Louis XIV and his successor, duty as commissioned officers in the army imposed a daunting financial burden on the men who seemed destined to that role in the "society of orders": namely, the sons of the oldest and most distinguished families of the provincial sword. All too often, these families were in straitened circumstances. Because the novel geopolitical needs of the state had to take precedence over old-fashioned considerations of pedigree, the Sun King and his royal great-grandson, after having turned to the old provincial noblesse and to sons of old and affluent court families as well, had again and again to avail themselves of the services of "new" nobles. The familial wealth of the last-named individuals, amassed from financial, administrative, and judicial service to the crown, and also from overseas trade and domestic industry, enabled them to purchase commissions and lead the increasingly luxurious style of life that seemed incumbent upon the king's military officers. Moreover, the Bourbon monarchs had at times to reach out even beyond these circles, to enlist into officer ranks out-and-out commoners whose wealth, gained much as fortunes were gained by nobles of recent vintage, accorded them preference in the military over the proud but impecunious sons of the country noblesse.[75]

But more than wealth was involved here. In the army, as in the civilian administration and the judiciary, state service increasingly required the mental discipline and specialized knowledge best imparted by a formal education. Artillerists and engineers like Bourcet and Gribeauval and commanders in the field like Favart and Simone Delorme may have drawn the sneers of military blue bloods for their lack of pedigree, but the army had a growing need for educated, technically knowledgeable, and enterprising men like these, and found them more frequently among the newer nobility of finance, justice, and trade, and even among the commonalty, than among the ancient sword noblesse.

Such tendencies in recruitment, however, were bound to foment discord among military men. With the spectacular defeats suffered by French forces at Rossbach and elsewhere in the wars of the mid-eighteenth century, this discord erupted into a major debate within military circles – and, to some extent, within society as a whole – over how the French army's officer ranks should be composed and what values they should embody.[76] If we leave out of our reckoning the hopelessly anachronistic yearning of some commentators for an armed force commanded exclu-

75 See André Corvisier, *Armies and Societies in Europe, 1494–1789*, esp. pp. 100–3, 162–66.

76 See Emile G. Léonard, "La Question sociale dans l'armée française au XVIIIe siècle," *Annales: E.S.C.* 3 (April–June 1948), pp. 135–49; and David D. Bien, "La Réaction aristocratique avant 1789: L'Example de l'armée," *Annales: E.S.C.* 29 (1974), pp. 23–48, 505–34.

sively by the sons of the old provincial nobility of the "sword," three schools of thought on this vexed matter require mention. First, reformist ministers like Choiseul and Saint-Germain and high-born writers like Vauvenargues and the chevalier d'Arc advocated a kind of Prussian style state service military elite, rewarding its members (who would preferably but not necessarily issue from the old sword noblesse) according to strictly defined criteria of military function and merit. Second, spokesmen for the moneyed noble courtiers and the affluent bourgeois unsurprisingly continued to chant the praises of venality in the commissioned ranks. Finally, there were those publicists (including, among their leading lights, Jean-Jacques Rousseau) who envisioned a citizen-army, modeled along classical Greco-Roman or idealized modern Genevan lines, whose members, hailing from all walks of society, would share a strong emotional tie to the *patrie*.

We have already appraised the immediate geostrategic implications of what Emile Léonard has called the "social question" in the eighteenth-century French army. The utter lack of consensus in France on such a fundamental issue was one of a number of ills afflicting the army and commensurately weakening the foreign policy of the country. But the social question bedeviling this great institution had a sociopolitical as well as a geopolitical significance. For, whether one argued for a meritocratic, a monetary, or a civic-republican criterion in envisioning the ideal French fighting force of the future, one was conceding the necessity, in the army as in other public institutions, to broaden the elite and modernize the constituent values of that elite. Affronted reactionaries in various quarters might reject all such prescriptions; what was sure, however, was that the inexorable pressures of international competition would sooner or later put all of these nostalgic Frenchmen (like their erudite conservative precursors Saint-Simon, Boulainvilliers, and Fénelon) out of court.

And so the modernization of elite French society derived in the first instance from state necessity. Yet, to round out this picture of enormous expansion of officialdom in France, it is important to remark that state necessity was more than eagerly embraced by new nobles and by the vastly more numerous bourgeois element in the kingdom. Doyle, citing what is "perhaps the most credible recent estimate, commanding confidence through the caution with which it is advanced," has suggested that the French bourgeoisie increased from 700,000 or 800,000 in 1700 to about 2.3 million in 1789. "This means that, over a century in which the number of nobles had remained fairly static, and the population as a whole had only risen by about a quarter the bourgeoisie had almost trebled in size." Additionally, while it is impossible to tell whether the bourgeoisie's share of national wealth increased in the sectors of landholding, industry, banking, and finance during the 1700s, we do know that the bourgeoisie predominated in the dynamic (if still secondary) sector of maritime trade, and we can also hazard the guess that they owned most of the capital sunk in the ever-critical stocks (*rentes*) of the war-waging and debt-ridden government.[77]

In light of their growing numbers and their continuing (and probably increasing) importance in the realm's economy, bourgeois Frenchmen were the most obvious "market" for the offices that the bellicose absolutist monarchy had, necessarily, to sell. Doyle, inquiring into the prices of venal posts in the eighteenth century, found that most if not all of them were rising rather than falling over that period. Inasmuch as assuredly there was no overall decrease in the number of venal offices during that time, their rising value suggests that bourgeois competition for them must have been growing. "In all categories which had always attracted bourgeois capital, from ennobling dignities at the top to petty clerkships at the base of the system, bourgeois pursuit of offices increased as the century went on. They were never more in demand than on the eve of their abolition." Thus, the appreciation of government posts reflected rising bourgeois competition for them as well as government fiscal exigency, and such a rivalry over offices in turn bespoke (among other things) a "bourgeoisie expanding in numbers, wealth, education, and ambitions."[78]

Bien has provided a dramatic illustration of these social realities in his research on the offices of *secrétaires du Roi*, which were especially coveted for their immediate conferral of transmissible nobility. The buyers of these prestigious sinecures were nearly all commoners – sons of merchants, municipal administrators, magistrates in *bailliages* and *sénéchaussées*, financiers, notaries, and so on. The number of these posts purchasable in provincial chancelleries rose from 104 in 1672, to 492 in the early years of Louis XV's reign, to about 500 later in the century. They cost only 5,000 livres apiece in 1672, but 20,000 or more by 1715, and four times that amount by 1789! As of 1789, there were also 300 of these sinecures at Paris yielding an aggregate "price capital" of 36 million livres to the state.[79] It would seem that there was no limit to bourgeois avidity for the offices that would admit their holders and their holders' families into the sunlit pastures of the social elite.

But there *was* a limit to the state's ability to satisfy the social aspirations of its subjects. François Furet has pointed to the importance of this

---

77 Doyle, *Origins of the French Revolution*, pp. 129–30.
78 Doyle, "Price of Offices in Pre-Revolutionary France," pp. 856–57.
79 Bien, "*Secrétaires du Roi*," pp. 153–68.

limitation of the old regime by arguing that it accounted for both the increase in bourgeois competition for ennobling offices and the heightening of tensions between old and new nobles:

These two phenomena . . . do not contradict but complement each other. Both were caused by the increasing inadequacy of the relatively narrow mechanism of social mobility developed by the absolutist State within the framework of the society of orders. To begin with, of course, the mechanism was quantitatively inadequate, considering the century's prosperity. But it was also qualitatively inadequate to the extent that the only avenue open to non-noble fortunes was integration into the State, its Court, its bureaucracy, its army and its magistracy.[80]

True, the continuing integration of successful bourgeois into the nobility was not entirely dependent on state service. As Furet himself has remarked, impoverished country squires always had the need to marry sons to the daughters of financiers and other prospering bourgeois, or to borrow their money, or to tap their managerial expertise in the stewardship of their lean properties; and those squires had ways of facilitating the entry of their bourgeois benefactors into the "best" local society. Furet has also argued that the rate of sales of seigneuries (presumably in most cases to aspiring commoners) accelerated during the eighteenth century. We may well suspect, in addition, that many a bourgeois family secured tax exemptions, honorific privileges, and eventual acknowledgment of "nobility" simply by buying and "living nobly" on handsome country estates.

Still, the increasingly acerbic debates within state-serving institutions like the army and the furious bourgeois concurrence for ennobling offices suggest that the Bourbon state was playing the pivotal role in promoting rising bourgeois expectations (as well as rising tensions within the nobility) that this state would eventually have to confront – particularly if it should persevere in its costly ways of war.

Furthermore, did not the tremendously widespread phenomenon of venal officeholding help to prepare the French people's minds in a yet more direct way for far-reaching changes? In an era more modern than that of the old regime, Ralph Giesey has contended,

the pursuit of noble status through officeholding . . . might be considered a contest for social mobility and its winners admired for their initiative and talent. Seen from that more complimentary viewpoint, self-interest implies not selfishness but self-fulfillment, and sycophancy not subservient performance for an absolute monarch but honorable public service. Patrimonial officialdom would thus be rehabilitated as a proto-republican civil service which the crown found itself forced to create in order to accomplish its goal of absolutism.[81]

And David Bien has sounded a similar note:

---

80 Furet, *Interpreting the French Revolution*, pp. 106–8.
81 Giesey, "State-Building in Early Modern France," p. 206.

Under the regime of corps and privileges local institutions grew and survived that at all levels of society may have preserved and even developed habits and ideas of local cooperation and participation. The shells of the narrower bodies once dissolved, these habits and ideas could be transferred to the national scale in 1789 and after. It is perhaps no accident that participatory democracy in Europe appeared first and strongest in the country where the corps had proliferated and flourished.[82]

Moreover, as Harold Parker and R. R. Palmer have pointed out, the schools of the eighteenth century attended by many *officiers* and other members of the professional classes in their youth placed a new emphasis on the classical Roman notion of civic virtue, of interest in and advocacy of the public weal.[83] The discharging of public duties in the government or in "constituted bodies" may therefore have enabled important numbers of educated Frenchmen to bring these civic values into the everyday world and, by associating them with honorable social status, to look forward in a general way to sociopolitical change in France.

Still, to contemplate venal administrators and sinecurists of prerevolutionary France "in isolation" would be to obscure a much broader fact: that these individuals constituted a strategic mediating element in a multifarious elite of "notables" that was starting to emerge from the cocoon of the "society of orders" in communities all over the kingdom.

In the case of Paris, Adeline Daumard and François Furet have carefully analyzed notarized marriage registers of 1749 and thereby cast light on the ties linking the capital's *officiers* with lawyers, with mercantile and fiscal agents of the crown – and with noblemen.[84] The existence of such ties may help to explain why, in the hectic spring of 1789, with the choosing of delegates and drafting of petitions of grievance for the Estates General very much the order of the day, the Parisian nobility would voice such a striking sentiment of solidarity with the bourgeois residents of the city.[85]

However, it is provincial archives that have yielded the most suggestive evidence of a partial transformation of nobility into "notability" in eighteenth-century France. Georges Lefebvre certainly discerned signs of such a phenomenon at Orléans:

82 Bien, *"Secrétaires du Roi,"* pp. 167–68. For further corroboration of this point, see Gail Bossenga, "From *Corps* to Citizenship: The *Bureaux des Finances* Before the French Revolution," *Journal of Modern History* 58 (1986), pp. 610–42.
83 See Harold T. Parker, *The Cult of Antiquity and the French Revolutionaries* (Chicago: University of Chicago Press, 1937); and R. R. Palmer, ed. and trans., Introduction, *The School of the French Revolution* (Princeton, N.J.: Princeton University Press, 1975).
84 Adeline Daumard and François Furet, *Structures et relations sociales à Paris au milieu du XVIIIe siècle* (Paris: Colin, 1961), esp. pp. 80, 87.
85 On this point, refer to Robert D. Harris, *Necker and the Revolution of 1789* (Lanham, Md.: University Press of America, 1986), pp. 369–72.

One has the impression that this upper class was an oligarchy. It did not form a compact bloc, but its diverse members shared a certain way of life; they all had the same respect for birth and wealth, the same horror of bad marriages, the same arrogance towards men of little property, and the same contempt for the populace. The system of corporate organisations obliged them to live side by side to some extent; in the *bailliage* and the *maîtrise des eaux et forêts* we find hereditary nobles, personal nobles and ordinary officials. They all met at the Academy of Sciences and Letters, in the Agricultural Society, in the Masonic Lodges, in the Philanthropic Society, and in the literary societies which were, in effect, their clubs. Lastly, they monopolized the urban administration. . . . These then were the "notables" who were to become the ruling class of France from the Consulate on.[86]

Lefebvre, it is true, cautioned that the privilege of nobility remained a "powerful internal barrier" within this upper class, "dividing men whom so many other bonds united." That he could nonetheless expatiate in a very un-Marxian fashion on the many "bonds" uniting respectable Frenchmen from the Second and Third Estates at prerevolutionary Orléans is arresting.

Robert Darnton has unearthed a fascinating description of Montpellier dating from 1768 that paints a similar picture. Here, the terms First Estate and Second Estate no longer designate the "prayers" and "fighters" of the antediluvian social schema but rather the *honnêtes gens* making up a mixed elite of cultured, affluent nobles and bourgeois. In the words of Darnton's anonymous commentator in far southern France:

Ever since people have begun to get rich rapidly from finance and trade, the Second Estate has won new respect. Its spending and luxury have made it the envy of the First. Inevitably the two have merged, and today there are no more differences in the way they run their households, give dinner parties, and dress.

"A new urban elite," Darnton has concluded, "was forming in opposition to the common people" at Montpellier.[87] This novel elite, battening upon government "finance" as well as upon state-promoted "trade," presumably could boast a substantial number of *officiers* discharging essential public functions.

At picturesque Bayeux in Normandy, Olwen Hufton has discovered a similar reality. "Urban nobles of comfortable rather than great means" constituted a group that "partly monopolized the government of the town and the surrounding district, helped the canons run the *bureau de charité*, and directed civic functions." These individuals were "big fishes in a very small pond and commanded the respect of the townspeople." We are not surprised to learn that most of these urban nobles, like their "notable"

86 Georges Lefebvre, "Urban Society in the Orléanais in the Late Eighteenth Century," *Past and Present* 19 (1961), pp. 50–51.

87 Robert Darnton, *The Great Cat Massacre and Other Episodes in French Cultural History* (New York: Vintage Books, 1985), pp. 131, 136.

counterparts elsewhere, were "nearer the wealthy *bourgeoisie* in their way of living than either the great houses who topped the noble scale of wealth, or the poorest nobles who could only be equated in wealth with the artisan class." But, once again, it is the *civisme* of these comfortably situated nobles, it is their competent participation in the management of local affairs, that most impressively argues for their membership in the embryonic *notabilité* of the kingdom. These urban nobles, in Hufton's own summation, were "carrying out useful public functions in the company of the professional sections of the *bourgeoisie* from whom some of them had originally been recruited."[88] Here, then, in this very old Norman community as elsewhere, a gradual fusion of birth, wealth, and public service was taking place.

A similar process was under way at Troyes and at Reims, lying to the east of Paris. Lynn Hunt has contended that

we can characterize the rulers of Troyes and Reims as political elites composed of local notables. They were elites – i.e., narrow and powerful cliques – because admission to their circle, though not closed, was carefully circumscribed. By the middle of the eighteenth century, wholesale merchants, lawyers, and doctors had been integrated into the ruling circle of royal officials and noblemen.

Like so many of her colleagues in social history, Hunt has underscored the community of interests forged among urban notables by the requirements of local governance. "Ruling linked noble and bourgeois, landowner and merchant; and their social alliances buttressed this pragmatic understanding. Political interests overshadowed underlying economic and status distinctions."[89] Here, then, are two more examples of nascent ruling elites foreshadowing such a vital aspect of the future in France.

Daniel Roche has depicted a like situation, though in more cautionary colors, at Dijon, Châlons-sur-Marne, Bordeaux, and twenty-nine other communities boasting provincial academies. His painstaking analysis of the recruitment to these institutions has pointed up the privileged role played in their host cities and towns by "an economically and politically influential noblesse" and by a "bourgeoisie of office, of administration, and of the liberal professions." Yet though Roche, too, has spoken of a "society of elites" prefiguring in many ways the proprietary elite of nineteenth-century France, he has also echoed Georges Lefebvre in stating that "nobles and bourgeois, however unified by the language of Enlightenment," could not ignore and never questioned the "barrier of privilege" within their academic societies. The "social order of the academicians"

---

88 Olwen H. Hufton, *Bayeux in the Late Eighteenth Century* (Oxford: Oxford University Press, 1967), pp. 46, 47–48, 56.
89 Hunt, *Revolution and Urban Politics in Provincial France: Troyes and Reims, 1786–1790* (Stanford: Stanford University Press, 1978), pp. 37–38.

was fated to be the principal beneficiary of the "social compromises of the future" – without, however, giving the twentieth-century historian any reason to believe that it would preserve its unity *in the short run* should the old regime founder in bankruptcy.[90]

The caution of scholars like Lefebvre and Roche regarding elite solidarity in this historical situation is well advised, for it raises a larger point. It is one thing to discern signs of the gestation of a "modern" elite in eighteenth-century France conjoining the administrative activities and life-styles of noble and bourgeois luminaries. It is quite another thing to prophesy that the much broader "upper crust" of "respectability" in the old regime – including within its ranks literally thousands of not very enlightened country squires – could survive as an identifiable class under the impact of an unprecedented crisis in national governance. Patrice Higonnet did well to cite Marcel Reinhard on this point: "The problem of the relations between elite and nobility [in 1789] was still unresolved. The resolution of this capital question was left to those who wanted to regenerate the kingdom."[91]

Still, even if we acknowledge this critically important point, we cannot ignore the evidence that the orthodox hierarchical values were being insidiously weakened in France. Economic change in the form of noble and bourgeois fortunes being made in maritime trade (which was protected and even subsidized by the state), in the textile and metallurgical industries (stimulated chiefly by state military requirements), and perhaps most of all in the booming business of state finance itself contributed substantially to this process, as private wealth continued to buy offices and lands and thus continued to pay off in terms of social advancement. But this is really to say that state geopolitical and derivative financial needs, more than anything else, drove the process onward. The crown had to find its resources where it could – and, hence, had to sell social recognition, social status, to those who could help it to finance its competition in the world at large.

Take, for example, some of the *lettres d'anoblissement* of this era found by Guy Chaussinand-Nogaret in the registers of the Paris Chambre des Comptes. In those given to Jean and Barthélémy Lecoulteux of Rouen in 1756, the government argued that "commerce has always been regarded as one of the surest and most fecund sources of the power of States," and underscored its own role of "assuring the nation that trade is honorable as well as useful."[92] Again, the *lettres* ennobling Jean-Abraham

90 Roche, *Siècle des lumières en province*, esp. pp. 255, 393–94.
91 As quoted by Higonnet in *Class, Ideology, and the Rights of Nobles During the French Revolution* (Oxford: Clarendon, 1981), p. 54.
92 Ibid., p. 47.

Poupart in 1769 alluded to "citizens whose industry can bring us the opulence of other nations and augment the luster and power of [our] State." And *lettres d'anoblissement* accorded (i.e., sold) to scientists, administrators, doctors, and even artists praised "talent," the "hours passed in studies," and "the merit that derives from personal qualities." It is probably not without significance, then, that Chaussinand-Nogaret should have found a much higher proportion of these official attestations of nobility going to "useful" Frenchmen after 1760 than before that date. Nor is it surprising that a royal edict of 1765 should have invited wholesale traders to purchase certain honorific privileges, such as the right to wear a sword, assimilating them, at least outwardly, to the "second estate."[93] Yet, again, the crown drew much of its capital from men trafficking in the fiscal affairs of government itself.

On the eve of the confrontation between Chancellor Maupeou and the parlements, then, retrospective analysis indicates a government dealing less and less consistently with sociopolitical realities at home as well as less and less effectively with geopolitical realities abroad. The crown that claimed in its ideology to epitomize divine-right absolutism could not stifle, and indeed in some ways helped to encourage, a constitutional discourse calling that venerable absolutism into question. And the crown that down to its revolutionary demise would stand by "its clergy" and "its nobility" was being driven by geopolitical and socioeconomic forces to sponsor (and was even starting fitfully to recognize) a social elite and elitist values that were at bottom incompatible with its most deeply rooted social convictions. But what specifically brought these royal governmental dilemmas closer to a convergence with geopolitical humiliation in 1770–74 was the onerous fiscal aftermath of unsuccessful warfare.

WAR, ABSOLUTISM, AND FISCAL CRISIS

The sinews of government, it has ever been said, are finances. The truth of this observation lay heavily for sure on the controllers-general of Bourbon France in the eighteenth century as they grappled with the increasing costs of an unprecedentedly ambitious foreign policy. That, in the event, they managed those expenses so poorly, and hence were instrumental in ushering in the political crisis at the end of Louis XV's reign, demonstrated even more dramatically than did constitutional and social developments that this kingdom's geopolitical and sociopolitical challenges were inextricably intertwined.

Louis XIV, we have seen, may have only narrowly avoided paying

93 Chaussinand-Nogaret, *Noblesse au XVIIIe siècle*, pp. 58–60; and "Aux Origines de la Révolution," pp. 267–70.

dearly in terms of his own absolute power for overblown international pretentions. Similarly extravagant French ambitions may have brought his great-grandson and successor uncomfortably close to the same precipice. No one has studied Louis XV more assiduously than Michel Antoine, and Antoine has given us a sobering portrayal of this monarch's limitations in the increasingly crucial domain of state finance:

Certain sovereigns had the inclinations or temperaments of bankers. . . . Louis XV did not possess these talents; to be sure, he held precise notions on the fiscal organization and financial state of his realm, but, he realized, "I really get out of my depth in projects of finance." Consequently he could not follow the operations and the initiatives of the department of finances with the same interest and competence and as closely as he could the other activities of the ministry. That was most unfortunate, because the administrative apparatus of the monarchy essentially depended upon the controller-general's domain.[94]

The "bureaucratic imperialism of the modern State" was developing apace and was doing so by virtue of decrees promulgated only in theory by the king's Council and stamped only in theory with royal approbation. Louis XV could have had little knowledge of the majority of such fiscal edicts and, like his ministers, could not have reckoned "how many thousands of them were being issued each year." The king, it would appear, kept a finger on the pulse of the diplomatic, parlementary, and religious affairs that so genuinely intrigued him; but he was less knowledgeable about fiscal problems failing whose resolution all these other matters might in time become academic.

These limitations on royal and ministerial competence in, and control over, financial matters especially haunted Versailles during and after the Seven Years' War. According to James Riley, involvement in this conflict cost the French more than twice as much on an annual basis as had their participation in the war of 1740–48. As a result, the kingdom's debt-insecurities was, by 1763, as large as it had been in 1714 after all of the Sun King's costly wars; and, if additional indebtedness such as that tied up in venal offices be taken into account, the national debt in 1763 was even huger than Louis XIV's debt "in terms of its constant value magnitude and perhaps its part of national output." Another indication of this turn of events: Whereas before the Seven Years' War the French government expended only about 30 percent of revenues upon debt-service, in the wake of that conflict servicing of the debt (meaning primarily interest payments) devoured more than 60 percent of revenue.[95]

Yet Riley and most other economic analysts would agree that the decision of the ministers at Versailles in 1755–56 to fund the latest war

94 Antoine, *Conseil du Roi*, p. 617.
95 Riley, *Seven Years War*, pp. 230–31, 236. See also Michel Morineau, "Budgets de l'Etat et gestion des finances royales en France au dix-huitième siècle," *Revue historique* 536 (October–December 1980), esp. pp. 317–18.

primarily from loans and only secondarily from taxes was not in itself illogical. All governments in that era found that raising imposts provoked a host of domestic difficulties, and even the heavy reliance in Britain on a system of customs and excise taxation tailored to that country's commercialized economy could not rescue London from increasing recurrence to long- and short-term credit in wartime. What the experts in the field cannot agree on is why, in the case of France, the accumulation of state indebtedness, though not nearly as great in per capita terms as in the British instance, should have had such catastrophic consequences.

Riley has sought to explain this conundrum by focusing on the decision of Controller-General Machault d'Arnouville and his ministerial colleagues to do for French finances during the Seven Years' War what Cardinal Fleury had been tempted to do during the War of the Austrian Succession – to convert "perpetual annuity" loans (*rentes perpétuelles*) into "life annuity" loans (*rentes viagères*). This policy, according to Riley, stemmed from a determination on the part of the authorities to "preserve the sanctity of the royal debt" by relying as much as possible on "self-extinguishing" loans rather than on those with no definite point of termination. And it is true that, in theory, repayment of life annuity loans by the debtor (in this case, of course, the crown) would cease with the deaths of the lenders or the individuals on whose lives the loans had been constituted, whereas borrowing in the form of perpetual annuities left the debtor with fiscal obligations extending indefinitely into the future. But in thus converting royal debt from *rentes perpétuelles* into *rentes viagères* on such a massive scale, Riley has contended, the ministers only revealed their ineptitude in matters of high finance, for such a reconstitution of government obligation actually increased the crown's annual interest charges.

Machault d'Arnouville and his successors, in effect, furnished a large number of speculators in the king's debt with a monstrous long-term windfall and failed to take measures that, falling safely short of a total repudiation of the debt, would have benefited the crown by reducing what it owed to its opportunistic investors in high-yield life annuities. Hence – at least in Riley's rendering – the existence, for the remaining years of the old regime, of a needlessly large public debt. It would inhibit all discussion of and efforts at political reform, require sustained taxation at unheard-of levels in peacetime as in wartime, drive up interest rates as the government perforce continued to borrow, encourage inflation, "squeeze out investment, and therefore . . . help transform the economic growth of the decades up to the 1770s into recession, and finally economic crisis."[96]

Yet this explanation of why heavy government debt had such dire

96 See Riley, *Seven Years War*, pp. 230–36, for this analysis.

consequences in France has been sharply challenged by other scholars in the field. David Weir, in particular, has faulted the "ministerial ineptitude" hypothesis by pointing out that a finance minister as resourceful and sophisticated as Jacques Necker himself would in later years finance French engagement in the American War by precisely the same primary means as his predecessors had utilized at the time of the Seven Years' War – namely, life annuity loans at interest rates of 8 percent or higher.[97] But as we shall see in Chapter 4 – and this is possibly the crucial point that even Weir has overlooked – Necker was only able to achieve success during his first ministry by assuring the monarch's creditors that a regimen of curbing wasteful expenditure, streamlining government fiscal administration, and maintaining strict auditing of royal finances would guarantee them a regular return on their investment in statist policies. Weir is correct to note that the abbé Terray, who in 1769 assumed the thankless duties of controller-general at Versailles, infuriated many holders of government annuities by his reforms of those obligations. Yet matters might never have arrived at such a critical impasse in the first place had Machault d'Arnouville and the other finance ministers of the 1750s and 1760s been willing and able to introduce the kinds of administrative and fiscal reforms that, from the time of Terray on, would almost surely give the belligerent Bourbon state its best chance to survive.

However this may have been, the mounting fiscal woes of the French government were undeniable in the bleak aftermath of the Seven Years' War. Furthermore, in the late 1760s those ills were compounded by (and perhaps contributed to?) a substantial downturn in the general economy that seems to many scholars to have heralded the "intercyclical recession" of the late 1770s and 1780s.[98] According to Steven Kaplan, those economic difficulties began in some regions, especially in the north and northwest, as early as 1765, and then, moving toward the south and southeast, "engulfed almost the entire kingdom."[99] A chain of events all too characteristic of France's ancien régime exposed the fragility of a subsistence economy pegged almost entirely to the cost of basic cereals. A succession of wet, cool summers led to poor harvests; the resultant high prices and scarcity of grain reduced the ability of hungry French people to buy any nonagricultural commodities; that in turn brought depression to the "pilot" textile sector of industry and produced the inevitable concomitant miseries of unemployment, lagging wages, and rising indebtedness; and,

---

97 David R. Weir, "Tontines, Public Finance, and Revolution in France and England, 1688–1789," *Journal of Economic History* 49 (1989), esp. pp. 118–24.
98 Consult again the basic works of Labrousse on trends in the economy of late eighteenth-century France.
99 Steven L. Kaplan, *Bread, Politics and Political Economy in the Reign of Louis XV*, 2 vols. (The Hague: Martinus Nijhoff, 1976), pp. 488–90, 692–94.

perhaps most crucially, that indebtedness spread through society's ranks, from artisans and small tradesmen to entrepreneurs in the textile and metallurgical industries, wholesale traders, and financiers.

Why was the phenomenon of indebtedness in the general population so critical? It was critical because it demonstrated with brutal clarity that the fiscal viability of a government unwilling or unable to reform its spending and administrative procedures in basic ways would continue to be every bit as fragile as was the subsistence economy to which that government in many ways remained chained. We have already noted that, as the French state continued to be caught up in the international competition of the eighteenth century, it remained reliant on a variety of "upwardly mobile" financiers: the Farmers-General, receivers-general, and treasurers-general. For these individuals, in addition to collecting, holding, and disbursing all kinds of royal revenue on royal command, invested increasingly in the crown's long-term debt and loaned the government the money it always seemed to need to survive on a short-term basis. Those indispensable short-term loans were secured on the following year's anticipated tax revenue. Therefore, in the economic hard times of the late 1760s and early 1770s, the Bourbon state was imperiled for at least three interrelated reasons: first, because it encountered mounting difficulties in collecting from desperate French citizens the tax revenue it needed as security for further loans from the financiers; second, because many of the financiers themselves, racked with business anxieties and in some cases suffering bankruptcies, proved less able than in earlier years to advance short-term credit, secured or unsecured, to the king's ministers; and third, because the most solvent financiers, due to their enhanced status in society and to their heavy investment in the government's long-term debt could not (like some of their predecessors) be bullied by the crown into disgorging their operational profits.[100]

By 1769, the controller-general of finances, Maynon d'Invau, "had a 55,000,000 livres deficit, eighty millions in arrears, and was meeting the needs of 1769 with the anticipated receipts of 1770"[101] – receipts that might never be forthcoming. Small wonder that he reported despairingly to Louis XV: "The finances of Your Majesty are in the most frightful state of collapse. . . . The situation is more than terrifying; it can continue no longer. We have reached the moment when it will drive the kingdom into the worst sort of catastrophe, for which there will be no remaining remedy. . . ."[102] Small wonder that, facing the real possibility of state

---

100 Refer again to Bosher, "French Crisis of 1770," pp. 17–30, and to Kaplan, *Bread, Politics and Political Economy*, pp. 488–90.
101 Ibid., p. 490.
102 As quoted in Durand Echeverria, *The Maupeou Revolution: A Study in the History*

bankruptcy, Maynon d'Invau surrendered his portfolio in December 1769, leaving Abbé Joseph Marie Terray to wrestle with the deepening financial crisis.

The abbé has acquired new defenders in the recent historical literature.[103] They have held, with considerable justice it would seem, that he was at least able to spare Louis XV the ignominy of a complete governmental fiscal collapse in his last years. Terray managed to do this through a combination of draconian reductions in crown expenditure, administrative reform resulting in greater royal control over the collection, management, and disbursement of royal funds, and enhancement of government revenue. He apparently was able thereby to produce for his aging sovereign a series of budgetary surpluses and, perhaps most importantly, cut into the crown's long-standing debt. This achievement, moreover, probably made it easier for the crown to return to its borrowing ways after Terray's downfall.

That the abbé himself, however, was sacrificed in the process – that is to say, in the wake of a crisis with major sociopolitical implications – tells us much. Assuredly he could, and did, reduce some of the crown's expenses by slashing interest rates on an array of government annuities, reducing pensions, and suspending the reimbursement of certain other royal obligations; but this, predictably enough, aroused the fury of a phalanx of *rentiers* and pensionaries. He could, and did, make some initial moves in the direction of systemic administrative reform by curbing the influence of certain financiers, abolishing other venal accountants' posts altogether, and in general, cutting waste in the management of the king's moneys; yet this brought down on his head the wrath of those individuals adversely affected by these useful reforms. And he could, and did, increase the government's revenue by eliminating a number of tax exemptions and prolonging important taxes that lay upon the land; but this, perhaps more than any other species of reform, was guaranteed to incense the population as a whole and raise serious new problems for the king and his embattled ministers.

The issue of taxation was already looming behind one of the causes célèbres of those years, the government's prosecution of the combative Breton parlementaire Louis-René de La Chalotais.[104] And there can be

of Libertarianism, France, 1770–1774 (Baton Rouge: Louisiana State University Press, 1985), p. 10.

103 They include Laugier, *Ministère réformateur sous Louis XV*, pp. 165, 341; Weir, "Tontines, Public Finance, and Revolution," pp. 121–22; and Eugene Nelson White, "Was There a Solution to the Ancien Régime's Financial Dilemma?" *Journal of Economic History* 49 (September 1989), pp. 548–55.

104 This controversy is examined from a wide variety of viewpoints in John Rothney, ed.,

no doubt that it was Terray's imperative need to increase taxation – and in particular his decision to make the first 5 percent impost (*vingtième*) upon the lands of lay nobles and commoners permanent and to extend the second *vingtième* to 1781 – that led him and his colleague Maupeou to challenge those everlasting opponents of higher taxation, the parlements. In the candid words of Maupeou's aide C. F. Lebrun: "We needed taxes, and in the face of existing attitudes we had to expect concerted resistance ... ; we resolved to forestall this opposition and to force the parlements to return to the recognized principles of the monarchy."[105] Hence, the government's assault in 1770–71 on the obstreperous parlements, an assault that entailed their neutralization by what those in authority hoped would be more docile institutions. The chancellor established a "supreme court" at the capital composed of councillors of state and a number of more or less complaisant magistrates. Provincial appellate courts arose at Arras, Blois, Châlons, Clermont-Ferrand, Lyons, and Poitiers. Justice, the government announced grandly, was henceforward to be meted out free of charge to the kingdom's subjects; venality of judicial office was to be abolished or at least curtailed; and various other ameliorations were promised to the *justiciables* of the realm. The parlements actually continued in existence, but the crown replaced the more refractory personnel with magistrates from whom it anticipated a greater receptivity to ministerial wishes. Thus, political obstructionism was to be purged from the hierarchy of tribunals, the king's judges would confine themselves largely to their proper roles in administration and the law, and the authorities would be unimpeded in the all-important domain of financial appropriations.

But these reforms touched off a veritable firestorm of constitutional protest. Indeed, Durand Echeverria, who has studied the controversy as methodically as anyone, has contended that the "propaganda war" of 1771 and subsequent years was "probably unequaled in French history until the Revolution."[106] The stricken magistrates and their adherents, styling themselves "Patriots," riposted against the crown with solemn remonstrances and decrees that in theory were confidential petitions to

---

The Brittany Affair and the Crisis of the Ancien Régime (New York: Oxford University Press, 1969).

105 Cited in Echeverria, *Maupeou Revolution*, p. 15. Taxes, it now appears, were already heavily affecting the properties of nobles as well as of commoners in rural France. On this and related matters, see Betty Behrens, "Nobles, Privileges, and Taxes in France at the End of the Ancien Régime," *Economic History Review*, 2nd ser., 15 (1963), pp. 451–75; and Peter Mathias and Patrick O'Brien, "Taxation in Britain and France, 1715–1810. A Comparison of the Social and Economic Incidence of Taxes Collected for the Central Governments," *Journal of European Economic History* 5 (1976), pp. 601–50.

106 Echeverria, *Maupeou Revolution*, p. 22.

the king but in reality were circulated in manuscript and in print to an ever more politicized reading public. These judicial protests, couched in dignified and formal language, were soon reinforced "by a flood of less restrained propaganda pieces – placards, engravings, satirical poems, jokes, and – principally – pamphlets ranging in length from a few pages to a hundred or more and varying in nature from the crudest libels to sober and reasoned political essays." Echeverria counted at least 167 writings of this kind published from 1771 to 1774, "in runs of up to 5,000 copies" apiece.

Of course, the government had its polemicists too.[107] Yet it is significant that, with the notable exception of Voltaire, nearly all the philosophes and most other lettered luminaries as well sided with the traditional magistracy in its confrontation with the crown. But it did not take the Patriots long to pass beyond the immediate issue of parlementary prerogatives and demand the resurrection of that keystone institution for which the prideful parlementaires themselves, if pressed to the wall, knew their tribunals to be only temporary substitutes: that ultimate of ultimates, the Estates General.

Waxing especially eloquent in the Patriot cause was that erstwhile protector of "Encyclopedism" Lamoignon de Malesherbes. Now chief of one of the sovereign courts, the Cour des Aides of Paris, Malesherbes used his company's remonstrances to launch a frontal attack on "ministerial despotism" and revive the specter of the Estates. "Originally," he reminded Louis XV on 17 August 1770, "taxes were established only by the consent of the people accorded in the assemblies of the Estates." And on 18 February 1771 he dared to address the monarch in this fashion:

King by divine right you may very well be, but you are also answerable for your power to your voluntarily obedient subjects. . . .
There are in France, as in all monarchies, some inviolable rights which belong to the Nation. . . .
Therefore, Sire, interrogate the Nation itself, for only the Nation can now be heard by Your Majesty![108]

Thus did Malesherbes go to the heart of the constitutional issue in France, as unambiguously as any Patriot could have wished.

And Malesherbes in the early 1770s had Patriot allies aplenty. Thus, Target insisted that the "parlements of France do not compensate for the loss of the States General. . . . They cannot in any sense replace them in the matter of taxes." Mey would have had the Estates give the necessary popular consent to taxation, initiate all legislation, and collaborate with

107 See D. C. Hudson, "In Defense of Reform: French Government Propaganda During the Maupeou Crisis," *French Historical Studies* 8 (1973), pp. 51–76.
108 Citations from Grosclaude, *Malesherbes*, pp. 233, 238–39.

the sovereign in the enactment of new constitutional laws. Morizot, unknowingly taking up the gauntlet thrown down by Turquet de Mayerne 180 years earlier, proposed the convening of a "General Diet of the nation" that would be much more broadly representative of "the people" than the old Estates General. This envisioned assemblage of the "true" mandatories of the nation would have the exclusive right to pass legislation and impose taxes. Saige, even more radical than this in a strictly constitutional sense, endorsed Rousseau's notion that the general will and hence the powers to tax and make laws were inalienable, even to the Estates General; still, he allowed that the Estates could claim the authority to function as the "organs" of the general will. Other writers – Augéard, Pidansat de Mairobert, Blonde, Clément de Boissy, various nobles, and any number of anonymous pamphleteers – argued along similar lines. So, too – and this may have been even more telling – did privileged institutions such as the parlements in Normandy, Languedoc, Burgundy, and Brittany. In fact the *Recueil des réclamations*, an enormous compilation of the protests issued by tribunals throughout the realm, stated in its preface that "the entire magistracy demands the convocation of the States General. . . . "[109] Thus did the warring Bourbons continue to be dogged by this apparition of representative governance from the past.

To be sure, this blizzard of constitutional commentary had its problematic aspects. Only a handful of authors like Morizot insisted on spelling out for their readers the "sociopolitical" implications of the crisis precipitated in France by Terray's and Maupeou's policies. Only those publicists, that is, forecast what Turquet de Mayerne had long before prophesied would be the case, that social and political change would require the "invention" of an altogether different, "modernized" sort of national representative assembly. Furthermore, the theoreticians in the Patriot party of 1771–74 "do not seem to have perceived the need for some mechanism for coordinating the judicial functions of the parlements, the legislative functions of the States General, and the executive functions of the crown, and for eliminating the destructive conflicts that plagued the existing constitution."[110] In these as in so many other respects, the final reckoning for ancien régime France would come, not now, but in 1789.

It is also true that the antiministerial firestorm had spent much if not all of its fury by the end of 1771. Some of the public interest in the clash between ministers and magistrates had been superficial all along, and by 1773, Durand Echeverria has conceded, the crisis "had long since ceased to dominate social conversations." Still, it is difficult not to concur with

109 Echeverria, *Maupeou Revolution*, pp. 85–86.
110 Ibid., pp. 87, 100.

the same author that the political crisis of 1770–74 was "a profoundly disturbing experience that set the French thinking about fundamental political questions with markedly increased seriousness and concern." As one contemporary reported: "Everybody wants to study the foundations of the national constitution. . . . People are questioning principles about which otherwise they never would have dared to think." Mesdames de Mesmes and d'Egmont informed Gustavus III of Sweden that Chancellor Maupeou was inadvertently "teaching the history of France to people who otherwise would have lived all their lives without knowing anything about it." Courses on "political science" were offered to the public; books on political topics continued somehow to see the light of day; and in August 1774, shortly after the disgrace of the chancellor and his associates, the Grimm-Diderot correspondence observed that "today there is scarcely a single young man who on leaving his college does not plan to establish a new system of government, scarcely an author who does not feel the obligation to instruct the powers of the globe on the best way to manage their estates."[111] It may not be too much to assert, then, that the political crisis of 1770–74 left literate, reflective Frenchmen with a sensitivity to public issues that they would retain in the years to come, and that this would make the new administration's navigation of the shoals of public opinion a more challenging task than it had ever been before.

Of more immediate significance was the fact that the ruling circles were themselves profoundly divided over Terray's and Maupeou's drastic reforms.[112] Any hope the chancellor might have had to master the king's Council was defeated when, in June 1771, the duc d'Aiguillon became secretary for foreign affairs and almost immediately began intriguing against Maupeou. Historians may have retrospectively painted Terray, Maupeou, and d'Aiguillon as making up a ministerial triumvirate, but, William Doyle has remarked, "they were as little united in reality as their original namesakes."

When the new parlements, especially that of Bordeaux, created so much trouble over Terray's tax increases in the spring of 1772, d'Aiguillon led an attack on Maupeou in the council, declaring that this resistance showed that the reform had achieved nothing. Terray and his ministerial colleague, Henri-Léonard Bertin, knowing the king's views, also came out against Maupeou by opposing vigorous action to crush the Bordeaux parlement. In 1773, when the famous lawsuit between the playwright . . . Beaumarchais and the counsellor Goëzman had brought down general public ridicule on the new parlement of Paris, d'Aiguillon and Bertin entered into negotiations with various exiled magistrates with a view to

111 Ibid., pp. 26–28.
112 See Doyle, "Parlements of France," esp. pp. 435–38; and Egret, *Louis XV et l'opposition parlementaire*, p. 202.

replacing the new parlement with members of the old. That any such change would involve the fall of Maupeou was taken for granted.[113]

Nor was Maupeou ever able to count on the undivided support of the court nobility. The Princes of the Blood themselves, with the adherence of many aristocratic hangers-on at Versailles, formally protested against Maupeou's overthrow of the old judiciary, and most of the princes, dukes, and peers boycotted the short-lived "Maupeou Parlement" at Paris. Rumor had it that even the immediate royal family was split over the issue of the chancellor's political survival by early 1774.

The French historian Jean Egret devoted much of a long and distinguished career to studying the struggle in the eighteenth century between the crown and the parlements. Nobody was more keenly aware of the defects of the parlementaires and of the justice they administered than was Egret. He was thus quick to acknowledge the potential utility of the judicial reforms of 1770–74. And yet Egret also concluded flatly that "the Parlement of Chancellor Maupeou, incapable of becoming a Court of Peers and of playing an honorable political role, could not have survived as it was."[114] Egret fully concurred in the scholarly opinion, already established on the basis of contemporaries' reports, that Louis XV was himself moving in the direction of dismissing Maupeou and abrogating his judicial reforms when he fell into his final illness in May 1774.

Jean Egret would not have disagreed with Durand Echeverria's subsequent recapitulation of the crisis of 1770–74:

Maupeou's experiment in absolutism failed not because there was no need for at least some of his proposed reforms, nor because Louis XVI made a stupid, gratuitous mistake in reestablishing the parlements, but because such a constitution was not viable in the face of the determined opposition of the nobility and the wealthy bourgeoisie and in the absence of active support from any other group except the church. Its philosophy and methods were inadequate to this moment in French history. . . . Louis XVI's dismissal of Maupeou in 1774 appears in hindsight the inevitable liquidation of an exhausted expedient.[115]

And Terray (paradoxically enough, given his own falling out with Maupeou) shared the chancellor's disgrace. In the final analysis, thoughtful Frenchmen in general – not just *rentiers*, pensionaries, and financiers – could not help but be uneasy about a government that might work its will without consultation of either the customary *corps intermédiaires* eulogized by Montesquieu and Le Paige or the historic if disused Estates General. Is it all that astonishing that even Louis XV, even the "absolute" monarch himself, could not in the end be isolated from such fundamental misgivings about the naked application of absolutism in France?

113 Doyle, "Parlements of France," pp. 437–38.
114 Egret, *Louis XV et l'opposition parlementaire*, p. 228.
115 Echeverria, *Maupeou Revolution*, pp. 34, 122.

It would obviously be absurd to claim, in summation at this point, that what we commonly term the "Maupeou revolution" of 1770–74 pointed to an unavoidable and violent "revolution from below" in Bourbon France's near future. Yet it does seem reasonable to conclude, on the basis of the historiography on early modern France, that two basic challenges had long been facing, and would most likely continue confronting, those exercising power in this realm. On the one hand there was the statist desire (shared, somewhat, by the public) to achieve and maintain French greatness on both the land and the seas in an increasingly competitive and global environment. On the other hand there was the need of the crown to fashion, in consultation with its wealthy, most articulate, and most aspiring subjects, a new kind of consensus on the allocation of political responsibilities and the definition of honorable social status in this ambitious country.

If this may with any degree of accuracy be deemed the "legacy of French history" up to the accession of Louis XVI, it would seem to enable those of us today seeking to understand the French Revolution's genesis to pose certain capital questions as we approach 1789 through a very careful reappraisal of the 1774–88 period. First, would the Bourbon state follow the advice of one of its most distinguished controllers-general, Anne Robert Jacques Turgot, to deny its cherished geopolitical mission, to forgo reengagement in the arena of international military competition? Second, if hallowed, centuries-old tradition should in this regard prevail over discretion, would the Bourbon state be able sufficiently to compensate wealthy, literate, and ambitious Frenchmen within the existing sociopolitical system for whatever support they might be required to bring to the resumption of the drive toward French security and greatness? Or – to rephrase this latter question in the terms of our overall thesis – would the bellicose Bourbon state become so isolated from evolving sociopolitical realities at home that it must face the genuine possibility of foundering? Upon the resolution of these questions might hinge the fate of the old France.

3

❧❧❧❧❧❧❧❧❧❧❧❧❧❧❧❧❧❧❧❧❧❧❧

The approaches to revolution, 1774–1788: the geopolitical challenge

Posterity's tribunal has judged France's ill-starred Louis XVI as lacking (among other qualities) the martial spirit of his most assertive Bourbon forebears. Yet, as a careful reconstruction of his early years by Pierrette Girault de Coursac has revealed, this prince did not escape indoctrination in the patriotic prejudices of the country he was destined to rule starting in May 1774 at the age of twenty. "A king of France," wrote the youthful and earnest duc de Berri seven years before his accession, "if he is always just, will always be the first and most powerful sovereign of Europe and can easily become arbiter of the Continent." As for France's neighbors: the Spanish might be "proud . . . noble and generous" and the Swiss "faithful," but the Italians were "clever, . . . vindictive and jealous," the Dutch "avaricious," the unduly thriving English "swelled up with pride, jealous, [and] presumptuous," and the Prussians (under Frederick II) ever seeking territorial gains at the expense of other kingdoms.[1] Such a prince as Berri, grown to manhood and garbed in royalty, might not wish to emulate his ancestors in the lists of combat – but could he effectively resist the notion that his realm must continue to pursue its destiny as a Great Power, as, indeed, the arbiter of Europe?

For such was the challenge placed before the young monarch by the new minister of foreign affairs, Charles Gravier, comte de Vergennes. As the foreign minister would later put it in a note to Louis reflecting back on the geopolitical situation they had inherited together in 1774: "The deplorable Peace of 1763, the partition of Poland, and many other equally unhappy causes had profoundly undermined the consideration due the crown of France, which in earlier days, had been the object of terror and

---

1 Pierrette Girault de Coursac, *L'Education d'un roi. Louis XVI* (Paris: Gallimard, 1972), pp. 152, 168, 171–72. For a somewhat more benign portrayal of Louis XVI's attitudes, see Robert R. Crout, "In Search of a 'Just and Lasting Peace': The Treaty of 1783, Louis XVI, Vergennes, and the Regeneration of the Realm," *International History Review* 5 (1983), pp. 364–98.

jealousy. . . . I confess, Sire, [that] all the arrogance and insults against which my heart revolted made me desire and search for the means to change a situation so little compatible with the elevation of your soul and the grandeur of your power."[2]

What young sovereign could have argued long against language such as this, or against the foreign policy likely to follow from it? Ultimately, of course, the weight of many decades of French diplomatic tradition lay behind the grand design that Vergennes, with Louis XVI's approbation, pursued from 1774 until his death early in 1787. In this chapter we must, first, reassess Franco-British relations and strategic developments on the Continent during 1774–88 and, then, underscore the anxious perception within France of a decline in Gallic power and prestige that continued despite all of Vergennes's efforts to check it.

THE CHALLENGE ON THE SEAS

"The explanation of Vergennes' tragedy," historian Jonathan Dull has said, "is the perilous disequilibrium of Vergennes' diplomatic universe. The moment of calm at Louis' accession presented to Vergennes not stability, but a brief opportunity to right that universe before disaster struck."[3] Student of the merciless ways of power politics through diplomatic service in Germany and at Constantinople and Stockholm, and successor at Versailles to Choiseul and d'Aiguillon, this urbane architect of Louis XVI's foreign policy was haunted by a vision of a France hard-pressed to retain a reasonably secure and prestigious role in the eternal competition of states. Keenly aware of and hotly resenting the crushing defeat inflicted on French colonial and mercantile interests by the English in the Seven Years' War, Vergennes brooded as well over the spoliation of the traditional Polish ally by the three eastern European powers and over the unrelenting pressure of Catherine the Great's Russia upon those other redoubts of Gallic influence to the east, Sweden and Ottoman Turkey. The French foreign minister, especially appalled by this latter "brave new world" of coercion and pressure applied on a massive scale in the west Eurasian interior, sought somehow to "restrain its forces."

Yet this was far more easily said than done. Those states supportive of France to the east, southeast, and northeast – from diminutive Genoa in Italy and Bavaria in Germany to the menaced outposts of Sweden, Poland, and Ottoman Turkey – could not possibly counterbalance Prussia, Russia, and Austria. Austria was a confederate of Versailles in name

2 Murphy, *Charles Gravier*, p. 217.
3 Jonathan R. Dull, *The French Navy and American Independence: A Study of Arms and Diplomacy, 1774–1787* (Princeton, N.J.: Princeton University Press, 1975), pp. 8–15.

only: Vergennes already anticipated the day when the ambitious and unstable Joseph II, ruling at Vienna alone upon the death of his mother and coregent Maria Theresa, would endeavor to enlarge the Hapsburg territories, hence further undermining the balance of forces on the Continent and straining Franco-Austrian relations beyond repair. There was, of course, the alliance of thirteen years' standing with Bourbon Spain; yet, as helpful as Spain might be to France in any resumption of maritime war against the British, Madrid was of little account in Continental affairs.

Where, then, could Vergennes find succor in his attempt to restrain what he regarded as unruly and dangerous forces on the Continent and restore that equilibrium most conducive to the security and prestige of France? As Jonathan Dull has explained, the paradoxical and problematic key lay, for this statesman, in reconciliation with England.

Such a reconciliation would permit diversion of French resources from the navy to the army. Of even greater importance, Anglo-French cooperation could greatly limit the power of the other continental powers which had great armies but not the finances to engage in major wars. Only from France or England with their numerous colonies and enormous trade could come subsidies. A half-century before, the England and France of Walpole and Fleury had cooperated as equals; ... but now England was the England of Pitt: arrogant, aloof, contemptuous of France. To reduce England to a position of equality, France had to take from her a share of her strength, her monopoly of American trade and markets.[4]

Thus, Vergennes, early on in his stewardship of French foreign affairs was groping toward a two-stage relationship with the British. First, Versailles might well work at humbling the "modern Carthage" by abetting the North American colonists in what looked very much like becoming a full-scale revolt against London; then Britain might somehow be enlisted in a campaign to counterbalance the covetous, unscrupulous geopoliticians at Berlin, Vienna, and St. Petersburg. In executing the first mission, Vergennes, his sovereign, and all their patriotic countrymen could fully indulge their prejudices against and revenge themselves on the English; in carrying out the second mission, they just might be able to restore that delicate equilibrium of European strategic forces best calculated to maximize French security and influence.[5]

There was, in retrospect, an unmistakably modern component in this diplomatic design. It clearly foreshadowed attempts by French and English statesmen during the revolutionary and post-Napoleonic eras to fashion in the west a bloc of "progressive" nations to hold the rapacious eastern powers in check; in a certain remote sense, it even prefigured the divisions between democratic "West" and totalitarian "East" in the twen-

---

4 Ibid., pp. 10–11.
5 Refer again to ibid., pp. 8–15, for the best exposition of the views held by the foreign minister. But consult also Murphy, *Charles Gravier*, pp. 211–21.

tieth century. But Vergennes's grand design, it is equally clear, rested on a host of debatable suppositions. It assumed, to begin with, that a British defeat in North America would automatically restore the power balance between France and England. It assumed, too, that Vergennes's colleagues in the naval department, having tasted the heady wine of success in North America against the longtime insular foe, would not desire to carry the campaign against London into other areas of the globe, or could at least be kept from indulging that desire. It furthermore assumed that the British, having been deprived of their cherished American possession by the French, would then see fit to join their victorious rivals in some sort of common effort against the powers to the east. Finally, it assumed that the French could implement such an ambitious (and necessarily costly) policy without fatally undermining social and political institutions at home. In the end, every one of these suppositions would be proven false.

Nonetheless, "the idea that France might support the colonists against England, following the plan of Choiseul, germinated to fruition in the mind of Vergennes by late 1775."[6] Like Choiseul before him, Vergennes sought through French ambassadors and chargés d'affaires at the various foreign courts all available information concerning London's relations with its American subjects, British efforts to recruit mercenaries for a possible campaign against the colonists, and the buildup and disposition of British naval forces. Louis XVI, intrigued by tales of geographic reconnaissance since childhood and genuinely interested as king in naval affairs, appointed, first, the brilliant Turgot and then Antoine-Raymond-Gualbert-Gabriel de Sartine as head of the naval department. Faithfully assisted by, among others, Charles Claret, chevalier de Fleurieu (himself fated to become naval minister during the Revolution), the methodical Sartine took on myriad tasks. They included curbing the factional infighting among naval personnel and the disorder in the management of ports that had afflicted the navy during Louis XV's final years; restocking the naval arsenals with masts, hemp, and other supplies; and fighting for greater naval appropriations. The French chargé d'affaires at London, Garnier, had reported in 1774 that England could boast 142 ships of the line, of which 72 were in service or serviceable at very short notice; the French at that time had no more than 64 ships of the line, 34 of them available immediately for service if needed. So much of Choiseul's work of rebuilding the French navy during the 1760s had been undone! At Louis XV's death, less than 25 million livres had been going annually to the naval ministry; but naval expenditure recovered to 34 million by 1776,

6 Singh, *French Diplomacy in the Caribbean*, p. 148.

would skyrocket to 100 million two years later, and by the early 1780s would be ranging between 150 and 200 million yearly.[7]

For Louis XV's successor, 1775 was apparently a year of soul-searching regarding the wisdom of permitting his country to plunge once again into combat on the high seas. Louis XVI might listen attentively to Controller-General Turgot's strictures against the ruinous expense of war, might perceive danger in the notion of a monarch by divine right abetting rebels, might resist being swept up in a stampede toward war; yet he shared his countrymen's prejudices against the English, and he was forever being reminded by Vergennes about the humiliation suffered by his regal grandfather in the Seven Years' War. It is not at all surprising, then, to find the French sovereign writing to Charles III of Spain in this ambivalent – indeed, self-contradictory – vein on 7 August 1775:

Perhaps there has never been a time when the appearances of war with England were less probable... but the unfortunate policies of that country are such that one cannot count upon it. England is much occupied with her American colonies and although I do not believe that they will ever come to terms with the mother-country, nevertheless England might try to go to war with us in order to escape her present difficulties. I think, therefore, that we should pay all our attention to preparations... in order to avoid war.[8]

The king's assertion that "England might try to go to war with us in order to escape her present difficulties" is especially striking, for it practically repeats verbatim a statement made by Vergennes in a major policy paper submitted to Louis the preceding year. In that memorandum of 1774, the newly created minister of foreign affairs had painted the English not only as "restless and greedy" but also as conniving to raise all of Europe against Versailles in order to escape the consequences of their own domestic and colonial problems. Vergennes's biographer Orville Murphy has commented that the foreign minister's diatribe against London exposed something of a "personal fatalism about the inevitability of war."[9] For reasons adduced above, Vergennes must have viewed a war with the power across the Channel, unavoidable or not, as likely to subserve his country's long-term strategic interests. In any case, what was not likely was that a monarch of tender age willing to endorse his foreign minister's cynical thoughts about the English in a letter to a royal

---

7 Dull, *French Navy*, pp. 11–15; Murphy, *Charles Gravier*, p. 245; Singh, *French Diplomacy in the Caribbean*, p. 148.
8 As quoted in Saul K. Padover, *The Life and Death of Louis XVI* (New York: Taplinger, 1963), p. 106.
9 See Murphy, *Charles Gravier*, pp. 215–17, for a discussion of this interesting memorandum.

cousin would be able very long to resist a formal and concrete argument for war.

That argument came the following April when Vergennes and the other principal ministers submitted memoranda to the king in what amounted to a debate within Council over the relative merits of war and peace. Dull has very carefully reviewed both sides in that fateful debate, and has best recapitulated what the foreign minister had to say:

> Vergennes'... "Reflections"... stressed the American Revolution as presenting France not with a danger to be avoided but with an opportunity she had no choice but to seize. [His "Reflections"] rationalized French intervention by reference to the "natural" animosity between the two countries, resurrected past injuries done by England, warned of the inevitability of war even if France did nothing, and offered to Louis the prospects of a share of American commerce and points of support for the Newfoundland fisheries.[10]

> Here, once more, the foreign minister was playing on the heartstrings of fatalism, invoking formidable diplomatic tradition, preaching the need for revenge against the old foe. And once more, Vergennes's capital (if dubious) argument was that "by depriving Britain of her possession of the American colonies France could so weaken her as to alter the balance of power."

> By ending Britain's monopoly of American trade France mistakenly believed she could seriously disrupt British "navigation" and thereby restrict the British navy's potential for wartime expansion. Ending this monopoly, just as denying Britain the use of American bases and opening American markets to foreign products, was believed by France ultimately to be contingent upon America's absolute independence from Britain.[11]

The deliverance of the American colonies would be the key to the reduction of Britain to parity with, if not actual subordination to, France. Such, in any case, was Vergennes's calculation.

Controller-General Turgot courageously argued against war. He warned that the precariousness of royal finances, and not the unfolding conflict in North America, should be engaging French minds. And he tried to chip away at the assumption that Britain really needed to maintain its hold on the North American colonies. In fact, he went so far as to suggest that a British victory in and military occupation of North America would so drain British resources as to work to the strategic advantage of the French!

But he spoke in vain. The king's first minister, Jean Frédéric Phélypeaux, comte de Maurepas (himself a former naval minister), and Sartine, current head of the naval department, took up the cudgels for war, offering in their "Reflections" arguments similar to those of Vergennes.

10 Dull, *French Navy*, pp. 36–37.
11 Ibid., p. 44.

Turgot, for his part, received no comparably persuasive support in these conciliar deliberations. Thus, he ultimately failed in his opposition to the reasoning of Vergennes, Maurepas, and Sartine. Dull has speculated upon the broader sociopolitical factors behind that failure:

> No one has as yet fully studied how the conjunction of the desires of unemployed military officers, Anglophobes, intellectuals, and expansionist businessmen reinforced the gradual acceptance of war by the king. The most penetrating judgment is still that of Albert Sorel, who wrote that Turgot failed because public opinion was divided on his reforms, and because the king did not have the strength to steadfastly support him, while Vergennes succeeded because he enjoyed the support of the public and because his program did not make demands on the king.[12]

The striking persistence of Anglophobic and pro-war sentiment in France will require elaboration later on. For now, the critical point is that Vergennes, increasingly sure of himself, encouraged the government's drift toward war. In the *Considérations* of 31 August 1776, which he addressed to the other pertinent ministers, Vergennes set forth a more explicit position on the "American question." He called for France and Spain to accelerate preparations for a possible conflict with England; he advocated the surreptitious provisioning of money and munitions to the rebellious American colonists; he urged eventual French recognition of the insurgents' cause contingent on their proclamation of independence; and he insisted on the need, at least for the time being, to deceive London as much as possible regarding the pursuit of all of these policies.[13]

Vergennes had his way. French agents at Madrid unceasingly prodded Charles III's government to upgrade Spanish naval forces, and never let slip an opportunity to remind the Iberian ally how vulnerable its yet vast overseas empire remained to British depredations. Louis XVI's government, utilizing its own trading and diplomatic personnel and turning to good purpose the pro-American (and anti-British) sentiments of aristocratic and bourgeois adventurers, supplied aid in a multitude of forms to the rebels in North America. And Vergennes and his representatives in London continued throughout 1776 and 1777 to assure George III's government of France's pacific intentions.

But this state of affairs obviously could not last forever. The British were aware of French efforts to assist the colonists; Vergennes and his associates knew about the mounting indignation of their counterparts across the Channel; and in the course of 1777, according to French scholar Jean-François Labourdette, the French foreign minister became "convinced that, no matter what the outcome of the Anglo-American conflict, the court at London would decide upon war against France to make her

---

12 Ibid., pp. 48–49. Dull's summation of Turgot's arguments is found on pp. 45–47.
13 Consult, on this memorandum, Singh, *French Diplomacy in the Caribbean*, p. 151.

pay dearly" for French machinations in America. Vergennes himself stated: "The question therefore comes down to this, would it be better to have war with the Americans on our side or at least neutral, or to have war against an Anglo-American combination restored by force of British arms?"[14]

Jonathan Dull's research has led him to hypothesize that the "preliminary decision for war was made by the end of July 1777." The French were, as ever, concerned about developments in eastern Europe. Nonetheless, a memorandum submitted to the king's Council that anxious summer by one of Vergennes's assistants contended that "however important it was to France to prevent the Russians from taking Constantinople, it was more important to weaken England and to open new markets in America." By the following January, Vergennes felt reasonably certain that there would be no renewal of Russo-Turkish warfare in the immediate future, and this "was probably the final factor freeing the council to act against Britain."[15]

The upshot was the treaty of friendship officially concluded between France and the youthful American republic on 6 February 1778. Vergennes, wishing to forestall any possibility of rapprochement between the British and the Americans and thus to render a full-scale war between the two unavoidable, had the Franco-American treaty announced formally in London on 13 March. Even so, the French foreign minister had had to argue Louis XVI out of last-minute misgivings about resuming the struggle on the seas, and, according to J.-F. Labourdette, had also had to overcome the opposition of the changeable Maurepas, War Secretary A.-M.-L. de Montbarey, and Turgot's successor Jacques Necker.[16]

And so France and England as of 1778 were once again locked in conflict, writing yet another chapter in the "Second Hundred Years' War." And this time, the French (if only in a Pyrrhic sense) prevailed. Although the French had to initiate hostilities without the support of their Iberian ally, Spain eventually rallied to Vergennes: Charles III's desire for Gibraltar, Florida, and Minorca and his ire over British incursions into his overseas empire in the end outweighed his scruples about associating his crown with subversive anticolonialist rebellion in North America. The Dutch, too, nursing their own grievances against London, in time joined the French and Spanish in their assault upon the English. Most crucial, however, was the fact that Vergennes succeeded where all his predecessors had failed: He was able to keep the war in the overseas

14 Jean-François Labourdette, "Vergennes ou la tentation du 'ministériat'," *Revue historique* 557 (Janvier—Mars 1986), pp. 89–90.
15 Dull, *French Navy*, pp. 84–86.
16 Labourdette, "Vergennes," pp. 89–90.

theater from spilling over into the Continental arena. The British found themselves, this time and this time only, isolated. Indeed, Catherine the Great, not having to reckon on this occasion with French involvement in European affairs, abetted Versailles's effort by forming a league of "neutral" states against the British lords of the seas.[17]

Thus it was that, before the end of 1781, Washington and Admiral de Grasse had caught Cornwallis at Yorktown and compelled him to surrender. The Americans, thanks to the assistance of two Bourbon states bent on old-fashioned revenge against their customary antagonist, were able to launch their decidedly novel experiment in popular governance. Vergennes's efforts had, seemingly, been crowned with success. Yet the decade of the 1780s was to expose the flaws in the foundation of the foreign minister's imposing strategic edifice. Reserving for the next chapter an examination of the consequences of Vergennes's foreign policy for sociopolitical developments within France, we need at this point to demonstrate the fallaciousness of his three key assumptions in the geostrategic realm. Those three assumptions were, to repeat: (1) that depriving England of her American colonies would restore the power balance between Versailles and London, if not actually subordinate the latter to the former; (2) that the French, having secured sweet revenge against their British competitors in North America, would not take up the grandiose dreams of earlier Gallic statesmen, would not carry the struggle against London into other areas of the globe; and (3) that the proud islanders, after having been bested for once in the American war, would somehow agree to join France in an effort to restrain the dangerous forces unleashed in Europe's eastern marches by the Hohenzollern, Hapsburg, and Romanov autocracies.

To begin with, the naval victory in April 1782 of Rodney and Hood over de Grasse in the Battle of the Saints helped dissipate British gloom over the surrender of Cornwallis at Yorktown the previous autumn.[18] This spectacular Caribbean triumph served as a reminder, if any were needed, that Britain's prowess on the seas remained fundamentally unshaken. This strategic reality was also reflected in the negotiations that ended the American war. The British and French made peace in 1783 on terms that hardly revealed any decisive shift in the power balance between the two feuding countries. Shelburne, the British foreign secretary, conceding the necessity to "deny France any further hope of using the rebellious colonies for its own purposes," dealt directly with the Americans

---

17 Refer again to Behrens, *Ancien Régime*, esp. pp. 138–62, for a discussion that illuminatingly places the American war of 1778–83 in the context of the "Second Hundred Years' War."

18 Franklin L. Ford, *Europe 1780–1830* (New York: Holt, Rinehart & Winston, 1970), pp. 63, 66.

prior to concluding peace with the Bourbon powers and the United Provinces. Under the terms of the separate pact of November 1782, the British recognized the Americans' independence, "acknowledged their claim to the Northwest Territory all the way to the Mississippi, and guaranteed them generous fishing rights off Newfoundland."

Having settled with the erstwhile American colonists, Shelburne then made peace with his country's French and Spanish antagonists. The general preliminaries to that peace, signed at Paris in January 1783 and sanctioned definitively by the Treaty of Versailles the following September, provided for the cession to France of Senegal in Africa, Tobago in the West Indies, and various fishing rights in the waters off Newfoundland in the North Atlantic. This was the extent of Versailles's gains as a result of involvement in the American war: Neither in Canada nor (more critically, perhaps) in India could the Gallic geopoliticians achieve a reversal of the embarrassing verdict of the Seven Years' War. For France's Spanish ally, too, this latest passage-at-arms with London yielded less than satisfactory results. Madrid obtained Florida and Minorca but not its most coveted prize, Gibraltar.[19] Finally, the British scored an outright triumph the following year at the expense of the Dutch, who, deserted by the French and the Spanish, had to cede to London both Negapattinam in southern India and trading privileges in the fabulously rich Moluccas in Far Eastern waters. Hence, the same war that, temporarily, cost the British some of their influence (although none of their genuinely vital strategic bases) on the Atlantic Rim actually fortified their position in the increasingly important Far East.

For Vergennes, on the other hand, the process of negotiating an end to the American war was fraught with disillusionment and augured more disappointment in the years ahead. Louis XVI's foreign minister had, first of all, to convince his Iberian ally that its most cherished goal, the recapture of Gibraltar, was beyond the reach of Franco-Spanish military capabilities. Moreover, he had to abandon France's Dutch confederate to the not so tender mercies of the British. Granted, Vergennes could derive a modicum of satisfaction from British cessions of territories and rights to France in Africa, the West Indies, and the North Atlantic, but in North America his policies over the long term reaped nothing but disappointment for Versailles.

There was the ironic case of Canada. As Ludwig Dehio has observed, the "local French Catholics feared the rule of their fanatically Puritan neighbors" to the south "more than the negligently tolerant regime of London." How, in fact, could the Canadians have known for sure "that the expansionist Yankees would never round off their huge territories by

19 Ibid., p. 67.

annexing Canada?"[20] Half a century before, fear of French-held Canada
had done much to bind the British colonists to their mother country;
now, misgivings about the emancipated ex-Britishers to the south tended
to bind France's erstwhile subjects in Canada to London!

But the greatest irony of all lay in Vergennes's frustration over those
"expansionist Yankees" into whose republican cause his country had
poured so much treasure. He drew no special pleasure from the prospect
of a United States solidly ensconced in North America: patently, an
insecure republic, still reliant on the French, hostile to London, and
perhaps challenging the British navy and British shipping upon the Atlantic, would better promote French strategic interests in that region.
Events, however, did not take this course: The Americans set out westward to develop their vast continental hinterland, and were quite content,
as a securely independent people, to resume commercial ties with the
English.

Durand Echeverria, among others, has reviewed in detail the difficulties
that arose in the Atlantic trade of the postwar era between France and
the young American republic.[21] French exporters attempted, immediately
after the war, to sell in the United States shoddy wares unsuited to
American buying habits, and did not in the ensuing years tailor their
goods (as did the British) to the specific needs and tastes of potential
American consumers. More seriously, perhaps, the French as a rule did
not (or could not?) extend to the Americans the long and favorable terms
of credit that the English habitually could extend to them. Those French
exporters who were exceptions to this rule sometimes lost their investments and their customers due to bankruptcies that were common in
America in the depressed economic conditions following the Revolution.
The Americans, for their part, "were discouraged from shipping their
products to French ports by the tobacco monopoly of the Farmers General, by the strangling mass of red tape which delayed unloadings, by
excessive duties on certain items, and by the lack of demand for a number
of important American products." Furthermore, individual American
firms conducting business in France often failed to honor debts incurred
toward the French, or in some cases went bankrupt altogether. In addition, the new American government, itself weighted down with debt,
was laggard in paying French military volunteers and moneylenders what
it owed them.

Further complicating Franco-American relations were commercial developments in the West Indies. In the course of the 1780s non-French

---

20 Dehio, *Precarious Balance*, pp. 122–23.
21 Echeverria, *Mirage in the West: A History of the French Image of American Society to
    1815* (Princeton, N.J.: Princeton University Press, 1956), pp. 130–32.

traders were permitted to import into the French Caribbean such commodities as salt beef, wheat, and salt fish from the United States and
other countries, and to deliver molasses, rum, and goods of French origin
to American ports. French shippers naturally condemned this arrangement, which in effect transferred considerable commercial profit from
French to American and English merchants.

Dull has pointed out that, over the 1784–89 period, average annual
British exports to the former North American colonies were already back
to 90 percent of the average yearly exports of 1769–74. Soon they would
be forging ahead to unheard-of levels.[22] British predominance in the
commerce with the United States was especially crucial in view of its
implications for the British leap into industrialization. H. J. Habakkuk
has rightly emphasized that the Americans, with their relatively high per
capita incomes, large aggregate wealth, and tendency to cluster together
in a very inclusive "middle class," provided an ideal market for the kinds
of goods – cotton and wool textiles and ironwares of everyday use – most
easily mass-produced by the emerging, steam-driven technologies.[23] Consequently, the British "defeat" in North America (as Turgot, had he lived
longer, would have been quick to observe!) turned out to be a victory in
economic terms. Relieved of the expense and worry of trying to maintain
political control over the Americans, England could now concentrate on
extracting maximum economic advantage from its new relationship with
a sovereign United States.

Moreover, the British were matching or besting their rivals during these
years in other regions of the globe as well. In the Mediterranean, British
fortunes, temporarily depressed during the war of 1778–83, rebounded
rapidly. Strategic Gibraltar remained in London's hands despite the long
and bloody siege of 1779–82; the rise of Lord Acton to power in Naples
boded well for British trade and ill for French trading interests in southern
Italy; and by 1784, London's commercial cause throughout the Italian
peninsula was in the ascendant.[24] In the Baltic, so crucial for its supply
of iron, hemp, and wood to the navies of the two competing western
powers, the research of Frank Fox has disclosed that imperial Russia's
merchants and landowners were highly reliant on British traders and

22 Dull, *French Navy*, pp. 340–41. See also Echeverria, *Mirage*, p. 130.
23 Habbakuk, "Population, Commerce and Economic Ideas," in *The New Cambridge
   Modern History*, Vol. VIII: *The American and French Revolutions, 1763–93* (Cambridge:
   Cambridge University Press, 1968), esp. pp. 40–45. See also on this point David S.
   Landes, "Technological Change and Development in Western Europe, 1750–1914," in
   The Cambridge Economic History of Europe, Vol. VI: *The Industrial Revolution and
   After* (Cambridge: Cambridge University Press, 1965), esp. pp. 353–69.
24 Anderson, *Europe in the Eighteenth Century*, p. 230; and Murphy, *Charles Gravier*,
   p. 430.

would remain so despite the signing of a Franco-Russian commercial treaty early in 1787.[25] Even at Constantinople, where commercial ties with France were a matter of nearly three centuries' standing, the gradual eclipse of Ottoman power by an expansionist Russia and the uneasiness of Franco-Russian relations did not augur well for the ability of French merchants to make hay at the expense of their British counterparts.[26] It is indisputable that the French West Indies – above all, the islands of Guadeloupe, Martinique, and San Domingo – produced about half of the western world's sugar and coffee in the late 1780s and secured for the metropolitan power much needed foreign exchange. Still, there was no demand in the French Caribbean islands for textiles and iron goods comparable to the demand for such mass-produced wares in the British-dominated markets of the United States, and as a result no spur to industrialization in France comparable to the stimulus to industrialization in England.[27] In addition, the British seem to have been transporting around twice as many African slaves to the New World by the late 1780s as were the French, were penetrating the markets of Spain and its American colonies, and were leading the way in exploiting the potentially rich markets of India and the Far East.[28]

As early as 1783, the volume of British trade worldwide may have been as great as at any time before the war. And over the years from 1782 to 1788 British merchant shipping apparently more than doubled. The value of British exports and imports, taken together, may have been increasing by the 1780s at a phenomenal annual rate of 4 to 5 percent. And the British share in overall global commerce must have been increasing – to the disadvantage, presumably, of France – even before the epochal struggle of 1792–1815 conferred insuperable advantages on the islanders' trade and industry.[29]

25 Frank Fox, "Negotiating with the Russians: Ambassador Ségur's Mission to Saint-Petersbourg, 1784–1789," *French Historical Studies* 7 (1971), esp. pp. 52, 62.

26 On the decreasing competitiveness of the French in the Levant in the 1770s and 1780s, see François Crouzet, "Angleterre et France au XVIIIe siècle: Essai d'analyse comparée de deux croissances économiques," *Annales: E.S.C.* 21 (Mars–Avril 1966), esp. pp. 263–64.

27 On the French West Indies trade, consult Jean Tarrade, *Le Commerce colonial à la fin de l'ancien régime* (Paris: Presses Universitaires de France, 1972); and Robert Stein, *The French Sugar Business* (Baton Rouge: Louisiana State University Press, 1988). But again, refer to Habakkuk, "Population, Commerce and Economic Ideas," pp. 40–45, on the relatively weak demand in the French colonies for industrial goods.

28 On these points, see again Crouzet, "Angleterre et France au XVIIIe siècle," pp. 263–64; and Habakkuk, "Population, Commerce and Economic Ideas," pp. 40–45.

29 On these points, consult Kennedy, *Rise and Fall of the Great Powers*, p. 120; Habakkuk, "Population, Commerce and Economic Ideas," pp. 40–45; Dull, *French Navy*, pp. 340–44; and Price, *Economic Modernisation of France*, pp. 132–33.

That the French were lagging behind their British rivals in commerce and other economic sectors was in part related to the fact that their sociopolitical and geopolitical purposes were less effectively meshed than were those across the Channel. A number of trade-related developments pointed up this reality in the course of the 1780s. There was, for example, the French government's decision in 1784 to open seven West Indian ports to foreign traders without fully consulting its own shippers. Then, again, there was the case of the ongoing Franco-Russian commercial negotiations, which made some French merchants in the Baltic markets envy their British competitors for the support they received from their own political leaders on mercantile issues.

But undoubtedly it was the furor over the Anglo-French trade pact of 1786 that most powerfully demonstrated the troubling implications for France not only of relative economic backwardness but also of governance unaccountable to such entrepreneurs as there were. C.-E. Labrousse and subsequent writers have argued plausibly that this agreement, which only went into effect in 1787, cannot be held responsible for an economic crisis in France whose origins extended as far back as 1778. Nonetheless, as J. F. Bosher, Orville Murphy, and others have shown, French traders and manufacturers had some reason to complain that their government, in negotiating this treaty, had not displayed nearly as much sensitivity to their needs as had the British government to the needs of its own entrepreneurs. Traders and industrialists in France could justifiably fear that a reduction of tariffs on grain, wine, and brandy exported from their country across the Channel would scarcely benefit a depressed French economy that had little in the way of those commodities to export, whereas a lowering of duties on English hardware and textiles imported into France could only damage the fledgling French industrial sector. The policy makers at Versailles, it now seems certain, should have reduced tariffs at the frontiers only after eliminating the innumerable internal tolls that were holding back French economic development – and only after ensuring for native French enterprises a decent opportunity to become competitive with like ventures in England. (Vergennes's lowering of tariffs on English goods may have testified primarily to his desire to improve Franco-English relations; paradoxically, the decision to retain tolls within France stemmed largely from the government's continued and war-related need for those tolls as guaranteed revenue.[30]) The acrimonious disputes among the French over this "Eden Treaty" of 1786 only served to high-

---

30 On these various trade issues in the 1780s, and what they reveal about the lack of harmonization of basic sociopolitical and geopolitical purposes among the French, refer to Echeverria, *Mirage*, pp. 131–32; Acomb, *Anglophobia in France*, pp. 117–120; Fox, "Negotiating with the Russians," p. 52; Bosher, *Single Duty Project*, pp. 82–83; and Murphy, *Charles Gravier*, pp. 443–46.

light the competitive disadvantage under which France, with constitutional arrangements unrepresentative of business interests and with a relatively underdeveloped economy (relative, that is, to that of England), had to labor.

Inevitably, Britain's economic strength vis-à-vis France was parlayed into military strength. Prime Minister Pitt was able to have thirty-three additional ships of the line constructed between 1783 and 1790, thus raising the peacetime power of the British navy to new heights.[31] "To be truly vulnerable," Franklin Ford has written, "the Royal Navy would have had to be crippled by an especially heavy desertion rate or by a more protracted interruption of its supply of timber for hulls and masts than any opponent had yet managed to inflict upon it."[32] In point of fact, any realistic expectation the French and Spanish governments might still have had of matching British forces upon the high seas was rapidly fading.

But if Vergennes overestimated the strategic impact of depriving England of its American colonies, he also overestimated the chances of achieving a postwar reconciliation between London and Versailles. And this latter disappointment stemmed at least in part from the French foreign minister's inability to restrain his warlike confrère in the naval department, Sartine's successor, Charles-Eugène-Gabriel de La Croix, Maréchal de Castries. All diplomatic scholars agree on this. In fact, as Murphy has been at pains to point out, Vergennes was having problems with his bellicose associate even before the end of the American war:

> While Necker intrigued for peace, the French "War Party," led by . . . Castries, . . . demanded escalation of the war. He insisted that France, too, make the American War for Independence a war of expansion, and urged the deployment of French soldiers and sailors with that idea in mind. Such a war was in clear contradiction to Vergennes' concept of Louis XVI's role in Europe and the world, but the fact that France's two allies were demanding additional territories gave Castries leverage in the Court and Royal Council. . . . As the negotiations began, the expansionist faction led by Castries incessantly bombarded Vergennes with memos and plans for extending French colonialism in India.

Vergennes might endeavor in Council to counter these aggressive designs with the hard realities of straitened royal finances; but Castries "never gave up."[33] Indeed, the naval minister fought to the bitter end to break off the peace talks with England and to find somewhere the financial means wherewith to resume and expand the struggle on the seas.

31 Dull, *French Navy*, pp. 340–44.
32 Ford, *Europe 1780–1830*, p. 63. As of 1783, according to Ford, Britain could boast 174 ships of the line together; France and Spain could not claim as many as 150. (These statistics may differ somewhat from figures adduced more recently by Dull.)
33 Murphy, *Charles Gravier*, p. 325. For corroboration on this point, see Labourdette, "Vergennes," pp. 91–92.

In the ensuing years, Castries returned to this theme time after time. In the autumn of 1785, for example, he argued in a memorandum that Asia was now the primary fount of British power and that, consequently, Asia should henceforth command the attention of French statesmen and France's Dutch allies.[34] Then, in November 1786, he brought to the Council (at a session attended by Vergennes) a memorandum severely critical of the foreign minister's policies. Castries made three cardinal points: (1) that British concessions in the strategic Newfoundland fisheries as a result of the American war had been inadequate; (2) that Vergennes had let slip the opportunity in that conflict to restore the French position in India to what it had been prior to the Seven Years' War; and (3) that the Anglo-French Commercial Treaty envisaged and indeed "required" by the Peace of 1783 could hurt and even ruin French manufactures.[35] Such charges obviously invoked the specters of bellicose Gallic policies of the past as well as anticipating troublesome issues of the future.

Castries's call for a more aggressive naval posture eventually bore fruit. Admittedly, as late as 1 January 1787, the French navy could still claim no more than sixty-two ships of the line: During the years after the American war, Jonathan Dull has stated, seventeen ships of the line were removed from service while twelve were being launched and seven more placed in construction. Still, as far back as 1781 the naval minister had spoken of his desire to see the navy built up to eighty ships of the line; and even before Vergennes's death, in 1787, "Castries had succeeded in reversing the trend toward a progressively tighter naval budget." Thus, the old pattern was fated to repeat itself: Just as French naval rearmament in times past, most recently during the 1760s and 1770s, had presaged the waging of maritime war against the Britannic antagonist, so now once again, in the mid-1780s, a quickening of activity in the French naval department foreshadowed hostilities against the islanders.[36]

Castries, like his immediate predecessor Sartine, was an industrious and capable administrator. E. H. Jenkins has described his labors during the 1780–87 period:

When the war [of 1778–83] was ending it was decided to introduce flint-locks for firing the guns, and every new ship built, or older ship coming into dock for a complete overhaul, was to be fitted with copper sheathing.... The ships had a first-class designer in Sané. Castries pushed ahead with the restoration of Dunkirk to its former usefulness, and started an extensive rebuilding of Cherbourg, whose harbor works had been destroyed by the British in 1758; and he got the king – his majesty's one "naval occasion" – to visit it. New ordinances in 1784–86 gave

34 Blanning, *Origins*, pp. 47–51.
35 Labourdette, "Vergennes," pp. 91–92.
36 Dull, *French Navy*, pp. 336–38.

the service a new organisation. Its ships and manning were divided into nine divisions, five based on Brest, two each on Toulon and Rochefort.

That Castries "intended the old defensive tactics to give way to aggressive ones" manifested itself plainly in his advice to Louis XVI to confer upon Suffren, one of the great French naval heroes, a fourth vice-admiralty: "the great honor and reward thereby given to that admiral made him an example for others to follow."[37]

In other ways as well, Castries signified his determination to restore France to a state of readiness for the waging of maritime war. He devised means for encouraging the recruitment of nobles (and some bourgeois) into naval officer ranks. As Paul Bamford has pointed out, he expended enormous funds for stocking French arsenals with masts, hemp, and other essential matériel, acquiring such supplies illegally, under the nose of the Turkish ally, through the Levant, as well as legally in the far northeastern ports of the Baltic. By 1785, Brest had six thousand masts on hand, and by the next year the dockyard at Toulon, traditionally difficult to provision because of its location in the far south, had twenty-three hundred masts in stock.[38] Most tellingly, perhaps, Castries tried to upgrade the seaworthiness of French naval forces – and probe for British weaknesses in the Far East – by sending a series of expeditions around Africa into the Indian Ocean. One, under the comte de Bussy, had set sail during the final two years of the American war; between 1784 and 1789, no fewer than ten expeditions followed in its wake. Moreover, the French formed a new Compagnie des Indes in 1785; maritime clashes between British and French forces actually took place in the waters off India the same year; and in 1786 the French government sent an agent to a local Indian prince, Tippoo Sahib, to proffer assistance in liquidating the debt he had incurred in the Mysore war against Britain.[39] Clearly, there were those in power at Versailles during these years who knew, as farsighted French statesmen had realized before and would comprehend again, that one of the keys to the future lay in the exploitation of the Far East.

And so Vergennes found that handling the English successfully was not a simple matter of first waging war against them and then "waging peace." The whole thrust of a century of French hostility toward British interests in the vast world beyond Europe was now working, in the twilight of the foreign minister's life, to thwart his dream of Anglo-French

---

37 Jenkins, *History of the French Navy*, pp. 199–200. Dull has affirmed that "Castries was a superlative administrator and by his reforms . . . made meaningful and lasting contributions to the navy." Dull, *French Navy*, p. 337.

38 Jenkins, *History of the French Navy*, pp. 199–200; and Paul W. Bamford, *Forests and French Sea Power, 1660–1789* (Toronto: University of Toronto Press, 1956), pp. 155–57.

39 See Blanning, *Origins*, pp. 47–51, on these French activities in the Far East.

rapprochement. And it was not only a matter of fire-eaters in the government like the Maréchal de Castries; Vergennes's own subordinates in the diplomatic service at London could not divest themselves of anti-British attitudes. What was more, the sentiments of the latter were more realistic than those of their superior insofar as they reckoned with, and responded to, the anti-French feelings of the British. Even as representatives of the two governments were laboring over the articles of what would become the Commercial Treaty of 1786 (an agreement destined to generate yet more misunderstanding and resultant hard feelings between the two countries), the French ambassador at the British capital, Adhémar de Grignan, and his chargé d'affaires, Barthélemy, were concluding regretfully: "It is an evident truth that the English are irreconcilable enemies. Rivalry, competition, jealousy, national hatred, spirit of vengeance, all are opposed to a *rapprochement* with this nation."[40]

Such a conviction, held by diplomats whose role it supposedly was at this time to calm the roiled waters of Anglo-French relations, was palpably counterproductive; yet would Louis XVI's foreign minister have been entitled to register any surprise at such a bleak assessment of English attitudes? After all, had he himself not been perfectly content to deceive London as to his diplomatic intentions during those pivotal two or three years in the preceding decade when the forces of anti-British insurgency were gaining strength in North America? And had the French not always shown themselves opposed to British interests throughout the world? Why, then, should Pitt and his colleagues have viewed even so significant a development as the signing of a trade pact as indicative of a fundamental change of attitude on the other side? The fact is that they did not. T. C. W. Blanning has put this as cogently as could any historian:

If the main motive of the French [in negotiating the pact] really was political rather than economic or fiscal, then their initiative was still-born. When congratulating Eden on the successful conclusion of the negotiations, the British foreign secretary, the Marquis of Carmarthen, added that French compliance on economic matters only made him more suspicious when it came to politics. Although Carmarthen was particularly Francophobe, his mistrust was shared by Pitt: "Though in the commercial business I think there are reasons for believing the French may be sincere, I cannot listen without suspicion to their professions of political friendship."[41]

And there appeared to the English to be all too many other disquieting portents of French expansionism in those years. As early as September 1783, "with the ink on the Treaty of Versailles barely dry," London was hearing rumors that the French were planning facilities for no fewer than

40 As cited in Murphy, *Charles Gravier*, pp. 434–35.
41 Blanning, *Origins*, p. 46. Carmarthen, according to Murphy, "suspected that Vergennes was plotting a sinister plan to ruin England." *Charles Gravier*, p. 436.

one hundred ships of the line at the artificial harbor under construction at Cherbourg. Did this augur an eventual strike across the Channel by the French? The Russian ambassador at London was certainly more than happy to convey to the British an intelligence report to this effect in August 1784; and, again, the ordinarily nontraveling Louis XVI made a highly publicized inspection of the works at Cherbourg just two years later. Then there was the formal alliance concluded between the French and the Dutch in November 1785. Since another French ally, Austria, possessed the intermediate Netherlands, did this presage a French strategic grip upon both the Channel and North Sea coasts? Furthermore, there were the numerous indications, some of them already noted, of French aspirations in the Far East. Since (as additional points in this connection) the French held the strategic islands of Bourbon and Mauritius in the Indian Ocean, and since their Dutch allies held the yet more crucial Cape of Good Hope at the southern tip of Africa and the superb harbor at Trincomalee on the northeastern coast of Ceylon, just off India, were the British not justified in feeling their sea links with India to be vulnerable and perhaps imperiled? As Blanning has observed, it is hardly astounding that Pitt and Carmarthen should have found it so difficult "to swallow the honeyed words of Vergennes."[42]

Thus, the premises on which Louis XVI's foreign minister based his policy toward Britain proved in the end to be flawed. Depriving the proud insular adversary of its American colonies did not restore the overall strategic balance between London and Versailles. What was more, Vergennes did not find in subsequent years that he could effectively curb aggressive anti-British tendencies in his country's foreign policy, tendencies that were not only rooted in the past but also (ironically) given new life by *his* victory (whatever its Pyrrhic aspects) over the British in North America. Finally, Vergennes (again for reasons of history and because of his own and his colleagues' policies) could not compass a fundamental Anglo-French reconciliation. Hence, the foreign minister found himself stymied in his ultimate design of involving an Anglo-French alliance in the worrying affairs of eastern Europe. For this and for other reasons, the late 1770s and 1780s brought as much frustration to the prerevolutionary Bourbon state in Continental politics as in overseas matters.

THE CHALLENGE ON THE CONTINENT

There was a curious analogy between the French experience in Continental affairs during the years preceding the "Maupeou revolution" and that during the years leading up to the greater upheaval of 1789. In each

42 Blanning, *Origins*, pp. 47–51.

situation the unceasing pressure of Romanov Russia on France's traditional friends in eastern Europe and the growth of Russia's presence in
international affairs in general accompanied and helped to hasten the
waning of French influence on the Continent; but in each situation it was
the other relatively new power to the east, Prussia (backed, naturally and
aggravatingly, by the British) that more directly humiliated the French.
The analogy was not by any means perfect; yet it remains incontrovertible
that, in the reign of Louis XVI as in that of his grandfather, France
suffered disappointment and even mortification in the west Eurasian theater of events.

We have already seen that, even in the act of deciding for a renewal of
war against England, Vergennes had a wary eye on developments in
eastern Europe. His assistant Rayneval conceded in July 1777 that "the
danger of war with Britain was that it deprived France of the ability to
act militarily on the European continent, above all to protect the Turks
from the Russians and perhaps even from Austria." Should the Russians
engage in war with the Turks and score gains at their expense, stated
Rayneval, it was to be hoped that those gains would somehow be "coun-
terbalanced by the reaction of the other European powers." As earlier
noted, the feeling in Louis XVI's Council that there would be no resumption of Russo-Turkish warfare, at least for the time being, was what
finally freed the king and his advisers early in 1778 for action against
London.[43]

Yet Vergennes and his confrères also had to worry about another potential crisis on the Continent at this very time. They learned in January
of the decease, without immediate heirs, of Maximilian Joseph, elector
of the south German state of Bavaria. This raised a sensitive issue for the
French. Bavaria had long been a redoubt of French influence in Germany,
and yet Versailles knew that its nominal Austrian ally Joseph II coveted
the duchy. Should a dispute over the Bavarian succession now erupt,
Joseph might take advantage of the situation to seize Bavaria. Such an
action would jeopardize France's historic role as the major guarantor of
the balance of power within Germany and might even touch off a central
European war.

Still, if the French really wished to devote an undivided attention to
events in America, they would have to rely on the Russians and Prussians
to defend the power equilibrium in central Europe against any Austrian
initiative that might upset it. Vergennes in this situation was limited to
warning the Austrian "ally" that his country would not support Vienna
militarily over the question of the Bavarian succession.[44] France, it ap-

---

43 On this point, refer once again to Dull, *French Navy*, pp. 84–86.
44 Ibid., pp. 95–96 and 101, n. 23.

peared, could no longer aspire to simultaneous greatness on the seas and on the Continent.

But ultimately it was a greater power than Joseph's Austria that profited most handsomely from the Bavarian imbroglio. Although the Treaty of Teschen, which ended a brief Austro-Prussian war over the Bavarian Succession by awarding minimal concessions to Vienna, resulted from Franco-Russian mediation, it was evident to observers that one mediating power had gained more than the other from this diplomatic intervention.

As a guarantor of the settlement Russia could claim to have achieved for the first time a formal *locus standi* in German affairs, and to have placed the influence she had exercised there since the reign of Peter I on a secure legal footing. In December 1778 the French representative to the Imperial Diet complained, with perfect truth, that Russia was now the dominant foreign influence in the politics of Germany, not, as for the last century and a half, France.[45]

Perhaps, as some have argued, Russia's formidable tsarina was especially intrigued by German developments because of her own Teutonic origins (in Anhalt-Zerbst). In any case, she made every effort to strengthen the Russian foothold in central Europe. She established a special department in her ministry of foreign affairs to deal with German politics; she increased her country's diplomatic representation in the Holy Roman Empire; and in early 1785, she was happy to have a Russian envoy, Count Romanzov, plead the Austrian case for the transfer of the Austrian Netherlands to the duke of Zweibrücken in exchange for the cession to Vienna of the Duke's recently established rights in Bavaria.[46] True, in this last connection a Prussian-sponsored "League of German Princes" intervened and ensured that the Hapsburg emperor was once again balked in his scheming after Bavaria. Still, it was a sign of the times that even the august Teutonic prince ruling at Vienna should have beaten a path to Catherine's door in search of Russian support in a German dispute.

The French could hardly look with equanimity on the growth of Russian influence in a region where they had viewed themselves diplomatically (and, in fairest season, militarily) ascendant ever since the conclusion of the Peace of Westphalia in 1648. In addition, growing Russian influence in a disunited Germany could also mean intensifying Russian pressure from the south and west on two of France's three traditional east European allies, Sweden and Poland. It might even prefigure a further partition of the hapless latter country. But what could Vergennes, given his preoccupation with the Anglo-French relationship, realistically have done to

45 Anderson, *Europe in the Eighteenth Century*, pp. 191–92. See also, on the Franco-Russian mediation in this conflict, Dull, *French Navy*, pp. 125–26.
46 Blanning, *Origins*, pp. 56–57.

counter this trend? Indeed, it bears reiterating at this point that France's very effort to defeat the British in the New World abetted the growth of the Russian presence in central Europe by encouraging Catherine to sponsor the formation of a league of "neutral" northern states. It may very well be true, as Anderson has insisted, that this "heterogeneous combination of states," which included Sweden, Prussia, Denmark, Portugal, the United Provinces, and Russia itself, and which intended primarily to oppose Britain for the way it defined and enforced its so-called maritime rights, had "little practical effect" beyond straining Anglo-Russian relations. Nonetheless, the same scholar has allowed: "It helped to consolidate in Western Europe the impression of Russia's power which had been developing . . . ever since Poltava." If diplomatic observers seemed entitled, in the wake of Teschen, to consider Russia the chief arbiter between Prussia and Austria in their Teutonic rivalries, they seemed almost as justified, at least for the duration of the American war, in regarding the huge Eurasian state as "arbitrating" between France and England in their struggle on the high seas, even as "dictating a new code of maritime laws to mankind!"[47]

But if Vergennes had reason to be nettled by Russian mediation in German affairs and to regard Russian intervention in maritime politics, anti-British though it might be, with some concern, he had far greater reason to be alarmed by developments in the early 1780s pointing toward a new and massive Russian assault on that other historic east European ally of France, Ottoman Turkey.

Here, in the ever unstable marches of southeastern Europe, was where the redoubtable empress of Russia especially dreamed of making her mark. And her dreams of glory were not small dreams. A visit by Joseph II to Russia in 1780 was followed up by an exchange of letters between the Romanov sovereign and her Hapsburg counterpart in 1781 that amounted to a secret pact of defensive alliance. On this basis Catherine proposed to Joseph nothing less than an Austro-Russian partition of the Turkish Balkans – and asserted Russian claims to the western Caucasus, the Crimean Peninsula, and the left bank of the Dniester. The tsarina's scheme envisioned the creation of a "restored Byzantine empire under a Romanov *basileus* or emperor." The Russian empress wished to groom her three-year-old grandson, who, as one historian has wryly commented, was "named Constantine not quite by accident," for this imperial role. He would, if all went as expected, rule Greece, Bulgaria, and Macedonia

---

47 Anderson, *Europe in the Eighteenth Century*, pp. 191–92. As Murphy has put it, Catherine's "shadow loomed ever larger over the map of Europe during the war, and began to eclipse Louis XVI in his role of arbiter. But, given the circumstances of the American War, Louis could hardly do anything but encourage her." *Charles Gravier*, p. 287.

some day from Constantinople after the Turkish capital had been "liberated" by the conjoined military efforts of St. Petersburg and Vienna.[48]

It is true that Catherine temporarily settled for something less than these prospects. Unaided by Joseph, who for many reasons was cool toward schemes entailing major warfare in the Balkans, but taking advantage of a Tartar revolt against her protégé the khan of the Crimea, the tsarina sent one of her armies into the Crimean Peninsula in 1783 and very soon was able to proclaim its annexation. At about the same time another Russian force, striking on the eastern side of the Black Sea, conquered much of Georgia in the western Caucasus. The Russian colossus, all too clearly, was once again on the move.

At Versailles, Vergennes watched with ever-mounting anxiety as these events unfolded. As far back as 1777, he had characterized the possible destruction of Turkey by Russia as one of the greatest calamities imaginable. Although his concern was motivated in part by economic considerations – the French might well fear the implications of a Russian domination of Turkey for their commercial privileges in the Levant – Vergennes's misgivings were above all strategic in nature. Nothing could more patently menace the delicate power equilibrium in Europe, and the French security and prestige deriving from that equilibrium, than unchallenged Russian aggression against Turkey. In the early 1780s, according to Dull, Vergennes feared a total dismemberment of the Ottoman Empire rather less than a scenario in which Catherine seized the Crimea and Joseph II of Austria took the Romanian principalities of Wallachia and Moldavia; but such a possibility was in itself sufficiently unnerving.[49] Having served as French ambassador at Constantinople from 1755 to 1768, Vergennes was acutely aware of Turkish strategic vulnerability; now, as war once again threatened and then broke out in southeastern Europe, the current French ambassador at Constantinople, the comte de Saint-Priest, reported back bluntly to Versailles that Turkish land and sea forces amounted to "nothing."[50]

As late as the autumn of 1782, Vergennes still entertained the wistful hope that Catherine might be forestalled through concerted action by the Bourbon states and Britain. But Versailles, London, and Madrid were still enmeshed in negotiations aimed at terminating the American war; and in any case, neither Spain nor Britain seemed that eager to take a hard line against Catherine. By June 1783, the French foreign ministry

48 Ford, *Europe 1780–1830*, pp. 70–71. For Joseph II's views of the various plans advanced by Catherine II for Russo-Austrian aggression against Turkey, see Karl A. Roider, Jr., *Austria's Eastern Question 1700–1790* (Princeton, N.J.: Princeton University Press, 1982), passim.

49 Dull, *French Navy*, p. 298.

50 Blanning, *Origins*, pp. 57–58.

had been formally notified of both the Russo-Austrian pact of 1781 and the Russian intention to annex the Crimea. According to Jonathan Dull, "France had resolved on war if Austria joined the Russians in despoiling the Ottoman Empire." It never came to that: As we have already seen, Joseph II held back at this juncture. But the Hapsburg emperor and his foreign minister Kaunitz, recalling no doubt the refusal of France to back Austria in various disputes of recent years such as that over the Bavarian succession, and wishing to preserve their new understanding with Russia, would in no way go so far as to intercede on France's (and Turkey's) behalf at St. Petersburg. Consequently, Vergennes could do no more than urge Constantinople to cut its losses by ceding the Crimea formally to Catherine. It did so in 1784; but French diplomatic influence in Turkey suffered accordingly.[51]

And so the Russian advance toward the Mediterranean halted, at least for the moment. As it was, Catherine could already draw immense satisfaction from the triumphs she had scored at Turkey's expense. As a consequence of the recent military engagements, her state had now tremendously expanded its Black Sea coastline, had acquired new bases or potential bases for a powerful Black Sea fleet, and was continuing to step up the pressure on the Caucasian frontier of the Ottoman Empire.

Yet these successes, arresting though they were, merely whetted the appetite of the empress of Russia. In 1786, while hosting her confederate Joseph II on her celebrated tour of the Crimea and the Dnieper Valley, the tsarina broached once again the idea of a joint assault upon the Ottoman Porte. Catherine was unable to arouse in her Hapsburg guest much enthusiasm for such an ambitious campaign. As Karl Roider has stressed, Joseph's strategic dilemma was that of any Austrian ruler in the eighteenth century: how to address simultaneously Prussian machinations within Germany and the projection of Russian power to Austria's northeast and southeast.[52]

For the Turks, however, Catherine's all too obvious designs portended the greatest imaginable peril. And, indeed, the Ottoman government, resenting its desertion by France over the issue of the Crimea, and desiring to counteract both the growing Russian military pressure in the Caucasus and the subversive activities of Russian consular agents within Turkish borders, decided on a desperate throw of the dice. It confronted Catherine's government with an ultimatum demanding an immediate end to its meddling in the khanate of Georgia. When this ultimatum was rejected, Turkey declared war on its foe to the north in August 1787. Initially, St.

---

51 Dull, *French Navy*, pp. 338–39. See also Anderson, *Europe in the Eighteenth Century*, pp. 236–37, on the weakening of French influence at Constantinople.
52 Refer again to Roider, *Austria's Eastern Question*, esp. pp. 189–96.

Petersburg, deploying poorly prepared armies in the field, and facing a new distraction in the form of a Swedish assault upon its holdings in Finland, went onto the defensive. This would not long be the case, however. By 1789, the Russians, at last abetted by an Austrian push into the Balkans, and aided further by the collapse of the Swedish military effort, would be resuming their long-term offensive against Turkey, thus threatening the precarious balance of power within Europe.

Vergennes died six months before this renewal of the Russo-Turkish struggle; yet, in light of his pessimism concerning political tendencies in eastern Europe, he would not have been astonished to see the chronic instability in that region once again eventuate in war. At the same time, however, it is important to note the existence in French policy toward Turkey of a strain of opportunistic speculation that ultimately merged with the expansionist bent in French overseas strategies. Blanning has commented upon this element in French calculations:

A growing number of French policy-makers began to have increasing doubts about the viability of the Turkish Empire... So the view gained ground in Paris that there might be more to be gained from the role of predator than [from] that of protector. Attention began to center on the soft target of Egypt, with Crete to be added as a naval base and entrepôt for the Levant trade. In the course of the 1780s, French diplomatic missions were sent all over the eastern Mediterranean to explore possibilities. For the time being, the temptation to share in a general partition was resisted, but the idea, once sown, never withered.[53]

As Blanning has also noted, calculating French businessmen could regard the growth of Russian influence in the Black Sea basin as offering economic opportunities rather than posing a political threat to their country. Indeed, a French trading company was founded at Kherson on the Dnieper River near the Black Sea in 1785. But beyond this, might not the entire Levant, if divided into Russian and French spheres of influence, provide a better market for French goods than a Levant ineffectually ruled, as was now the case, by the Turks? And then, inevitably, there was the chance that geostrategic benefits might accrue to France from some sort of accommodation with Russia in that region. For instance, with Russia now in control of the mouth of the Dnieper, France might be able to divert the important timber resources of Poland and western Russia from the Baltic — and therefore from the British — to the south. And in fact, the French were able to ship several consignments of masts, spars, and hemp through Kherson to their southern port of Toulon before Russo-Turkish warfare, flaring up once again in 1787, brought an end to that commerce.[54]

53 Blanning, *Origins*, pp. 57–58.
54 See, on these issues, Bamford, *Forests and French Sea Power*, pp. 204–205; and Blanning,

Some of this audacious thinking, which obviously linked developments in Franco-Turkish and Franco-Russian relations with the ongoing global struggle between France and Britain, may have been reflected in the negotiations that led to the signing of a commercial treaty between Versailles and St. Petersburg in January 1787. Certainly, there were those observers at the time who saw this pact as an indication that France, having abandoned the Turks to the Russians twice in the preceding twenty years, were about to do that once again, this time in a more definitive manner. Yet Vergennes himself most assuredly did not see the trade agreement in this light. As the French foreign minister's principal biographer has correctly pointed out, Vergennes considered the commercial treaty to be a means for increasing Louis XVI's leverage in his dealings with Catherine, especially in the matter of attempting to moderate her ambitions against Constantinople, and not as a means for facilitating the breakup or subversion of the Ottoman Empire. "French interest in the preservation of the Ottoman Empire," Murphy has in fact stated, "remained an unsurmountable obstacle to a true Franco-Russian *rapprochement* and Vergennes was not willing to relinquish that interest."[55]

Because of this, the Franco-Russian pact of 1787 undeniably mirrored what Murphy has called "the deep ambiguities of Franco-Russian relations on the eve of the French Revolution." But it reflected more than this. Although its articles defining commercial relations between France and Russia may have accorded to French merchants most of the privileges long enjoyed by their English counterparts in Russia, nearly half of its provisions dealt with the prerogatives of maritime powers in times of war and peace. Those latter clauses "echoed the rights demanded by Catherine, in her Armed Neutrality of 1780. . . . In this respect, the treaty represented Louis XVI's recognition that Russia was now a permanent part of the European international system."[56] Just four decades before, the disdainful French had refused to allow Russian participation in the talks at Aix-la-Chapelle marking the finale of the War of the Austrian Succession. Much had changed during the intervening years, not least of all the relative standing of France and Russia in the system of competing Continental powers.

But if events during the period from 1774 to 1788 demonstrated that France's power status vis-à-vis Russia was continuing to decline, they also pointed up a continuing (if somewhat less fundamental) "migration"

Origins, pp. 57–59. Both authors appropriately stress the ambivalence in French attitudes toward the apparently tottering Ottoman Empire in the 1780s.

55 Murphy, *Charles Gravier*, pp. 453–54. See also Fox, "Negotiating with the Russians," pp. 70–71, for a similar view of the obstacles to a genuine Franco-Russian accommodation in the Levant.

56 Murphy, *Charles Gravier*, pp. 453–54.

of power from Versailles to Berlin. This time, on the very threshold of the revolutionary era, there would be no repetition of Rossbach, no humiliation visited upon French troops by the formidable Prussian army; yet Prussia would no less grievously wound the French sense of military honor.

The fact that Gallic martial pride had taken such a drubbing on the battlefields of the Seven Years' War helps to explain efforts by Louis XVI's military advisers to modernize the French army. Samuel F. Scott has described the reforms, instrumental toward that end, of the comte de Saint-Germain, minister of war from 1775 to 1777:

> The number of infantry companies per battalion was reduced from 17 (of 25 men each) to 6, thus reducing the excessively high proportion of officers to men. . . . Towards the same end, increased efficiency, Saint-Germain cut the strength of the royal household by disbanding the Musketeers and Horse Grenadiers and reducing the number of Gendarmes and Light Horse.

Saint-Germain also created a military health service, and struck out of the army's codes at least some of the more barbaric punishments. Arguably of greatest importance, however, were his efforts to rehabilitate the military status of the sons of the old provincial noblesse. Not only did Saint-Germain address their educational needs by establishing military schools in the provinces; he also aimed to facilitate their selection by the king as officers (and thus consummate one of Choiseul's designs) by suppressing venality in military ranks.[57]

Reform in the army continued under a subsequent war minister, the marquis de Ségur. The notorious Ségur law of 22 May 1781, requiring as it did that all commissioned army officers possess at least four generations of nobility, complemented Saint-Germain's campaign to give the king "control over all ranks of the army," and in particular to enable him to choose his officers from among his "brave and ancient nobility."[58] Yet, even as early as 1781, contemporary observers could have legitimately questioned whether the army's long-term needs would permit the monarch forever to favor such men over *anoblis* and bourgeois in commanding ranks.

Of greatest moment in this whole area, however, were the reforms promulgated in 1787–88 by a special council of war that Louis XVI convened. Again, Scott is our guide:

> Besides a number of tactical and organizational reforms, e.g. the decision to use columns for movement and lines for combat and the reorganization of chasseur units, the council improved conditions of military service. A new pay-scale was

---

57 Scott, *Response of the Royal Army*, pp. 27–29.
58 Ibid., pp. 29ff. Also, on this subject, refer again to Bien, "Réaction aristocratique avant 1789," pp. 23–48, 505–34.

established which raised the pay for all grades, but most of all for the officers.
. . . Officers and N.C.O.s were forbidden to inflict any punishment except those
authorized by regulations; they were likewise prohibited from mistreating their
men. . . . Punishment by blows with a sabre flat was, however, maintained. Each
regiment was required to establish a school for candidates to the N.C.O. ranks
which would teach the men to read, write, and count.[59]

In general, the council of war continued the process, dating from Choiseul, of rationalization of roles within the army. The royal bodyguard
was further reduced, and the Gendarmes were eliminated altogether; the
excessive number of general army officers was reduced somewhat; and
although the council of 1787–88 upheld the monopoly of the court aristocracy over the grades of general officer and colonel, it required that
these noblemen put in longer service before advancement to rank of
colonel, and guaranteed for provincial nobles promotion to general (*maréchal de camp*) after twenty years' service in lieutenant colonel rank.

Yet the undoubted industry of Saint-Germain, Ségur, and the military
specialists in the famous war council of 1787–88 did not bear significant
fruit – not, in any case, in time to contribute to the salvation of the ancien
régime. This was in part due to the fact that the reforms, albeit urgently
needed from a military point of view, exacerbated tensions and jealousies
within the social hierarchy, pitting established court aristocrats, provincial
squires, newly created nobles, and ambitious, affluent commoners against
each other. "Witnesses all agree," Jean Egret has commented with respect
to the 1787–88 reforms, "on the profound malaise produced in the army
by the drastic treatment applied to it. . . . It is easy to imagine, if difficult
to measure, the disarray and exasperation produced among officers, especially older ones, by a reform that threw everything into question."[60]
Still, however true this may have been, France's military power upon the
Continent during the 1774–88 period, as in the preceding reign, was
crippled above all by lack of adequate funding. Indeed, this was perforce
even more the case under Vergennes's stewardship of foreign affairs than
it had been under his predecessors; Vergennes, after all, devoted most of
his attention to overseas rather than to European politics. Hence, the
comte de Saint-Germain and the marquis de Ségur found it difficult to
compete with the naval ministers Sartine and Castries for largesse from
the government's various treasuries. And then, in 1787, when France
would especially need to be able to field an army, the government would
be hovering on the brink of a general bankruptcy.

The French need to mobilize a land force in 1787 arose from Versailles'

---

59 Scott, *Response of the Royal Army*, pp. 27–33.
60 Jean Egret, *The French Prerevolution, 1787–1788*, trans. Wesley D. Camp (Chicago:
   University of Chicago Press, 1977), pp. 47–54. See also Scott, *Response of the Royal
   Army*, pp. 27–33, for a detailed corroboration of Egret on this point.

involvement in the troubled domestic politics of the United Provinces. This involvement began, at least in part, as an offshoot of the perdurable Franco-British rivalry, but it was fated as well to become an issue of Continental balance-of-power politics. The French, whose effort in the American war had been seconded by the Dutch, committed themselves in November 1785 to a more formal alliance with the States General of the United Provinces, whose leaders, the Patriots, were able to seize power in 1787 from the pro-British stadtholder William V of the house of Orange. The British, for their part, fearing the possibility of French strategic control of the Channel and North Sea coasts, wished to restore the stadtholder to power on terms that would destroy French influence at The Hague. Crucially, the British were able in this instance to count on the strong arm of Prussia. The death of the aging and cautious Frederick II in August 1786 had brought Frederick William II to power, and the new Prussian sovereign, who was brother-in-law to none other than the Dutch stadtholder, had no desire to see his own sister, the Princess of Orange, and her husband William V humiliated by the pro-French Patriot party in the United Provinces.

Orville Murphy has recapitulated a developing diplomatic and military crisis that could only spell chagrin for the French:

The obvious response to such a turn of events was a coalition of Prussia and England, and a military intervention to protect the Orangists. . . . France, in 1785 and 1786, [had] played a dangerous game in the United Provinces . . . that could be won now only if France committed herself militarily. The Patriots expected support from France, but would not be controlled by her. Since the French treasury was exhausted, and French domestic affairs were rapidly approaching chaos, warnings from Versailles that France would support the Patriots militarily, were interpreted as bluffs, as indeed they were.[61]

Events rapidly came to a head in the summer of 1787. The princess of Orange was stopped on the road at Schoenhoven on the frontier of the province of Holland by a party of Patriots on 28 June; her royal Prussian brother sent the duke of Brunswick with an army of twenty thousand men into the United Provinces six weeks later; Amsterdam capitulated on 12 October; and William V, reinstated by what was in essence an Anglo-Prussian stroke of power politics, repudiated the Franco-Dutch pact of 1785. Thousands of defeated and angry Dutch Patriots went into exile.

The French, paralyzed by impending bankruptcy, could do absolutely nothing on behalf of their Dutch republican protégés. What was more, they had to watch from the sidelines, impotently, as a new diplomatic alliance arose from the ashes of their Dutch policy. An Anglo-Prussian

---

61 Murphy, *Charles Gravier*, p. 471. On the crisis in the United Provinces, see also Blanning, *Origins of the French Revolutionary Wars*, pp. 50–51.

convention was signed at the start of October; Anglo-Dutch and Prusso-Dutch treaties of alliance were concluded on 15 April 1788; and a formal defensive alliance was signed between Britain and Prussia on 13 August 1788. "A powerful Anglo-Prussian combination had now emerged as a factor in European affairs for the first time since 1761 and seemed likely to take a hand in the affairs of the Near East."[62]

But if a confrontation between the British and Prussians on the one hand and the Russians and Austrians on the other seemed very much a possibility in the twilight of the 1780s, such a scenario was premised in part on the likely absence of the erstwhile "arbiters of Europe" from the stage of high politics. To the men in the French foreign ministry who, in the wake of Vergennes's demise, attempted wearily to salvage some shreds of their country's former prestige, the recent geostrategic developments must have seemed dishearteningly reminiscent of events in the later years of Louis XV. Once again, France had been embarrassed by the waxing power of Russia, humiliated by an Anglo-Prussian cabal, and unaided by an Austrian "alliance" that seemed hardly worth the paper on which it was inscribed. Moreover, just as in the earlier period, so now in the late 1780s, the acid of patriotic frustration ate into domestic support for the Bourbon government.

THE LATE WINTER OF FRENCH DISCONTENT

Although the subject of elite and popular attitudes toward international affairs in the twilight of the ancien régime awaits a definitive treatment, we can already cite suggestive evidence concerning those attitudes. It appears that a significant number of Frenchmen outside governing circles were now, as in the preceding reign, sensitive in some measure to their country's role in the world at large. In fact, the growing phenomenon of public opinion probably ensured that Vergennes and the other ministers would find it harder than had any of their predecessors to keep French foreign policy successes – and failures – from acquiring a broad resonance in society.

The man who stood at the very apex of French society surely set an example for unempowered subjects to follow when it came to passing judgment on the English. Louis XVI may have offered some resistance during 1775–77 to the idea of resuming the global struggle with the new "Carthage," but he displayed little patience with those of his subjects given to singing the praises of the people on the other side of the Channel. When, in 1774, the duc de Lauzun returned to court from a sojourn in London and, in the royal presence, compared his own country's ways

---

62 Anderson, "European Diplomatic Relations, 1763–90," pp. 274–76.

unfavorably to those of the English, Louis XVI reportedly cut him short with the tart observation that "those who so admire the English should live among them and serve them."[63] This was, we should recall, the same individual who, as the youthful duc de Berri seven years before, had penned some highly unflattering comments about the British national character and who, as king, was shortly to warn his royal cousin at Madrid that war with London, however undesirable, might not be avoidable.

And apparently the French people in many walks of life were ready, nay, hungering for a return match with the supercilious British. French intervention in America seemed to them a grand opportunity to settle old scores with the national enemy. "When the interventionist movement is looked at from the angle of its relation to the structure of French society," Frances Acomb has affirmed, "it is seen to have been – this is abundantly evident – of a general or national rather than a class character."[64] Nobles, to be sure, were especially conspicuous in the ranks of those demanding military action against George III. That was only natural, in light of their military ethos and prominence in society. But French patriotism in these challenging times hardly confined itself to aristocratic circles:

According to the journalist Louis-Sebastien Mercier, who vividly described the society of Paris at the time of the war, the beau monde and the bourgeoisie were virtually at one in their ideas about the ease with which the English could be defeated and in their general enthusiasm for the war. Fine ladies talked glibly about the freedom of the seas, he said, while all the cope-makers of the Tuileries and the Luxembourg spoke of nothing but the hoped-for invasion of England.[65]

"In the cafés," said Mercier, "one hears people who, the *Gazette de France* in hand, affirm upon the slightest advantage gained that the English people is reduced to extremities. . . . It is a corner grocer who meditates on sugar and coffee who makes these fine prophecies; he will tell them in the evening to his wife, who hates the English because they are heretics."[66]

It is noteworthy that even an author of a study devoted to signs of "Anglomania" in late eighteenth-century France has had to stress the prevalence of Anglophobic attitudes in the late 1770s among the people. In the words of Josephine Grieder:

Particularly in 1777–1779 there is abundant testimony to their irritation. The people "ne rêve et ne parle que guerre," says a reporter, while the "plus nombreux et ardents partisans" of the Americans are "les militaires et les seigneurs." . . . In

63 Josephine Grieder, *Anglomania in France, 1740–1789* (Geneva: Droz, 1985), pp. 19–20. My own translation from Grieder's text.
64 Acomb, *Anglophobia in France*, p. 86.
65 Ibid., pp. 86–87.
66 Ibid., p. 87.

the beginning of 1778, "on ne respire ici que guerre et vengeance!"... A year later the atmosphere is still the same: "il s'agit d'humilier l'orgueil Anglois et de rendre à la France son égalité et sa supériorité sur la mer."[67]

In 1777, a new coiffure dedicated "to the Insurgents" was reportedly all the rage, and satirical cartoons about the British circulated freely. And when, in November of the following year, a number of statues in the royal park at Marly were vandalized, the public "did not fail to attribute that outrage to Englishmen."[68] Such were the variegated manifestations of undying Anglophobia among the French.

At least one reflective Frenchman, J.-M.-A. Servan, was sufficiently struck by his countrymen's patriotism during the American war to conjure it up heatedly years later:

The war we have recently suffered, that abyss of so much money, the greatest cause of our financial disorder and of the evils with which France is now assailed... – in short, gentlemen of the Third Estate, who wanted that war, who asked for it? You yourselves, who, in your homes, in your public places, in your cafés, and even in your taverns, saw in imagination the whole English navy swallowed up, and drank in long draughts, in advance, the pleasure of vengeance.[69]

Servan's outburst furnishes compelling additional testimony, were it needed, to the fervor of Anglophobia among the loyal French subjects of Louis XVI.

Yet these observations, referring as they did to finances and war, and coming as they did in the hurly-burly of a new kind of politics in 1789, also recall our central thesis that French foreign and domestic politics converged ultimately in revolution. And in this connection it is also most enlightening to note the gradual fusion, during and after the American war, of Anglophobic nationalism in France with liberal constitutional commentary. To be sure, there were those theorists like Mably who thought that the proper glory of France lay in Continental rather than in overseas conquest; and hindsight indicates such individuals as prophets of the Napoleonic imperium so soon to come. But what Acomb has called "the Anglophobe doctrine of the sovereignty of the nation" was a more prominent credo in the waning years of the old regime.

In the 1780s, as political opinion moved to the left, the older conservative nationalism became much less conspicuous, while the demand for reform... became the way in which French nationalism was most usually and vigorously expressed. Reformers invoked the love of country and the pride of nationality. They wished France to achieve, so they said, the destiny which nature had intended for her, but which the tissue of abuses that constituted the old regime had thus far prevented her from attaining.[70]

67 Grieder, *Anglomania in France*, pp. 19–20.
68 Ibid. My own translation from Grieder's text.
69 Acomb, *Anglophobia in France*, p. 86.
70 Ibid., pp. 113–21.

Moreover, as the decade advanced, and as it began dawning on the French that their "success" in North America had not, after all, cowed and diminished the eternal foe across the Channel, the political reformists were prominent in the ranks of those registering patriotic disappointment at this turn of events. Often deriving inspiration from the works of Rousseau and Mably, they included luminaries like Mirabeau, Dupont de Nemours, and Lafayette; somewhat less renowned figures like J.-B. Mailhe and A.-J.-J. Cérutti; and writers mostly forgotten today such as Chavannes de la Giraudière, Fantin des Odoards, and Lescène Desmaisons. It was they who censured the administrative practices of the British East India Company, belabored the British for their treatment of the Irish, excoriated London for denying French merchants easy access to colonies in the West Indies and elsewhere, and deplored the immolation of the Dutch Patriot cause on the altars of British and Prussian ambition. And it was they who, increasingly, brought together in their correspondence, essays, and other writings "the two ideals of the political and martial glory of France and the freedom of the citizen."[71] They were, had they but known it, heralding a sociopolitical upheaval that would indeed revive the fortunes of France abroad (at least on the Continent) even as it empowered unprecedented numbers of French people at home.

But it was not only radical men of letters who lashed out at the British, and decried their own government's impotence, as the Revolution neared. French shipowners and merchants, for example, trading out of ports like Nantes, Le Havre, and Bordeaux, loudly assailed both London and Versailles for permitting British and other foreign traders to penetrate their markets in the West Indies while gainsaying them access to the colonies of George III's government.[72] French merchants in the Baltic, as we have already had occasion to note, bitterly complained about commercial privileges accorded to their British counterparts in Russia by Catherine's government.[73] Moreover, hostility to the British (and criticism of the French government's policies) flared up again in metropolitan France in the wake of the signing of the Eden Treaty of 1787. The parlement of Rouen, in Normandy, voicing a general suspicion, attributed the current economic recession to the commercial pact signed with the English.[74]

---

71 Ibid. On this phenomenon of patriotic or nationalist sentiment in prerevolutionary France, see again Palmer, "National Idea in France before the Revolution," pp. 95–111; and see also Jacques Godechot, "Nation, Patrie, Nationalisme et Patriotisme en France au XVIIIe siècle," *Annales historiques de la Révolution française* 43 (1971), pp. 481–502.

72 On this point, refer to Echeverria, *Mirage*, pp. 131–32; and consult Acomb, *Anglophobia in France*, pp. 117–18.

73 Refer again to Fox, "Negotiating with the Russians," esp. pp. 52 and 62.

74 The judges did this in a letter sent to the monarch on 3 May 1788. Their complaints

Normandy's chamber of commerce "asserted that the English had been well aware, during the negotiations, that they were dealing French industry a serious blow, for without protection it would be a very long time before French manufactures could compete on equal terms with those of England." At textile centers like Lyons and Rouen, Frenchmen and their wives were invited to attend "patriotic balls" dressed ostentatiously in habiliments of French manufacture; there and elsewhere it became patriotic to "buy French."[75]

Louis XVI and his counselors were aware of this discontent, but it was the humiliation suffered by France in the United Provinces in 1787 that affected them most profoundly, in the process reminding them (and their compatriots) that the British were not their only rivals. The chief authority on the "prerevolution" of 1787–88 has shown that the Dutch crisis drove a wedge into the king's Council itself. The war minister, Ségur, seconded by the naval minister, Castries, urged the mobilization of twenty-five battalions under the command of Lieutenant General Rochambeau for possible action in defense of the Dutch Patriots; but Finance Minister Loménie de Brienne, obsessed by the state's mounting fiscal woes, vetoed this proposition. Ségur and Castries resigned in disgust. The strong-willed naval minister had "never ceased predicting resumption of the war with England after what he felt was the premature signing of the Treaty of Versailles in 1783." He probably thought, as noblemen such as Alexandre de Lameth and the Baron de Bésenval claimed then or subsequently, that a war in 1787 could have rallied army and people to the king, turned all minds away from domestic controversies, and encouraged all Frenchmen in a burst of patriotism to accept higher taxes.[76]

It appears that the duc de Montmorency-Luxembourg, incensed at the retreat of his government before the coalition of England and Prussia, spoke for many in his class:

Abandoning the Patriots served to demonstrate the inexperience, the weakness, and the incompetence of the first minister [i.e., Brienne] and the foreign minister [i.e., Montmorin, Vergennes's successor], prompting scorn for alliances with France and disgust with her conduct; she was the plaything of the will of others.[77]

It was all very well for Louis XVI to hope in April 1787 that his finance minister could curtail expenses "without cutting the army or the navy."[78]

---

are discussed in Stone, *The French Parlements and the Crisis of the Old Regime* (Chapel Hill: University of North Carolina Press, 1986), pp. 248–50.

75 Acomb, *Anglophobia in France*, pp. 117–20.

76 Egret, *French Prerevolution*, pp. 40–42.

77 Ibid., p. 41.

78 Ibid., p. 32. In justice to Louis, however, Egret has noted that he was "trained by an already long experience" not to "share the general illusion concerning the extent of possible cutbacks in expenses."

It was, again, all very well for Loménie de Brienne himself to assure Sweden's anxious ambassador to France, the baron de Staël, in late September of that year, that his reforms would eventually allow France to "play the role that becomes her" in the world's affairs.[79] And it was all very well for Keeper of the Seals Lamoignon to address the Paris Parlement in these sanguine terms just two months later:

> In the midst of the Estates of his realm, His Majesty, surrounded by his faithful subjects, will confidently present to them the comforting picture of . . . a formidable navy, of the army regenerated by a more economical and more military constitution, of . . . a new port built on the [English] Channel to insure the glory of the French flag.[80]

For the time being, only one thing really mattered: the glaring fact that mighty France, erstwhile and would-be-again arbiter of Europe, had been reduced to the status of nonentity in international affairs. The Austrian ambassador to France, Mercy-Argenteau, could well write to Kaunitz, in reference to Dutch developments: "It is not credible that the Versailles ministry, in such straits, would risk getting involved in a war that would make bankruptcy inevitable."[81] This, and not the smooth assurances of harried statesmen like Brienne and Lamoignon, was France's ignominious "bottom line" as 1787 ended and the new year began. And in 1788, things would only grow progressively worse, as the new foreign minister, Montmorin, found himself constrained to desert both Sweden and Turkey in their struggle with avaricious Romanov Russia.

In summing up the geopolitical developments of the 1774–88 period and France's role in them, we have to emphasize the continuing decline of the Gallic state relative to most of the other Great Powers. As of 1788, Britain had rebounded from its temporary isolation of the American war years and, in alliance with Prussia and a United Provinces remodeled according to British wishes, seemed poised to intervene if it so desired in the volatile situation in eastern Europe. At the same time, Catherine the Great seemed capable of interfering as suited her purposes in the feud between the Germanic powers, Prussia and Austria, all the while playing her own ruthless game from the Black Sea to the Baltic. But as for the situation of the French? The sorry record speaks for itself. Louis XVI's government had, in just the few years since the signing of the purportedly glorious Treaty of Versailles, "abandoned its Turkish protégé twice, . . .

79 Ibid., p. 42. The Swedish ambassador "stressed" in his conversation with Brienne "the lamentable effect on Europe . . . of the current weakness of the French court." He must have had especially in mind the vulnerable situation of his own country.
80 Ibid., p. 107. Lamoignon was addressing the parlementaires at the soon to be notorious "royal session" of 19 November.
81 As quoted in ibid., p. 41. A letter of 15 September 1787.

deferred to Frederick the Great in the matter of the Bavarian succession, allied itself with Sweden only to refuse Gustavus III any help in Finland, . . . and allowed London and Berlin to manoeuvre the Dutch into an unforeseen alliance."[82] And even this summation, mortifying enough for the French, leaves out the fact of greatest global import: that in the race for the unparalleled riches of the extra-European world, a bounty ever translatable into power upon the Continent itself, the British were relentlessly forging ahead.

Contemporary statesmen were, unavoidably, quick to take note of France's decline. The Prussian diplomat Hertzberg wrote that "France has lost the alliance of Holland and the remnants of her prestige in Europe." Observed Joseph II of Austria: "France has just fallen, and I doubt whether she can be raised up." "This shows," he commented in a letter to his brother Leopold, "in how short a time so considerable a state, with great resources, position and possibilities, can lose credit, influence, vigor and power through the want of a capable leader and lack of order." And Catherine of Russia, so successful an aggrandizer of power herself, wrote contemptuously: "One cannot say that Louis XVI is flattered. Everything has been done to persuade him to accept guidance and to convince him that he understands nothing of his task. . . . If they [i.e., the French] have retreated and are not going to jump, then goodbye to the reputation acquired through two hundred years! And who will believe in people who have neither will, vigor, nor enterprise?"[83] This last testimony, coming as it did from one whose imperial predecessors had scarcely been recognized by haughty Versailles, serves especially well to underline the collapse of France's international credibility on the eve of the Revolution.

Yet Catherine the Great, whatever her triumphs in the merciless power politics of west Eurasia, undoubtedly overlooked the "will," "vigor," and "enterprise" of ordinary French people who had not yet been admitted into the precincts of power in their own country. The enfranchisement of such people, many of whom possibly were as distressed as nobles like Ségur, Castries, and Montmorency-Luxembourg over their country's foreign policy reverses, might have made France somewhat more competitive, even if we concede the exorbitance of French ambitions. It is intriguing in this connection that Vergennes, however much committed to absolutism, should nonetheless have unhappily admitted during his ministry that the British constitutional system had much to recommend it. In writing to his eventual successor Montmorin on 7

82 Ford, *Europe 1780–1830*, pp. 74–75. M. S. Anderson has characterized the state of affairs much the same way in "European Diplomatic Relations, 1763–90," pp. 274–78.
83 Quotations are from Sorel, *Europe and the French Revolution*, pp. 502–503.

September 1782, Vergennes acknowledged that England "has, in its constitution and in the establishments which it has permitted her to form, resources which are lacking to us."[84] Eight weeks later, he revisited that theme in his correspondence with Montmorin, stating, even more explicitly on this occasion, that England's "constitution gives her . . . advantages *which our monarchical forms do not accord us.*"[85]

Vergennes's shrewd observations pointed up a glaring discrepancy in the old France – that between the aims of its foreign policy and the national means actually summoned forth to accomplish those aims. But even as the foreign minister committed his misgivings to paper, a fundamental sociopolitical evolution was continuing among his countrymen that, once it had helped to destroy the outmoded institutions of the old regime, would reinvigorate some aspects of France's international mission by conferring a new status, new rights and duties, upon unheard-of numbers of French people. It is to that process of sociopolitical change, responding to, influencing in turn, and ultimately combining with the process of geopolitical change over the years from 1774 to 1788, which we must now turn.

84 Cited in Dull, *French Navy*, p. 304.
85 Cited in ibid., pp. 316–17. A letter dated 1 November 1782. My emphasis.

4

The approaches to revolution,
1774–1788: the sociopolitical challenge

If the future Louis XVI absorbed in childhood his country's patriotic pride and prejudices, he absorbed as well its ethos of absolutism and social inequality. The duc de Berri's preceptor, La Vauguyon, taught him to "know the whole extent both of your authority and of the obedience due to you from your subjects. . . . Uphold all the orders of the State and each of them in particular in its rights, properties, honors, distinctions, and privileges. . . . alter nothing . . . except after the most profound re-flection and most scrupulous examination."[1] At thirteen or fourteen, the sovereign-to-be wrote that "there was no person more proper than himself . . . to manage his State, God having destined him, and no other, to that function."[2] Here, capsulated, was the philosophy of the world in which this prince, like his predecessors, was formed – a world that, tragically for him, was being steadily undermined by the converging geopolitical and sociopolitical requirements of the modern France.

In his imposing overview of the institutions of old regime France, Pierre Goubert has asserted: "The financial problem of the Ancien Régime is not really distinct from the problem of the State, which itself is hardly more distinct from that of society. These are three practically synonymous expressions of the same reality."[3] For analytical purposes, however, we will treat these three "problems" separately, acknowledging even as we do so that they are, indeed, very closely interrelated. The following pages deal, first, with the attempts by Louis XVI's financial advisers to manage the costs of French foreign policy during 1774–1788; second, with the trend toward a more consultative form of governance that inhered in these war-related efforts at fiscal management; and third, with war-related evo-lutionary tendencies within the French elite that contributed a profound

1 Girault de Coursac, *L'Education d'un roi*, p. 121.
2 Ibid., p. 176.
3 Goubert, *L'Ancien Régime*, vol. 1, pp. 150–51.

social resonance to this kingdom's brewing fiscal and constitutional crisis. Here in sum was the sociopolitical challenge to the monarch and his government that, in combination with the geopolitical challenge analyzed in Chapter 3, made some measure of revolutionary change in France all but unavoidable by August 1788.

THE FINANCIAL PROBLEM

"After the partial bankruptcy of 1770," Eugene Nelson White has observed, "reform ministers made numerous economies and restructured the government's financial administration. These changes allowed the Crown to finance its deficits successfully by borrowing until the middle of the 1780s. The origins of the ancien régime's collapse are not to be found in the debt burden acquired either during the American War for Independence or before. Instead, it is the return of the venal financial aristocracy after 1781 that began the monarchy's problems."[4] These comments quite accurately suggest (as has the scholarship of Robert D. Harris and J. F. Bosher[5]) that the policies of Louis XVI's finance ministers in general and of wartime Finance Minister Jacques Necker in particular must be appraised within the context of the overall credibility of the French government's fiscal and administrative procedures.

As we noted in Chapter 2, the abbé Terray was able, perhaps just barely, to stave off governmental fiscal collapse in Louis XV's final years through a combination of brutal cutbacks in government expense, revenue enhancement, and administrative reform translating into increased royal control of expenditures, revenues, and accounting.[6] White's reconsideration of the pertinent financial data (which largely corroborates even as it goes beyond that of French historian Lucien Laugier[7]) seems to demonstrate convincingly that Terray was able to produce a series of budget surpluses and, perhaps most crucially, reduce the government's outstanding debt. This accomplishment was certainly a key factor enabling the crown to resume its borrowing policies in subsequent years. Yet the fact that Terray (along with the other members of the so-called triumvirate of the early 1770s) was brought down in the wake of a domestic crisis with serious sociopolitical implications did not augur well for the future, especially if that future should be burdened, as the past so frequently had been, by war-related indebtedness.

4 White, "Was There a Solution?" pp. 545–46.
5 Refer again to Harris, *Necker: Reform Statesman of the Ancien Régime*; and Bosher, *French Finances, 1770–1795*.
6 See Bosher, *French Finances*, pp. 148–53, for a review of Terray's policies.
7 White, "Was There a Solution?" esp. pp. 548–55; and Laugier, *Ministère réformateur sous Louis XV*, pp. 165, 341.

Terray's successor as controller-general, the Physiocrat and former humanitarian intendant of Limoges Anne-Robert-Jacques Turgot, capitalized on the fact that France was temporarily at peace by holding to a policy of budget surpluses and debt retirement through 1775–76.[8] Even though Turgot, too, like Terray, incurred the enmity of venal accountants and many other parasitical individuals through a variety of reforms and eventually fell from power, his brief successor Bernard de Clugny was able to report an adjusted budgetary surplus of seven million livres for 1776.[9] The government of Louis XVI, then, clearly could produce annual surpluses and reduce royal debt during peacetime – but what would happen if and when the Gallic state returned to its ways of war?

This question necessarily dominated the first finance ministry of the Protestant and Genevan banker Jacques Necker. He (and his successor Jean-François Joly de Fleury) would have to keep the government financially afloat even as it waged a war costing approximately one billion livres.[10] Necker (like Turgot before him) saw his true métier in the promulgation of peacetime administrative and social reforms; unhappily, however, Turgot's failure to dissuade Louis XVI from taking up his country's gage of combat against London had denied that role to the Genevan in advance.

Significantly, Necker, sharing Vergennes's loyalty to French absolutism in the late 1770s and early 1780s, also shared the latter's awareness of the war-making benefits conferred on the British by their unique constitution. The yearly publication of government accounts on the other side of the Channel, and their submission to Parliament, so obviously furnished creditors with vital information concerning the financial health of the British state. In his renowned treatise of 1784 on the administration of finances, Necker paid explicit tribute to the constitutional wellsprings of fiscal stability at London:

The strong bond between citizens and the state, the influence of the nation on the government, the guarantee of civil liberty to the individual, the patriotic support which the people always give to their government in times of crisis, all contribute to making the English constitution unique in the world.[11]

Yet Necker, who because of his specific duties had to delve more deeply into these matters than did Vergennes, sought to make absolutism in France compatible with that confidence of investors in royal bonds failing which the foreign minister would have no chance to achieve his goals.

---

8 See White, "Was There a Solution?" pp. 555–57, on Turgot's fiscal policies.
9 Ibid., p. 556.
10 For particularly careful calculations of these war costs, see Harris, "French Finances and the American War, 1777–83," *Journal of Modern History* 48 (1976), pp. 233–58.
11 Harris, *Necker: Reform Statesman*, p. 121.

Henceforward, the director-general of finances knew so well, the crown would have to reject forthrightly the bad habits of the past: defaulting repeatedly on obligations to its creditors, borrowing carelessly at onerous rates of interest, and allowing revenue to be siphoned off and expenditure to be gratuitously swollen by the venal accountants' stranglehold on royal fiscal operations.

Perhaps the crux of the matter for the Genevan was the truly painstaking attention he devoted to the relationship between "ordinary" revenues and "ordinary" expenditures and to the distinction between these "ordinary" funds and the "extraordinary" moneys. We should, on this critical point, let Necker speak once again for himself:

Ordinary expenditures must be balanced by fixed and constant revenues. It is a great error, both politically and morally, not to observe the proper distinction between this type of expenditure and needs that are extraordinary, because there is danger of raising permanent taxes to the level of temporary expenditures. It is necessary therefore to provide for extraordinary and momentary needs by resources that are also extraordinary and momentary; and if one chooses the recourse of loans, the interest on the loan must be classified among the ordinary expenditures.[12]

This last point was really the capital one. Necker had no particular fondness for borrowing as such, but he realized that, just as the British used loans to fuel their war effort, so also must the French.[13] But because creditors of the French state could not, like their counterparts in the British case, rely on an elected and responsible institution like Parliament, they *must be assured at all times that the French government at the very least could meet its interest charges out of its ordinary revenue.* Interest on loans, in other words, would always have to be reckoned at Versailles as ordinary or fixed expenditure, the kind of expenditure that, as a matter of priority, would require redemption to creditors in a publicized fashion, and on a strict schedule. "The most unjust as well as the most dangerous of all fiscal policies," wrote Necker in his famous *Compte rendu* of 1781, "is to borrow money without having assured the interest payments on it, either by economy or by increasing revenue."[14] The director-general even believed (unlike some other eighteenth-century finance ministers) that amortization payments on such debt should also be categorized (at least in most cases) as ordinary expenditure, to be met out of fixed or ordinary income.

Here, then, was the challenge for Jacques Necker as France became ever more deeply involved in the North American conflict. As Harris has put it:

12 Ibid., p. 122.
13 Ibid., p. 120.
14 Ibid., p. 123.

The great drama of Necker's first ministry was whether he would succeed in keeping the ordinary accounts balanced, as new war loans were piled on ever more loans. Would he be able to balance the ordinary accounts of the royal finances through improvement of administration, the elimination of waste and inefficiency, the reduction of costs of collecting taxes, the reductions of pensions and gratifications, and all the other measures that came under the heading of ameliorations? Would he be able to escape, in the end, the recourse to new taxes? It was by no means a foregone conclusion.[15]

Still, although he did insist in 1777–78 on revising the basis for the assessment and collection of *vingtiéme* taxation on the lands of commoners and secular nobles so as to derive greater income from that quarter (in the process arousing the anger of the parlementaires at Paris and elsewhere),[16] Necker was indeed able to avoid saddling the French with new taxes even as he raised huge loans on the international money markets. He achieved this success by implementing "ameliorations," ranging from the curbing or elimination of courtiers' pensions and gratifications to the streamlining of the financial administration.

It was in this last area that Necker labored most rewardingly for the future, even though, in doing so, he planted some of the seeds of his first ministry's downfall. "How could the Minister of Finance and his department manage the royal finances efficiently," J. F. Bosher has reasonably queried, "when nearly all the collecting and spending was in the hands of accountants who were independent of administrative control because they owned their own offices? Here was the main problem. Several hundred venal accountants ... held practically all government funds and behaved more like private businessmen than public officials."[17] In particular, the long-term as well as short-term indebtedness of the government was held hostage by men who, even though owing much of their influence in society to their roles as quasi-public managers of "public" funds, could still bring ruin to the crown as well as to themselves through bankruptcies in their private business dealings. And now, of course, there was the added fact that the king's advisers, not yet able to discipline such protobureaucratic individuals through the modern means of continuous administrative supervision, had nonetheless lost the older weapon of legal process against them. No longer could chambres de justice be instituted against accountants who, in general, had purchased their way into the aristocracy by the later decades of the century.[18]

As Bosher has demonstrated, the overhauling of the French financial

---

15 Ibid., pp. 123–24.
16 See Georges Lardé, *Une Enquête sur les vingtièmes au temps de Necker: Histoire des remontrances du Parlement de Paris* (Paris: Letouzey et Ané, 1920); and Stone, *Parlement of Paris*, esp. pp. 77–82 and 96–100.
17 Bosher, *French Finances*, pp. xi-xii.
18 On this point, consult again Bosher, "*Chambres de justice* in the French monarchy," pp. 19–40.

system took place in two stages. The first began with Terray, continued with Turgot, and reached its apogee with Necker's first ministry. During the Genevan's tenure, "the paying caisses were very much reduced in number, concentrated in fewer hands and obliged to account to the Keepers of the Royal Treasury; the accounting system was revised on Colbertist principles to give the Minister more knowledge and control; the excise taxes (*aides*) and stamp duties were taken away from the General Farm of Taxes and established as a government agency (*régie*); and the Receivers General, after being made responsible for the accounts of the *Receveurs particuliers*, were reduced from a corps of 48 independent accountants to a Crown company (*régie*) of 12."[19] Granted, these and other reforms so infuriated the venal accountants and sybaritic courtiers adversely affected in their incomes that without much trouble we may descry here one reason for the Genevan's disgrace in 1781. But, as Bosher, Harris, and others have observed, Necker, deliberately adopting the long view during his first ministry, tirelessly explained in the preambles to his fiscal edicts and in his other writings the motives behind his revamping of the fiscal system and his curbing of pensions and gratuities. In so doing, he helped prepare that increasingly potent force in society known as public opinion for the second phase of financial reform that got seriously underway with Loménie de Brienne's ministry in 1787.[20]

In the meantime, however, France had to defray its enormous foreign policy expenses, and its finance minister had to secure loans to that end. Under the circumstances, he appears to have discharged this task well. When wrangling later on with one of his successors, Charles-Alexandre de Calonne, over fiscal issues, Necker stated (and the latest research appears to bear out his calculations) that he had borrowed a total of 530 million livres for the crown during his wartime ministry. The average yearly cost of those loans, including both interest and amortization, had been 8.375 percent. This meant for Louis XVI's government an additional annual fixed expense of about 44.4 million livres. But the Genevan had had to add to this sum 24 million livres of deficit left over, in his accounting, from Clugny's short ministry, as well as nearly 15 million livres in supplemental fixed or ordinary expenditure unrelated to the war loans. The upshot of all this was that Necker somehow had to find, through established taxation, ameliorations, and other means, the wherewithal in terms of increased annual ordinary income to balance the increase of approximately 83.4 million livres in annual fixed expenses.[21]

That he was able to do this, and even more, he purported to show in

19 Bosher, *French Finances*, pp. 142, 145.
20 On this point, see ibid., p. 145; and Harris, "Necker's Compte rendu of 1781: A Reconsideration," *Journal of Modern History* 42 (1970), pp. 161–83.
21 Harris, *Necker: Reform Statesman*, pp. 118, 134–36; and White, "Was There a Solution?" pp. 558–60.

his *Compte rendu* of 1781. This reckoning of royal finances, positing a current excess of 10.2 million livres in ordinary revenue over fixed expenditure, provoked controversy at the time and has occasioned scholarly debate ever since.[22] The documentation available today suggests that Necker's calculations were essentially correct and that his detractors' criticisms were not. In fact, as E. N. White has pointed out, various projected reimbursements of funds into the royal coffers would have raised the surplus in this fixed budget to more than 27 million livres.[23] More importantly, however, as Necker so clearly recognized, the demonstration to the crown's creditors that ordinary royal finances remained in the black and that the interest on their advances of capital would therefore continue to be paid *out of ordinary income* encouraged them powerfully to keep up their loans to the warring Bourbon state. Admittedly, not even Necker could secure for his royal master the low interest rates prevailing across the Channel; the French government, after all, did not possess the creditworthiness anchored in Britain in a long tradition of parliamentary activism and funded debt policies.[24] The really crucial fact, however, is that men possessing ready capital could confidently make it available to the authorities at Versailles so long as the Genevan's fundamental precepts held sway there.

Yet there were storm signals on the horizon. The director-general's detractors were forever questioning whether publicizing the royal accounts, monitoring the relationship between ordinary revenue and ordinary expenditure, curtailing courtiers' monetary favors, and forcing rural nobles to pay their fair share of *vingtième* taxation were really policies suitable for such a country as France. Were these not rather "mean-spirited" devices, most appropriate for some small "bourgeois" republic like Geneva? Did not their employment in France somehow

22 See, for example, how George Taylor (*Journal of Economic History* 40 [1980], pp. 877–79) and Charles P. Kindleberger (in his *A Financial History of Western Europe* (London: Allen & Unwin, 1984), p. 172) have challenged Robert Harris's interpretation of the *Compte rendu*, and how Harris has reacted to their criticisms in *Necker and the Revolution of 1789*, pp. 188–91.
23 White, "Was There a Solution?" p. 559. This was, of course, only a projected surplus, and did not take into account extraordinary revenues and expenditures. Only the retrospective accounts known as the *états au vrai* could determine, definitively, the overall balance between ordinary and extraordinary income and outlays.
24 It is also only fair to note some scholarly criticism of the yields Necker offered to purchasers of the *rentes viagères*. See James C. Riley, *International Government Finance and the Amsterdam Capital Market, 1740–1815* (Cambridge: Cambridge University Press, 1980), pp. 175–78. Yet both Harris and White would seem to reject such criticisms. For further discussion of the interest rates on loans to the British and French crowns in this period, see again Morineau, "Budgets de l'état et gestion des finances royales," pp. 289–336; and Brewer, *Sinews of Power*, esp. pp. 88–134.

diminish the *gloire* of the Gallic sovereign and his throne?[25] Indeed, to Necker's ruin, his ideas on finance, grounded as they were in a philosophy of governmental accountability (which will require fuller analysis later on), alienated not only his more libelous foes – that, after all, was to be expected – but even responsible parties ranging from Turgot to the king himself.[26] These factors, abetted, to be sure, by Necker's own political miscalculations, led to his dismissal in May 1781.

It was from this point on, it now appears, that financial affairs began to escape the control of those in power at Versailles. It was not that Necker's immediate successor, Jean-François Joly de Fleury, failed to grasp the need for strict accounting procedures. In fact, this scion of one of France's most distinguished robe families drew up his own careful records of government fiscal operations, and, prior to his resignation on 30 March 1783, served for a brief time on a Committee on Finance established by Vergennes for the express purpose of accounting for outlays of royal funds.[27] Unfortunately, however, Joly de Fleury lacked his predecessor's appreciation of the imperative need to curb venal officeholding in the financial administration and to restrain the concession of special favors to sybaritic figures at court and the taxpaying rural noblesse.

As a result, many of Necker's most salutary reforms were abandoned. "The 48 receivers-general who collected the direct taxes for the royal treasury were restored. . . . Even offices abolished by Necker's predecessors, Turgot and Terray, were restored by Joly de Fleury. The alternate receivers of revenue in the *élections* numbering 204 . . . [and] the offices attached to the Bureau of Finance and the Chamber of the Domain. . . . were all restored. . . . These offices included the 36 Treasurers of France." Joly de Fleury would have even restored the six intendants of finance in the Contrôle Général had the king not vetoed that idea.[28] The numerous officers in the king's household had their privileges reinstated; strategies used in earlier times by opulent landowners to evade their fair share of *vingtième* taxation reappeared; and Joly de Fleury and his even more misguided successors discarded Necker's practice of having all pensions and other gratuities from royal coffers publicized – and hence (at least in theory) exposed to royal review and criticism. "All the old abuses are returning in a flood," wrote Mercy-Argenteau to Joseph II as early as

---

25 These criticisms are discussed in Harris, *Necker: Reform Statesman*, pp. 88, 230–31.
26 On the misgivings of Turgot and Louis XVI, which appertained especially to Necker's provincial assemblies, see Jean Egret, *Necker: Ministre de Louis XVI, 1776–1790* (Paris: Honoré Champion, 1975), pp. 132–33.
27 On Joly de Fleury, see Harris, *Necker and the Revolution of 1789*, pp. 31–39; and White, "Was There a Solution?" pp. 560–61.
28 Harris, *Necker and the Revolution of 1789*, p. 34.

October 1781. The inundation would reach new heights in the years to come.

All of this naturally had implications for Joly de Fleury's budgetary calculations. True, he was able to continue funding French involvement in the American war (and other, largely geopolitical expenses) through loans. By the end of 1782, he seems to have raised 251.7 million livres on the money markets. Yet, because he had jettisoned so many of his predecessor's curbs on wasteful expenditure, Joly de Fleury had an increasingly difficult time maintaining the all-important balance between ordinary income and fixed outlays of royal moneys. It is unclear whether the finance minister's budget for 1783 was as reliable a reckoning of the king's finances as Necker's might have been; such as it was, however, it disclosed an *ordinary deficit* of 52 million livres, and even with all reimbursements from the tax farmers and other officials taken into account, the ordinary books for 1783 would at best barely balance.[29] Joly de Fleury was only able to maintain crucial investor confidence in the French government by appealing to the Parisian parlementaires for new revenue in the form of loans and taxation; and it did not bode well for the future that the judges, in reluctantly acceding to his requests in wartime, cautioned that they would be less amenable to such pleas after the conclusion of peace between France and England.[30]

It was also an ominous sign that, when Joly de Fleury resigned at the end of March 1783, he reportedly did so due to his inability to control other ministers' spending.[31] The crown's carefully nurtured, and publicized, ability to pay the interest on its loans *out of a surplus in its ordinary income* was now starting to erode rapidly. This was surely one of the factors behind the early and resounding failure of the next finance ministry, that of Henri-François de Paule III Le Fevre d'Ormesson. This youthful controller-general, who shared Necker's frugality up to a point, worked with Vergennes in his select Committee on Finance to resist the courtiers' never-ending clamor for pensions and other royal largesse and was apparently willing to abolish some obviously useless venal offices. Still, Le Fevre d'Ormesson either would not or could not return to the wholesale administrative cost cutting of the Necker era. At the same time, however, he could not realistically anticipate parlementary sanction of new taxes now that peace was returning in the west. In desperation, he secretly secured a loan of 24 million livres from the Discount Bank, whose purpose it had never been to bail out insolvent ministers of finance; and,

29 White, "Was There a Solution?" p. 560.
30 Stone, *Parlement of Paris*, pp. 83–86.
31 White, "Was There a Solution?" p. 561.

still in search of additional income, he tried to alter the lease of the powerful Farmers-General. Both of these ploys damaged his credibility in financial circles when they became known; the latter action in addition provoked a panic among those who had invested in the General Farms. Ultimately, these two setbacks pointed up Le Fevre d'Ormesson's inability to restore the government to Neckerite standards of fiscal trustworthiness and supplied the controller-general's foes with much of the ammunition they needed to engineer his disgrace. That event occurred in November 1783.[32]

But if the French government's ability to retain the confidence of its domestic and foreign creditors began insidiously to slip away under Joly de Fleury and Le Fevre d'Ormesson, it collapsed altogether under the latter's successor, Charles-Alexandre de Calonne. With some justification Harris has portrayed this former parlementary lawyer and provincial intendant as "the consummate courtier of the *ancien régime* . . . [whose] most important talent was not to exercise independent thought and command, but to please the king and those who were powerful at court."[33] It is revealing that Calonne should have been one of the pamphleteers deriding Necker in 1781 for his "bourgeois" emphasis upon careful accounting and frugality in royal financial administration. A "splendid" kingdom like France had to spend lavishly to keep up appearances; and would not such expenditures, in combination with measures promulgated to liberate the productive forces of the economy, foster the impression and ultimately the reality of prosperity for all? So the future controller-general had argued then, and so Calonne continued to think as he assumed his portfolio late in 1783; but events were soon to certify that a state guided by such a philosophy, and burdened still by the wages of global competition, courted disaster by risking the forfeiture of its vigilant stockholders' confidence.

From the start of his ministry, Calonne bent every effort to generate prosperity for his country – as well as a windfall of favors for sundry acquaintances. He hoped to stimulate the economy by freeing internal trade from its various shackles, raising the number of free ports, inaugurating public works, suppressing some indirect taxes, and negotiating a new trade compact with England. He avoided the various technical blunders of his youthful predecessor Le Fevre d'Ormesson. He opened loan after loan at onerous rates of interest and found ready subscribers to those loans not only at home but also abroad, in part because the

---

32 On Le Fevre d'Ormesson, see Harris, *Necker and the Revolution of 1789*, pp. 39–43; and White, "Was There a Solution?" pp. 561–62.

33 Harris, *Necker and the Revolution of 1789*, p. 45.

troubled relations between London and The Hague helped, temporarily, to divert Dutch capital from England to France.[34] Then, again, he allowed the venal accountants to reclaim more and more of the administrative-financial territory so sagely denied them by Terray, Turgot, and Necker, and channeled government funds to members of the royal family and courtiers at Versailles.

Yet this was a primrose path that could only lead to disaster. By borrowing more than 650 million livres *in peacetime*, the controller-general added another 45 million livres in annual interest charges to the budget.[35] By opening the gates to prodigal spending and throwing strict accounting procedures to the winds, by allowing himself to become per-ilously reliant on fortuitous shifts in international capital flows, and by reinstating the venal *comptables*, Calonne ineludibly found himself con-fronting the situation against which Necker and others had repeatedly warned: France was now saddled with a permanent *ordinary* deficit – and this, in time of peace. No longer could investors have the assurance that they would ever see the interest on (let alone regain the capital of) their loans – and what would happen to their extended assets should the his-torically bellicose Gallic state drift once again into war?

To their credit, the Parisian parlementaires, so implacably opposed to reforms in other areas of public policy, repeatedly sounded the alarm in this domain. On at least three occasions – very late in each of the years 1783, 1784, and 1785 – the judges attached to their grudging endorsements of major loans remonstrances over the increasing dilapidation in royal finances. By December 1785, the magistrates, stridently critical of Ca-lonne, were trying to foist upon Louis XVI a blueprint for a more efficient administration of his government's finances, and the crown's *rapporteur* or political spokesman within the tribunal, the influential judge Adrien Louis Lefebvre d'Amécourt, lost that semiofficial post in a heated con-frontation with the king and his finance minister at Versailles.[36] By early 1786, Calonne was no longer on speaking terms with the directorate of the most powerful law court in the land. Austrian ambassador Mercy-Argenteau, ever attuned to developments at Versailles, wrote at about this time to Kaunitz: "The present government surpasses in weakness, disorder, and extortion the previous reign, and it is morally impossible for this to continue without a catastrophe."[37]

34 On Calonne's policies, see White, "Was There a Solution?" pp. 562–65. On the move-ments of foreign (and especially Dutch) capital in this period, see Riley, *International Government Finance*, p. 185; and "Dutch Investment in France, 1781–1787," *Journal of Economic History* 33 (December 1973), pp. 733–57.
35 Harris, "French Finances," p. 238.
36 Stone, *Parlement of Paris*, pp. 85–89.
37 As cited in Harris, *Necker and the Revolution of 1789*, p. 77. Similarly dire predictions,

Joseph II's ambassador proved to be all too prophetic. For Calonne, 1786 was a year of fruitless attempts to bridge the dangerous and ever-widening gap between expenditures and revenues in the ordinary accounts. The controller-general had willy-nilly to extend two *rente viagère* loans issued by his predecessors, that of March 1781 by 52,260,000 livres, with a yearly charge of more than 5 million livres, and that of January 1782 by 36 million livres, adding more than 3.6 million livres yearly to the crown's debt. Calonne had already borrowed 25 million livres from the *pays d'états*, and could expect no additional assistance from that quarter. He extracted 24 million livres from the city of Paris, and another 10 million livres from the creation of yet more venal posts! Soon the harassed finance minister would be forced into the embarrassing position of having to resort, in imitation of his maligned predecessor Le Fevre d'Ormesson, to solicitations of loans from the Discount Bank. Yet however resourceful Calonne proved himself to be in employing all of these expedients, the gap between fixed expenditure and fixed income – in this year of peace – was passing inexorably beyond 100 million livres.[38]

But perhaps the most unmistakable sign of approaching crisis for Calonne in late 1786 and early 1787 was the government's increasing dependence on the short-term credit notes issued to it by the venal accountants and other financiers in anticipation of future tax revenue. These anticipations, as late as the end of 1783, had amounted to "only" 176 million livres, which was already a sufficiently troubling sum; but by early 1787 this short-term credit had ballooned to a total of 255 million. This was, as Robert Harris has rightfully noted, "the most onerous of all types of government loans, the one that Necker tried most to keep limited."[39] What this (and the other developments enumerated above) augured for France was a rerun of the crisis that had bedeviled Terray fifteen years before. But this time the crisis was going to spiral out of control.

For this there were many reasons. Some of them were more or less financial in nature. As Taylor, Bosher, and Harris have stressed, many of the accountants and bankers upon whose short-term advances of capital the crown had increasingly to live day by day were using both public and private funds to speculate as never before on the Parisian stock exchange; and they themselves were, in a number of cases, on the verge of ruin or in actual bankruptcy at this time. A "severe general crisis" in financial circles was plainly shaking "public confidence in the financial

from the Swedish ambassador Baron de Staël and from the British Minister Plenipotentiary Hailes, appear on pp. 78–80.
38 For these statistics, see ibid., pp. 80–81; and White, "Was There a Solution?" pp. 562–65.
39 Harris, *Necker and the Revolution of 1789*, pp. 80–81.

system."[40] This general crisis, in addition, owed some of its severity to the larger economic recession of the post-1778 period studied carefully by C.-E. Labrousse and those following in his wake. Adversity for wine producers and textile workers meant a growing resistance to tax collectors. That in turn, by endangering the credit of venal accountants who relied in part on continuing returns from diverse forms of indirect taxes, accelerated the trend toward failures among their number and hence toward the insolvency of a government dependent in turn on these financier-accountants. (Concomitantly, the crown suffered in a more direct fashion since its direct tax revenue, brought in by its various fiscal agents, was also reduced by the recession.) Again, as White has pointed out, the ranks of government creditors within France had continued to swell during the 1770s and 1780s. As a result, any effort by the finance ministry to break the stranglehold of venal accountancy and fixed peacetime deficits by returning to Terray's expedient of partial bankruptcy would have affronted a powerful coalition of *rentiers*.[41] And that coalition would have surely found a resonant voice in a Paris Parlement still wrathfully associating the partial government default of 1770 with its own political oblivion of 1771–74.[42] It is equally clear that French policy makers, now unable for all the foregoing reasons to bring back the days of balanced ordinary finances, could not have expected to be rescued by a new influx of capital from the Dutch or any other foreign money markets.

Yet, as the next two sections of this chapter will demonstrate, the situation by 1786 and 1787 was growing more worrisome from the government's standpoint for other reasons as well, reasons transcending finances. For it was becoming questionable whether any controller-general could now have restored a situation of balanced ordinary budgets (and, hence, domestic and foreign investor confidence) without consulting ever wider circles of Frenchmen about governmental fiscal operations. And to discuss financial issues would most likely mean broaching the possibility of constitutional innovation, which in turn could very easily lead to speculation about redefining the social elite in France.

True, in February 1787, Calonne belatedly attempted to stabilize the situation. He presented a program of economic stimulation and tax reform

---

40 Bosher, *French Finances*, pp. 189–90. On the various elements of this crisis, see also Taylor, "The Paris Bourse on the Eve of the Revolution, 1781–1789," *American Historical Review* 67 (1962), pp. 951–77; and Harris, *Necker and the Revolution of 1789*, pp. 80–81.

41 White, "Was There a Solution?" p. 566. A major point as well for Weir, "Tontines, Public Finance, and Revolution," passim.

42 The judges attacked the venal accountants but championed the broader cause of the *rentier* class in 1787–88. See, for some information on this subject, Stone, *French Parlements and the Crisis of the Old Regime*, pp. 106–16.

to an Assembly of Notables. But this body responded almost immediately by clamoring for an institutionalized public review of royal finances that would be incompatible with absolutism as practiced in this land. Calonne fell from power soon thereafter.

Calonne's successor in the finance ministry, Cardinal Etienne Charles Loménie de Brienne, strove mightily from April 1787 until August 1788 to succeed where his predecessor had failed, to resuscitate the crown's finances within the sociopolitical framework of the ancien régime. This outspoken critic of Calonne and confidant of Jacques Necker resumed the Genevan's abortive campaign for a centralized bureaucratic control over the king's finances and the elimination of the venal *comptables*. Toward this end, Loménie de Brienne endowed the old Royal Council of Finance and Commerce with a role of strict supervision over the government's major financial operations; and, under its aegis, he established a single royal treasury (*caisse*) and the principle of annual, publicized budgets (*comptes rendus*).[43] Unfortunately, however, the first of these budgets, published on 28 April 1788, revealed the same old problem of ordinary revenues and expenditures that would not balance; and, although specialists differ even today on the precise amount of the ordinary deficit (as well as on the size of the extraordinary shortfall),[44] it is a somber fact that by August of that year the cardinal-minister and his colleagues had run out of ways to cover the fixed deficit.

The immediate problem seems to have been that a significant proportion of the government's income, because it was in the form of anticipations on future revenue, was becoming progressively less secure as the government's public credit sank. As Harris has put it: "The drop in value of government securities on the bourse meant that financiers who normally granted short-term credit in the form of anticipations of future tax revenue, were unable to come forth with more money... [they] were dependent upon the government's credit in order to raise that capital in the money markets."[45]

The government's credit, in turn, was collapsing (at least in the most immediate sense) because of Loménie de Brienne's inability to demonstrate clearly, in his *compte rendu* for 1788, how future loans or other measures would enable the crown to balance its books. But the year before, the authorities had also tacitly linked the government's credit to the eventual summoning of the Estates General. Thus, financial and con-

---

43 On these reforms, see Egret, *The French Prerevolution, 1787–1788*, trans. Wesley D. Camp (Chicago: University of Chicago Press, 1977), pp. 60–64.

44 See, for example, Harris, *Necker and the Revolution of 1789*, pp. 233–36, and White, "Was There a Solution?" p. 565. Yet both would agree that those deficits were very large.

45 Harris, *Necker and the Revolution of 1789*, pp. 264–65.

stitutional questions had already been joined, fatefully, in public opinion *before* the treasury crisis of August 1788. This is why, on 8 August, Brienne could only attempt to restore the government's credit on the bourse and thus renew the flow of anticipations by promising (in a royal decree) to call the Estates for 1 May 1789. This is also why, when the government's credit did not improve over the subsequent week, the finance minister had to promulgate the decree-in-council of 16 August that suspended payment on some of the debt, converted much of the rest into paper money, and once again portrayed the Estates General as the surest guarantor of the king's solvency.[46] When Loménie de Brienne, at his wit's end, resigned nine days later, this action cleared the way for Necker's return to power – and, predictably, one of the first things on which the reengaged Genevan insisted was the need to confirm the state's pledge to revive the historic organ of national consultation.

At first glance, it might seem sufficient to conclude that the ancien régime sank beneath the burden of its largely geopolitical expenses due to the return of venal accountancy and fixed peacetime deficits in the 1780s. But was the return of the financiers and of inefficiency in the management of royal funds fortuitous, or was it perhaps built into the sociopolitical order of things in Louis XVI's France? The second and third sections of this chapter will argue the latter case by showing that Turgot and Necker, and after them Calonne and Loménie de Brienne, found it impossible to disassociate the technicalities of fiscal administration from broader sociopolitical questions in this globally oriented kingdom.

THE PROBLEM OF THE STATE

There was an almost dialectical relationship between fiscal and constitutional issues in France during the 1774–88 period. Financial questions, because they constituted the most immediate domestic legacy of the kingdom's ongoing drive for international greatness, and because their insolubility after 1786 ushered in a constitutional crisis, have required initial consideration here. Yet to a large extent the financial problem itself first became a serious threat to the old regime after 1781 due to an old constitutional problem in France: the breach between the government and the governed, especially the elite among the governed. Some of the statesmen at Versailles acknowledged that problem, yet several among their number were also instrumental in aggravating it after 1781. This boded especially ill for the crown in light of the fact that constitutional questions now resonated more broadly and deeply than ever in educated society.

---

46 Ibid., esp. pp. 233–36 and 264–65. See also Egret, *French Prerevolution*, pp. 182–85.

We have already seen how Vergennes, principal architect of French foreign policy during most of this period, uneasily ruminated in wartime on his country's constitutional deficiencies. Yet, even earlier, in a memorandum to Louis XVI of 1774, this minister had identified a cardinal player in what would become the constitutional drama of a new France. "Opinion, it is said, is the queen of the world. The government that can establish it to its own advantage doubles with the idea of its real strength the consideration and the respect that have been, and ever will be, the reward of a well-directed administration and the most certain guarantee of its tranquillity."[47] It is not all that surprising, therefore, that Vergennes, having so willingly genuflected before the tribunal of public opinion, should have so readily subsidized the publication of tracts endorsing the American insurgents' cause in ideological terms. He may have been a committed royalist; but he was also bent on revenge against the British, and knew that, in this age, an appeal to a popular audience would be more conducive to that end than any invocation of absolutist canons.

It is revealing that so many of Louis XVI's advisers early on – not only Vergennes but also Turgot, Malesherbes, and Necker – should have acknowledged in one way or another the rising force of public opinion. With Jacques Necker in particular, challenged to find all possible means to finance war resumed on the high seas, the issue became a veritable obsession. The Genevan, it has been correctly observed,

> recognized [public opinion] as an awesome power that had grown up in the eighteenth century along with the expansion of commerce, education, and enlightenment. He was convinced that public opinion had become so powerful in France that it could no longer be ignored even in the most absolute of monarchies. ... The royal government would either rule with the support of public opinion or attempt to rule against it. He agreed with Malesherbes that the French people in the second half of the eighteenth century were too intelligent, too well educated, too *sensible* to submit to despotism.[48]

Hence, this minister's cultivation of a certain "style" in office – that of the astute, dedicated public servant staunchly opposed to unmerited grants of public funds to private persons. Hence, his painstaking efforts, in *comptes rendus*, preambles to royal edicts, and treatises on finance, to educate the public about the king's purposes. And hence, his insistence on assuring the crown's creditors or prospective creditors that a fiscally sound administration in France, always capable of paying them interest on their loans out of ordinary revenue, would always deserve their trust.

And Necker, by all reckonings, met with an extraordinary response in polite society. Of first and most patent concern to the authorities, this translated into the Genevan's fabled ability to raise huge amounts of

47 Cited in Baker, "Politics and Public Opinion," p. 240, n. 99.
48 Harris, *Necker: Reform Statesman*, p. 86 (italics in original).

money for the waging of war without having to devise new taxes. Yet it was also reflected in the prodigious popularity of his diverse writings on public administration. A case in point was the *Compte rendu* of 1781. "You never saw such a crowd," noted the duc de Cröy amazedly of the Parisian throngs besieging the printers for copies of this rendering of the royal budget. "Three thousand copies at a time were printed, and they were snapped up instantly. Soon 20,000 copies were sold. There was good reason to run there. Never before had one seen the finances of the kingdom laid bare, the king giving an accounting, so to speak, and a very faithful accounting, to his people."[49] Before long, it seems, 100,000 copies of the work had been purchased, at three livres per copy. Whether or not Harris is justified in speculating that the *Compte rendu* may have been "more widely read and more influential than the *Contrat social* of Rousseau," he is undoubtedly correct in averring that it "became the political handbook for a generation, as far as public administration of the finances were concerned."[50] We know as well that Necker's more general discourse on royal finances, appearing three years later, evoked a similar reaction from the reading public.[51]

For the Genevan, taking notable Frenchmen into the crown's confidence, and thus working toward healing the breach between government and elite governed, also meant – as, earlier, it may have possibly meant for Turgot – establishing provincial assemblies in the kingdom. Turgot's ideas on the subject were, it seems, contained in the famous "Memorial on Municipalities," written by his confidant Dupont de Nemours in late August 1775.[52] This treatise advocated the creation, in the provinces or *généralités*, of three-tiered hierarchies of representative assemblies of landholders. Members of primary assemblies at the parish level would send deputies to secondary assemblages at the *élection* level, from which mandatories would be selected to gather at convocations in the capitals of the various provinces. The dome of the whole edifice would be the "great municipality of the kingdom," a national assembly of landowners. These bodies, working in the future on the basis of a universal *cadastre* or survey of taxable lands in the parishes, *élections*, and *généralités*, would receive from the king's Council the quota of taxation to be assessed and would then parcel it out, ultimately, among individual landowning parishioners. They would also take over from the intendants and subdelegates local responsibilities for road maintenance and social welfare.

49 Cited in ibid., p. 217.
50 Ibid., p. 219.
51 See Egret, *Necker*, p. 187; and Henri Grange, *Les idées de Necker* (Paris: Klincksieck, 1974), pp. 38–52.
52 See Douglas Dakin, *Turgot and the Ancien Régime in France* (London: Methuen, 1939), passim; and Harris, *Necker: Reform Statesman*, esp. pp. 77–83.

Whether the controller-general would actually have submitted this project to the Council had he not fallen from power in 1776, and whether and to what extent he envisaged it as a rein on administrative absolutism in France, are questions that have long perplexed specialists in the field.[53] Of equal or greater significance is the fact that, subsequently, Jacques Necker did try to make provincial assemblies one means of bridging the gap between policy makers at Versailles and respectable Frenchmen in the provinces. He was able to establish two such bodies at the *généralité* level, in Berri and Haute-Guyenne, and enact legislation for two others as well, before he in turn was cashiered by Louis XVI in 1781. Although Necker (like his predecessor, apparently) was concerned lest such experimentation get out of control, and hence made it clear that his assemblies, like those mooted by Turgot, would merely allocate royal taxes and not question their amount or purposes, the bodies in Berri and Haute-Guyenne did in fact remove a substantial array of local responsibilities from the intendants' hands and thus heralded "radical changes in administration at the provincial level."[54] The members of the two assemblies, it seems, worked at their tasks with a will and "won substantial support in public opinion."[55]

And so the ministers in prerevolutionary France (like their counterparts who sponsored provincial and local *zemstvos* in prerevolutionary Russia) strove to close the long-standing breach between rulers and ruled, to mesh, at least a bit, the interests of state and subjects. Yet the reformist spirit of the age, sensitive at all times to the waxing tribunal of public opinion, was hardly confined to the corridors of power at Versailles. Whereas a number of the intendants, understandably hostile to Necker's innovations in provincial administration, joined the ranks of the director-general's enemies, others spoke (and acted) in quite another wise. As early as January 1778, Douet de la Boullaye, intendant in Auch, invoked "the opinion of the people" to justify the labors of social melioration projected for the provinces of southwestern France. Eight years later, Bertrand de Boucheporn, newly installed as intendant for Navarre in the far south, declared to the parlementaires at Pau: "We no longer live in times when men consider that mode of governance to be perfect which is most com-

---

53 For an interpretation of Turgot as a "republican by preference" and of his envisioned assemblies as protorepublican institutions, see Gerald J. Cavanaugh, "Turgot: The Rejection of Enlightened Despotism," *French Historical Studies* 6 (1969) pp. 31–58. Yet neither Dakin (*Turgot*, pp. 277–80) nor Harris (*Necker: Reform Statesman*, pp. 77–83) is willing to go that far. They stress, instead, the complexity and ambiguity of much of Turgot's political thought.
54 Harris, *Necker: Reform Statesman*, pp. 182–84.
55 Ibid., p. 98. On the provincial assemblies, see also Pierre Renouvin, *Les Assemblées provinciales de 1787: Origines, développements, résultats* (Paris: A. Picard, 1921).

plicated and most shrouded in mystery, or which endeavors to distract or altogether deceive the people."[56] The research of Paul Ardascheff, Douglas Dakin, Maurice Bordes, and others goes far to establish the generalization that the administrative toil of the intendants (and perhaps of their subdelegates as well?) was increasingly actuated by "enlightened" considerations in this era, whatever the misgivings of certain intendants up to 1781 regarding trends in Neckerite policies.[57]

Furthermore, the Enlightenment itself, however we define it, was now capturing the ministerial strongholds of the old France. Certainly this is what Robert Darnton has discovered in following the fortunes of the *Encyclopédie* into the reign of Louis XVI.

The Enlightenment and the French state have often been interpreted as enemies; and the official condemnation of the *Encyclopédie*, notwithstanding Malesherbes' success in saving it, has often been cited as the supreme example of their enmity. That interpretation fails to take account of a change in the tone of French administration during the last fifteen years of the old regime. The persecution of the *Encyclopédie* in the 1750s turned into protection in the 1770s. Malesherbes' successor, Le Camus de Néville, actively promoted the quarto editions. And Panckoucke, the successor to the publishers of the first edition, based his speculation on the support of the government. From his first skirmishes with the pirates of Lyons, Geneva, and Avignon to his final settlements with the consortia of Liège, Lausanne, and Berne, Panckoucke relied on a strategy of official protection and privilege to defend his market against interlopers.[58]

Panckoucke's final edition of this great collaborative effort of the philosophes, the *Encyclopédie Méthodique*, "was printed openly in almost every shop in Paris, advertised and sold as a quasi-official publication, and written by men who not only owed their careers to the State but also included a heavy proportion of royal censors." Administrators like Le Camus de Néville, Vergennes, and the lieutenant-general of police, Lenoir, not to mention Turgot, Malesherbes, and Necker, "sympathized with the rational, reformist principles that the *Encyclopédie* had come to embody."[59] Had they really any choice in the matter, especially those among them who (correctly) saw the rationalization of finance, justice, and administration at home as a capital prerequisite for upholding the French state's competitiveness in the world at large?

Yet it was one thing to sympathize with "rational, reformist principles"

56 Maurice Bordes, *L'Administration provinciale et municipale en France au XVIIIe siècle*, pp. 152, 157.

57 Paul Ardascheff, *Les intendants de province sous Louis XVI*, trans. Louis Jousserandot (Paris: Alcan, 1909); Dakin, *Turgot*, esp. pp. 27–28; and Bordes, "Les Intendants éclairés de la fin de l'ancien régime," pp. 57–83.

58 Robert Darnton, *The Business of Enlightenment: A Publishing History of the Encyclopédie 1775–1800* (Cambridge, Mass.: Harvard University Press, 1979), p. 538.

59 Ibid., pp. 538–39, 537.

and quite another to accept what might turn out to be their exceedingly subversive constitutional (let alone social) implications. Tensions within ruling circles over constitutional issues emerged almost from the start of Louis XVI's reign and contributed to the defeat of the ameliorative policies that characterized his early years on the throne.

Those tensions may have been foreshadowed on the day (11 June 1775) the new monarch took his coronation oaths at Rheims. Turgot had suggested that these solemn and ritualized pledges be updated and secularized so as to spare the sensibilities of Protestants within France. Louis had rejected the controller-general's advice, but, so Keith Baker has alleged, "when the service reached the stage of the royal oath to exterminate all heretics within the realm, the king apparently found it less embarrassing to mumble an unintelligible phrase." Although the veracity of this story has been challenged, it does seem that, at a later point in the proceedings, the bishops of Laon and Beauvais, rather than "presenting" the newly crowned sovereign to the peers and popular throng to solicit their "acceptance" of his kingship, dispensed with this custom altogether.[60] Such incidents (if, indeed, they actually took place) may have been significant insofar as they betokened some uncertainty in the government over the precise limits of the youthful monarch's authority.

Louis XVI was to be troubled by constitutional questions of a more concrete nature in the early, reformist years of his rule. When, in early 1776, the Council debated a proposal to resurrect the Estates General, both Turgot and his confederate Malesherbes reportedly opposed it on the ground that such an institution might play into the hands of the "privileged classes," hobble the king, and engender violent conflicts in society. Soon thereafter came the dismissal of Turgot; and the king's doubts about the "constitutionality" of certain reforms sponsored by the controller-general (such as the abolition of the Parisian guilds and of certain tax exemptions of noble landowners) seem to have played a role in this royal decision.[61]

Then, less than two years later, Louis XVI reacted dubiously to a confidential "Memorial" from Finance Minister Necker on the subject of his envisioned provincial assemblies by penning this question: "Is it more expedient to hand over . . . control of administrative affairs to administrative bodies, or is it [not] wiser to keep such affairs in the hands of the constituted judicial bodies?"[62] As Jean Egret, in citing this royal

---

60 Baker, "French Political Thought at the Accession of Louis XVI," *Journal of Modern History* 50 (1978), pp. 280–81. For another version of the coronation story, see Merrick, *The Desacralization of the French Monarchy*, pp. 152–53, n. 34.

61 On all of these matters, see Dakin, *Turgot*, p. 280; and Edgar Faure, *La Disgrâce de Turgot* (Paris: Gallimard, 1961), passim.

62 Cited in Egret, *Necker*, p. 132. My translation.

query, rightfully pointed out, the king, as inheritor of a nearly two-centuries-old tradition of administrative absolutism in Bourbon France, could hardly fail to scent danger in any proposal, however limited, to involve assembled subjects in the business of public administration. Several of the intendants, whose administrative powers in the provinces were to be reduced if the director-general established his new assemblies, shared their monarch's misgivings.

One of the most prestigious and powerful of the "constituted judicial bodies" alluded to by the king in his comment on Necker's memorandum, the Paris Parlement, had already clashed with the director-general over his reform of *vingtième* taxation.[63] When this court received from one of the Genevan's foes a copy of his "Memorial" and saw that it was highly critical of judicial activism in administrative matters, its indignation – or at least that of its deans – knew no bounds, and the embattled Necker had now to reckon these Parisian magistrates among his most unyielding adversaries.[64] Ironically enough, the judges might have been confirmed in their righteous anger had they known that even their old nemesis Turgot was, from the sanctuary of retirement, voicing his own doubts regarding the propriety in an absolutist state of representative bodies of landowners.

In light of all this, it was only natural that a plethora of individuals whose interests were menaced by the Genevan's reforms should have seen the constitutional questions posed by his revision of *vingtième* taxation, his provincial assemblies, and his writings on royal finance as so many weapons to use against him.[65] By the spring of 1781 the director-general had to fend off not only the criticisms voiced directly to Louis XVI by antagonized justices and intendants but also the slings and arrows of anonymous foes (including future Finance Minister Calonne) who spared no opportunity to depict Necker as recklessly dabbling in republican ideas. That the finance minister actually hailed from a republican city-state only made his detractors' task that much easier.

And so Necker, like Turgot before him, was abandoned by the king. The Genevan fell from grace in May 1781, in part because of his own political miscalculations, it is true, but primarily because his enemies had known at the critical moment how to turn against him his efforts to bridge the gap between the rulers and the notables among the ruled in this land. Nor did the issue, once raised, leave him to rest. Four years after his dismissal, a prominent judge, Président de Coppons, insisted in a lengthy and unfriendly commentary on Necker's 1784 treatise on French finances

---

63 On this controversy, refer again to Lardé, *Une Enquête sur les vingtièmes*, and Stone, *Parlement of Paris*, pp. 77–82 and 96–100.

64 Harris, *Necker: Reform Statesman*, pp. 86–98; and Stone, *Parlement of Paris*, pp. 68–70, 77–79, 113–19.

65 Harris, *Necker: Reform Statesman*, pp. 82–83; and Egret, *Necker*, pp. 132–33.

that "secrecy, not publicity, was the true principle of the French monarchy"; and another writer retrospectively anathematized Necker's *Compte rendu* of 1781 by declaring rhetorically to Louis XVI that it would be "a long time before Your Majesty heals this wound inflicted upon the dignity of the throne."[66]

The burgeoning scholarship upon French finances during the 1774–88 period has established 1781, the year in which Necker's first ministry foundered, rather than 1776, the year of Turgot's downfall, as the moment of truth for the old regime. The intendants, avatars of old-style absolutism, seized back their administrative functions in those provinces where, under Necker, they had briefly been constrained to share them with newfangled assemblies of landed proprietors. The crown's accountability to public opinion for its finances began to slip away. And, as we have already seen, the ensuing conjuncture of war-imposed indebtedness and fiscal dilapidation was to lead the king and his counselors down the road toward ruin. That this was the case, however – that, in more concrete terms, the crown's credit ran out – was in some measure due to the fact that the constitutional questions ventilated within the power structure itself continued also to resonate in the much broader milieu of educated society.

Clearly the "sovereign courts" played a central role in defining a political culture increasingly at odds with absolutism after 1774. It is striking that the Parlement of Paris, rather than meekly accepting as the price for its reinstatement in 1774–75 restrictions upon its future political behavior reminiscent of those that Louis XIV had been able to impose upon the same institution a century earlier, brushed the new curbs aside. It even heard one of its illustrious peers, the duc de La Rochefoucauld, conjure up the nation's "imprescriptible rights" and call for the revival of "those national assemblages [i.e., the Estates General] without which all is irregular and illegal."[67] In sparring with the crown over the coming years, the judges in the kingdom's most influential court would still show traces of the radical Jansenist ecclesiology that, in the 1750s and 1760s, had held the king to be but "minister" or "mandatory" of the secularized "nation." They would, moreover, draw on both the manuscripts and the constitutional advice of retired President Durey de Meinières, who in 1775 prophesied the rebirth of the nation's sovereignty in the Estates General.[68]

---

66 Harris, *Necker: Reform Statesman*, p. 88; see also ibid., p. 230, and Egret, *Necker*, pp. 132–33, for further discussion of this anti-Neckerite literature.

67 Carcassonne, *Montesquieu et le problème de la constitution française*, pp. 466–67.

68 On the Jansenist theme, consult Van Kley, "The Jansenist Constitutional Legacy in the French Prerevolution, 1750–1789," *Historical Reflections/Réflexions Historiques* 13 (1986), pp. 393–453; and Merrick, *Desacralization of the French Monarchy*, pp. 125–

Meanwhile, in April 1775, Malesherbes, still first president of the Paris Cour des Aides, insisted on identifying for Louis XVI the three key defenses against "despotism": written laws "available to all," an independent system of primary and appellate tribunals, and "public opinion." He also voiced the hope that the king might "listen to the Nation itself assembled, or at least... permit assemblies in each province."[69] (Appointed to a ministry soon thereafter, Malesherbes would drop any advocacy of the Estates General but would continue to favor the concept of provincial assemblies.) As the reign progressed, parlementaires from Rouen to Grenoble to Bordeaux, protesting to Versailles over a legion of issues, filled the air with denunciations of "arbitrary" or "despotic" government agents and with invocations of the rights of taxpayers and *justiciables.*[70]

Reinforcing this ideological assault on absolutism by the high judiciary was a constitutional commentary flowing from a multitude of private sources. Barristers in the parlements, drawing on their experience during the Maupeou crisis, their professional training and eloquence, and the legal briefs they could publish without preliminary censorship, emerged as spokesmen for public issues extracted from private litigation.[71] Periodicals such as the Dutch *Gazette de Leyde*, Pidansat de Mairobert's *Journal historique*, and Simon-Nicolas-Henri Linguet's *Annales Politiques* accustomed their readers to a political discourse that in many ways heralded the dizzying political experimentation of the Revolution.[72] The *Encyclopédie*, as edited now by Panckoucke, continued to disseminate its message that "rational standards, when applied to contemporary institutions, would expose absurdity and iniquity everywhere" among "a general public of lawyers, officials, and local notables."[73] A pamphlet literature, taking its cue from the antiministerial polemics of the early

64. On Durey de Meinières, see again Hudson, "Parlementary Crisis of 1763," pp. 113–15; and Baker, *Inventing the French Revolution*, pp. 34–36, 75.

69 Cited in Harris, *Necker: Reform Statesman*, pp. 74–76.

70 Consult, on these themes, Amable-Pierre Floquet, *Histoire du parlement de Normandie*, 7 vols. (Rouen: E. Frère, 1840–42); Egret, *Le Parlement de Dauphiné et les affaires publiques dans la deuxiéme moitié du XVIIIe siècle*, 2 vols. (Grenoble: Arthaud, 1942); and Doyle, *The Parlement of Bordeaux and the End of the Old Regime 1771–1790* (New York: St. Martin's, 1974).

71 See Sarah Maza, "Le tribunal de la nation: Les mémoires judiciaires et l'opinion publique à la fin de l'ancien régime," *Annales E.S.C.* 42 (1987), pp. 73–90; and David A. Bell, "Lawyers into Demagogues: Chancellor Maupeou and the Transformation of Legal Practice in France 1771–1789," *Past and Present* 130 (1991), pp. 107–41.

72 Popkin, "The *Gazette de Leyde* and French Politics Under Louis XVI," in J. Censor and J. Popkin, eds., *Press and Politics*, pp. 75–132; and Popkin, "Prerevolutionary Origins of Political Journalism," in Baker, ed., *Political Culture of the Old Regime*, pp. 203–23.

73 Darnton, *Business of Enlightenment*, pp. 539–40.

1770s, anatomized the concept of the social contract developed by writers like Rousseau and extolled the Estates General as the embodiment of the popular will in France. In more general terms, the pamphleteers of this period represented a diversity of elite interests "willing to appeal to the growing force of public opinion to settle their disputes."[74] In the meantime, at a more visceral level, the pornographic *nouvelles à la main* that were in these years pouring from the presses of Grub Street mocked the king for his sexual impotence and used causes célèbres like the "diamond necklace affair" to pillory decadence and despotism in high places.[75] As Mona Ozouf has suggested, public opinion may have derived some of its growing influence on the eve of the Revolution from serving (at least in some people's minds) as a replacement for a kingship whose sacral qualities could no longer be assumed.[76]

Paradoxically, the government contributed to this "contamination" of the political culture at home by pursuing its geopolitical goals abroad. Vergennes was warned by a number of individuals in and out of the ministries that his support of anticolonialist insurgency in America, and in particular his subsidization of pro-American propaganda, could undermine his own country's credo of absolutism and social inequality.[77] Frances Acomb has explored one aspect of this process by analyzing the mutual reinforcement of Anglophobic and liberal constitutional perspectives in France during and after the American war.[78] Yet reflective Frenchmen could draw a powerful inspiration from events in America without concerning themselves unduly about the old enemy across the Channel. "Liberals and intellectuals," Durand Echeverria has argued,

identified the American struggle against British oppression with their own battle against autocracy. The word *liberté* was a constant refrain in every panegyric of America, and to a great extent the American example was used as an excuse to

74 Citation from Popkin, "Pamphlet Journalism at the End of the Old Regime," *Eighteenth-Century Studies* 22 (1989), p. 363. See also Carcassonne, *Montesquieu*, pp. 553–54; Baker, "French Political Thought," pp. 281–82; and Roger Barny, *Prélude idéologique à la Révolution française: Le Rousseauisme avant 1789* (Paris: Les Belles Lettres, 1985).

75 Darnton, *The Literary Underground of the Old Regime* (Cambridge, Mass.: Harvard University Press, 1982); and "The Facts of Literary Life in Eighteenth-Century France," in Baker, ed., *Political Culture of the Old Regime*, esp. pp. 276–82. See also the stimulating essays on Marie-Antoinette by Sarah Maza and Lynn Hunt, in Hunt, ed., *Eroticism and the Body Politic* (Baltimore: Johns Hopkins University Press, 1991).

76 Mona Ozouf, "L'opinion publique," in Baker, ed., *Political Culture of the Old Regime*, pp. 419–34. Also, refer back to Baker, "Politics and Public Opinion," pp. 204–46, for other thoughts on this subject.

77 See Baker, "Politics and Public Opinion," p. 240, n. 99; Bernard Fay, *The Revolutionary Spirit in France and America*, trans. Ramon Guthrie (New York: Cooper Square, 1966), esp. pp. 484–85; and Higonnet, *Sister Republics*, passim.

78 Acomb, *Anglophobia in France*, passim.

express ideas which otherwise could not have been voiced. . . . The American War was for the *ancien régime* a sort of Pandora's Box out of which poured a cloud of books and articles advocating equality, republicanism, liberty, and constitutionalism, and attacking both the aristocratic principle and monarchical absolutism.[79]

The writings of Franklin, Paine, and Dickinson, the Declaration of Independence and Articles of Confederation, the constitutions and bills of rights of the various American states, and the resolutions and acts of the American Congress were widely reprinted and disseminated in France. Franklin, of course, shrewdly cultivated for American purposes the image of the innocent, rustic republican during his embassy to the Gallic kingdom, and was lionized by the Parisians. But perhaps it should have more seriously concerned those wielding power at Versailles that a presumed pillar of the status quo like the Paris Parlement, feuding with Necker over his reform of *vingtième* taxation in its remonstrances of January 1778, could invoke the principle of no taxation without representation that the magistrates, like many other educated Frenchmen, knew to be guiding the insurgents in America.[80] It is true that during the 1780s a sort of anti-Americanism set in, not only among opponents of domestic sociopolitical change but also among those French intellectuals genuinely skeptical about the long-term prospects for self-government in America.[81] Yet this seems to have been a tendency only of a minority – all the smaller a minority in that the opposite, pro-American tendency still accorded so easily with imperishable Gallic suspicions regarding the British.

Such were the tributaries flowing during these years into the great stream of ideological challenge to Bourbon absolutism. It is true that the institutions and individuals upholding that absolutism occasionally noted and sounded alarms over this challenge. As early as 1775, the Assembly of the Clergy alerted the authorities to what it termed "the restless and inquisitive examination which everyone is making of the Government's operations, of its prerogatives and the limits of those prerogatives."[82] The Paris Parlement, too, however much it might in other ways contribute to the national disputation over constitutional principles, lashed out occasionally at "pernicious" pamphleteers who dared to question the king's writ in France. And even Vergennes, mastermind of the foreign policy that ensured the triumph of republican canons in America, came to fear the resonance of subversive ideas in French public opinion. "In 1782 and 1783," according to Darnton, the foreign minister "wrote as many letters

---

79 Echeverria, *Mirage in the West: A History of the French Image of American Society to 1815* (Princeton, N.J.: Princeton University Press, 1956), p. 42.
80 Ibid., pp. 71–72, 140, 152–57, and 161; and Stone, *Parlement of Paris*, pp. 81–82.
81 Echeverria, *Mirage*, pp. 62–64, 125–28.
82 Carcassonne, *Montesquieu*, p. 551.

to England about the need to suppress a smut factory run by émigré French *libellistes* as he did about the diplomatic preliminaries to the Treaty of Paris."[83]

It was not unreasonable for Vergennes to fear the impact of filthy literature on public opinion and thus to crack down on underground publishing, for in the relatively restricted world of court politics personal reputations ultimately counted for more than did substantive policies, and reputations were all too easily marred by adverse publicity. But the lesson that Vergennes, the king, and the other authorities at Versailles should have learned from this was that the government, by abandoning the reformism associated up to 1781 with Turgot, Malesherbes, and Necker, was only sapping itself. It might try to suppress offending literature, and it might even pay its own court to public opinion by buying over hacks like the comte de Mirabeau and Jacques-Pierre Brissot – but could such tactics effectively replace institutionalized reforms as a means of cultivating the public confidence in government so indispensable to this globally minded state?

The answer today must be that they could not. And this was Calonne's tardy conclusion as well when, in August 1786, he submitted his fateful memorandum to Louis XVI recommending a host of fiscal and administrative reforms.[84] However, the king's finance minister almost immediately became caught up in an uncontrollable dialectic of ministerial initiative and public response. Sensing that he could not hope to ram the crown's program through parlements, at Paris and elsewhere, that had for some time (and with very good reason) been denouncing his profligate fiscal policies, Calonne advised the king to call an Assembly of Notables to consider the proposed reforms. According to the controller-general, such a forum, in which "it is the most important and enlightened magnates of the realm to whom the king is pleased to communicate his views," would be less dangerous to royal authority than the dread Estates General, in which "it is the representatives of the nation who remonstrate, petition, and consent."[85] Yet, given the potency of public opinion, and the literate nation's "memory" of Estates General sporadically convening in earlier centuries, how likely was it that the French people's recovery of consultative institutions could have stopped with the summoning of an Assembly of Notables?

It is not that the royal reforms first submitted to the Notables in late February 1787 would have failed, in execution, to revive the financial

83 Darnton, *Literary Underground*, p. 195.
84 On Calonne's memorandum of August 1786 and the reforms it advocated, see Egret, *French Prerevolution*, chap. 1.
85 Ibid., p. 4.

sinews of the bellicose Bourbon state. In fact, this was exactly the problem from the viewpoint of Frenchmen *still subject to the whims of that absolutist state*. What might landholders not fear from a "territorial subvention" whose yield was undetermined and whose duration was unfixed? What public purposes could hierarchies of provincial and subordinate assemblies of landowners in the *pays d'élections* serve if, in apportioning taxation decided upon at Versailles, and in dealing with other administrative matters, such bodies (to a greater extent than Necker's) would have to obey those henchmen of absolutism the intendants? How could Frenchmen effectually protest the extended stamp tax of such a renascent state? And why should they enthuse over the elimination of internal tolls and duties, the reduction of the various salt imposts, the liberation of the internal commerce in grain, and the conversion of the peasants' obligatory road work into cash payments, if such measures, by stimulating taxable agriculture and trade within the realm, merely refilled the coffers of absolutism?

Calonne, servant of the monarchy as it had existed ever since 1614–15, had failed to anticipate how quickly the informed citizenry would discern constitutional issues behind the government's reform initiatives. And on the more immediate question of government solvency, he had also miscalculated. The public, already accustomed to regarding him as a frivolous courtier, as "a combination of all the abuses he wanted to reform,"[86] would not accept his revelation to the Notables of a fixed annual deficit of more than 100 million livres.

It was inevitable that the Notables, on learning that Necker's reported budgetary surplus of 1781 had now become a running deficit, would demand to see the government's fiscal records; and it was inevitable that their examination of the controller-general's proposed reforms would radicalize their thinking on all public questions. "Their assigned role was as loyal councillors," Vivian Gruder has commented, "but they fast became prosecuting attorneys and soon assumed the guise of quasi-representatives of the nation, trying to make their consultative assembly into a virtual legislature."[87] When put to the ultimate test, that of deciding whether or not to endorse the crown's legislation, the Notables, as Gruder has lucidly explained, could only continue to stake out an ever more radical position:

When refusing to grant final approval, especially to tax measures, they denied having political power, contending they were appointed, not elected, mere private

---

86 This was Pierre Victor Malouet's subsequent characterization of Calonne, cited in ibid., p. 29.

87 Gruder, "Paths to Political Consciousness: The Assembly of Notables of 1787 and the 'Pre-Revolution' in France," *French Historical Studies* 13 (Spring 1984), p. 348.

persons, not deputies. Instead they believed that other institutions, other instruments of the nation already established or to be called into existence, should have the task of consenting to laws. They turned the Crown's constraints on their functions, which they often criticized and tried to break, into an argument for conferring the larger role to which they aspired on another and more effective body. . . .

And though the members of this assemblage might offer various institutional alternatives to their convocation, it was predictable that some among their number should have urged upon the authorities "an estates-general, which they looked upon as the fullest embodiment of the nation's will, in the past as in the future."[88] Indeed, Leblanc de Castillon, a distinguished jurist from Provence, had declared early on in the Notables' discussions that the Estates General would ultimately have to sanction any new taxes; and Lafayette was to issue a clarion call for the resurrection of this historic consultative organ on the eve of the Notables' dissolution. The Bourbon state could not, even now, lay the ghosts of venerable constitutional precedent.

That the dialogue between the government and the Notables engendered such a radical discourse owed much to the concurrent politicization of the educated public. The abbé Morellet spoke to this point in a letter to Britain's Lord Shelburne:

A slight fever has gripped the country. As soon as the public has seen the Notables seriously occupied with its interests, opinion has given them a power which they would not have had by the manner in which they were convened. The Nation has, so to speak, recognized them as its true representatives, although they were assembled with quite a different intention, and by reason of the confidence acquired they have become like the deputies of our old States General.[89]

The Notables, doubtlessly aware that hawkers in the streets were selling dolls to the raucous refrain "Notables for sale!" and cognizant as well of popular cartoons depicting them as guileless geese about to be devoured by the ministers, wished at all costs to avoid playing a role of subservience to the government. Hence the blunt warning of the prince de Beauvau to his fellow Notables that if their assemblage served "only to levy taxes," it would be "compromised in the eyes of the nation"; thus the final agreement of all the standing committees in the Assembly that, in the pivotal matter of consent to taxation, they could not possibly fill the shoes of either the parlements or the Estates General.[90]

But the Notables were not the sole pleaders before the tribunal of public opinion; the ministers, too, had willy-nilly to appear there. Indeed,

---

88 Ibid., pp. 349–50.
89 Quoted in Harris, *Necker and the Revolution of 1789*, p. 134. See also the discussion of the public's political awakening in Carcassonne, *Montesquieu*, esp. pp. 554–57.
90 Harris, *Necker and the Revolution of 1789*, p. 134; Egret, *French Prerevolution*, p. 34.

Calonne precipitated his own disgrace in March by appealing over the heads of his adversaries to the literate public. In a pamphlet obviously intended for such an audience, the controller-general vehemently attacked "privileges" and then posed these audacious questions:

> But... why not make known all of the minister's projects? Why should their publicity not serve as a shield against his enemies' attacks? What is this strange darkness that surrounds the administration when all it wishes is to be just and beneficent?... Should the people's minister work in obscurity?[91]

The "people's minister" – in an absolute monarchy? Small wonder that Louis XVI saw fit to fire his finance minister. Yet Louis himself handed over to the Notables the fiscal accounts they had been demanding, and the new steward of the crown's imperiled finances, Loménie de Brienne, chosen in a conciliatory gesture from among the Notables themselves, tried to mollify the Assembly further by more carefully defining several of the government's proposed reforms and by rescinding others altogether.

It is true that the authorities, finding the Assembly still to be recalcitrant, dissolved it and bent their efforts toward forcing their edicts – above all those aimed at augmenting revenue – through the Paris Parlement. Brienne and the new keeper of the seals, the ex-parlementaire Chrétien-François II de Lamoignon, hoped to appeal to the ordinary French people by devising provincial assemblies that, some day, might provide part of the personnel for an Estates General, by stimulating economic growth, and by providing a simpler, less expensive, and more humane system of civil and criminal justice. Yet they were reckoning, as Calonne earlier had reckoned, without the explosive force of public opinion, a public opinion for which the whole five-month saga of the Assembly of Notables had just served as a riveting primer in constitutional principles. Could the ensuing struggle between the ministers and the Parisian parlementaires have done anything other than open that Pandora's box even wider?

And, predictably, the judges in the capital, loath to appear any more amenable to ministerial desires than had the Notables, hesitated not a whit to invoke the cause of the "constitution" on the day (2 July) they received from the crown its legislation extending the stamp tax. "A similar type of tax had served as pretext for the insurrection of the English colonies against the mother country," reminisced one observer. "Orators of the Paris Parlement were proud to have to reiterate the arguments of the American publicists."[92] (Thus, yet again, did the French state's international mission come back to haunt it.) The Parlement rejected the stamp tax, and insisted,

91 Ibid., p. 22.
92 Ibid., p. 94.

as had the Notables, on review of the government's fiscal accounts and projections. By 25 July, the tribunal was calling for the convening of the Estates-General, and two days later its printed protests making that portentous demand were selling openly on the streets of Paris. When the ministers (without yielding on the stamp tax issue) sent the justices their edict levying a "territorial subvention" on the landowners of all three orders, they again elicited a defiant magisterial call for the Estates General. By mid-August the recusant judges, having dared to condemn the government's compulsory registration of its financial decrees at a *lit de justice* staged on the sixth, had been banished to Troyes.[93]

But the parlementaires, like the Notables before them, seem in retrospect to have been riding what Harris has called "a gigantic tidal wave of public opinion." Mercy-Argenteau, who as Austrian ambassador to France in a season of impending crisis in the Balkans had every reason to be monitoring closely the domestic situation of Vienna's nominal western ally, wrote to Kaunitz in July:

The evil is greatly magnified because of the increasingly excited state of public opinion. Little by little... the agitation is reaching all classes of society. And it is this ferment which is giving the Parlement the power to persevere in its opposition.... The fever has become so general that even if people were put in prison by the thousands the evil could not be overcome; that would exasperate their anger to the highest pitch and riots would erupt. This is what the police are saying.[94]

That this anxious diplomatic observer should have depicted the situation in such somber hues was not all that surprising. Yet the perspicacious Malesherbes said much the same thing, and more besides, as he surveyed the entire kingdom:

I say that the Parlement of Paris is... merely the echo of the Parisian public, and that the Parisian public is the echo of the whole nation. The Parlement is speaking because it is the only body that has the right to speak, but we must not blink the fact that if any assembly of citizens had this right, they would make the same use of it. We are dealing therefore with the whole nation, [and] it will be to the nation that the king replies when he replies to the parlement.[95]

By August 1787, according to Jean Egret, "everyone was calling for the Estates General, and some daring journalists were already speculating about its potential composition... and about the task it would have to accomplish."[96] A pamphlet literature descanting freely on the basic constitutional issue of the breach between government and governed in France was already flourishing: Ralph Greenlaw has traced nearly three hundred

---

93 Ibid., pp. 95–102.
94 Cited in Harris, *Necker and the Revolution of 1789*, p. 279.
95 Cited in Egret, *French Prerevolution*, p. 98.
96 Ibid., p. 103.

of these tracts to the period from January to November 1787 and has found their rate of production steadily increasing over that period.[97] Moreover, the ministers, who had also had to exile Bordeaux's parlementaires to Libourne because of their long-standing resistance to royal policies, were showered in late August and September with protests from courts all over the realm voicing solidarity with the Parisian and Bordelais tribunals and swelling the national chorus of demands for the Estates General.

Fearing in such a highly charged atmosphere for the government's credit in the financial markets, let alone for his long-term program of reform, Brienne had little choice but to bargain with the Parisian magistrates. Yet, in effect, he was attempting to square the circle. The judges allowed themselves to be temporarily bought off in September by a ministerial pledge to withdraw the *subvention territoriale* and stamp tax in return for reimposition of the more conventional *vingtième* taxes, but insisted no less on reaffirming the necessity of the Estates General's consent to taxes in France. Two months later, at the tumultuous royal session of 19 November, the ministers promised the parlementaires that the Estates General would convene by 1792 – if the justices would ratify a series of loans designed, in combination with Brienne's administrative reforms, to restore the state's financial health. But the authorities' attempt to secure passage of the first of these loans without allowing the customary judicial vote on the measure led the duc d'Orléans to denounce the proceedings as illegal to the king's face. The following day Orléans was exiled for his temerity, and two of the more defiant magistrates were incarcerated. Over the next six months, as relations between the monarch and his most influential court of law deteriorated yet further, and as the provincial parlements multiplied their attacks on "ministerial despotism," the constitutional crisis ineluctably deepened. By early May 1788, the Paris Parlement, echoed in much of this by its provincial counterparts, had progressed from a denunciation of the specific ministerial actions of 19–20 November 1787 to a more sweeping condemnation of the "despotic" *lits de justice, lettres de cachet*, and taxes of the old regime and to an invocation of the "fundamental laws" supposedly hedging in the prerogatives of French kings. Clearly, the government, finding its revenues, its reforms, and its very legitimacy called into question by these pronouncements, would have to strike back if it were to have any chance to survive.

And strike back the government did, endeavoring with its May edicts

97 Ralph W. Greenlaw, "Pamphlet Literature in France During the Period of the Aristocratic Revolt (1787–1788)," *Journal of Modern History* 29 (1957), p. 353.

to break the parlementary opposition for good.[98] Henceforth, a plenary court made up of the senior Parisian parlementaires, the princes and peers, and divers other notables was to assume the parlementary role of endorsing fiscal acts and, for that matter, all legislation affecting the kingdom as a whole. The new tribunal could protest royal edicts up to a point, but in essence the sovereign courts' political role would be nullified. The parlements would also be diminished in their purely judicial function, for they were now to share it with newly created *grands bailliages* at the intermediate level and with presidial courts in first instance. Concomitantly, seigneurial courts and certain specialized tribunals would be weakened or eliminated altogether, and a new judicial ordinance, long meditated by Lamoignon, would mitigate the rigors of criminal justice.

The finance minister and the keeper of the seals envisioned these reforms as opening new careers to the jurists, barristers, and proctors of the Third Estate and as facilitating justice for all litigants. And of course the May edicts were but one way in which the authorities, at the eleventh hour of the ancien régime, were desperately attempting both to enhance the efficiency of the Bourbon state and to involve the respectable citizenry in its designs. Brienne, Lamoignon, and their associates were, in these same hectic days, trying to renovate the military, reduce venality and establish modern accounting procedures in the administration of finances, invigorate agriculture and commerce, and grant a civil status to the country's Protestants. Additionally, and as the first fruit of their sweeping overhaul of royal finances, they could unveil the confidence-building capstone of all their efforts: a published budget for 1788. Through such an innovative program, might it not be possible for the French government to carry on its daunting international mission (and realize a new legitimacy at home as well) without sacrificing absolutism altogether?

Yet, once again, the evidence suggests that both the reform-minded crown and its immediate antagonists in the judiciary were being rapidly overtaken by an awakening political "nation" whose constitutional demands would soon leave monarch and magistrates far behind. Even before the *séance royale* of 19 November 1787, that attentive British observer Arthur Young, moving in fashionable circles at Paris, was discovering a general conviction that the "existing ministry" should "immediately call to its aid the Estates General." At almost exactly the same time, the abbé Morellet, even though one of Brienne's most loyal collaborators, was informing the finance minister flatly: "We need some bar to the repetition of abuses: we need the Estates General or the equivalent. That is what

98 Egret, *French Prerevolution*, pp. 145–69, discusses the government's promulgation of those edicts and the controversy to which they gave rise.

people everywhere are saying."[99] And soon after the dramatic session of
19 November, a perturbed Mercy-Argenteau wrote to Kaunitz: "Despite
the wealth of France, nothing is in its place. The revolution that is so
evident in the national spirit threatens some momentous change in the
constitutional principles of the monarchy."[100] Austria's high envoy at
Versailles could not have been more prescient.

The execution of the government's coup against the refractory judiciary
provoked widespread outrage in society. The most luminous members
of what now became known as the antigovernment Patriot party – Lafayette, Target, Barnave, Bergasse, Condorcet, Mirabeau – disparaged
the plenary court as an emanation of "despotism," whatever reservations
they might have harbored about the old magistracy.[101] After a slight
decline during the winter months, the output of pamphlets discoursing
on constitutional questions registered a "spectacular upswing" in May
1788 and thereafter, according to Greenlaw. He counted 534 of them
during May–September 1788, and in reading them was struck by "the
overwhelming preponderance of opinion hostile to the policies and activities of the royal government."[102] Many of the pamphleteers scoured
French history for precedents regarding past convocations of the Estates
General and other representative bodies that could serve now as arguments
for demanding the restoration of the nation's political rights.[103] In addition, numerous polemicists, by fusing "historic-mythic" concepts of
the "nation" with Enlightenment notions about the "general will" and
the "social contract," developed a constitutional schema that would require the king, hitherto the embodiment of the absolute state, to rule
henceforth in partnership with the French people.[104] Reinforcing this
ideological onslaught on absolutism were periodicals such as the *Gazette
de Leyde*, which now likened French Patriots to the revolutionaries in
America and to the Patriots in Poland and published large numbers of
antigovernment resolutions.[105]

It was precisely the censorious resolutions issuing from assemblages of
incensed notables all over the realm that most concerned Louis XVI's
advisers. At its quinquennial convocation of 1788, a formerly docile clergy

99 Ibid., p. 108.
100 Cited in Harris, *Necker and the Revolution of 1789*, p. 280.
101 Egret, *French Prerevolution*, pp. 161–62.
102 Greenlaw, "Pamphlet Literature in France," p. 353.
103 This is pointed up by Kenneth Margerison, "History, Representative Institutions, and
    Political Rights in the French Pre-Revolution (1787–1789)," *French Historical Studies*
    15 (Spring 1987), pp. 68–98.
104 See again Furet, *Interpreting the French Revolution*, pp. 33–36; and Margerison, "His-
    tory, Representative Institutions, and Political Rights," pp. 72–73.
105 Popkin, "The *Gazette de Leyde* and French Politics Under Louis XVI," esp. pp. 102–
    104.

not only refused adamantly to give the crown anything like the eight million livres requested from it as its "free gift" but also endorsed remonstrances that anathematized the plenary court, called for the reinstatement of the parlements, and implored Louis XVI to "listen to the voice of the nation" in formulating all of his policies. Noblemen convened in Brittany and Béarn castigated the ministers and their reforms; the Bretons resolved as well to send delegates to Versailles to petition for retraction of the May edicts. In Provence, the celebrated *avocat* Pascalis prevailed, first on the general assembly of the Third Estate of Provence and then the intermediary committee of the recently revived Provençal Estates, to protest the ministers' stroke against the magistracy. In Dauphiné, the representatives of the three orders who met without governmental authorization at the Château de Vizille in July demanded not only the restoration of the old magistracy but also the revival of their own Estates and – ultimate of ultimates – the Estates General. The authorities could still rely on troops to secure order in those areas where elitist defiance of the royal will touched off popular rioting. Yet such action by itself could not restore ministerial credibility in the public sphere.

In view of all this, it would have been astonishing had Loménie de Brienne and Lamoignon been able to rally the designated judges of their plenary court and *grands bailliages* and the legal auxiliaries of those new tribunals to the crown's banner; and in fact they achieved little success on this front.[106] The senior parlementaires at Paris and many of the other notables who were supposed to serve on the plenary court refused to have anything to do with this "illegal" creation. As for the justices of the *grands bailliages*, Philip Dawson has incisively described their dilemma:

The inner turmoil of conflicting duties, the anxiety over the future actions of parlements and royal ministers, and the factional divisions in the judicial profession were all intensified in their effects by being presented to public criticism. It was the explosion of pamphlets during the spring and summer of 1788 which especially marked the entrance of the leading bailliage magistrates on the political stage, where many of them were cruelly treated by the audience.... Although about half, perhaps more, of all the bailliage magistrates may have genuinely supported Lamoignon's entire program, a far greater number were profoundly troubled by the necessity of making an important political choice and frightened or irritated by the violence of political passions swirling around them.

As a result, most of the *grands bailliages* "moved from delay to equivocation, taking refuge in procedural formalities, registering the new measures while noting that they were forced to comply with the royal will, and avoiding any clear commitment throughout the summer."[107] Natu-

106 Egret, *French Prerevolution*, pp. 163–69.
107 Philip Dawson, *Provincial Magistrates and Revolutionary Politics in France, 1789–1795* (Cambridge, Mass.: Harvard University Press, 1972), pp. 149, 146–47.

rally, those jurists deprived wholly or in part of their powers by the May edicts – the provincial parlementaires, for example, and the members of presidial courts not elevated to *grand bailliage* status – added their voices to the antiministerial hue and cry. Nor did the crown win greater adherence from the barristers, some of whose major urban confraternities trumpeted their solidarity with the stricken parlements.[108] The judicial reforms of 1788 were, in essence, stillborn.

The government only further undercut its own position in the crisis of 1787–88 by courting public opinion (as it patently felt it had to) through hired publicists.[109] Some of these propagandists optimistically predicted the transformation of the plenary court into a representative body, an "intermediary committee" of the Estates General; a greater number of them assailed the parlementaires and even set upon clerics, high nobles, and the wealthy in general as foes of the public interest while lauding the king and his advisers as the true friends of the people. Yet how long a step was it from all this to a rediscovery of theories of popular sovereignty? The king's own polemicists assuredly helped to prepare the way for the abbé Siéyès and other purposefully revolutionary writers and politicians in the years to come.

By 30 June 1788 the Parisian bookseller and journalist S.-P. Hardy was fearing the advent of civil war in the kingdom, and in July, Mercy-Argenteau wrote to Joseph II that "the French nation at this moment is seized with such a spirit of *vertige* that it is difficult to say on which side there is more delirium . . . on the part of those who should command, or on the part of those who ought to obey."[110] In such impossible circumstances, absolutism in France had to retreat – had, in the end, to sign its own death warrant. By 5 July, the government in a conciliar decree was inviting "all Frenchmen, through provincial Estates or assemblies, to make known their opinions on the appropriate rules to be followed" in the summoning of the Estates General. The harried finance minister was apparently still hoping to stave off immediate recourse to this institution; but as July faded into August, the crown's irredeemable loss of credit, registered as we have seen on the indispensable stock exchange, finally caught up with Loménie de Brienne. On 8 August, a royal edict informed the nation that the Estates General would convene on 1 May 1789, and on 16 August, yet another decree, in effect announcing the government's

---

108 Egret, *French Prerevolution*, pp. 164–69.
109 As pointed up in ibid., pp. 161–62; by Van Kley in "Jansenist Constitutional Legacy in the French Prerevolution"; and by Gruder, "The Bourbon Monarchy: Reforms and Propaganda at the End of the Old Regime," in Baker, ed., *The Political Culture of the Old Regime*, esp. pp. 368–69.
110 Hardy and Mercy-Argenteau are cited in Harris, *Necker and the Revolution of 1789*, pp. 282 and 280, respectively.

"temporary" bankruptcy, also promised the crown's creditors that the upcoming assembly of the kingdom's Estates would permanently secure their investments. Not long after having thus intertwined fiscal and constitutional issues in the eyes of the nation, the cardinal-minister gave way to Necker.[111]

Yet the fabric of the Bourbon state's sociopolitical failure over the period from 1774 to 1788 was necessarily woven of social as well as of financial and constitutional threads. Accordingly, it is those threads of ongoing social evolution in the late ancien régime that must now engage our attention.

THE PROBLEM OF SOCIETY

In the years after Louis XVI's accession, as during the preceding century or so, the absolutist and globally oriented French state provided the basic prerequisites for (and principal motive force behind) the modernization of domestic elite society. The research of the Labrousse school may have fixed this as a time of "intercyclical depression" for the French economy as a whole; yet French overseas and European trade, depressed during the American war, picked up again after 1783, and French state finance necessarily remained a lucrative business throughout. As a result, numerous traders, tax collectors, and financiers, emulating earlier compatriots, made a virtue of state diplomatic necessity by purchasing their way into the nobility. Yet if the government in this way contributed to the further development of a "society of notables" whose public opinion camouflaged socially progressive and socially conservative points of view, it ensured by the same token the survival of privileged *corps* feeding on state administration and finance and harboring their own clashing social perspectives. Thus, the reforming ministers of this era had to deal simultaneously with public opinion and private interests and with socially innovative and socially preservative attitudes that heralded genuine social polarization within the elite. Absolutism thereby conjured up its own social nemeses in the 1770s and 1780s.

Of course, the ongoing modernization of the elite meant, to begin with, that the shift from old to more recent noblesse was continuing within the civilian and armed services of the government. François Bluche has clearly projected this as a trend for the entire eighteenth century in the bureaux of the secretaries of state at Versailles, even though his prosopographical research has focused primarily on the secretaries holding

111 Egret, *French Prerevolution*, pp. 183–85.

office under Louis XIV.[112] Gruder has demonstrated a similar tendency among the intendants. "At the end of the eighteenth century," she has observed, "more of Louis XVI's intendants were newer to the nobility and to the robe and pen" than had been true of their predecessors under the aging Louis XIV, "and they were still in the process of being assimilated and accepted in the highest ranks of the social hierarchy."[113] It might be impossible to document a shift from relatively old to relatively new nobility in the high judiciary during the eighteenth century, but even here, the last fifteen years of the old regime reveal a magistracy more intent on aggrandizing power within familial "dynasties" of the robe than on boasting escutcheons of "ancient" lineage.[114] Finally, there is the case of the army. As David Bien and Emile Léonard, among others, have convincingly shown, noble officers whose imposing genealogies belied their straitened economic circumstances directed their frustration not so much at bourgeois aspirants to placement or promotion within the army as at the wealthy *anoblis* whose easy purchases of officers' posts were (they charged) adulterating the spirit of the ranks. Here, too, then, the shifting of influence from venerable to recent noblesse was the cutting issue: the notorious *loi Ségur* of 1781 specifically targeted *anoblis* and not bourgeois as such.[115]

Thus, noblemen of recent bourgeois extraction were parlaying their capital into advancement within the officialdom of prerevolutionary France. At the same time, aspiring commoners were continuing to break into the lower echelons of administrative, judicial, and military service (and into the Second Estate itself) by turning to this purpose wealth earned in commerce, manufacturing, stock exchange manipulations, and the management of royal funds. In his celebrated treatise of 1784 on French finances, Necker estimated that more than four thousand offices at that time conferred hereditary nobility upon Frenchmen, either at the time of purchase, or after a period of service, or in the second or third generation. Bien has calculated that 2,477 heads of bourgeois families bought themselves into the elite during the 1774–89 era.[116] In the bellwether case of the *secrétaires du Roi*, Bien has been able to uncover 266 purchases of these coveted sinecures at Paris and about 600 in the provinces during

---

112 Refer again to Bluche, "Social Origins of the Secretaries of State," pp. 90, 95–96. See also his "L'Origine sociale du personnel ministériel français au XVIIIe siècle," in *Bulletin de la Société d'Histoire Moderne* (1957), pp. 7–12.

113 Gruder, *Royal Provincial Intendants*, pp. 205–6.

114 Information on this point is marshaled in Stone, *French Parlements*, pp. 28–45.

115 See again Bien, "La Réaction aristocratique avant 1789," pp. 23–48 and 505–34; and Léonard, "La Question sociale dans l'armée française," pp. 135–49.

116 As cited in Behrens, *Society, Government and the Enlightenment*, p. 52.

the final fifteen years of the old regime, and has found nearly all the buyers, as before 1774, to have been commoners.[117] It was altogether foreseeable that William Doyle should have found the prices of "certain ennobling offices in towns where bourgeois capital was abundant" to be "soaring" on the eve of the Revolution; as he inferred from his data, the "demand for ennoblement was positively growing" among Louis XVI's good bourgeois subjects.[118]

The mania for nobility that gripped opulent commoners in the twilight years of the ancien régime evidenced itself in various ways. Attesting to the lure of elite status were the bourgeois purchases of seigneuries, the marrying off of bourgeois daughters to the sons of penurious but pedigreed rural squires, and the unabashed bourgeois aping of noble fashion and fanfare.[119] In illustration of this last point, Patrice Higonnet has observed that "the names of commoners like Roland de la Platière, Creuzé de la Touche, Brissot de Warville, de la Révellière de Lépaux (all of them Girondins of sorts), or of Montagnards like Barère de Vieuzac, d'Anton, de Robespierre, and de Saint-Just, or even of future *enragés* and feminists like Leclerc d'Oze, Taboureau de Montigny, Théroigne de Méricourt, and Etta Palm d'Aelders speak for themselves."[120] Indeed, they do.

Yet, again, it is well to keep uppermost in mind those successful men of the Third Estate who, through purchase of office, acquired noble status or set themselves on the road toward its acquisition; for, under Louis XVI as under his regal grandfather, these aspiring *officiers* figured centrally in that urban elite of luminaries that could never be altogether reconciled with the monarch's cherished vision of "prayers," "fighters," and "workers." When Adeline Daumard and François Furet detected the formation of such a nontraditional social grouping at Paris, and when Georges Lefebvre, Robert Darnton, Olwen Hufton, Lynn Hunt, Daniel Roche, and a host of other specialists discerned a like development at Orléans, Montpellier, Bayeux, Troyes and Rheims, Bordeaux, Dijon, Châlons-sur-Marne, and elsewhere, they were plainly describing a process as characteristic of the 1770s and 1780s as it had been of the 1750s and 1760s.

It may be true, as Roche has maintained, that the *officiers* and other notables whose public responsibilities, urban investments, and intellectual pursuits brought them frequently together in the scientific and literary academies of the era were not fundamentally alienated from the political

117 Refer again to Bien, "Secrétaires du Roi," pp. 153–68.
118 Doyle, *Origins of the French Revolution*, p. 130.
119 Elinor Barber has presented much literary evidence to this effect in *The Bourgeoisie in 18th Century France* (Princeton, N.J.: Princeton University Press, 1955), esp. chap. 4.
120 Higonnet, *Class, Ideology, and the Rights of Nobles*, pp. 49–50.

and social structures of their age.[121] What is indisputable is that these noble and bourgeois elitists loomed very large in that novel tribunal of public opinion that the ministers of prerevolutionary France had ever more zealously to woo. Undeniably, they furnished some of the crown's most accomplished administrators and technical advisers; they counted in their ranks (most notably at Paris) increasing numbers of *rentiers* holding shares in the royal debt;[122] and they sponsored some of the principal forums in which talented and educated Frenchmen could debate the compelling public issues of the day. It was from their milieu that Turgot thought of recruiting, and Necker, Calonne, and Brienne actually did recruit, a fair number of the provincial assemblymen whose institutions were designed to coordinate more closely the government and the governed in this land. It was from these notables, moreover, that Louis XVI's ministers hoped to elicit an especially positive response as they drafted preambles to royal acts explicating the meliorist intentions behind those acts. And, most critically of all, perhaps, it was from these luminaries' quarter that issued quite a few of the "Notables" called by Calonne to Versailles in late 1786 and early 1787 to weigh his proposed solutions to the crown's mounting problems.

What is especially fascinating in this last connection is the way in which the "first" Assembly of Notables betrayed opposing views on the matter of social privilege that would soon tear the country's elite apart. On the one hand, Gruder, who has of late been thoroughly reappraising Calonne's convocation, has argued that, for the Notables in early 1787, the term *noblesse* "was a covering term for the new ruling class they intended to constitute in the provinces" as well as (presumably) at the center of state power. In Gruder's rendering, the Notables were looking optimistically ahead to a society in France that was to be "rigidly divided" into two basic groups: "those of rank, property, and power – nobles and clergy, public officials, landowners, even businessmen – who were educated, reasonable, by tradition or culture trained to govern, [and] those who engaged in physical labor, in mechanical work or in vile trades, uneducated, uncultivated, prone to unreason and disorder."[123]

121 Roche, "Académies et politique au siècle des lumières: Les enjeux pratiques de l'immortalité," in Baker, ed. *Political Culture of the Old Regime*, esp. pp. 340–43.
122 On this important subject, see Michel Vovelle and Daniel Roche, "Bourgeois, Rentiers, and Property Owners: Elements for Defining a Social Category at the End of the Eighteenth Century," in Jeffry Kaplow, *New Perspectives on the French Revolution* (New York: John Wiley and Sons, 1965), pp. 25–46; Roche, *The People of Paris* (Berkeley: University of California Press, 1987), esp. pp. 79–82; and Weir, "Tontines, Public Finance, and Revolution," pp. 122–24.
123 Gruder, "Class and Politics in the Pre-Revolution: The Assembly of Notables of 1787," in E. Hinrichs et al., eds., *Vom Ancien Régime zur Französischen Revolution*, pp. 229–30. She has enlarged upon these ideas in "A Mutation in Elite Political Culture: The

What have we here, if not a schema of notables and nobodies faithfully reflecting realities already in place in many communities of the realm? It is surely arguable that the most progressive Notables were prepared to apply this vision to France as a whole – with the accompanying understanding that the new political elite of *notabilité* would speak for the French king as well as for the French people. And indeed, once the citizens of this land had navigated the treacherous and incarnadined waters of the revolutionary era, this was largely the way they would order their society and its politics. The problem lay, of course, with the interim period. As Michael Fitzsimmons has pointed out in a cursory but telling critique of Gruder's scholarship on the Notables, many of that body's members harbored behind their constitutional liberalism a stubborn adherence to privilege as the essential "superintending" principle of society. They could, for example, defend their own fiscal prerogative of undertaxation relative to rural plebeians in constitutional terms as a "bulwark against despotism"; but, if pressed to the wall, they would probably have also championed that privilege, like all privileges, in *social* terms as well. That this was the camouflaged stance of many (perhaps most?) of the Notables at their initial convocation early in 1787 could likely be inferred from their more explicit advocacy of estate and corporate privilege at their second meeting a year and a half later.[124]

And so there was a real potential for polarization within the elite. Yet the Bourbon state under Louis XVI continued to sanction (at least to a limited extent, in a certain bureaucratic fashion) the social evolution that its unending geopolitical and derivative financial needs so powerfully promoted. Of the 476 *lettres d'anoblissement* that Guy Chaussinand-Nogaret located in the registers of the Paris Chambre des Comptes for the period 1712–87, nearly 75 percent went to their affluent purchasers after 1760. During 1774–87, as during the 1760s, these expensive attestations of nobility witnessed more particularly to the increasingly utilitarian criteria of elite status in France. Administrators and men of business, artists and scientists were acquiring a nobility that the government no longer reserved (at least exclusively) to the martial and judicial professions.[125] Turgot was commenting upon one aspect of this evolutionary process when he observed in 1776 that "privilege" differentiated now between the "rich" and the "poor" rather than, as before, between "illustrious families" and "commoners." Eleven years later, in his *Considérations sur les richesses et la luxe*, Sénac de Meilhan made much the

French Notables and the Defense of Property and Participation, 1787," *Journal of Modern History* 56 (1984), pp. 598–634.

124 Michael P. Fitzsimmons, "Privilege and the Polity in France, 1786–1791," *American Historical Review* 92 (1987), pp. 274–75.

125 Chaussinand-Nogaret, "Aux Origines de la Révolution," esp. pp. 267–70.

same point, but with greater force. "Neither rank nor privilege," he declared, could now resist the "sovereign power" of wealth.[126] Yet, just as plainly, the *officier's* discharge of public responsibilities was advancing arm-in-arm with the possession of wealth as an attribute of the developmental elite of notables in the ancien régime. That, among many things, emerged clearly from the discourse of the Assembly of Notables in the late winter of 1786 and spring of 1787.

And so the government of Louis XVI, driven by the necessity inherent in its self-imposed international mission, continued to encourage the formation of a novel elite in France, and thereby consolidated the social base of the public opinion that challenged its administrative operations and undermined its constitutional and social philosophy. But this was only half of the process by which the Bourbon state helped to generate the social origins of its own revolutionary demise. The other half consisted in the fact that the monarchy, by continuing to finance its policies in part by selling an enhanced social status and various public functions to members of privileged *corps*, gave a new lease on life to a horde of special interests predisposed to obstruct the ministers' campaign for greater government efficiency.

Among those special interests, none, belike, was more immediately dangerous to the government than that represented by the financiers. Yet, in the final analysis, it was the revenue-hungry crown that had made it so. To take only the most notorious example: By selling nobility to the *fermiers-généraux* (86 percent of whom had gained access to the Second Estate by 1786), the authorities had deprived themselves in advance of the ability to discipline these individuals and divest them of their (frequently sizable) gains.[127] But to an extent varying, of course, with individual cases, nearly all traffickers in royal funds had become untouchable by the time of Louis XVI. And this cardinal fact of life became especially obvious whenever the finance ministers of the 1770s and 1780s, driven increasingly to distraction by the fiscal difficulties of the state, tried to remove these venal (and now frequently noble) accountants from power and rationalize administrative procedures. Naturally, Terray in 1774, Turgot in 1776, Necker in 1781, Le Fevre d'Ormesson in 1783, Calonne in 1787, and Loménie de Brienne the following year did not fall from grace exclusively because of the opposition they stirred up among the financiers; still, on each of those occasions this opposition played its role in the sorry denouement.[128]

---

126 Both Turgot and Sénac de Meilhan are quoted in Higonnet, *Class, Ideology, and the Rights of Nobles*, p. 47.

127 On the nobility of the *fermiers-généraux* in the 1780s, see Durand, *Les Fermiers-Généraux au XVIIIe siècle*, p. 295.

128 On Turgot, for instance, refer again to the works of Douglas Dakin and Edgar Faure already cited.

Of course, the financiers, whenever they came under ministerial fire, would argue that their collecting and disbursing of royal revenues certified them as unwaveringly loyal to the crown. The kingdom's most privileged courts of law, the parlements, proclaimed a similar fidelity; yet they, too, by obstructing so much of the government's modernizing legislation during the 1770s and 1780s, helped to bring down the reformist cause and, with it, the entire ancien régime. At Paris and in the provinces, these high tribunals championed to the bitter end the privileges and corporate structure of the old society. In 1776, Antoine-Louis Séguier, the redoubtable avocat-général of the Paris Parlement, reacted in the royal presence to Turgot's campaign against the prerogatives of noble landowners and the Parisian guilds by exalting all privileged groups:

All your subjects, Sire, are divided into as many different bodies as there are different conditions and professions in the Kingdom: the Clergy, the Nobility, the sovereign courts, the inferior tribunals, the universities, the academies, the companies of finance, the companies of commerce, indeed living bodies in all parts of the State, which one can regard as the links in a great chain, the first one of which is in the hands of Your Majesty, as chief and sovereign administrator of all that constitutes the body of the Nation.[129]

A few years later, one of Séguier's professional counterparts at Besançon, in Franche-Comté, the erudite François-Nicolas-Eugène Droz des Villars, said much the same thing in poking avuncular fun at the egalitarian philosophy of his century:

I cannot make myself believe that our ancestors were imbeciles and that we should be on guard against imitating them. Equality, uniformity, liberty: these are grand words, but how to apply them and reconcile them with the monarchy, subordination, customs founded upon local circumstances.... I leave all these grand views to more clever minds...[130]

All of the parlements, in expostulating with the crown about its eleventh-hour reforms in 1787–88, were inspired by this antiquated vision of society. Typical was the sovereign court at Rouen as it riposted against the authors of the May edicts of 1788:

These rash innovators have dared to advance the fatal project of bringing everything into a system of *unity* which, no doubt rejecting the diversity of social ranks, of privileges, of prerogatives, of capitulations of provinces and cities, as it must reject the diversity of customary laws, will leave all France no longer with a cherished King and faithful Subjects but rather with a feared master and debased, cowering slaves.[131]

The magistrates did not, as some historians have charged, advocate an "aristocratic revolution" in the final years of the old regime; they had

---

129 Cited in Stone, *Parlement of Paris*, pp. 122–23. On the *corps* in general, see William H. Sewell, Jr., *Work and Revolution in France: The Language of Labor from the Old Regime to 1848* (Cambridge: Cambridge University Press, 1980), esp. pp. 1–77.
130 Quoted in Stone, *French Parlements*, p. 171.
131 Cited in ibid., p. 174 (italics in original).

too much of a stake in the status quo to endorse insurgency on the part of any order in society.[132] Still, in a sense, what they did cling to in these critical years – namely, a world that must remain atomized into privileged groups of every imaginable description – was basically inimical to the survival of the monarchy as these judges had always known it. For how could Turgot or Necker, a tardily reformist Calonne or Loménie de Brienne, have possibly slain the hydra of parasitical privilege that was suffocating the monarchy? No one has explained their dilemma more lucidly than their contemporary Rabaut Saint-Etienne:

> Every time one creates a corporate body with privileges one creates a public enemy because a special interest is nothing else than this. . . . Imagine a country where there are a great many corporate bodies. The result is that . . . one hears talk of nothing but rights, concessions, immunities, special agreements, privileges, prerogatives. Every town, every community, every province, every ecclesiastical or judicial body, has its interest to defend in this confusion. . . . A minister who wants to disentangle the wires does not know where to begin because as he touches them he makes the interest cry out to which they are attached.[133]

The special interests indeed cried out in this fashion whenever menaced by reformism under Louis XVI, and all too frequently they could depend on the sovereign courts of the kingdom to espouse their cause. Yet the fact remains that the *corps* of *privilégiés* in France had purchased (and often been compelled to repurchase) their prerogatives and influence from the absolutist government itself. Now, that government was patently unable to reverse this insidious process.

The parlementaires sometimes found it useful to remind the crown of its folly. To cite just one example: In defending the Parisian guilds against Turgot's attempt to abolish them in 1776, Avocat-Général Séguier of the Paris Parlement wryly observed to Louis XVI that

> the price of a great portion of these masterships . . . has been paid directly to the royal treasury, and if the other portion has been given to the societies, it has been used to reimburse the loans that those societies had to make to the State; that resource, which the government has perhaps availed itself of too frequently, but which has always been useful in urgent circumstances, will from now on be closed to Your Majesty, and the public revenues will themselves be quite considerably reduced.[134]

Séguier, it is true, was ignoring here the fact that the legislation in question provided in various ways for the liquidation of the guilds' debts; still, in a more general sense, he had palpably scored. Turgot, reformer that he

---

132 Egret, *French Prerevolution*, p. 203, for example, attributes this design at least to some of the parlementaires in 1787–88; but my own research (e.g., Stone, *French Parlements*, pp. 94–106 and 170–207) shows, fairly persuasively I think, that neither the Parisian nor the provincial jurists were so motivated.
133 Quoted in Behrens, *Ancien Régime*, p. 179.
134 Cited in Stone, *Parlement of Paris*, p. 125.

was, would have dearly loved to buy all *corps* out of their special concessions, for he realized all too well how effectively those privileges bolstered
opposition to royal policies and, in so doing, denied the government
some of the revenue it might otherwise have collected. But, alas, he had
not the wherewithal to do so. And even if he had, another question would
have been lying in wait for him: whether his master the king could have
resigned himself to a world in which *privilège* no longer served to anchor
that hierarchy, that inequality in whose venerable tradition he had since
childhood been socialized.

Thus the crown in large measure engendered the social origins of its
own demise. By conferring venal posts and their associated public duties
and influence on its subjects in such huge numbers, it consolidated the
social bases of two worlds: that of public opinion and that of private
corporate interests. And, just as an incipient constitutional liberalism and
clashing social notions within the former world tended to chip away at
the elitist ideological solidarity undergirding the ancien régime in France,
so also did analogous developments within the latter, associated *monde*
of privileged corporations.

That public opinion had for some time been articulating subversive
constitutional ideas and (at least through the vehicle of the Assembly of
Notables) disclosed ambivalence on social issues we noted earlier. However, that a number of the privileged corporations (in addition to the
academies and other cultural bodies) were similarly being tugged and
pulled in opposing ideological directions – especially in the "prerevolution" of 1787–88 – requires a degree of elaboration at this point. Assuredly
the parlements, by lashing out at the ministers and their "despotic" taxes,
lettres de cachet, and *lits de justice* in 1787–88, strode even farther down
radical paths than they had before. Moreover, at Paris in particular, the
junior parlementary chambers in these stirring times rang with youthful
magistrates' idealistic renunciations of selfish corporate privilege and invocations of the reawakening nation's rights.[135] But equally interesting
(if not yet as methodically studied) were similar ideological tendencies in
the lower echelons of French venal officialdom. Gail Bossenga, for instance, has found that on the eve of revolution growing numbers of the
trésoriers de France staffing the *bureaux des finances* in many communities
of the realm reacted to the crown's manipulation of their offices (and of
the capital sunk in those posts) by jettisoning their old sociopolitical
notions altogether. These *officiers*, at least – and how many functionaries

---

135 The radical ideas embedded in the parlementary discourse of 1787–88 are discussed in
   Stone, *French Parlements*, esp. chaps. 2 and 3; but see also the analyses of judicial
   radicalism in William Doyle's and Jean Egret's books upon the parlements at Bordeaux
   and Grenoble, respectively.

at other levels of the bureaucracy did likewise? – began to think of *privilège* as most properly rewarding service to the state, and of control of that state as destined, rightly, to be vested in the "people."[136] The "prerevolution" hence induced some *officiers* to set forth radical sociopolitical canons. And had not such canons long inhered, in a way, in the very exercise of public office in France?

To some extent the worlds of public opinion and corporate opinion actually joined hands in the crisis of 1787–88 and challenged outright the constitutional (if not yet the social) tenets of the monarchy. They did so, driven by the inexorable logic of the kingdom's situation, despite the personal misgivings of many of the individuals caught up in their coalition (most notably, if not exclusively, the parlementaires). That both worlds, furthermore, were populated (especially at Paris) by growing numbers of *rentiers* holding shares in the burgeoning royal debt made their tactical alliance in 1787–88 all the more dangerous to the crown.

Some historians, desirous of preserving the primacy of social factors in their interpretations of the Revolution's causes, have sought for and played up ways in which progressive and reactionary notables and *privilégiés* flew at each other's throats in French society prior to 1788–89. And, to be sure, it is not only in the situations discussed above that we can descry signs of nascent social polarization within this kingdom's elite. Georges Lefebvre, we recall, never lost sight of the "privilege of nobility" that remained a "powerful internal barrier" within the "oligarchy" of clerical, noble, and bourgeois notables that he discovered at prerevolutionary Orléans.[137] Again, noble and bourgeois academicians exchanging intellectual views at Dijon, Châlons-sur-Marne, Bordeaux, and twenty-nine other communities studied by Daniel Roche could not ignore and apparently never challenged the "barrier of privilege" within their learned societies.[138] Additionally, the move toward professionalism within many of the institutions of the old regime, by excluding from those bodies Frenchmen not deemed to be suitably prepared to exercise whatever corporate functions they discharged, sparked friction between those within such privileged institutions and those on the outside. Thus, some bourgeois notables doubtlessly resented their exclusion from parlements that insisted anew on genealogical and other qualifications for membership.[139] The *loi Ségur* of 1781, insisting as it did on the possession of at

---

136 Refer once again to Bossenga, "From *Corps* to Citizenship," esp. pp. 637–42.
137 See again Lefebvre, "Urban Society in the Orléanais," pp. 50–51.
138 Refer again to Roche, *Le Siècle des lumières en province*, pp. 255, 393–94.
139 These resentments, and related sentiments, are explored in a number of works. See, for example: Maurice Gresset, *Le Monde judiciaire à Besançon, de la conquête par Louis XIV à la Révolution française, 1674–1789*, 2 vols. (Lille: Service de réproduction des thèses de l'Université, 1975), Vol. 1: pp. 1161–95; L. R. Berlanstein, *The Barristers*

least four generations of nobility as a prerequisite for an officer's commission in the army, antagonized some *anoblis* and bourgeois notables.[140] And the crown, it now seems, incurred the enmity of some of the great sword families at Versailles by shutting them out of the king's councils, bureaucracy, and armed forces.[141] It is also plausible to assume that those bourgeois able to translate wealth gained in trade or royal finance into instant nobility (often through purchase of the office of *secrétaire du Roi*) aroused the envy of less opulent squires and bourgeois, and that respectable French people frequently disliked each other in other connections as well.[142]

Nevertheless, it appears in retrospect that such tensions, however meaningful they may have been as harbingers of the 1788–89 struggle within the elite over privilege as the key organizational principle of Gallic society, did not in actuality constitute autonomous causes of revolution in France. As François Furet shrewdly pointed out, many of these frictions derived from "the increasing inadequacy of the relatively narrow mechanism of social mobility developed by the absolutist State within the framework of the society of orders."[143] The crown, in other words, by sanctioning something like "a new ruling class by State fiat and money"[144] out of sheer fiscal need – thereby contravening its own historic adherence to the hoary schema of three estates – encouraged nobles and bourgeois to argue among themselves about just how a ruling class should be constituted, both locally and nationally, in their country. This would come into its own as a catalytic issue once absolutism had collapsed in 1788. For the years prior to 1788–89, however, it is best to reiterate our thesis that the government itself generated such social origins of revolution as existed, first by consolidating the social bases of public opinion and

of *Toulouse in the Eighteenth Century (1740–1793)* (Baltimore: Johns Hopkins University Press, 1975), pp. 11–23; Doyle, *Parlement of Bordeaux*, pp. 160–61, 189; and Egret, *Parlement de Dauphiné*, 2: 85–89.

140 See Bien, "The Army in the French Enlightenment: Reform, Reaction, and Revolution," *Past and Present* 85 (1979), pp. 68–98; and Corvisier, *Armies and Societies in Europe*, esp. pp. 169–70.

141 Daniel L. Wick, "The Court Nobility and the French Revolution: The Example of the Society of Thirty," *Eighteenth-Century Studies* 13 (Spring 1980), pp. 263–84; and *A Conspiracy of Well-Intentioned Men: The Society of Thirty and the French Revolution* (New York: Garland, 1987).

142 On the widespread resentment aroused by the *secrétaires du Roi* in the upper and middle reaches of French society, see Bien, "Manufacturing Nobles: The Chancelleries in France to 1789," *Journal of Modern History* 61 (1989), esp. pp. 445–46. Colin Lucas, in "Nobles, Bourgeois, and the Origins of the French Revolution," has cited other signs of friction among the notables of prerevolutionary France. So, too, has Doyle, in *Origins of the French Revolution*, chaps. 6 and 7.

143 Furet, *Interpreting the French Revolution*, p. 108.

144 Ibid, p. 107.

corporate or private opinion and then by rendering itself vulnerable (through fiscal exhaustion) to attack from these (eventually coalescing) quarters of elite society.

Let us sum up. Over the years from 1774 to 1788 in France, constitutional issues joined with social issues and – in particular after Jacques Necker's fall from power – with financial issues to overwhelm Louis XVI's reformist ministers, one after another. Turgot, to begin with, was disgraced in 1776 due at least in part to misgivings in high places about the constitutional and social implications of his reforms. But a more pivotal juncture for the monarchy likely came in 1781, when Necker was undone by a king and by intendants, judges, and courtiers who purportedly saw his provincial assemblies, *vingtièmes*, and *Compte rendu* as constitutionally subversive and by financiers and courtiers whose private interests were menaced by his administrative reforms. Six years later, Calonne was toppled by a similar confluence of issues, to which a genuine fiscal crisis was now added. In view of Necker's resounding failure, it is hard to see how Calonne could have forever averted recourse to a consultative body like the Assembly of Notables even if (uncharacteristically) he had resolved at the outset of his ministry to revive the Genevan's confidence-building policies; that he did not resolve to do so merely affected the timing of the crisis to come. Once Calonne had been forced to call the Notables to Versailles, his decision in March 1787 to appeal over their heads to public opinion alienated not only the Notables themselves but also Louis XVI, who saw such an appeal as subversive of his authority, and the privileged classes, which found themselves singled out for attack in that appeal. Finally, Loménie de Brienne and his collaborator Lamoignon were overthrown by a crisis in which fiscal, constitutional, and social issues had become so tightly interwoven as to deprive the crown of its last shreds of domestic legitimacy and, thus, of its very solvency.

Yet, in the final analysis we need to situate the converging fiscal, constitutional, and social developments of the 1774–88 period in an international context. For we cannot help recalling (1) that a staggering 75 percent or more of state fiscal needs projected for 1788 was, directly or indirectly, related to war,[145] and (2) that similar fiscal needs had, right up to 1788, loomed behind much of France's sociopolitical evolution. And this in turn points to a crucial decision that Louis XVI would have to confront, once he had (with all too obvious distaste) recalled Necker to power. If he was prepared to abandon his kingdom's age-old pursuit of international greatness, he could avoid having to ask his subjects to continue subsidizing enormous government expenditures and thereby

145 See, for example, Goubert, *L'Ancien Régime*, Vol. 2: pp. 137–39.

avoid having to consult them on a broad range of public questions. But if, on the other hand, cleaving to his country's geopolitical traditions, he should opt for the alternative, he would then have to accommodate at least some of the sociopolitical ambitions of his most affluent, articulate, and enlightened subjects. And in that case, how far down the road of compromise Louis XVI would be willing to venture would be critical in determining how "revolutionary" France would have to become.

5

The onset of revolution: from August
1788 to October 1789

On the eve of the July Days of 1789, Georges Lefebvre contended, the French court "certainly intended to dissolve" the Estates General. The court, in this view, could rely henceforward upon the support of the parlements and "resign itself to bankruptcy."[1] Yet such conjecture seems wildly unrealistic when we regard the onset of the Revolution from a global-historical perspective. Any French monarch in late 1788 and 1789, not only Louis XVI, would have been impaled on the horns of a dilemma fairly reminiscent of that which had faced Charles I of England and strikingly anticipatory of that which would confront Nicholas II of Russia. In each of these situations the sovereign was challenged by history, by the conventions of his own upbringing, and by contemporary events to maintain the international credibility of his state; and yet to do so, in each situation, required his endorsement of domestic reforms inimical to the public philosophy by which he and his ancestors had always lived! Cruel predicaments, for sure – and, in the French case, this was the ultimate challenge looming behind the developments that took the Bourbon polity from the threshold of revolution in August 1788 into the initial stages of revolution proper by the summer and autumn of 1789.

We can best analyze those developments under four headings: (1) the critical geopolitical context of the events of 1788–89, (2) the failure of the king to compromise with the patriotic and progressive notables, (3) the polarization within the "respectable" ranks of society, and (4) the upheaval of the urban and rural masses. The task here is twofold: first, to discuss these explanatory factors in depth, and, second, to show how they interacted in such a fashion as to commit Louis XVI and his approximately twenty-eight million subjects to the rough and uncharted waters of revolutionary change.

1 As cited in Lefebvre, *Coming of the French Revolution*, p. 91.

196

THE CRITICAL GEOPOLITICAL CONTEXT

During the period extending from the French government's announcement of insolvency in August 1788 to the October Days of the following year, foreign affairs provided an ominous backdrop to politics in the Gallic kingdom. M. S. Anderson has commented that the "effective separation of the politics of eastern Europe from those of the west which became visible after 1762–63 began to disappear in the later 1780s. The outbreak of . . . war between Russia and the Ottoman empire . . . began a sequence of events which had produced by 1789–90, for the first time in a quarter of a century, a crisis of European as distinct from merely regional dimensions."[2] That France should have fallen into revolution in such a time of threatening European-wide instability only underscored its urgent need to resynchronize its governmental and social-elitist values and ambitions. There are signs, moreover, that Frenchmen came once again to perceive a challenge in this sphere. In other words, the politicization of society that took place during 1788–89 as a result of France's converging fiscal, constitutional, and social crises revived embers of popular patriotism that would blaze as of old in the years of *la grande nation* so soon to come.

As Bourbon absolutism was unhappily drifting on the shoals in France, Europe as a whole was becoming polarized between two potentially antagonistic power groupings. On the one hand there was the combination, prefigured in October 1787 and formalized in August 1788, of Britain and Prussia. On the other hand there was the older alliance of Austria and Russia that finally bore full fruit in 1788 with Joseph II's decision to join Catherine the Great in a military assault on Ottoman Turkey. The Austro-Russian initiative threatened to destabilize the power balance in eastern Europe radically; for that very reason (and because of the endemic Teutonic rivalry between Berlin and Vienna), there was a real possibility of the British and Prussians being drawn into war with St. Petersburg and Vienna over the Near East.[3]

It was equally clear that France, long accustomed to deeming itself arbiter of Europe, was utterly incapable of intervening on either side in this tense situation. Yet even if bankruptcy had not precluded an active French role in the international politics of the day, could the policy makers at Versailles have gravitated happily toward either of the coalitions now existing in Europe? On the one side, an Anglo-Prussian combination had mortified the French twice since midcentury. Now, Vergennes's succes-

---

2 Anderson, "European Diplomatic Relations, 1763–90," p. 274.
3 For a classic account of all this, see Sorel, *Europe and the French Revolution*, esp. pp. 502–5, 514–17.

sor, Armand-Marc, comte de Montmorin, held fast to the tradition of French distrust toward London and Berlin. The new foreign minister, according to Albert Sorel, could not help but suspect the eternal adversary across the Channel of working for the further diminution of French power. "This government is jealous of us and hates us," Montmorin wrote on 8 February 1789; "if we are friendly with them they will want to dominate us; if we resist their desires they will not scruple to betray us . . . " And the foreign minister was "no less suspicious of the secret machinations of Prussia."[4] Yet, on the other side, what reasons had France to endorse the actions of its nominal ally Austria and of voracious Russia in the Balkans? It is true that Montmorin's colleague Saint-Priest later claimed in his memoirs that he, the foreign minister, and all the other members of the Council save for Necker had advocated in the early months of 1789 Versailles's entrance into a "quadruple alliance" conjoining France, Austria, Russia, and Spain.[5] Such a diplomatic gambit by Versailles would no doubt have been one way of spiting the British and Prussian authors of the French humiliations of 1757 and 1787. Additionally, it would have subserved the purposes of those in France who still envisaged a vastly expanded sphere of Gallic influence in the eastern Mediterranean. Still, adoption of such a policy at Versailles could not have been squared with the age-old French commitment to the security of Turkey, Poland, and Sweden, and it would have redounded chiefly to the geopolitical advantage of the already dangerously successful Catherine of Russia.

Therefore, even a powerful, self-confident France in 1788–89 would have found it practically impossible, as it had always found it impossible, to master both the west Eurasian and the overseas spheres of power politics. (Britain, we recall, was already well on the way to becoming a global power at this time; for France to have taken on the Anglo-Prussian coalition in 1788–89 would thus have entailed, even more than before, a challenge to state power generated on the high seas as well as on the Continent.) In point of fact, however, the French were not even capable of essaying the impossible as they had so often essayed it in the past. The king, the queen, and Necker realized only too well that governmental insolvency ruled out for the time being any kind of French assertiveness in foreign affairs. Apart from the possibility that an alliance between Versailles and St. Petersburg could hinder rather than promote any French effort to mediate between Austria and Turkey, Marie-Antoinette reminded her countryman Mercy-Argenteau, it would require new expenditures on the French side and would give the impending Estates General

---

4 Ibid., pp. 514–15.
5 Harris discusses this in *Necker and the Revolution of 1789*, pp. 304–306.

an excellent excuse to trespass on the king's domain of foreign policy.[6]
As for Necker, Mercy-Argenteau reported somewhat simplistically and
unfairly to Joseph II in April 1789 that the director-general of finances
saw "only the financial problems to which he subordinates all else."[7]

It is certainly true that Necker, backed in this instance by the royal
couple, prevailed in conciliar debates over militants like Saint-Priest, who
held in 1789 (much as Nicholas II's advisers would contend, more effectively if not more wisely, in 1914) that resort to warfare abroad might
bank the rising fires of sociopolitical insurgency at home.[8] The Genevan
therefore succeeded in blocking what otherwise would have likely become
a costly new French involvement in the Byzantine alliance politics of the
Continent. This did not at all signify, however, that Necker, as the
statesman of the moment at Versailles, was unmindful of resplendent
French diplomatic tradition, or of the implications of stability at home
for power abroad. In the Council decree (*Résultat du Conseil*) of 27
December 1788, which attempted primarily to arbitrate the dispute within
the kingdom over procedural matters relating to the upcoming assembly
of the Estates, the director-general made this sanguine prophecy to the
monarch:

If there is established in Your Majesty's finances an immutable order, if confidence
soars, as one may hope, if all the forces of this great kingdom are become vitalized,
Your Majesty will enjoy in his external relations an ascendancy which adheres
much more to real and well-ordered power than to an authority that is irregular.[9]

And less than five months later, in his eagerly awaited address of 5 May
1789 to the Estates General of the realm, the Genevan returned to this
fundamental theme:

You will not forget that the financial needs of the government are not separate
from your own; they are one and the same because the expenditures for defense,
for policing the kingdom, treating the creditors of the government justly, rewarding truly meritorious service, and the needs of maintaining the dignity of
the foremost throne in Europe, all these expenditures ... concern the nation as
much as the monarch.

Necker somberly reminded his audience that modern warfare could not
be financed solely out of ordinary revenue; that if France should reenter
the lists of combat, loans would again be requisite; and that, as a result,

6 Ibid.
7 Ibid.
8 Saint-Priest, for one, was explicit on this point in his later memoirs and recalled as well
   that he had advanced the same argument eighteen months earlier in connection with the
   Dutch crisis. Ibid., p. 305.
9 Quoted in ibid., pp. 330–31.

the fiscal stability of the crown was a matter of national security and honor.[10]

Like Loménie de Brienne and Lamoignon before him in the turmoil of the "prerevolution," so now Necker in the opening months of the Revolution itself was both advocating and prophesying the convalescence of France at home and abroad. Yet all his exhortations and promises could not alter the brutal reality of French impotence in 1789. "The virtual paralysis of France as a factor in international relations," Anderson has noted, "did a great deal to free the hands of Britain and Prussia for possible action against Russia and Austria."[11] Moreover, by treating so timidly with Russia over its envisaged quadruple alliance and then lamely rejecting the concept, Versailles only excited contempt in the courts of Europe. Wrote French ambassador Ségur from St. Petersburg on 22 May 1789:

> By our rapprochement with Russia we have embittered the league (England, Prussia, Holland), Poland, Sweden, and Turkey. By not signing the alliance, we have given the two imperial courts a grievance. Thus we have got out of the alliance all the kicks and none of the halfpence. This is what our domestic troubles have brought us to. If England and Prussia are skilful, they can procure a peace advantageous to Russia, win her over, and completely overthrow our influence here.[12]

Ségur's anxiety over the possibility of a reconciliation between London and Berlin, on the one hand, and St. Petersburg, on the other, may not have been altogether unfounded: Mercy-Argenteau had voiced a similar concern in his correspondence with Austrian Chancellor Kaunitz four months earlier.[13] Yet the paramount fact here was not so much the diplomatic uncertainties attending the Near Eastern crisis as the utter inability of the erstwhile arbiter of Europe to have anything effective to say about it.

Those holding the diplomatic and military portfolios at Versailles – Montmorin, Saint-Priest, Puységur, and La Luzerne – must have tasted especially bitter frustration as events now unfolded rapidly in eastern Europe. In the spring of 1789, Joseph II's forces, rebounding from setbacks of the preceding year, again seized the offensive, sweeping through Turkish-held Serbia; by that autumn they would be in Belgrade. Sweden's daring attack on Russia's northwestern flank soon fizzled out, due as much to mutiny in Guastav III's army and to discontent within his kingdom as to Denmark's sudden strike against Sweden. Meanwhile, Catherine's gifted General Suvorov led a relentless Russian assault on Turkish holdings in eastern Romania. Sweden, deserted by its traditional French

10 Cited in ibid., pp. 421–23.
11 Anderson, "European Diplomatic Relations," p. 275.
12 As quoted in Sorel, *Europe and the French Revolution*, p. 517.
13 See Harris, *Necker and the Revolution of 1789*, pp. 305–306.

confederate in 1789, would feel fortunate to be able to make peace with Russia upon a status quo ante basis the next year; Turkey would cede its Black Sea territories down to the Dniester River to the Romanov colossus; and Poland would feel more vulnerable than ever to its rapacious neighbors.

As a result of these developments, Anderson has concluded:

The structure of international relations... had undergone at least two radical changes. Russia... had shown a greater capacity for territorial expansion than any other European state and was now the greatest power on the continent. [And] France... now appeared to be doomed for many years to relative impotence in international affairs; the real nature of the change she was undergoing was still misunderstood by nearly all observers.[14]

In the meantime, Austria, deserted by France in its rivalry with Prussia, had gained temporarily at the expense of Turkey (also abandoned by France) and might look to achieve further security in the always perilous reaches of eastern Europe through participation in a new partition of Poland – yet another polity for which Versailles could do nothing more. Prussia still had its pact with London, and at the same time was not about to be outdistanced in demanding new territorial concessions from the Poles. Finally, the British, able in 1789–90 to preserve a judicious distance between themselves and the inhabitants of the Continent, were moving ahead ever more resolutely into industrialization and consolidating their commercial links with the vast and inviting world beyond Europe.

Were the French to be left behind by the detested "modern Carthage" in the competition for the immeasurable resources of the extra-European world? And (in part as a result of *that* failure) would they have to acquiesce without a murmur in a continuing shift of power on the Continent from a Gallic west toward a Slavic-Teutonic east? Necker made it clear in the *Résultat du Conseil* of 27 December 1788 and in his address to the Estates General on 5 May 1789 that he was as sensitive as any of the other ministers to the worrying implications for French foreign policy of the sociopolitical crisis at home. International affairs challenged the director-general as manifestly in 1788–89 as they had ten years before. Moreover, just as in the heady days of the French intervention in British North America, so now ministerial efforts to resurrect the war-making capabilities of France could reasonably draw some encouragement from the xenophobic patriotism of the general public.

That patriotism, ever smoldering in the land, flamed defiantly as the prerevolutionary crisis ripened toward revolution. François Furet's perusal of 230 pamphlets published between February 1787 and March 1789

---

14 Anderson, "European Diplomatic Relations," p. 278. See also Ford, *Europe 1780–1830*, pp. 73–74, for additional discussion of these events.

has revealed a literate "nation" in the process of recovering its historical identity even as the king's ministers lurched desperately from one expedient to another:

"Germanic" freedoms, formerly a monopoly of the nobles, [had] become the mythic patrimony of the entire nation in its decisive struggle for *restoration*. More than half the pamphlets include references to the history of France, which, when analyzed in their context, amount in most cases to a genuine historical plea for the rights of the "nation." The powerful appeal of that new national awareness can also be read in the rejection of all foreign models, on the rare occasions when they are invoked. The authors of that literature invoke English, Swiss or Dutch institutions only to point out that they are inapplicable to France, given the country's special features... and its tradition.[15]

Furet was notably struck by the publicists' resolve to "make the history of France begin with the Franks." No longer would it be acceptable, as it had been for the abbé Dubos earlier in the century, to exalt the supposed link between the imperial tradition of ancient Rome and the unbridled sovereignty of the subsequent French kings. The "nation," a "human community both historical and mythical," had arisen out of a Frankish past, and must now reign in partnership with a king who would consequently remain "head" of that nation only in a carefully qualified sense.[16]

And from a "nation" enfranchised as never before could issue "nationalism," a force that has come, perhaps more than any other, to shape the world bequeathed to us by the French Revolution. It is true that the nationalism animating the French at the outset of their revolution was not the monstrous ideology we associate today with early twentieth-century fascism. Beatrice Hyslop's pioneering analysis of the *cahiers de doléances* of 1789 led her to conclude cautiously that the "*patrie* of most Frenchmen in 1789 was a unity of king and nation augmented by national traditions, enhanced by Gallicanism, conditioned by cosmopolitanism, reenforced by economic patriotism, and tempered by a peaceful and unaggressive spirit."[17] Yet how long could this liberated national consciousness retain its cosmopolitan and peaceable qualities in the crucible of Continental and extra-Continental power politics? Again, Hyslop:

The idea of the brotherhood of all men irrespective of nationality and patriotism was not remote from a belief in a national mission in the world's evolution, and a desire to extend the blessings of the French regime to other less fortunate nations. Several cahiers expressed the superiority of French institutions or looked upon France as the foremost power in Europe, or even of the entire world. A few

15 Furet, *Interpreting the French Revolution*, pp. 33–34 (italics in original).
16 Ibid., pp. 33–36.
17 Beatrice Hyslop, *French Nationalism in 1789 According to the General Cahiers* (New York: Octagon, 1968), pp. 194–95.

cahiers combined statements of superiority with suggestions that France was an example to the world.

This "messianic psychology," as Hyslop called it, already prefigured in 1789 the chauvinistic oratory of the Legislative Assembly of 1791–92 and, beyond that, the "spirit of war" of 1793–94.[18]

Moreover, a "messianic psychology" was already discernible in such institutions as the army and the National Assembly. Of course it is scarcely surprising that this should have been the case in the military. "Whether common or noble," Jean-Paul Bertaud has written, "those who occupied responsible posts [in the army] and thought of themselves as military professionals all wished to produce a professional army, thoroughly trained and ready for revenge against Prussia."[19] However divisive status considerations may have been within army officer ranks in 1788–89, the stinging memory of Rossbach tended contrariwise to forge within those ranks a patriotic consensus.

More intriguing were the sentiments of the neophyte politicians who transformed the Estates General into the National Assembly during the summer of 1789. It is perfectly true that the members of this body were little inclined at the time to hurl anathemas at the crowned heads of Europe. They had more pressing problems upon their hands, including the drafting of a constitution for France. Yet it is worthy of note that the assemblymen betrayed their underlying patriotism even as they went about this pacific task. "They have so much national vanity," observed a Swiss publicist of the Assembly's delegates, "so much pretension, that they will prefer all kinds of stupidities of their own choice to the results of British experience."[20] Said Robespierre in the course of the constitutional debates: "The representatives of the French nation, knowing how to give their country a constitution worthy of her and of the wisdom of this century, were not delegated to copy servilely an institution [i.e., the English constitution] born in times of ignorance, of necessity, and of the strife of opposing factions." Predicted Camille Desmoulins brazenly: "We shall go beyond these English, who are so proud of their constitution and who mocked at our servitude."[21] And Alexandre de Lameth queried incredulously: "Well! Do we not have the precious advantage over England of being able to assemble all the parts of our Constitution at the same time?" Even Jean-Joseph Mounier, noted for his Anglophile opin-

18 Ibid., pp. 172–73.
19 Jean-Paul Bertaud, *The Army of the French Revolution: From Citizen-Soldiers to Instrument of Power*, trans. R. R. Palmer (Princeton, N.J.: Princeton University Press, 1988), p. 21.
20 Cited in Acomb, *Anglophobia in France*, pp. 120–21.
21 Quoted in ibid., p. 121.

ions, conceded defensively that it was in the power of France "to have a Constitution superior to that of England."[22] Such rodomontade in the Constituent Assembly, like much of the rhetoric in the *cahiers* of the early Revolution, served to adumbrate "a spirit that would joyfully assume the mission of carrying that Revolution to other nations as well, by force of arms."[23]

But for these politicians, pride in country went hand in hand (as it does for most people in most historical situations) with an anxious distrust of the outside world. Consequently, the men striving to fashion a new France could not escape the misgivings and fears that derived then, as they would derive throughout the revolutionary era, from the international context of their efforts. Through the eyes of Périsse-Duluc, a deputy from Lyons to the self-proclaimed Constituent Assembly, Lefebvre enabled us to perceive how that context could be rendered into the apprehension of articulate bourgeois:

At the end of June and beginning of July it was currently believed that the comte d'Artois, if he failed to have his way, would leave the country and ask for aid from foreign sovereigns. What could be more natural? Was not Louis XVI the brother-in-law both of the Emperor and of the King of Naples, and in addition the cousin of Charles IV of Spain? Were not his two brothers sons-in-law of the King of Sardinia? Périsse-Duluc recalled having foreseen, before the opening of the Estates-General, that the French aristocracy might follow the example of the counterrevolutionaries in Holland, who had called in the Prussians to win a victory over their own countrymen.

"Collusion of the aristocracy with foreign interests," Lefebvre affirmed, "was regarded as a fact from the beginning, and in July 1789 there was already fear of an invasion."[24] If it may be forcing matters to believe, with this luminous historian, that the entire Third Estate subscribed in 1789 to the theory of an aristocratic plot against the public weal, it seems indisputable that many commoners did – and the exposed, "Continental" situation of France must have played a role in promoting that conviction.

"Commoners," of course, meant artisans, urban laborers, and peasants, as well as affluent and lettered bourgeois. For all of these inhabitants of the realm, mistrust and outright fear of the world beyond France – and memories of how French kings had always raised troops to combat that world – interacted with and magnified a whole complex of economic, social, and political concerns in the course of this turbulent year. Again, Georges Lefebvre:

---

22 Lameth and Mounier are cited in Egret, *La Révolution des notables: Mounier et les Monarchiens* (Paris: Colin, 1950), p. 149.
23 Acomb, *Anglophobia in France*, p. 123.
24 Lefebvre, *Coming of the French Revolution*, pp. 100–1.

It was maintained from an early date that the aristocracy favored the hoarding of food, that it held back its grain in order to crush the Third Estate and that for the same reason it was not displeased to see the harvest pillaged or the crops cut down before they were ripe. Those who feared that the aristocrats were resorting to arms naturally expected them to recruit followers among vagrants and vaga-bonds, just as the kings' recruiting officers enrolled their men among the lowest classes. . . . And since the nobles were expected to call on foreign troops, it was thought natural that they would also draw on "brigands" from neighboring countries. . . . This supposed collusion was what spread the "fear of brigands" to the nation as a whole, giving it a social and political significance.[25]

Townspeople and countryfolk reacted fearfully and at times violently to rumors about the emigration of nobles, the movements of brigands, and the diabolical preparations of the British, Spanish, Piedmontese, and other foreigners to invade France.

It is important to note that the incendiary passions of the populace also reflected international pressures in ways that were less obvious. For instance, popular hearsay in 1788–89 frequently ascribed the widespread suffering occasioned by the industrial recession to the commercial agree-ment recently concluded with the nefarious English. Although subsequent scholarship has not been altogether supportive of that contention, it *has* viewed the recession as aggravated by the dislocation of markets for French goods in eastern Europe – and this latter phenomenon resulted from the military strife involving Russia, Austria, Turkey, and Sweden.[26]

There were, in sum, innumerable ways in which international competi-tive pressures were part and parcel of the revolutionary process in France from the very start. The king and his advisers were bound to resent the con-tinuing decline of their country's standing among the Great Powers. It is difficult to see how they could have failed to assign a fairly high priority to the long-term task of ensuring the basic security and (beyond that) resusci-tating the traditional greatness of France in the world at large. Furthermore, a determination at the ministerial level to remain true to this international mission could only draw encouragement from an elite and popular citizenry agitated (in part) by pride in France and mistrust of foreigners. But the de-cisive question remained: Would Louis XVI be psychologically capable of accepting the sort of sociopolitical compromise at home that would guar-antee for his state security and continued influence abroad?

THE FAILURE OF THE KING TO COMPROMISE

There can be no doubt that the process of change in France in and after 1789 would have been different – among other things, probably, less

25 Ibid., pp. 108–9, 146.
26 See ibid., pp. 104–5, for references to these additional sources of anxiety and anger within French society.

violent – had Louis XVI been able to relinquish in unequivocal fashion his commitment to absolutism and the old society of privilege. Yet such speculation is as bootless in connection with Louis XVI as like conjecture would be in the cases of England's Charles I and Russia's Nicholas II. The whole course of events from August 1788 to October 1789 demonstrated that this monarch, like his counterparts in the other revolutions, simply would not bend to the degree required by evolving realities. Some of the country's brightest luminaries tried to convince the king that basic sociopolitical reform was unavoidable and that he, as sovereign, would in fact be a prime beneficiary of that reform; and Necker, the statesman who for the moment attracted most patriotic and progressive hopes, assuredly argued and acted in the same sense. But Louis, confirmed in his conservative sociopolitical leanings at critical moments during 1789 by reactionaries in the kingdom's splintering social elite, would not heed voices counseling compromise. He thereby helped inescapably to radicalize the situation within the realm.

In the late months of 1788, some of France's most thoughtful observers, motivated by their allegiance to and concern for the royalist cause, spoke out on the pressing need for the crown to sponsor domestic reform. The retired chancellor, Maupeou, wrote to Louis XVI that the nation lacked integrative principles that could focus its latent loyalties. "Hence ... the eternal condemnation [of the government] ... which is nearly always absurd ... the continual tendency towards the fragmentation of desires which if united would make for the strength and prosperity of the monarchy. The people, almost everywhere left to itself, sees in the government only the force which restrains and represses it."[27] Even more intriguing was a memorandum forwarded to the king from another minister in retirement, Malesherbes, as soon as the Estates General became the object of serious discussion in the conclaves of power. Malesherbes, in language summarized by the barrister Pierre-Louis Lacretelle, exhorted Louis to convene a new kind of national consultative body:

Seize people's imagination with an institution that will surprise them and please them, that the nation will approve and in which it can more easily prevail. . . . Let a king at the end of the eighteenth century not convoke the three Orders of the fourteenth; let him call together [instead] the proprietors of a great nation renewed by its civilization. . . . A constitution should correspond to the best ideas produced and tested by discussion. Create the constitution of your century; take your place in it, and do not fear to found it on the rights of the people.[28]

Sage counsel – and, apparently, quite similar to confidential advice that Mirabeau was later to tender the king.

27 Quoted in Behrens, *Society, Government and the Enlightenment*, p. 164.
28 Cited in Egret, *French Prerevolution*, p. 188.

And numerous were the publicists who argued in like vein for a natural compatibility of royal and popular interests. Insisted Lanjuinais: "The king is the supreme motor, the repository of executive power. He gives the laws, consented to by the nation, the seal of public authority. He is the necessary support of the people, the foundation stone of our social edifice." Observed Lacretelle: "The august monarchy fits our physical situation and our moral nature. Our aims and principles do not tend to weaken it; we wish only to regulate it in order to strengthen it." And Servan riposted sarcastically against those *privilégiés* who would stand between the sovereign and his people: "There now exists in France a sedition of about 20 million subjects of all ages and sexes, who ask only to unite with their king against two or three hundred magistrates, a few hundred great lords, the sacred little legion of bishops, and fellow-plotters who, in the name of the 1614 convocation [of the Estates General], would reduce the people to an extremity."[29]

Such individuals, eager to see the crown rejuvenated through a constitutional process (a process that "respectable" citizens presumably would control), pinned most of their hopes on the Genevan financier recalled to power at Versailles in August 1788. And there is every indication that Necker, whatever his faults, labored honestly to fulfill their expectations. The resultant tension between a minister endeavoring to restore the French monarchy upon a new foundation and a sovereign passively resisting those efforts constituted one of the dominant themes in this time of transition from prerevolution to revolution in France.

From the very start of his second ministry, Necker perceived as clearly as did the Maupeous, Malesherbes, and Mirabeaus the urgent need of France for a new constitution – in other words, for a reintegration of public purposes and private talents and ambitions. He argued, then, all the more strongly that the crown, having already tied its legitimacy explicitly to the convocation of the Estates General, must now proceed with that body and must try to make of it the "single great enterprise ... that would ensure public regeneration." Remarked the director-general:

Tired of continual vicissitudes in the fundamental principles of government, the kingdom would like to see a proper and durable balance finally established between incomes and expenses, cautious use of credit, sensible distribution of taxes, a general plan of public charity, an enlightened system of legislation, and above all, a constitutional guarantee of civil liberty and political liberty.[30]

But Necker also knew all too well that "the kingdom" was composed of a plethora of political and social interests that would have to compromise

29 For these citations, see ibid., pp. 196–97 and 210.
30 Cited in ibid., p. 189.

on specific issues were France to attain these objectives. "Throughout his second ministry," Robert Harris has written with much justification, "Necker's role was that of mediator, attempting to find the right compromise that would be not only acceptable but just to all sides, and reasonable in the light of the circumstances."[31]

Thus, after the deliberations in the reconvened Assembly of Notables in the late autumn of 1788 drove a wedge between progressives and conservatives over the composition and procedures of the upcoming Estates General, the director-general announced in his *Résultat du Conseil* of 27 December several governmental decisions intended to heal the divisions over this imminent convocation.[32] For instance, deputies of the Third Estate were to be as numerous as all clerical and noble representatives taken together. Such a measure, in addition to pleasing all progressive spectators in the throng of public opinion, would ensure the presence in the assembly of men of affairs who could offer the government much valuable advice on economic and administrative matters. Again, voters would be able to deputize to the assembly at Versailles men hailing from any of the three orders, and not only individuals from their own Estates. Necker hoped that this concession would be particularly efficacious in fostering a spirit of national solidarity among the delegates and their constituents.

It is true that the Genevan in other respects accepted the recommendations of the "second" Assembly of Notables, disappointing in the process many of his partisans. Most notoriously, Necker stated that, in the impending convocation as in its predecessor of 1614, deliberation and voting would be by order rather than by head unless the king and the three orders should in unanimity decide otherwise. Yet Necker manifestly hoped that if the three orders should deadlock on certain issues they might agree to meet in common to resolve their differences. Furthermore, and of far greater moment, the finance minister used the *Résultat du Conseil* to proclaim in so many words the "abdication of Louis XVI as an absolute monarch." According to the controversial *Résultat*, the king had informed his ministers that he would never levy another impost without the Estates General's sanction; that he would consult with the approaching convocation about its periodicity in the future; that he would seek its advice on the means for ensuring henceforth a competent management of public finances; and that he would invite the Estates to debate such questions as the use of *lettres de cachet*, freedom of the press, and the publicizing of the government's acts.

Necker's most recent and authoritative biographer has asserted that the

---

31 Harris, *Necker and the Revolution of 1789*, p. 325.
32 For the most recent analysis of the *Résultat du Conseil*, see ibid., pp. 323–33.

Genevan at this time saw fiscal issues as the cardinal obstacle to consensus among the three orders. "It will never enter the minds of the Third Estate," the director-general confidently predicted, "to seek to diminish the prerogatives, either seignorial or honorific, of the first two orders, or their property, or their persons. There is no Frenchman who does not recognize that these prerogatives are as respectable a property right as any other, that several are intimately linked to the essence of a monarchy."[33] Such an assessment, however, was in the end to prove overly optimistic: Conservatives and liberals in the course of the following year would be falling out over a daunting array of issues. In addition, as Harris has conceded, the Genevan underestimated the difficulties attendant upon creation of a durable balance between the executive powers to be retained by the crown and the legislative role to be gained by the new national assembly. Thus Necker, however sincerely he intended through promulgation of the conciliar decree of 27 December 1788 to overcome discord within the emerging body politic of the kingdom, failed to anticipate the intractability of both constitutional and social questions.

The director-general nonetheless pursued his policy of domestic conciliation in addressing the opening session of the Estates General on 5 May 1789. Apparently with his noble auditors in mind, he urged that "those distinctions which pit citizens in opposition to one another because of status or birth" be subordinated at least for the time being to the public welfare. "We do not ask you to forget them entirely; they even make up the social order, they form that chain so necessary for the regulation of society. But these rival considerations must be suspended for a time, and their sharpness mitigated, to be returned to only after a long period has been spent working in common for the general interest."[34] Necker, it seems, was looking for accommodations on social and constitutional issues to be reached in France as he believed they had been achieved on the other side of the Channel. According once again to Harris:

By comparing... his May 5 speech with his other writings... it is possible to see that what Necker wanted to come out of the "great enterprise" was a constitution similar to the British. It would allow full executive powers and functions to the king; it would provide for a periodically assembled legislative of two chambers exercising full legislative powers. The upper house would not represent the privileged orders. It would be appointed by the king from a pool of public-spirited citizens regardless of social status who had served the country with distinction.[35]

Yet, in light of what we know today of the Anglophobic sentiments in the Constituent Assembly – sentiments that, Necker himself informs us,

33 Quoted in ibid., p. 328.
34 Cited in ibid., p. 426.
35 Ibid., pp. 434–35.

the king largely shared in 1789 – it was not likely that constitutional arrangements drawing upon British experience would find many adherents in France.[36]

There is still considerable scholarly debate over the wisdom and forcefulness of Necker's stewardship of public affairs during these critical months. Virtually no one today will deny that the director-general succeeded in temporarily resuscitating the royal finances. Yet some specialists have faulted him for having unrealistic expectations of the Estates General and thus for leaving the nation without adequate direction on the basic problems it had to confront.[37] Alternatively, others have suspected him of trying to turn the schism between the conservatives and Patriots to the king's, or to his own, benefit.[38] There may be some truth to both of these charges. Regarding the former criticism, Necker arguably could have acted more decisively than he did at certain points – for instance, by prescribing the vote by head for the Estates in the *Résultat du Conseil*, by sponsoring government candidates for that assembly, and by laying out an elaborate program of reforms during the electoral campaign in the spring of 1789. With regard to the latter charge: If the authorities in the summer of 1788 had unashamedly sought to foment dissension among their critics as part of an effort to delay the summoning of the Estates General, their successors were, at least in theory, just as capable of resorting to divisive tactics the following spring. Still, whatever justice may adhere to such strictures – and they have been vigorously combatted by Robert Harris in his latest volume[39] – they may in a very real sense be beside the point. For in the final analysis Necker, like any other minister of Bourbon France, had to defer to his royal master; and there is no evidence whatsoever that Louis XVI was at bottom ready to concede what it was probably necessary for him as sovereign to concede on the cutting sociopolitical issues of the day.

To be sure, the king and queen seem to have been sufficiently angered by aristocratic opposition to the reforms of Brienne and Lamoignon in the summer of 1788 to have rallied to the Genevan at the summer's end. The king may have accepted Necker back into the conclaves of power at Versailles with patent reluctance, but he and Marie-Antoinette could perceive that Necker's enemies had also been Brienne's detractors, and

---

36 Necker's characterization of Louis XVI's prejudice against all institutions British is cited by Egret, *Necker,* p. 323. See also, on the same subject, ibid., p. 351.

37 See, for example, Doyle, *Origins of the French Revolution,* pp. 139, 150.

38 Consult, for instance, Fitzsimmons, "Privilege and the Polity in France," pp. 278–79, regarding the crown's issuance in January 1789 of regulations for the convening of the Estates General.

39 See Harris, *Necker and the Revolution of 1789,* esp. pp. 315 and 325, for remarks in defense of the finance minister.

in any case only this reputed master of financial wizardry could now attract French and international capital back to the thoroughly discredited "arbiter of Europe." Hence, the Genevan, at least for the time being, and above all for geopolitical reasons, was empowered once more in France.

Come the stalemate in the Estates General in June 1789, however, the king had, finally, to divulge his deepest convictions. Georges Lefebvre rightly observed that Louis XVI's exposition of those reforms he deemed acceptable for France at the 23 June *séance royale* of the Estates General "is of the utmost interest because it shows clearly what was at stake, not only in the following weeks but in the whole Revolution."[40] Whether, however, the king was as "willing to become a constitutional monarch" as Lefebvre claimed he was, and hence betrayed inflexibility only on social questions, is less certain. We can best elucidate this matter by contrasting Necker's ideas on reform, submitted to the royal Council on 19 June, with those articulated by the king at the royal session four days later.

Necker was certainly not at this crucial juncture advocating an unconditional surrender by the crown on all substantive points raised in recent days by liberal assemblymen and propagandists.[41] He would, for instance, have had the king insist that the future legislature be bicameral, have all its acts royally sanctioned, and acknowledge his retention of "the plenitude of executive power." The finance minister suggested, moreover, that the public be barred from the Assembly's deliberations and urged that the honorific privileges of the nobility be declared sacrosanct. Nevertheless, in other respects the Genevan called for a fundamental break with the past.

The king would command the reunion of the orders and the vote in common on all matters of general interest. These would include the financial measures, taxes and loans, and accountability. The king would no longer ask the privileged orders to give up their fiscal privileges but would abolish them himself. Also, and the most significant clause, the deliberations on the new constitution would be done in the common assembly and the vote taken by head.

Necker would have had the king satisfy many of the most salient demands in the Third Estate's *cahiers*. Thus, Louis XVI would admit qualified commoners to all civilian and military employments, abrogate the tax (*franc fief*) on plebeian owners of fiefs, and make it possible for peasants to redeem the feudal payments they owed to their seigneurs. In addition, he would recognize the individual's rights to security and property, free-

---

40 Lefebvre, *Coming of the French Revolution*, p. 87.
41 For this discussion of Necker's and the king's ideas on reform in June 1789, consult especially Harris, *Necker and the Revolution of 1789*, esp. pp. 506–7 and 514–18.

dom of assembly and of the press, and "in fact all the rights later appearing in the Charter of 1814."

Had the French monarch announced these reforms to the self-proclaimed National Assembly on 23 June 1789, and stood by them thereafter, the whole course of the Revolution might have been different. But, inevitably, he was lobbied by the queen, by his brothers, and by conservative ministers and courtiers – all of them to one extent or another caught up in the politics of polarization within the country's social elite – to follow what was likely his own inclination and reject Necker's ideas. And indeed Louis's message to the assemblymen on 23 June diverged considerably from that formulated by his director-general of finances.

At that fateful session, the king commanded the deputies of the "Estates General" (as he continued to call this body) to retire to their respective chambers. They were to deliberate and vote by order on all questions save those for which the unanimous consent of the three estates and the sovereign secured discussion and suffrage in common and by head. Thus, everything – the form of the constitution, the structure of society, even the fiscal immunities of the clergy and nobility – was in effect to be held hostage by the members of the first two orders. True, Louis did reiterate his "exhortation" of 5 May that the three orders come together "for this session of the States-General only" to discuss matters of public interest. But he expressly designated as off-limits to deliberation and suffrage in common some of the most pivotal issues: "the feudal and seigneurial rights of the fief-owners, the economic and honorific privileges of the first two orders, all matters concerning religion and ecclesiastical organization, . . . " and, perhaps most sweepingly of all, "the future organization of the States-General, in other words, the Constitution."

In light of this message, proclaiming as it did restrictions that were to be imposed upon meaningful change in this war-prone realm, it was simply not enough for Louis XVI to announce grandly that the Estates General would henceforth be convened periodically; that it would supervise and control the finances of the crown and wield full legislative power; and that he, as monarch, would grant all the basic rights and liberties invoked in the *cahiers*. It would have been amazing had the representatives of the Third Estate not feared that the adoption of the royal program could drastically curtail their public roles in the new France. The king's parting threat – to send the delegates home if they should prove recalcitrant and take upon his own shoulders "the regeneration of the kingdom" – only added fuel to fires of legislative rebellion that, in alliance with the blaze of popular rage in city and countryside, would soon incinerate the sociopolitical institutions of the old France.

Perhaps the specific issue in all of this that most starkly exposed the difference between Necker's vision of France and that of Louis, and at the same time exposed the ultimate inseparability of constitutional and social questions, was that of access to public employments. When Necker spoke out on behalf of the concept of meritocracy in the royal council on 19 June, the war minister Puységur "especially protested against any measure by which the king's hands should be tied in the appointment of army officers, and the king, much disturbed by this possibility, blamed Necker for having even thought of it."[42] Here were both a constitutional question of *power* – should the executive continue to monopolize control of the kingdom's armed forces? – and a social question of *defining that kingdom's power elite* – should all Frenchmen qualified to serve their country in its positions of public responsibility be allowed to do so irrespective of their provenance in society? But the controversy over appointments to the army in 1789 also draws our attention again to an issue transcending domestic matters: the connection between the foreign and internal policies of the French state. The controversy reminds us that the Revolution's origins lay above all in the need of France to harness its people's aspirations and talents to its geopolitical and other statist requirements.[43]

Over the next four months Louis XVI would be coerced on no fewer than three occasions to retreat publicly from the position he had staked out at the *séance royale* of 23 June. He retreated immediately after the *séance* itself in order to retain the services of Necker, who was riotously championed by the populace of Paris and Versailles; and of course he abandoned the field again after the July and October Days. But although this sovereign in 1789 neither raised the standard of civil war in the provinces in imitation of Charles I nor ordered his troops to mow down his countrymen in unknowing anticipation of Nicholas II, he did refuse, in the sullen depths of his conscience, to accept the tremendous sociopolitical changes that this dramatic year wrought in France. Louis XVI reacted to the decrees pushed through the Constituent Assembly on the tumultuous night of 4 August, decrees that measurably reduced feudal and particularist privileges in the kingdom, by writing to the archbishop of Arles: "I will never consent to the spoliation of my clergy or of my nobility. I will not sanction decrees by which they are despoiled."[44] And he condemned all the concessions wrung from him over the summer in

42 As reported by Lefebvre, *Coming of the French Revolution*, pp. 83–84.
43 Vivian Gruder has taken the postulation of a commingling of constitutional and social questions on 23 June 1789 a step farther. She has argued that the crown actually defended the concept of separate estates more out of concern for its own authority than out of concern for the traditional social hierarchy as such. Gruder, "The Bourbon Monarchy," pp. 352–58.
44 Cited in Lefebvre, *Coming of the French Revolution*, p. 185.

a secret statement sent to his Spanish cousin Charles IV soon after the
October Days had forced the royal family's removal to Paris:

> I owe it to myself, to my children, to my family and to my entire dynasty, not
> to . . . let the royal dignity, confirmed in my dynasty by the passage of centuries,
> become debased in my hands. . . . I have chosen Your Majesty, as head of the
> second branch [of the House of Bourbon], to receive my solemn protest against
> all the acts contrary to my royal authority extracted from me by force since 15
> July of this year, and, at the same time, to witness my determination to fulfill
> the promises I made in my statement of 23 June.[45]

This was the credo of someone schooled since childhood to believe in
the divinity of his rule and of the old society of estates and *privilège*.
Louis was never to deviate from this philosophy; and his constant refusal
to do so was one of the factors that in 1789 and subsequently led respectable Frenchmen favoring the recovery of Gallic strength abroad and
progressive reformism at home to endorse a degree of revolutionary violence that they otherwise would never have sanctioned.

To allude to "respectable Frenchmen" in this connection is to acknowledge our next task: to situate the tension between Necker's vision
and that of the king in 1788–89 in its proper social context. We can begin
to do this by asserting that the director-general and Louis XVI, in dis-
agreeing over crucial public issues, in part were responding to, and in
part helped to further, the process of polarization within the country's
aroused elite of "notable" Frenchmen – that is, clerics, lay nobles, and
bourgeois.

THE POLARIZATION WITHIN THE SOCIAL ELITE

Just as the fiscal breakdown of the French government, intolerable in
view of that government's international mission, forced Louis XVI and
his chief minister to debate the precise nature of the reforms needed in
the kingdom, so it unleashed a parallel debate within respectable ranks
of society over constitutional and social change. Historians seem generally
to agree today that only the electoral campaign in the spring of 1789 and
subsequent events fully translated the tensions long latent within those
social ranks into revolutionary (and counterrevolutionary) politics. Yet
those politics were clearly foreshadowed in the preceding autumn and
winter, when clerical, noble, and bourgeois Frenchmen were forced by
their awareness of the imminence of the Estates General to begin crys-
tallizing their sociopolitical philosophies.

The authorities from July 1788 on cleared the way for a national discussion of public issues by granting broad freedom to the press, liberating

---

45 Cited in Egret, *Necker*, p. 372. My translation.

"all booksellers, pedlars, [and] merchants arrested and imprisoned lately for distributing tracts opposing ministerial policies," and tolerating clubs and other societies in the capital and elsewhere. Jean Egret has effectively summarized the clubs' diverse activities:

The clubs published and distributed the most famous Parisian pamphlets of the National Party and particularly those of the Abbé Siéyès.... They established liaison with the provinces in order to help "spread simultaneity of ideas, to prepare simultaneity of aims and forces," in Rabaut Saint-Etienne's own words. It is certainly beyond doubt that they contributed to the extraordinary diffusion of works by such provincials as the Comte d'Antraigues, Rabaut Saint-Etienne, and the barrister Albisson, all from Languedoc; Lenoir-Laroche and Jean-Joseph Mounier from Dauphiné; Volney from Brittany; and Servan from Provence.[46]

Prominent among these activist organizations was the Society of Thirty. Some of the members of this group, courtiers of the old aristocracy, became sociopolitical liberals because they had lost out in the competition for government posts and patronage to families of the provincial squire-archy; others, whether issuing from the military noblesse, the judiciary, or even the bourgeoisie, acted out of genuine idealism.[47] In any case, from such clubs, and from the outpouring of pamphlet literature associated with them, emerged the challenge of the National or Patriot party to the status quo in France at the end of 1788.

Speaking as constitutionalists, some in this Party – such as Huguet de Sémonville, Beauvau, and Démeunier – looked hopefully to institutionalized Estates General and revivified provincial Estates to deliver the kingdom from the yoke of "despotism." Others, such as Mounier and Rabaut Saint-Etienne, spoke of adopting the English constitution. The most radical among them, like Siéyès, located the nation's sovereignty squarely and without appeal in a hypothetical unicameral legislature.[48]

But to raise the constitutional question was ineluctably to broach the social question as well. Declared Mirabeau: "War on privileges and privileged, that is my motto. Privileges are useful against kings but detestable against nations, and ours will never have a public spirit until delivered from them." Exhorted Target: "Provinces, cities, courts, companies, Orders – oppose the king with your privileges, but strike them [down] before France assembled." And Cérutti pierced to the heart of the matter as the Patriots perceived it: "It is said that the people are conspiring on all sides against the nobility, the clergy, and the magistracy. Here is the conspiracy: excluded from brilliant careers in the army, they are allowed only to die there. Excluded from high dignities in the church, they are allowed

---

46 Egret, *French Prerevolution*, p. 193.
47 On the Society of Thirty, refer again to Wick, "The Court Nobility and the French Revolution," pp. 263–84; and *A Conspiracy of Well-Intentioned Men*.
48 Citations in Egret, *French Prerevolution*, p. 194.

only to work there. Excluded from important positions in the courts, they are allowed only to plead there. Excluded from the legal share of legislative authority in the Estates General, they will be allowed only to pay there." It does not seem that, at this (relatively early) point, most Patriots were consciously advocating the abolition of the old schema of orders, either within the impending Estates General or within society as a whole. But they assuredly were envisioning a France in which social rank would reflect merit rather than genealogy; and double representation for the Third Estate and voting by head in the approaching assembly of the nation were in their minds prerequisites to that end. "The fate of the nation is at stake," warned Target. "With such great issues every uncertainty is a danger; every worry, a torment; every truth, a duty."[49]

It is important to stress that support for modernization of the Estates General's composition and procedures and for the idea of meritocracy was also coming now from the grass roots all over France. "The nobility's privileges are truly properties, all the more respected because we are not excluded from them but may acquire them," observed the barristers of the Burgundian town of Nuits. "Why should anyone suppose we would think of destroying the seeds of emulation, the lodestar of our labors?" At Rouen in Normandy, bourgeois citizens in huge numbers signed a petition to the king invoking the need for deliberation in common in the Estates. In Provence, nineteen towns and villages and nine parishes drafted petitions demanding doubling of the Third. By 30 December, one *nouvelliste*, generally well informed, could claim that "the number of demands from Provinces, Cities, Communities, and Corporations for the doubling of the Third Estate is immense, and some put it at more than 800 without reckoning those arriving here daily from all quarters."[50] It is perhaps needless to add that many of these manifestos called as well for voting by head in the Estates and for "careers open to talent" in the renascent kingdom. Moreover, as Greenlaw and Margerison, among others, would remind us, a polemical literature drawing very specifically upon French historical precedents was now inundating the realm with the same demands.[51]

In late 1788, however, champions of such ideas had to shout across an ever-widening divide at "notable" compatriots committed still to the survival of the ancien régime. Spearheading the conservative defense of the old France was the Paris Parlement, which reacted to the Patriots' clamor for sociopolitical change on 25 September by recommending that

49 These quotations are from ibid., pp. 195–96.
50 Ibid., esp. pp. 206–43.
51 See Greenlaw, "Pamphlet Literature in France," p. 353; and Margerison, "History, Representative Institutions, and Political Rights," esp. pp. 95–98.

the Estates of 1789 be modeled in composition and procedures on the convocation of 1614. The judges, in other words, raised the specter of a national deliberative body in which equal contingents representing the three estates, voting on all issues by order rather than by head, would effectively stymie all meaningful reform. Although Van Kley may be right to divine in this cautionary pronouncement a vestige of this tribunal's Jansenism and Gallicanism,[52] it probably constituted more than anything else a conservative reflex against a perceived threat of destabilizing change. This was the interpretation of the Parlement's action given later by two of the magistrates who had attended the court's session of 25 September.[53] The parlementaires wished, however quixotically, to preserve the balance of constitutional and social forces characterizing the France they had always known, and saw an Estates General functioning in 1789 as its predecessor supposedly had in 1614–15 as instrumental toward that end.

From 6 November to 12 December a similar message emanated from the second Assembly of Notables, called by Necker to advise him on the constitution and procedures of the Estates. Only one of the Assembly's six committees, that chaired by the king's brother the comte de Provence, endorsed a doubling of the Third (and that by the threadbare margin of 13 to 12); the Notables even more overwhelmingly rejected the notion of suffrage by head. They would concede to the National party fiscal equality and nothing else. What was more, they went on the offensive against their progressive foes. The crusty and reactionary prince de Conti inveighed against "scandalous writings spreading disorder and dissension throughout the realm," and in the last days of the Assembly the Princes of the Blood presented a manifesto to Louis XVI restating the Notables' opposition to all changes other than those in the domain of taxation. "Prejudices, pretensions, caution, habit, all appear to be so deep rooted in most heads," despairingly commented Beauvau, one of the outvoted liberal Notables, on 10 November, "that I have no illusion that the simplest logic could ever penetrate there."[54]

Even when the Paris Parlement attempted in a decree of 5 December to restore its popularity, shattered by its earlier invocation of the 1614 Estates General, it stood stubbornly by its guns insofar as suffrage by order in the national convocation was concerned. Moreover, J.-J. Duval d'Eprémesnil, author of this latest parlementary pronunciamento, can-

---

52 See Van Kley, "The Estates General as Ecumenical Council: The Constitutionalism of Corporate Consensus and the *Parlement*'s Ruling of September 25, 1788," *Journal of Modern History* 61 (March 1989), pp. 1–52.

53 These testimonies (by Louis François de Paule Le Fevre d'Ormesson and Guy Marie Sallier) are discussed in Stone, *French Parlements*, pp. 102–103.

54 See Egret, *The French Prerevolution*, pp. 199–202, on the subject of the second Assembly of Notables.

didly signaled his unwavering support of "the just prerogatives of the Nobility and the Clergy" in a pamphlet he had published on 7 December.[55] The Patriots saw this as "outmoded, ridiculous, and intolerable"; they might as well have said the same of the Parlement's decision later in the month to take the eminent anatomist J. I. Guillotin to task over his championship of the Parisian Third Estate.[56]

It was against this backdrop of deepening division between the advocates and the opponents of political and social change in France that the hard-pressed Necker promulgated his conciliatory *Résultat du Conseil* on 27 December 1788 and soon thereafter set forth electoral procedures for the Estates General. Yet it was probably beyond the abilities of any individual to reverse the process of polarization within the elitist ranks of French society. In these last days of 1788 and early weeks of 1789, Georges Lefebvre has written,

> the nobility of Lower Poitou came together spontaneously to protest. The Parlement of Besançon drew up remonstrances. On January 6, 1789, the Provincial Estates of Franche-Comté, assembling under the ancient forms, protested likewise. In Provence the nobility did the same, with the result that the Third Estate refused to sit in the Provincial Estates. In Brittany the class conflict degenerated into civil war. . . . Bands of men recruited by the nobles, on January 26, 1789, came into conflict with the law students. . . . The students won the battle and besieged their opponents in the hall of the Breton Estates. The young men of Nantes took arms on learning the news, and marched off to bring aid to the patriots at Rennes.

Rabaut Saint-Etienne, partisan as recently as October of British-style bicameralism, was calling by December for a unicameral legislature and for voting by head. Siéyès, in his renowned *What is the Third Estate?*, poured cold scorn upon the aristocracy. And Mirabeau, excluded by ancien régime snobbism from the Estates of Provence, took to the printed page to lionize Marius, "less great for having vanquished the Cimbrians than for having exterminated the order of nobility in Rome."[57]

Of course, none of this goes to show that compromise between conservatives and liberals would have been impossible at this time, had the former been willing to concede the entrance of affluent and ambitious commoners into the purlieus of power and status in France. The Dauphinois assemblies of 1788, at Vizille and Romans, had shown that deliberation in common and voting by head on substantive issues could be reconciled with the conventional hierarchy of estates.[58] And certainly

---

55 On the parlementary decree of 5 December 1788 and its aftermath, refer again to Stone, *French Parlements*, pp. 104–6.

56 On the incident involving Guillotin, the six merchant guilds of Paris, and the Parisian parlementaires, see Egret, *French Prerevolution*, p. 204.

57 Lefebvre, *Coming of the French Revolution*, pp. 60–62.

58 On the politics of Dauphiné in 1788, refer to Egret, *Révolution des notables*, passim.

analysis of the *cahiers de doléances* has divulged a widespread willingness among the electors to the Estates General in the spring of 1789 to proceed on the same basis. "Many cahiers deemed the division of the French nation into three classes as fundamental to the French constitution," Beatrice Hyslop noted. "Comparatively few cahiers . . . attacked the class system at its root. The majority accepted class divisions and worked for equalization among them."[59] Even in focusing exclusively upon commoners' grievance lists, George Taylor has had to conclude that "in no *cahier* . . . outside Paris appears a twinkle of the idea that the three orders must go, that to vest sovereignty in something called the nation required that the estates be abolished. Even the electors who in their *cahiers* called the Estates General a national assembly implied that in the future, as in the past, each of the three estates would choose its own deputies."[60]

Yet it is also clear that the Third Estate (and progressives in the clergy and noblesse as well) viewed a substantial widening of access to power and status in France as essential. In nearly 36 percent of the general *cahiers*, Hyslop discovered

[a] demand for the abolition of ennoblement by purchase, and the substitution of ennoblement for service of France. Members of all classes would thereby be eligible on the basis of merit. . . . This demand was not an attack on the old hereditary nobility, but its application would gradually transform aristocracy into an *elite* of public servants, to which distinction all alike could aspire.[61]

We know from our analysis of the old regime, however, that this was hardly what most nobles were visualizing when they railed against purchase of nobility and advanced their conception of a state-service noblesse. The majority of them, obdurately wedded to the past on this as on so many other questions, were therefore bound to see voting by order in the approaching convocation at Versailles as a crucial bridle upon change in France.

And, indeed, scholars such as Roger Chartier and Guy Chaussinand-Nogaret, however eager to unearth in the *cahiers* evidence of a fusion of nobles and bourgeois on the threshold of the Revolution, have had to concede a real difference between the noble and Third Estate *cahiers* on the issue of voting in the Estates. Chartier discovered a general insistence on the part of commoners upon the vote by head, whereas, by contrast, he found only a small proportion of the nobles' *cahiers* pronouncing unambiguously for such an arrangement.[62] Chartier's colleague Chaussinand-Nogaret, focusing more narrowly on the Second Estate's *cahiers*,

59 Hyslop, *French Nationalism in 1789*, p. 83.
60 Taylor, "Revolutionary and Nonrevolutionary Content in the *Cahiers* of 1789," p. 494.
61 Hyslop, *French Nationalism in 1789*, p. 88.
62 Roger Chartier, "Cultures, Lumières, Doléances: Les Cahiers de 1789," *Revue d'histoire moderne et contemporaine* 28 (1981), esp. pp. 90–91.

arrived at similar conclusions regarding the nobility.[63] Furthermore, passing beyond the immediate procedural issue of voting in the Estates, Chaussinand-Nogaret admitted forthrightly that only a "radical fringe" of noble *cahiers* accepted "the access of all, without distinction of birth and status, to public and military employments, [and] the suppression of distinctions and formalities humiliating for the Third Estate."[64] Again, both Chartier and Chaussinand-Nogaret cited a significant divergence between noble and bourgeois grievance lists on the subject of seigneurial dues and justice. In light of all this, François Furet's assertion that the *cahiers* of the nobility were "on the whole somewhat more 'enlightened' than those of the Third Estate" must strike us as inaccurate.[65] It seems, rather, that the electors' writs of grievance, however impressively testifying to a consensus among French notables on a variety of constitutional, administrative, and economic issues, witnessed also to the continuing potential divisiveness of privilege, and especially *social* privilege, in the politics of the realm.[66]

The electoral process itself helped to ensure that this latent divisiveness would become actual discord. William Doyle, himself synthesizing the germane scholarship on the elections of 1789, has shown how those contests within the Second Estate played generally into the hands of nobles unlikely to meet aspiring bourgeois halfway on contentious social issues:

Everywhere, only nobles with full and transmissible nobility received a summons to the electoral assemblies. This excluded several thousand *anoblis*, members of rich and ambitious families who had paid good money to escape from the third estate and now found themselves brusquely pushed back into it. . . . The noble elections were a triumph for the natural but hitherto silent majority among the nobility – provincial, poor, relatively inarticulate, politically inexperienced, but determined to use this unlooked-for opportunity to disavow those who had formerly usurped the role of their spokesmen. Not surprisingly, it was a conservative majority, and the anti-noble agitation of the preceding six months had only stiffened its conservatism.[67]

By the same token, the electoral process within the Third Estate ensured that the untitled laity, too, would enjoy a resolute advocacy in the debates of the Estates General. No one has explicated this more clearly than George Taylor:

---

63 Chaussinand-Nogaret, *Noblesse au XVIIIe siècle*, p. 190.
64 Ibid., p. 219.
65 Furet, *Interpreting the French Revolution*, p. 41.
66 See again, on this point, Fitzsimmons, "Privilege and the Polity in France," esp. pp. 279–80.
67 Doyle, *Origins of the French Revolution*, pp. 152–54. See also James Murphy and Patrice Higonnet, "Les Députés de la Noblesse aux Etats Généraux de 1789," *Revue d'histoire moderne et contemporaine* 20 (April–June 1973), pp. 230–47.

Those who deliberated in city and *bailliage* assemblies had already helped compose the *cahiers* of parishes or corps, and one may suppose that at each stage of discussion.... they gained a sharper sense of needs and goals, greater skill and precision in expounding them, and more ideological awareness than appears in the grassroots documents. Those who reached the Estates General, therefore, had been schooled in a series of revolutionary seminars. Also, the voters tended to choose as deputies not only prominent and influential men respected for good judgment, but others who had the talent, finesse, and ardor needed to formulate the *doléances* of the group in a style that commanded regard and gratitude.... The electoral process, in other words, returned to the Estates General the sifted and seasoned nucleus of a national revolutionary elite.[68]

That the First Estate, the Gallican clergy, was split internally along ideological lines by its own contests for the Estates General only enhanced the likelihood of strife in that body over the months to come.[69]

It was in these circumstances, not very auspicious from the point of view of Jacques Necker, that the Genevan resumed the mediating role he had earlier taken up in promulgating the *Résultat du Conseil.* Yet, as Harris has shown in almost excruciating detail, the bottom fell out of the director-general's designs from the start of the convocation at Versailles. Necker, obsessed as ever by a fiscal emergency grounded primarily in the unrelenting exigencies of international politics, had hoped that each order would verify its members' credentials and constitute itself as a deliberative body with all due speed; that the first two orders would then renounce their financial privileges; and that the three estates would then decide quickly on which substantive issues they could deliberate in common and vote by head. What actually happened, of course, was markedly different. The nobility certainly proceeded straightway to validate its delegates' credentials, but in doing so it was rejecting the Third Estate's call for verification of credentials in common. The clergy, divided internally over this question, failed to follow the nobility's example; and the Third Estate similarly refused to constitute itself as a separate body. Activists on both sides rightly descried behind this immediate dispute the ultimate question of how much change might conceivably come to France. The conservatives naturally feared that conceding the principle of validation of credentials in common would be to open the floodgates to plenary sessions of the Estates voting by head on all questions; the Patriots just as understandably feared to set what might become an unbreakable precedent for deliberating and voting by order on public issues. Thus, deadlock set in – and with deadlock, during May, June, and early July,

68 Taylor, "Revolutionary and Nonrevolutionary Content," p. 500.
69 Consult, on the clergy, Ruth F. Necheles, "The Curés in the Estates General of 1789," *Journal of Modern History* 46 (1974), pp. 425–44. See also, on the electoral campaign of 1789, the papers by Furet and Ran Halévi in Baker, ed., *Political Culture of the Old Regime.*

the extremists in both ideological camps could only harden their positions.[70]

Yet we can see, with benefit of hindsight, that sooner or later the leaders of the Third Estate were likely to force the question. They knew that Lafayette and other progressive deputies in the Second Estate and the majority of parish priests in the first order were keen to break ranks and join them; they sensed that the ever more potent force of public opinion was on their side; and, paramount fact, they knew that the crown's bankruptcy held public affairs at their mercy. Thus, the commoners' momentous decision on 17 June, by a lopsided vote of 491 to 90, to rename the Estates the National Assembly and declare "that it is in the power of this assembly, and this assembly alone, to represent the general will." The self-styled National Assembly promptly took it upon itself to legitimize royal taxes (lacking which sanction, it stated, those imposts would be "illegal"). It also announced on 17 June that it would examine and consolidate the nation's debt and review the urgent question of popular subsistence. Then, three days later, all deputies in the chamber save for one swore the famous Tennis Court Oath that they would not disband until they had drafted a constitution for the new France. And on 23 June, the day of Louis XVI's fateful *séance royale*, the delegates of the Patriot party endorsed Mirabeau's defiant motion threatening with the charge of *lèse-nation* anyone who should lay hands on any of the National Assemblymen.[71]

It is true that the king, constrained for the time being to keep Necker from resigning and taking with him the government's credibility in the financial markets, commanded his ideological brethren in the first two estates to join the rebellious commoners. But, however obedient to this royal summons, the conservatives left no doubt as to the constancy of their attitudes. On 25 June, the recalcitrant majority in the second order vowed in a letter to the sovereign "that the Nobility would continue to insist on the right, granted by the king himself at the Royal Session, to ... exist as a separate order and to have its own assembly for deliberation and voting on matters that concerned the Nobility." Two days later, the cardinal de La Rochefoucauld touched off an uproar in the Assembly by informing the representatives that the clergy, though acquiescing in the

---

70 See Harris, *Necker and the Revolution of 1789*, pp. 445–96. Also very helpful on this period is Fitzsimmons, "Privilege and the Polity in France," esp. pp. 279–81; and Timothy Tackett, "Nobles and Third Estate in the Revolutionary Dynamic of the National Assembly, 1789–1790," *American Historical Review* 94 (April 1989), pp. 271–301.

71 Harris, *Necker and the Revolution of 1789*, pp. 486–89, 509–10, 519–20. See also, on the constitutional debates within the Assembly during this period, Baker, *Inventing the French Revolution*, esp. pp. 252–305.

king's order to join in common deliberations on questions of urgent national interest, nonetheless reserved its "right, according to constitutional laws of the monarchy, to assemble and to vote separately." Early in July, conservatives in the Second Estate passed a resolution reaffirming their stance on corporate privilege.[72]

In mid-July, the deepening schism in "respectable" society played a patent role, along with other factors already discussed or yet to be considered, in precipitating the July Days. The king, drawing encouragement from an increasingly reactionary element at court and in the Assembly whose philosophy (albeit irreconcilable with continuing French prominence in worldly affairs) meshed in essence with his own, tried to overthrow the reformists in the government and legislature. The result, as all the world knows, was a defeat for the king and his ideological confederates and a victory for a "nation" that would soon be reviving Gallic prestige abroad even as it forged a new social compact at home.[73] Yet, because Louis XVI remained, even in the wake of his reverse, at the heart of Versailles's opposition to sociopolitical change, the forces that had loomed behind events from 5 May to 14 July continued to shape affairs from late July until early October.

In particular, the deputies in the National Assembly continued to be driven toward what we would today call extreme leftist and rightist positions. On the left, the Patriots prompted the Assembly on 14 July to declare that the ministers would be held criminally liable for any actions contravening its decrees or, in general, the nation's rights. The Assembly also ringingly reaffirmed its proclamations of 17, 20, and 23 June; set about drafting a declaration of rights and a constitution; and on 21 July ratified Siéyès's assertion that "all public powers without exception are an emanation of the general will, all come from the people, that is to say, the Nation."[74] Then, on the memorable night of 4 August, the aroused Patriots in the legislature dealt at least a glancing blow to the rural regime of seigneurial servitudes, payments, and justice – and they altered much else:

The tax exemptions of the Nobility and the Clergy were now unequivocally renounced, and the royal taxes were to be levied on all classes and in the same manner. The entire system of venality of office was abolished as was the separate status of the . . . *pays d'états*. The prelates abandoned church tithes. Both Nobility and Clergy accepted the principle of the career open to talent. . . . In short, the

---

72 Harris, *Necker and the Revolution of 1789*, pp. 536, 539–40.
73 On the background to and events during the July Days, see (among myriad studies) Jacques Godechot, *The Taking of the Bastille, July 14th 1789*, trans. Jean Stewart (New York: Scribner's, 1970).
74 Harris, *Necker and the Revolution of 1789*, pp. 576, 601.

entire system of privilege upon which the *ancien régime* was based, was officially "abolished" by the National Assembly on that dramatic night.[75]

The following month, the Patriots, energized anew by the passive resistance of the king and by the not so passive opposition of certain courtiers and assemblymen to the changes they were implementing, ran roughshod over attempts in the Assembly to grant the aristocracy an upper chamber in the new legislature and to give the monarch an absolute veto. On 8 September, bicameralism went down to crushing defeat by a vote of 849 to 89; and just three days later, by a margin of 673 to 325, a "suspensive" rather than an absolute veto was accorded the king.[76]

On the other side of the ever-widening ideological gulf, a sulky defiance in the face of these initial forays into sociopolitical renovation ran deeper than ever. "Throughout the month of July," Timothy Tackett has written, "the organization of the recalcitrant privileged faction seems never entirely to have dissolved, despite the popular upheavals and the temporary flight of many of its adherents. Even after the meeting halls of the Nobles and the Clergy had been closed . . . a core of the most conservative noblemen and bishops continued to meet in the homes of individuals. . . . Significantly, it was toward the beginning of August that several Patriots first took note of the 'cabal' of nobles and clergy that was opposing them and voting as a bloc."[77]

We can see the fury of the conservative delegates (and of their constituents, too) over the reforms of 4 August mirrored in one noble assemblyman's confidential denunciation of "a revolution which in fact destroys nobility and fiefs, deprives 500,000 families of their property and prepares France for fetters which we are amazed to see borne by Orientals." As late as 10 August, the marquis de Thiboutot, deputy from Caux, endeavored to defend in the Assembly "the special law of fiefs and the honorific prerogatives of manorial lords" and to assert his order's eternal right to "the distinctions that characterized it."[78] As August wore on, moreover, religious issues – the suppression of tithing without redemption, for example, and proposals for the nationalization of church property and for other ecclesiastical changes – seemingly helped crystallize opposition to the Patriots in a number of quarters.[79]

Yet what most alarmed the Patriots in August and September was the attempt by Jean-Joseph Mounier and some of his Monarchist or Anglophile friends, advocating like Necker a British-style variety of constitutionalism, to fashion a coalition of moderate and reactionary deputies

75 Ibid., pp. 627–28.
76 Egret, *Necker*, pp. 353, 357.
77 "Nobles and Third Estate," pp. 285–89.
78 Lefebvre, *Coming of the French Revolution*, pp. 165, 156–57.
79 Tackett, "Nobles and Third Estate," pp. 287–89.

against changes they could all deem too precipitate and radical. It is true that, in the event, the Patriots need not have worried unduly about the obstructive potential of such a grouping on the right. As Jean Egret astutely observed, "The majority of the Nobility and high Clergy . . . felt nothing but hatred and contempt for these Monarchists," whose slightest signs of political moderation they stigmatized as betraying the good old ways of the past.[80] Yet the very fact that so many secular nobles and high ecclesiastics felt this way, and were even ready to join their ideological opposites the Patriots in sabotaging the efforts of Mounier and other Monarchists in the Assembly to secure a bicameral legislature, suggested in itself how far to the right the events of 1788–89 had driven many of the conservatives. These ever more reactionary deputies, hailing in most cases from the relatively impoverished and "unenlightened" countryside, detested the prospect of an upper legislative chamber dominated by cosmopolitan notables like Mounier as much as they abhorred the thought of a unicameral deliberative body controlled by noble and commoner Patriots.

And so the dream of solidarity on the moderate to extreme right held by Mounier and confederates like Lally-Tolendal, Virieu, Clermont-Tonnerre, and Malouet remained but a dream. Yet this was far from obvious at the time to those on the left.

The deputies of the Left clearly believed themselves under siege from late August to early October. Lombard wrote home that "our party is absolutely in the minority." Louis-Prosper Lofficiel was convinced that, without the support of about forty clergymen and a hundred or so liberal nobles, "we would certainly be defeated on every vote." Périsse estimated that as many as two-thirds of all the deputies were influenced by the "cabal" – although fortunately half of these were open-minded and could sometimes be won over.

The celebrated deputy from Anjou, Volney, saw the Assembly as so divided, so menaced by aristocratic machinations, that it needed to be dissolved immediately and replaced by a new body whose membership, excluding most clerics and nobles, would more faithfully reflect the composition of French society. At one point the delegation from Brittany, already storied for its radicalism, considered walking out of the Assembly for good.[81] And Barnave, on the very eve of the October Days, despairingly informed an unknown correspondent that "almost all of the governing part of the Nation," having become "our enemy and the enemy of liberty," was poised to restore the old order and give it "the means to annihilate us, almost without combat."[82] This anxiety was only too obviously sharpened by Patriot memories of the king's abortive resort to

80 Egret, *Révolution des notables*, pp. 227–28, 126.
81 Tackett, "Nobles and Third Estate," p. 289.
82 Cited in Egret, *Révolution des notables*, p. 168.

military intimidation in July. Is it any wonder, then, that Louis's refusal to sanction the Assembly's revolutionary acts now sufficed to drive the Patriots once again into the arms of the "people"?

Privilege, which in the ancien régime had placed a barrier between "notable" Frenchmen even in the cultivated world of the academies, drove them much farther apart in 1788–89, once the collapse of the central government forced them to crystallize their ideas on government and society. This polarizing tendency both responded to and undermined Necker's mediatory role; and it sapped his efforts at mediation in part because it also responded to and helped to confirm the king's rejection of systemic sociopolitical change. All of this in turn prolonged the paralysis of France in a world whose mobilized state power was continuing to migrate away from the Gallic realm, overseas and into easternmost Europe. Yet the polarization evident in respectable French society interacted dialectically as well with the discontents and outright insurrection of the laboring masses. Because this was the case, and because it was only with their muscle power that the erstwhile arbiter of Europe could eventually recover its Great Power status, we need to reassess the role of plebeian Frenchmen (and Frenchwomen) in the advent of the Revolution.

THE MOBILIZATION OF THE URBAN AND RURAL MASSES

The intervention of the kingdom's artisans, shopkeepers, urban workers, and peasants in the epochal quarrel between conservatives and Patriots in 1788–89 was, like that quarrel itself, only made possible by the breakdown of a government overtaxed by its grandiose international mission. Yet, like the schism between conservatives and progressives in elitist France, the uprising of the country's humbler folk had certain roots in the ancien régime. For people who had always been absorbed primarily by the task of keeping themselves and their dependents alive from one day to the next, the antecedents to revolutionary insurgency had to be first and foremost economic in nature, although other factors were in play here as well. Come the unanticipated political void of 1788–89, the king's most industrious and necessitous subjects would be more than ready to add their harsh voices to the national outcry for change.

On more than one occasion we have noted that the French fell on hard economic times in the late 1770s and 1780s. Doyle, summarizing the findings of specialists in this general area, has observed (among other things) that, though the harvests of 1779, 1783, and 1787 were fairly good, there were in 1778, 1782, 1784, and 1786 "serious deficiencies affecting several provinces at once, and in 1788, for the first time within living memory, the harvest was poor to catastrophic almost everywhere."

Yields and revenues, it must be emphasized, were unstable over this period in all sectors, not just in that of cereals.

In 1778, the vintage failed completely, depriving many small cultivators of an important supplement to their revenues. Subsequent years were abundant, and by the mid-1780s there was a wine glut. These wild fluctuations deprived the market of all stability. In 1785 and 1786 there was also a general shortage of hay, making it impossible to obtain adequate fodder for livestock at reasonable prices, and thereby forcing sales of cattle and sheep in an oversupplied market. Only one thing remained steady and inexorable throughout these see-saw years, and that was the rise in rents.[83]

With more peasants than ever in a century of population growth vying for lands, agricultural rents, indeed, could only soar – and this at a time when the same demographic pressures also ensured that the wages earned by plebeian cultivators as supplemental income fell ever farther behind the prices they had to pay for supplemental foodstuffs. And how many unlettered countryfolk owned sufficient land to profit from rising agricultural prices, let alone from skyrocketing agricultural rents?

To refer to wages is to conjure up the question of the industrial sector in France. The fact that manufacture played second fiddle to agriculture in this typically premodern society meant that hardship in the latter sector all but guaranteed tribulations in the former domain. Again, Doyle:

The most important industry in France, accounting for half of all industrial production, was textiles. And after food, clothing was the largest item in most people's expenditure. . . . And so, the wild ups and downs of the harvests in the 1770s and 1780s were reflected in equally spectacular variations in the textile trades born of unstable demand. The effect on weaving towns like Rouen, Amiens, Nîmes, or Lyons was devastating. Weavers tended to be laid off at exactly the times when the price of bread was already straining their limited wages. And in the countryside peasants impoverished by the agricultural crisis found that they could not rely on weaving in order to make up for their losses.

As if this were not enough, the dearth of hay and other fodder crops in the mid-1780s restricted the supply of flax and hemp to workers in a variety of textiles; and the silk harvest failed in 1787. Whether the Anglo-French Commercial Treaty of 1786 actually aggravated the crisis by allowing English woolens and cottons to compete in France with the products of such textile centers as Rouen, Lyons, and Amiens is still moot; yet this trade agreement certainly did nothing to alleviate the woes of French spinners and weavers, and they naturally saw the treaty in the worst possible light.[84]

In any case, the disastrous harvest of 1788 not only wiped out or severely reduced the subsistence margin of many peasants; it also wreaked

83 Doyle, *Origins of the French Revolution*, pp. 159–60.
84 Ibid., pp. 160–61.

havoc on textiles and other industries whose wares could no longer be purchased by townspeople and rural folk constrained to spend their funds upon ever more expensive food. This development led in turn to widespread unemployment and underemployment in the industrial sector, so that by late 1788 and through most of 1789 the difficulties in agriculture and industry were mutually reinforcing. Furthermore, the bitterly cold winter of 1788–89 and subsequent spring floods worsened the economic crisis by impeding the milling of grain and the transport within France of fuels, foodstuffs, and other essential commodities.[85]

It is not surprising, then, that by 1789 laboring French people should have been caught up (even more than they usually were) in the toils of dire need. The price of bread at Paris, on the rise ever since the preceding August, passed fourteen sous for the four-pound loaf by the spring of 1789 and was absorbing as much as 88 percent of the average worker's salary at times. In provincial France, the towns and peasant communities, traumatized by the fear of famine, fought to preserve local stores of grain; riots erupted in market places, and millers and bakers were assaulted; and grain was often seized on the roads. The most serious disturbances prior to the events of the summer occurred in March and April in Flanders, Provence, Franche-Comté, Dauphiné, Languedoc, and Guienne. At Versailles, Necker, bedeviled by the subsistence crisis as well as by the sociopolitical impasse, had to spend hard currency and credit (desperately needed elsewhere by the straitened crown) to import grain, subsidize merchants in Paris and other communities, establish charitable workshops for the unemployed and starving in the capital, and pay troops overseeing the transport of grain through the countryside. Government and people alike were adversely affected by the economic crisis.[86]

These economic troubles alone would have provided ample incentive for the humble folk of urban and rural France to intervene in the constitutional and social wrangles of their betters. Yet other influences were also inclining them in that direction. For example, as George Rudé demonstrated with particular clarity, contesting elements within the "dominant classes" at Paris took to appealing to the populace during the prerevolutionary crisis with printed and verbal attacks against each other and with antiministerial invocations of liberty and social justice. The artisans and shopkeepers whom history would soon know as the sansculottes developed early on the habit of championing one courtier faction against another, one institution (such as the Paris Parlement) against

85 Ibid., pp. 160–67.
86 On Necker's handling of the subsistence crisis in his second ministry, see Harris, *Necker and the Revolution of 1789*, esp. pp. 273–74, 544–59.

another (such as the government itself), and so by 1789 were already psychologically prepared to burst into the arena of politics.[87]

In the countryside, too, factors other than the economic downturn of the late 1770s and 1780s were destabilizing the population. Theda Skocpol, for example, has pointed out that "the potential for the peasant revolts that erupted in 1789 was inherent in an agrarian social structure peculiar to France (and to the western parts of a disunited Germany) within eighteenth-century Europe." Subject to the constraints of the seigneurial regime, French peasants controlled the utilization of much more of the arable land than did the increasingly enserfed peasantry of eastern Europe or the "dispossessed agricultural lower strata" of England. Concomitantly, the peasant communities of France, "shaped through centuries of struggle for economic security and administrative autonomy," had by the eighteenth century emerged as formidable competitors with their lords for local agrarian rights and influence. And the crown played an important role in this process – as in so much else in French history.

The penetration by the royal administration into the localities had gradually edged aside the seigneur, leaving him merely the "first subject of the parish." He, or his agents if he was an absentee (as was often the case), did retain the control of seigneurial justice; yet this was a right with much economic but little political significance. Otherwise the peasants, with the aid of the local priest, handled their own local affairs – responsible to the *intendant* through his subdelegate.

Though the village assemblies more often than not were "informally dominated by the well-to-do peasants," they could still function, and frequently did function, as "vital arenas for the discussion of local affairs by all family heads; and their decisions controlled key aspects of village life."[88]

Generalizing from his research into lord–peasant relations in prerevolutionary Burgundy, Hilton Root has argued along similar lines, although affirming even more explicitly that "the rise of the bureaucratic state" and resultant "absorption of the village into the bureaucratic structure" of that Bourbon state gave the peasant community "a new self-image" and the confidence to challenge its seigneur as it had never challenged him before. Vaunting this new confidence rather than responding to any novel demands on the part of the local lord, the rural village tapped the burgeoning talents of the legal profession to launch a "devastating" critique not only of specific seigneurial rights but also of "the historical

---

87 See George Rudé, *The Crowd in the French Revolution* (New York: Oxford University Press, 1959); and *Paris and London in the Eighteenth Century* (New York: Viking, 1973).
88 Skocpol, *States and Social Revolutions*, pp. 118–21.

and moral foundations of seigneurial authority" itself.[89] Whether the primary emphasis in this structuralist rendering of rural history in the late ancien régime falls on the paternalistic role of the Bourbon state or upon the autonomy or semiautonomy of the peasants' communities, their psychological preparedness for an active role in the politics of 1789 seems as evident as does that of the Parisians and townsfolk in general.

Thus, ideological and structural as well as economic realities made it likely that the "people" would rise up in 1789 – were they given the chance to do so.[90] That opportunity came with the central government's collapse in 1788–89. And, although we have thus far been accentuating the broad fiscal, constitutional, and social aspects of that collapse, we need now to recall that, in this as in many subsequent revolutionary situations, the inability or unwillingness of the old regime state to employ its instruments of physical coercion – most notably, its army – to forestall or suppress potentially revolutionary unrest played a very definite role in triggering revolution.

Assuredly, the monarchy had impaired its ability to use the French army to this purpose, at least over the short term, by implementing in 1787–88 reforms that exacerbated existing tensions within that institution. Court aristocrats, provincial nobles, *anoblis*, and opulent commoners feuded among themselves – and vented their frustration and anger at times upon the government itself. As Samuel Scott has commented, the crown's policy "contributed to the deterioration of morale within the Royal Army, especially among officers." The polarization within the overall "society of notables" in 1788–89 must have compounded this problem insofar as it drove "notable" officers within the army even farther apart. Yet, as Scott has also observed:

Of even greater importance in determining how the army would react to crisis was its day-to-day functioning. . . . What ultimately incapacitated the army and led directly to the collapse of both royal and noble authority was the breakdown of the discipline exercised by officers over their men. This failure arose primarily

89 See Root, "En Bourgogne: L'état et la communauté rurale, 1661–1789," *Annales: E.S.C.* 37 (March–April 1982), pp. 288–303; and "Challenging the Seigneurie: Community and Contention on the Eve of the French Revolution," *Journal of Modern History* 57 (December 1985), pp. 652–81. This interpretation receives additional support in Jones, *Peasantry in the French Revolution*, passim; and John Markoff, "Peasant Grievances and Peasant Insurrection: France in 1789," *Journal of Modern History* 62 (1990), pp. 445–76.
90 There is currently a debate regarding the relative merits of "structural" and "historical" (i.e. economic) explanations of peasant behavior in revolutionary situations. See J. Craig Jenkins, "Why Do Peasants Rebel? Structural and Historical Theories of Modern Peasant Rebellions," *American Journal of Sociology* 88 (1982), pp. 487–514.

from the conditions of military life, particularly the relationship between soldiers and officers.[91]

On more than one occasion during 1788 and early 1789, officers hesitated to order their troops into action against rioters, or the troops themselves proved reluctant to march against their countrymen; and such failures on the part of the army in a number of areas marked by unrest reflected in some measure the lack of empathy between noble officers and soldiers of humble provenance. When, in addition, we recall that officers and soldiers alike wore themselves out policing the countryside in a time of subsistence crisis, and were often underpaid and hungry themselves, it becomes even easier to understand the diminishing reliability of the army as an instrument of social control in 1788–89.[92]

Yet even after all these points have been taken into consideration, there remains the question of how, in reality, the king could have used military coercion, even assuming its momentary efficacy, to solve the bedrock geopolitical and sociopolitical problems that had bankrupted his government in the first place. Necker's warnings against any such employment of the army – and the sane misgivings of the king himself on the subject – can only confirm our suspicion that the situation in France had by now evolved far beyond the point at which a military coup could have served any positive long-term design.[93]

It is not our purpose here to relate the gripping story of the seizing of the Bastille on 14 July or to chronicle the insurrections in the other communities of the realm. Historians without number have done that, and done it very well. What we need to do is to account, in broad analytical terms, for the municipal and peasant upheavals of 1789 and gauge their significance in helping to launch France irreversibly upon its momentous revolutionary adventure.

Lynn Hunt has reminded us that the "municipal revolution was a national movement because it occurred all over France, not because it was centered in Paris." Her research into this matter has shown that twenty of the thirty communities in the kingdom boasting populations of twenty thousand or more witnessed the formation of revolutionary committees during the latter half of July, to be followed by six additional towns in August. "Grenoble and Lille," she has conceded, "had committees for only a few days in July; Toulouse and Clermont-Ferrand never introduced committees. But even though a few municipal govern-

91 Scott, *Response of the Royal Army to the French Revolution*, pp. 27–33.
92 On the army's problems in 1788–89, refer also to Bertaud, *Army of the French Revolution*, esp. pp. 22–29.
93 For some very thoughtful observations on the role (and political options) of Louis XVI in the July and October Days, consult Harris, *Necker and the Revolution of 1789*, pp. 577–78, 691–93.

ments retained their position and power, most local governments changed dramatically in some way during the summer of 1789."[94] They did so because urgent political and economic issues, though we know them best in connection with the pivotal insurrection at Paris, were truly national in character.

Four factors, according to Hunt, were particularly influential in determining the extent of change in a given municipality: its socioeconomic structure, the recent political behavior of its ruling elite, the impact of the economic crisis, and the closeness of its ties with other towns. Of these four variables the first was the most important; yet all four of them "worked together to limit the political options available in each town." Revolutionary change, it turns out, was least likely "in administrative towns, whose ruling elites had either opposed the monarchy or opened their ranks in 1787–88, in which prices did not continue to climb in 1789 (the south) and which were not in close contact with revolutionary centers." Revolution was likeliest to erupt "in manufacturing, military, and naval construction towns. Committees claimed more power where ruling elites had refused to open their ranks, especially during the meetings to elect deputies to the Estates General; where prices rose steeply in 1789 (the north); and where the local leaders of the revolution had close contacts with other revolutionary centers." Displaying the most ambivalent politics in 1789, according to Hunt, were commercial and in particular port towns:

They established committees, but the committees rarely took complete control, except in those towns where the ruling elite showed itself to be rigid and closed prior to the Revolution. Port towns often had the best access to foreign grain sources, so their prices rose less steeply than did prices in the hinterland. Contact with other towns was also different for the port towns: their merchants had national and international connections, but they were much less subject to the influence of revolutionaries in Rennes, Dijon, or even Paris, than were the political leaders of the smaller towns of the hinterland.[95]

Because of its unique status, Paris did not in all respects fulfill the criteria for revolutionary upheaval adduced on these pages. Nonetheless, it is easy to see why the capital, with its politicized judges, *officiers*, and men of letters, its intransigent municipal elite, its economic difficulties, and its exposure to the rumors (and eventual reality) of counterrevolutionary measures coordinated at nearby Versailles, should have exploded in July and October. It is, furthermore, easy to understand why so many other communities across France, which did more or less satisfy these revolutionary criteria, should also have revolted. And the brawn in most

94 Lynn Hunt, "Committees and Communes: Local Politics and National Revolution in 1789," *Comparative Studies in Society and History* 18 (July 1976), p. 324.
95 Ibid., pp. 327, 328–29.

of these uprisings was furnished by small shopkeepers, craftsmen, jour-
neymen, and unskilled toilers, some of whom had participated in the
spring in the "consciousness-raising" tasks of electing delegates to the
Estates General and drafting protests to the king, and all of whom harbored throughout 1789 fears of starvation, aristocratic plots, and foreign
invasion.[96]

With the kingdom's populous capital lost to its king, then, and with
other cities and towns, like Paris, setting up revolutionary committees,
forming citizen militias, and obeying only such orders from the National
Assembly as sorted with their own local political concerns, power effectively shifted from monarch, ministers, and intendants to Assembly and
even, to some extent, from Assembly to local municipalities. But that
historic transference of power only engaged the majority in the realm
with the coming of the peasant upheaval in the summer.

In rural as in urban France, the electoral campaign in the spring of
1789 did much to awaken the masses.

In each rural community, every man 25 or older who paid any amount of taxes
was eligible to participate in a meeting that both elected representatives to the
bailliage assembly and drew up a *cahier de doléances*. . . . Extraordinary as it may
seem, every peasant community was invited by order of the king to ruminate
collectively upon its troubles. The result surely was, on the whole, to heighten
possibilities for the peasants to rebel, especially against seigneurs and nonlocal
recipients of the tithes.[97]

Significantly, insurgency in the countryside began to develop at this time,
well in advance of the uprising at Paris:

During the spring, . . . peasants began to go beyond bread riots to attack the
seigneurial system. "The first wave of rural uprisings was . . . aimed mainly at
tithes, feudal rights, and the men who received them . . . " Very often the target
was the feudal records of the local seigneur, but there were also seizures of
"hoarded" grain stores. Even these early outbreaks were widespread, occurring
in Anjou, Dauphiné, the Paris region, Picardy, Hainault, and the Midi.[98]

But only with the summer did this phenomenon become nationwide in
scope, culminating in the "Great Fear" of late July and early August.[99]
At this time, rural cultivators, obsessed by fears that brigands in the pay
of foreigners and/or native aristocrats would cut down the crops ripening

96 On the elections to the Estates General, refer again to the papers of Furet and Halévi
    in Baker, ed., *Political Culture of the Old Regime*. On the beliefs of the townspeople
    in 1789, see Lefebvre, *Coming of the French Revolution*, esp. chap. 6.
97 Skocpol, *States and Social Revolutions*, p. 123.
98 Ibid., p. 122. A point also emphasized recently by Jones, *Peasantry in the French
    Revolution*, esp. pp. 60–62.
99 The authoritative work on this fascinating subject is still Georges Lefebvre, *The Great
    Fear of 1789: Rural Panic in Revolutionary France*, trans. Joan White (New York:
    Pantheon, 1973).

in their fields, banded together for defensive purposes and then passed on to an assault upon the manorial archives of their lords.

Clearly, the uprising in the countryside, as a national development, was made possible by, and then reacted back upon, the municipal revolution. The authorities had been unwilling or unable to employ the royal army against the revolutionaries at Paris; the *intendants* were deserting or had been chased from their posts; what military coercive power still existed was passing in all areas into the hands of civic militias; and peasant soldiers, allowed to return to their home provinces to assist in harvesting the crops, were spreading there the news of revolt in cities and towns across the realm.

Yet, as Skocpol has suggested, the most decisive factor in this situation may have been the ambivalence of the Patriots in the Assembly and in the rebellious municipalities regarding the use of force: "If (as many would have preferred) they used militias or called upon the royal army to protect property rights in the countryside, they would play into the hands of autocratic reaction. This was a chance that most were unprepared to take. Only in a few localities did urban forces act against the peasants."[100] Progressive notables who themselves believed in foreigner-aristocratic plots against the new France they were attempting to create, and who had just received in the July Days evidence of the king's unyielding hostility to their meliorist endeavors, could hardly afford – yet – to turn against their rural plebeian supporters. Hence, the National Assembly not only refused in this epochal summer to adopt such a course of action but also tried on the night of 4 August to meet the peasantry halfway by reforming (if not, for sure, abrogating altogether) the seigneurial regime in rural France.

Furthermore, with unrest in town and countryside persisting through August and September due primarily to the continuance of the economic crisis, the more radical Patriots in the Constituent Assembly and their adherents at Paris and in the provinces remained under popular pressure (had they needed it) to defend the Revolution as it had developed up to that point. Here, then, was yet another calculation behind the Parisian insurrection of early October that secured the residence of the sovereign, and that of his legislature, in the capital of the awakening Gallic nation.

After all is said and done – after we have fully reviewed the convergent forces impelling France into revolution in 1788–89 – we must still acknowledge the paramount importance in this situation of a discrepancy between the crown's grandiose international ambitions and the socio-political resources it was willing to mobilize to realize those ambitions. Louis XVI was sufficiently alive to his geopolitical responsibilities to

100 Skocpol, *States and Social Revolutions*, p. 124.

accord Necker a free hand in convoking the Estates General in 1789; yet, in the end, he could not bring himself to accept the reforms that, by fully integrating his "respectable" subjects into public affairs, would enable his country to resume its quest for security and greatness. He was encouraged in his propensity to uphold his forebears' canons by the queen, his brothers, the courtiers, and those ecclesiastics and lay nobles in the Assembly and the kingdom at large driven ever farther to the right by the prospect of basic sociopolitical change. Thus, Bosher's gallant characterization of Louis as "liberal to some extent, almost won over to the revolutionary cause" must yield to Simon Schama's description of the king at this moment of truth as "either feebly submissive . . . or deviously reactionary."[101] But the radicalized Patriots within and outside the Assembly, many of whom owed their public positions and aspirations at least in part to the government's past waging of war, profited from that same government's paralysis (and from the anxieties and actions of working French citizens) to take control of civic affairs in October.

Indeed, October marked the end of the "coming of the French Revolution" and the beginning of the fully mature revolutionary process. At least, so would many fine historians argue today, concurring in this with Georges Lefebvre. "Nothing could disguise the fact that political authority had shifted decisively," D. M. G. Sutherland has written. "Unlike July when Parisians' actions had been essentially defensive, the October Days represented the first . . . occasion when direct Parisian intervention decisively affected national politics." Most portentously, "Parisians had begun to learn the lessons of insurrectionary politics."[102] Colin Lucas has held in similar fashion that "it is October rather than July that appears . . . more significant . . . in shaping the revolutionary crowd." Now, and only now, the "crowd" invaded "both seats of national government – the royal palace and the Assembly – rather than merely the seat of municipal government." Now, and only now, it secured the person of the king "as a permanent, political solution to a perennial problem rather than a temporary solution."[103] For better or for worse, the Revolution was under way in France, and it would unfold, as the old regime had developed and then foundered, under a dialectic of external and internal pressures for change.

101 Citations from Bosher, *French Revolution*, p. 148; and Simon Schama, *Citizens: A Chronicle of the French Revolution* (New York: Knopf, 1989), p. 419.
102 D. M. G. Sutherland, *France 1789–1815: Revolution and Counterrevolution* (New York: Oxford University Press, 1986), p. 85.
103 Lucas, "The Crowd and Politics Between *Ancien Régime* and Revolution in France," *Journal of Modern History* 60 (1988), pp. 448–49. Yet another historian viewing the October Days as a turning point is Egret, in *Necker*, p. 377. Admittedly, Doyle, in his *Origins of the French Revolution*, prefers to break the story off with the events of August 1789.

Conclusion

If this study is essentially correct, the French Revolution began in 1789 as the result of a convergence in the Gallic kingdom of statist geopolitical and sociopolitical needs rooted deeply in the past. On the one hand, Bourbon statesmen were long mesmerized by the vision of a France not only perdurably secure in the endless competition of the European states but also uniquely positioned to achieve greatness on both the high seas and the Continent.[1] On the other hand, the policy makers who sought to realize this vision found, as time went on, that pursuing it forced them to sponsor a kind of domestic change that was ever more difficult to square with the social and political tenets undergirding the ancien régime. By 1789, the French crown was irretrievably undone by its coalescing failures in the foreign and domestic realms: that is to say, its failure to achieve anything remotely approaching its historic goals abroad and its failure to maintain control over rising sociopolitical expectations at home that, paradoxically, owed much in the first place to the crown's very pursuit of international greatness.

Although the unfolding of the Revolution itself lies manifestly outside the purview of our inquiry, we cannot help noting how deep a shadow was cast over the sanguinary French landscape of 1789–99 by the historical forces that had so long conditioned developments in the old regime. This is emphatically not to posit an unbroken continuity extending from pre-revolutionary days to and through the epochal period of the Revolution. As Lynn Hunt, Maurice Agulhon, Mona Ozouf, Simon Schama, Joan Landes, Emmet Kennedy, and others have shown in their compelling

---

1 To repeat what was said earlier, such an interpretation cannot attribute much significance to the natural frontiers concept, which would have had Bourbon France limited to the space occupied by ancient Gaul, and which can hardly account for the opportunistic dynamism that characterized French foreign policy before (as, indeed, after) 1789. But refer again to Sahlins, "Natural Frontiers Revisited," pp. 1423–51, for a stimulating discussion of this concept.

works, the Revolution gave rise to a new popular politics and political culture. Ordinary Frenchmen and Frenchwomen were for a few unforgettable years after 1789 set adrift in a void created by a truly historic collapse of central authority in this traditionally well-ordered polity. How they dealt with that void, how they fashioned through rhetoric and ritual and raw human action a new identity for themselves in a world briefly turned upside down – that is assuredly one of the most fascinating and portentous stories of the revolutionary decade in France.[2] And nothing in that ancien régime so assiduously studied by latter-day historians could have altogether prepared the men and women of 1789–99 for the revolutionary occurrences they were to witness, for the revolutionary turns their own humble lives (in so many cases) were to take.

Yet, this having been said – and it is a point worth dwelling on – the fact remains that in the Revolution, as in the old regime, the destinies of ordinary Frenchmen and Frenchwomen were ineludibly caught up in the dialectical interplay between statist geopolitical and sociopolitical requirements.

How could this not have been the case, given the weight of a century and a half of Gallic expansionism on land and sea, given the undiminished need of French statesmen for domestic legitimacy, and given the emergence of a host of "popular" politicians ready to take up the age-old challenge of meshing foreign and domestic policies? And, granted these realities, the waging of war was likely now, as before, to be the crucial catalyst of change. In this connection, Theda Skocpol has unerringly refuted the assertion by François Furet and Denis Richet that the drift back to war in the 1790s was somehow a fortuitous development that threw the Revolution off course:

To believe this is to suppose that the Revolution could have proceeded, let alone broken out, in a France somehow suddenly and miraculously ripped out of the context of the European states system in which it had always been embedded. Neither the domestic actors in the French revolutionary dramas nor the foreign spectators, kings and peoples, ever succumbed to such an illusion.

Warfare was, in fact, "far from extrinsic to the development and fate of the French Revolution; rather it was central and constitutive."[3]

2 See Lynn Hunt, *Politics, Culture, and Class in the French Revolution*; Maurice Agulhon, *Marianne into Battle: Republican Imagery and Symbolism in France, 1789–1880* (Cambridge: Cambridge University Press, 1981); Mona Ozouf, *La Fête révolutionnaire, 1789–1799* (Paris: Gallimard, 1976); Simon Schama, *Citizens: A Chronicle of the French Revolution*; Joan Landes, *Women and the Public Sphere in the Age of the French Revolution* (Ithaca, N.Y.: Cornell University Press, 1988); and Emmet Kennedy, *A Cultural History of the French Revolution* (New Haven, Conn.: Yale University Press, 1989).
3 Skocpol, *States and Social Revolutions*, p. 186. Isser Woloch even more recently has taken François Furet (and a number of his compatriots) to task for maintaining in their

This was so in at least three senses. In the first place, there was the sheer inherence of war in the global context of the Revolution. After all, the patterns of war as the revolutionaries waged it arrestingly recalled the patterns of competition in the ancien régime. This was notably if not exclusively the case in the Terror of 1793–94. In the Continental sphere of geopolitics, the resumption of the ancient struggle with enemies to the east entailed a return to conventional methods of diplomacy. As Robert R. Palmer has written, "the French Republic . . . entered into secret negotiations with the Turkish Empire. French officers went to Constantinople to instruct the sultan's sans-culottes. A sum of 4,000,000 livres was offered to the Turks to attack the Hapsburg dominions along the Danube."[4] This might have been the Sun King (or even, 150 years farther back, Francis I!) attempting to apply pressure on the Austrian foe from the rear – save that, now, the French had also to deal with the Prussians and were ever aware as well of the Russian tsarina's anti-Jacobin fury. And in the maritime theater of power politics, too, very little had changed. Again, Palmer:

The Committee of Public Safety clung to its project of attacking England. . . . The modern Carthage remained the true enemy of mankind, and especially of Frenchmen. France through all its avatars, Bourbon monarchy, revolutionary Republic, military empire, carried on its modern Hundred Years War with the nation of shopkeepers.[5]

When Robespierre or Bertrand Barère or one of the other Jacobins wielding power in the Terror banged the deafening drums of patriotism in the National Convention over the supposed turpitude of the British, what were they doing if not resurrecting (and manipulating) the Anglophobia of the old regime?

And tacitly informing both Austrophobia and Anglophobia in Gallic ruling circles was the most deeply rooted conviction of all: that France, due to its unique geographic situation, was uniquely entitled to aspire to supremacy or at least to a pivotal role in both maritime and Continental arenas of power politics. And this did not always remain an unarticulated

scholarly works the "French blanket denial that circumstances shaped the revolution or that 'revolutionary necessity' could ever justify acts that were inexcusable by ordinary standards of liberal principle or morality." See Woloch's review article "On the Latent Illiberalism of the French Revolution," *American Historical Review* 95 (1990), pp. 1452–70. Under review here is François Furet and Mona Ozouf, eds., *A Critical Dictionary of the French Revolution*, trans. Arthur Goldhammer (Cambridge, Mass.: Belknap/Harvard University Press, 1989). See also, on this issue, the remarks by David Bien, Donald Sutherland, and Furet himself in "François Furet's Interpretation of the French Revolution," *French Historical Studies* 16 (1990), pp. 777–802.

4 Robert R. Palmer, *Twelve Who Ruled: The Year of the Terror in the French Revolution* (Princeton, N.J.: Princeton University Press, 1941), p. 104.

5 Ibid., p. 218.

conviction. Stunningly consistent with all that had gone before on this capital point was the Committee of Public Safety's apotheosis (in a letter of 2 January 1794) of France – France, "which alone of all European states can and should be a power on both land and sea."[6] How could 150 years of Gallic pretensions in the world's great affairs have been more effectively summed up? Robespierre and his cloud-compelling confederates might soon fall from power in one of the final hecatombs of this bloody upheaval; but their successors would carry on the hallowed tradition of warfare on the land and dream the heady old dream of humbling Albion on the seas.

In the second place, war was central to and constitutive of the French Revolution on the level of day-to-day domestic politics. Skocpol has accurately noted that "conflicting groups were repeatedly tempted (like Court cliques under the Old Regime) to use for factional purposes preparations for wars, and the anticipated or actual consequences of successful campaigns."[7] Thus, J.-P. Brissot and some of his impetuous associates in the Legislative Assembly courted a general war in 1791–92 in order to overthrow the constitutional monarchist or Feuillant faction in the ministries. (After some hesitation, the reactionary party at the court took up the same cause, promoting it as an instrument of its own, counterrevolutionary, aims.) Thus, in the course of 1793, the Robespierrist Jacobins, initially divided over the prospect of going to war, used the Brissotine faction's bungling of the military campaign against a swelling coalition of European states to replace that coterie of politicians in the councils of power. And thus again, during the years immediately subsequent to the demise of the Robespierrists, shifting combinations of politicians and generals seeking to advance their own agendas took full advantage of what was by now a predominantly aggressive rather than defensive bellicosity inspiriting the French. Bonaparte, of course, was to be the most successful of these individuals – a politician and consummate general rolled into one.

Finally, war was central to and constitutive of the Revolution in the sense that the ruling progressive notables, driven by their need to conduct war successfully, sharply accelerated (at least temporarily) the heretofore gradual trend within their country toward meritocracy and a more inclusive politics.

It is perfectly true that the revolutionaries, particularly those of the years culminating in the Terror, were not actuated in their domestic policies solely by geopolitical concerns. They had their own idealistic and humanitarian goals to pursue. Moreover, they had to respond to endog-

6 Ibid.
7 Skocpol, *States and Social Revolutions*, p. 186.

enous sociopolitical, economic, and religious developments that (in addition to influencing their foreign policies) were conducive to a far more radical transformation of politics and society in revolutionary France than had occurred (for example, and by way of contrast) 150 years earlier in revolutionary England.

For one thing, since France's renovators did not, like their counterparts in England, inherit a national representative assembly long accustomed to mediating the diverse political, social, and regional interests in the kingdom, and were not themselves versed in the difficult arts of governing (at least on a stage of national politics), they inevitably came to blows over how to fashion a stable parliamentary system that could accommodate France's myriad interest groups. For another thing, the totally unanticipated peasant uprising of 1789 – and the endemic popular insurrectionism of subsequent years – subjected the ruling notables in France to pressures that the "dominant class" in the English Revolution had not known and helped further to divide these "respectable" Frenchmen. Then, again, the differences between proclerical and anticlerical deputies in the successive assemblies of revolutionary France helped to ignite a civil war that affected many more individuals than had the civil struggle in the England of the 1640s, and thus generated a much greater fund of both revolutionary and counterrevolutionary fervor.[8]

To these domestic factors adduced in partial explanation of the "revolutionizing of the Revolution" the historian of political culture would add endogenous cultural processes. Lynn Hunt, indeed, has insisted flatly that "the origins of democratic and revolutionary republicanism must be sought in political culture, where all the strands of the polity came together."[9] For Hunt, political competition within the Third Estate from 1789 on, more intense than anything of the kind in the English Revolution, and feeding on rhetorical, ritualistic, and symbolic representations of sociopolitical realities, enlarged the possibilities for and quickened the pace of political mobilization in this land, thus radicalizing the Revolution well into the 1790s.[10]

Nonetheless, whatever the significance of internal factors – sociopolitical, economic, religious, and cultural – in driving the Revolution in France ever leftward, it was above all war that brought this about. For, in the final analysis, there is no reason to believe that the bewigged and

---

8 See Theda Skocpol's discussion of these and other factors in ibid., pp. 180–85.
9 Hunt, *Politics, Culture, and Class*, pp. 234–35.
10 François Furet has stressed in like fashion the role of cultural factors in radicalizing the Revolution. Refer again to *Interpreting the French Revolution*, passim. Along these lines, see also the essays in Colin Lucas, ed., *The Political Culture of the French Revolution* (Oxford: Pergamon, 1988) and the pertinent essays in Hunt, ed., *Eroticism and the Body Politic*.

comfortable notables who governed the country in the early 1790s would have even marginally empowered the urban sans-culotterie, not even to score points in their factional bickering, had they not become needful of popular support in their undertaking of war against virtually all of Europe. True, the Terror of 1793–94 was, in an immediate sense, directed as much against those who fomented civil war at home as against those threatening France from abroad.[11] Yet, in fact, the two perils could not be separated; and, ultimately, the French of whatever rank and station who viewed the crushing of counterrevolutionary rebellion at home as a crucial means toward the preservation of sociopolitical reform were the same individuals most patriotically determined to restore French security and greatness in the world at large.

Hence, for the authoritarian government of the Terror, its imposition of some of the political and socioeconomic demands of the sans-culottes on the entire country was, first and foremost, the price it had to pay for popular participation in the war effort. And let there be no mistake about it: The war effort was what really mattered. "The armies of France expanded enormously," and the men on the Committee of Public Safety labored tirelessly at "selecting and advising new generals for the armies, propagandizing the troops, and bending all of the government's powers to the enormous problems of supplying the armies." The Montagnard authorities requisitioned and/or arranged for the purchase of foodstuffs and other commodities for the troops and urban dwellers, organized the weapons industry, and regulated prices and wages. Only through such extraordinary efforts could the government not only "relieve popular economic distress" but also provide adequately for the revolutionary armies.[12]

That the waging of war had once again, but now to an even greater extent than before, become the function of French governance most affecting the population as a whole is suggested by the language (however overblown it may have been) in the proclamation of the famous *levée en masse* of August 1793:

All Frenchmen are in permanent requisition for army service. The young men will go to fight; the married men will forge arms and carry supplies; the women will make tents and uniforms and will serve in the hospitals; the children will shred the old clothes; the old men will be taken to the public squares to excite the courage of the combatants, the hatred of royalty and the unity of the Republic.[13]

---

11 For an interpretation of the Revolution that places considerable emphasis on the interplay between domestic revolutionary and counterrevolutionary forces, consult again Sutherland, *France 1789–1815*, passim.
12 Skocpol, *States and Social Revolutions*, p. 189.
13 Cited in ibid.

Predictably, the ruling notables' sensitivity to the needs of laboring Frenchmen and Frenchwomen waned in Thermidor and under the Directory, for the military emergency seemed, by then, to have passed forever. Yet the very fact that revolutionary sentiment henceforth resided most securely in France's increasingly aggressive armies serves to underscore the dialectical relationship between geopolitical and sociopolitical imperatives in the "process" of the French Revolution.[14]

In summation, we can at this point regard the French Revolution as having continued the thrust of the ancien régime toward both a modernized, militarily more puissant state and a partial empowerment of previously unheeded Frenchmen. And as the Revolution furthered the agenda of the old regime, so the Napoleonic era advanced the agenda of both prerevolutionary and revolutionary France. For it was only when all inhabitants (at least, all male inhabitants) of France had been granted certain social, religious, judicial, and economic rights – if not, assuredly, full political liberties – that a modernized state, controlled by a military genius who knew how to tap the basic patriotism of his subjects, could come closest to realizing the boldest geopolitical dreams of both the old regime and the Revolution. That Napoleon, like other conquerors before and after him, failed to break strategically out of the heartland of western and central Europe only showed how exceedingly difficult it was and ever would be for any warlord arising in this region to deal simultaneously with the state power generated in the overseas world and with that engendered in the Eurasian hinterland.[15]

But at least the revolutionary and Napoleonic eras made some headway toward resolving in the French state the deeply embedded contradiction between geopolitical pretensions and sociopolitical principles. "Modern" statist ambitions to preserve security and greatness in a nascent system of global power politics required, and had now secured, some degree of statist sensitivity to, and accommodation of, the hopes and needs of ordinary French people. And this conclusion may serve as well as a prescription for comprehending the Revolution's overall significance in the emergence of modern France.

"The Revolution," Lynn Hunt has affirmed provocatively, "was not just an example of the violence and instability caused by modernization,

---

14 Jean-Paul Bertaud, in *The Army of the French Revolution*, remains perhaps the outstanding authority upon this fascinating subject. Yet, admittedly, we should beware of exaggerating the strength of republican sentiments in the armies. See, on this issue, Alan Forrest, *Conscripts and Deserters: The Army and French Society during the Revolution and Empire* (New York: Oxford University Press, 1989); and *The Soldiers of the French Revolution* (Durham: Duke University Press, 1990).

15 On this subject, consult, in Dehio, *The Precarious Balance*, the lengthy chapter on the revolutionary and Napoleonic eras.

or an essential step on the road to capitalism, or a link in the birth of totalitarianism. . . . More centrally, it was the moment in which politics was discovered as an enormously potent activity, as an agent for conscious change, as the mold for character, culture, and social relations." Along lines implied by such an assessment, Hunt goes on to assert forthrightly that in "many respects . . . democratic republicanism was the most important outcome of the Revolution," in terms of both "its immediate impact and its long-term influence."[16] Yet, while admiring much in Hunt's politico-cultural analysis of the Revolution and its aftermath, we may feel that it requires (as, for that matter, does Skocpol's structuralist analysis) some modification.

Our examination of the long-term and immediate origins of the French Revolution suggests that two things were supremely at issue in France before, during, and after the cataclysm of 1789–99. We can call these two things "state competitiveness" and "state-sponsored social justice." The former, in our construction, necessarily preceded the latter. In other words, the historic Gallic state, like all states, was, first of all, concerned to maintain its competitive status vis-à-vis rival powers of the time; and chiefly because of this prior and unalterable concern it was eventually persuaded to bring about a greater measure of social justice (and its indispensable concomitant, state power) by conferring various rights and status recognition on unprecedented numbers of its subjects. Hence, the dynamic foreign policy and radical domestic reforms of the revolutionary and Napoleonic years.

But hence, as well, the subsequent achievements of the Gallic state in both the foreign and domestic spheres of policy. If, on the one hand, there had been no revolution to make French government more efficient, to harness to its purposes the tremendous intelligence and devotion and energy of the French people, could France have preserved any substantial portion of its Great Power status? Could it have warred yet once more against Vienna – and done so successfully – in 1859, and mounted any major effort against the more formidable Prussia of Bismarck in 1870? Could France have resumed the old colonial rivalry with Great Britain after 1870 and carved out a new empire in the overseas world? Could it have seriously considered vying with Vienna and Berlin, now closely allied, for preeminence in western and central Europe in the early years of the twentieth century? And could it have endeavored, with the usual Gallic flair and pride, to parlay its geographic situation and its nuclear *force de frappe* into a semiautonomous role of mediation between the American and Great Russian empires in the years after 1945? Anti-Marxian revisionist scholars may remind us, and properly so, that the

16 Citations from Hunt, *Politics, Culture, and Class*, pp. 236 and 224.

Revolution in some ways retarded economic modernization in France, thus setting certain limits on the country's ability to project power beyond its borders. Yet capitalism in all of its multifarious forms did eventually take root in France; and, in any case, the ability of the French to reassert themselves in international affairs after 1815, to reassume at least part of their keystone geostrategic role of the 1648–1815 era, speaks for itself.

On the other hand, the French state has in postrevolutionary times been obliged, as it was during the 1790s, to link its strategic ambitions with the sociopolitical expectations of its own citizenry; and, as warfare has become more total and thus more dependent on cooperation between state and society, and as a humanitarian welfare state ethos has by slow stages emerged in the west, the ordinary French citizens' requirements and rights have gained an increasing recognition from their government. To this extent, Lynn Hunt, and all others who accentuate the durability of the democratic-republican legacy of the Revolution, are right on the mark. A second Bonapartist emperor ruled for a time in the nineteenth century, and a far uglier species of authoritarianism briefly prevailed in France during the bleak days of the occupation in World War II; but a republicanism increasingly leavened with governmental concern for the public weal has, despite all of its vicissitudes, rooted itself tenaciously in this country's political soil and has triumphed to the present day.

Such conclusions regarding the postrevolutionary and post-Napoleonic experience in France are consistent with our explanation as to why revolution came to this land in the first place, and ultimately derive, as does our overall analysis, from what we have defined on these pages as a global-historical perspective. In keeping with that perspective, we should probably complete our inquiry by situating the French Revolution as a whole in the broadest possible comparative historical context. We may discover that, by doing so, we can also achieve a tentative insight into the pro-democracy movements that have been appearing in recent years in areas ranging from eastern Europe to China.

To begin with, we can view the Revolution of 1789 as having been, in the most fundamental sense, a "transitional upheaval." The transition referred to here was one from revolutions, such as those in mid-seventeenth-century England and eighteenth-century British North America, which took place in insular societies under minimal pressure from the outside world, to revolutions of the twentieth century, such as those in Russia and China, which have occurred in societies under severe exogenous pressures. The cataclysm in France may have differed from both of the earlier revolutions in some of its domestic aspects – indeed we pointed this up before with specific regard to the English Revolution – but it differed from them most strikingly in its geographic and geopolitical aspects. True, we noted earlier that international credibility was far from being a negligible concern for Charles I in 1640. Still, the French in 1789, unlike their revolutionary forerunners, were striving to live up to a very old tradition of supremacy or at least "greatness" in the chief geostrategic theaters of the world; and they were essaying this in the teeth of the armed opposition of much of Europe. Is it at all surprising, in light of these realities, that the Terror of 1793–94 had no real equivalent in either of the earlier revolutions? On the other hand, the upheaval in France was less brutal and involved less thoroughgoing sociopolitical change than either the Russian or the Chinese Revolution. This was so primarily because the Russians and Chinese in the first half of the twentieth century faced, in Germany and Japan, respectively, greater external threats to their existence than the French confronted in the 1780s and 1790s, and did so, in part, because of greater relative technological backwardness than the French had to overcome in the late eighteenth century.

And so the winds of change that gusted across the French landscape during 1789–99 were pivotal in what we might call the world history of revolution. Although the cataclysm in France has sometimes been viewed as the last and most profound of the liberal or presocialist revolutions of the early modern west, it also looked forward to the socialist or communist upheavals of the twentieth century. The imperative driving the French toward sociopolitical modernization was, for sure, not so much a dire threat to Gallic existence from one or several expansionist and vastly more advanced rival powers as it was a vision, "imposed from within," of continuing Gallic greatness in the competitive world at large; but it was an imperative nonetheless. Moreover, once the Revolution in France had gotten under way, it launched a challenge to the monarchical-feudal world of its time comparable in many ways to the challenge hurled later at the liberal-capitalist world by the revolutions in Russia and China. And, like those upheavals, and others that have taken place in this century on a less vast scale, it survived despite the violent efforts of its enemies to destroy it.

The analysis that we have developed in this study, suggesting as it has certain parallels between the French Revolution and upheavals in other times, may also serve as an explanatory key to the pro-democracy movements of the past few years in the socialist countries of Eurasia. Here it is necessary to distinguish explicitly between countries, such as Russia and China, in which revolution has resulted "naturally" from a classic convergence of international and indigenous forces, and countries, such as those in eastern Europe and what used to be Soviet central Asia, for which revolution has most genuinely (and, of course, much more recently) meant the overthrow of Soviet-imposed communism.

It is arguable that even in the cases of Russia and China (as in the earlier classic cases of England and France), revolutionary parties have remained or are likely to remain in power only so long as they have subserved or are likely to subserve with demonstrable success permanent statist and societal purposes that are ultimately independent of revolutionary ideologies as such. More specifically, those parties have helped to rationalize the concerned states' administrative and fiscal procedures, establish a closer identity between statist purposes and the aspirations of ordinary citizens, and restore thereby the international standing of the states involved.

Thus, the mid-seventeenth-century English state first used and then jettisoned its Puritans; the French state at the end of the eighteenth century first turned to its purposes and then discarded its Jacobins; the Great Russian state today has, at least tentatively, resolved to dispense with its Bolsheviks, seventy years and more after their dramatic elevation to power; and there are even premonitory signs that the historic Chinese state, with the passing of another political generation, will subject its Maoists to the same unceremonious treatment. In the latter two situations, the same changeless and interlocking needs for state competitiveness and state-sponsored social justice that earlier legitimized, respectively, Leninist-Stalinist and Maoist parties, may definitively push those parties aside. If this happens, it will be because those unalterable needs will require the emergence of new leaders, less ideologically inclined and more pragmatic than the old, for whom a more competitive mix of participatory politics and partially socialistic, partially free-market economics will seem to be the key to the future.

As intimated earlier, the initial stages of this process (at least as they concern the former Soviet Union) have been attended by the "revolutions" in eastern Europe and central Asia whereby the peoples of those regions have regained their political autonomy (or, in the special case of East Germany, their membership in a larger fatherland). We are painfully aware today that this has not been an unalloyed blessing: indeed, the so-called end of the Cold War has conjured up old nightmares of German hegemonism and intractable nationalistic, ethnic, and religious hatreds. Yet few of us, it is probably safe to say, would wish to relinquish the new travails and uncertainties in order to return to the potentially catastrophic and ruinously expensive nuclear stalemate of yesterday.

These observations logically take us back to the philosophical question we raised at the start of our inquiry: whether human beings can make their own revolutions, or whether it is bureaucratic states, activated by statist concerns, that make socially ameliorative upheavals possible. Having reexamined the roots of revolution in France, and having noted the parallels between that cataclysm and revolutions in certain other countries, we have to reaffirm our first response to this question – but, in doing so, we can also offer comfort to protagonists on both sides of the issue. It remains as indisputable as ever that in France, as later in countries such as Russia and China, the humiliating failure of the state to remain competitive was the key that unlocked the door to revolutionary betterment of the human condition. Thus, ordinary subjects of such states have never been able, like Beethoven, to "seize Fate by the throat," to engage and alter their own destinies. They have had to wait on developments in the secretive cabinets of power. This having been said, however, it is also true by the same token that states wishing to remain competitive – and sooner or later all states do – have had willy-nilly to reach out to their own people, to acknowledge their abilities and their grievances and their dreams, so as to be able to assimilate their energies to the sinews of governance.

Has this been an especially difficult, vicissitudinous process in countries like Russia and China? Undoubtedly so, as the worst excesses under Stalin and Mao and their successors pointedly remind us. Yet let us not forget that, even in the earlier and somewhat less brutal cases of England and France, the despotic tendencies of Charles II and James II, of the Bonapartes and three postrevolutionary Gallic kings, and the revolutionary aftershocks of 1688, 1830, 1848, and 1871 intervened between those countries' initial revolutions and their emergence on the highroad of stable, participatory, and humane governance. In light of all this, and for all the reasons adduced earlier, the men and women who continue to hazard and sometimes sacrifice their lives for revolutionary causes that all human beings can understand and love are likely always to have history on their side.

Suggestions for further reading

Over the past seven years I have had to consult an enormous number of works in constructing this reinterpretation of the French Revolution's genesis. My intention in this bibliographical essay is to point the interested reader toward some of the classic studies in the field as well as some of the most important scholarship of recent years. I have divided the essay into the following six sections: Revolutionary Historiography and Theory; Diplomatic and Military History; Administration, Finance, and Politics; Social History; Ideas and Ideologies; and Economic and Demographic History. Naturally, these are not hard and fast categories; consequently, the reader not locating a particular source under one rubric may find it discussed under a related heading. Additional sources appear in the footnotes.

REVOLUTIONARY HISTORIOGRAPHY AND THEORY

The reader might find it helpful first of all to peruse a number of general interpretations of the Revolution and its origins. Of lasting significance among nineteenth-century works is Alexis de Tocqueville, *The Old Regime and the French Revolution*, trans. Stuart Gilbert (New York: Doubleday, 1955). The classic Marxian or neo-Marxian rendering of the Revolution's causation remains Georges Lefebvre, *The Coming of the French Revolution*, trans. R. R. Palmer (Princeton, N.J.: Princeton University Press, 1947). Alfred Cobban initiated the revisionist assault on the long-regnant socioeconomic paradigm with, among other efforts, *The Social Interpretation of the French Revolution* (Cambridge: Cambridge University Press, 1964). Two books that in subsequent years have placed a notable stress on geopolitical antecedents to the Revolution are C. B. A. Behrens, *The Ancien Régime* (London: Harcourt, Brace & World, 1967); and Theda Skocpol, *States and Social Revolutions: A Comparative Analysis of France, Russia, and China* (Cambridge: Cambridge University

248

Press, 1979). William Doyle has emphasized domestic politics and deemphasized social and economic causation in *Origins of the French Revolution*, 2nd ed. (Oxford: Oxford University Press, 1988), and in *The Oxford History of the French Revolution* (Oxford: Clarendon, 1989). The recent scholarly accentuation of political culture in old regime and revolutionary France is reflected provocatively in François Furet, *Interpreting the French Revolution*, trans. Elborg Forster (Cambridge: Cambridge University Press, 1981); and Lynn A. Hunt, *Politics, Culture, and Class in the French Revolution* (Berkeley: University of California Press, 1984). Three recent surveys of the revolutionary era showing substantial interpretive depth are D. M. G. Sutherland, *France 1789–1815: Revolution and Counterrevolution* (New York: Oxford University Press, 1986); J. F. Bosher, *The French Revolution* (New York: Norton, 1988); and Simon Schama, *Citizens: A Chronicle of the French Revolution* (New York: Knopf, 1989). For a variety of stimulating perspectives upon modernizing aspects of the revolutionary process in France, consult Ferenc Féher, ed., *The French Revolution and the Birth of Modernity* (Berkeley: University of California Press, 1990).

Historians are wont at times to pass critical judgment on each other's interpretations of historical events. Nowhere has this tendency yielded more fascinating insights than in the debate over the French Revolution's causation. Elizabeth Eisenstein, for instance, faulted aspects of Georges Lefebvre's "class" rendering of the Revolution's origins in "Who Intervened in 1788? A Commentary on *The Coming of the French Revolution*," *American Historical Review* 71 (1965), pp. 77–103. Much more recently, François Furet has anatomized the Marxist paradigm – and has tried to rediscover what Marx himself had to say on the subject – in *Marx and the French Revolution*, trans. Deborah Kan Furet (Chicago: University of Chicago Press, 1988). William H. Sewell, Jr., and Theda Skocpol have clashed over the centrality, or marginality, of ideological causes of revolution. See Sewell, "Ideologies and Social Revolutions: Reflections on the French Case," *Journal of Modern History* 57 (1985), pp. 57–85; and Skocpol, "Cultural Idioms and Political Ideologies in the Revolutionary Reconstruction of State Power: A Rejoinder to Sewell," *ibid.*, pp. 86–96. Thomas E. Kaiser has reassessed scholarly attempts to link the Enlightenment to the Revolution in "This Strange Offspring of *Philosophie*: Recent Historiographical Problems in Relating the Enlightenment to the French Revolution," *French Historical Studies* 15 (1988), pp. 549–62. On another key issue for historians of revolution, the etiology of peasant upheaval, see J. Craig Jenkins, "Why Do Peasants Rebel? Structural and Historical Theories of Modern Peasant Rebellions," *American Journal of Sociology* 88 (1982), pp. 487–514. Finally, for a comparative evaluation of the surveys on the revolutionary era by Sutherland,

Bosher, Schama, and Doyle, refer to Jack R. Censer, "Commencing the Third Century of Debate," *American Historical Review* 94 (1989), pp. 1309–25.

DIPLOMATIC AND MILITARY HISTORY

There are a host of general works on the evolution of international affairs in seventeenth- and eighteenth-century Europe. Among the most useful are the following: M. S. Anderson, *Europe in the Eighteenth Century 1713–1783* (New York: Holt, Rinehart & Winston, 1961); Jeremy Black, *The Rise of the European Powers 1679–1793* (London: Arnold, 1990); Ludwig Dehio, *The Precarious Balance: Four Centuries of the European Power Struggle*, trans. Charles Fullman (New York: Knopf, 1982); Paul Kennedy, *The Rise and Fall of the Great Powers: Economic Change and Military Conflict from 1500 to 2000* (New York: Random House, 1987); Derek McKay and H. M. Scott, *The Rise of the Great Powers 1648–1815* (London: Longman, 1983); and Albert Sorel, *Europe and the French Revolution: The Political Traditions of the Old Regime*, trans. Alfred Cobban and J. W. Hunt (Garden City, N.Y.: Doubleday, 1971).

Prior to concentrating on themes in French diplomatic and military history, the reader might wish to get a sense of how international and domestic affairs interacted in the other Great Powers of the era. Particularly valuable regarding Great Britain is John Brewer, *The Sinews of Power: War, Money and the English State, 1688–1783* (Cambridge, Mass.: Harvard University Press, 1990). For Prussia, the best work in English may very well still be Hans Rosenberg, *Bureaucracy, Autocracy, and Aristocracy: The Prussian Experience, 1660–1815* (Cambridge, Mass.: Harvard University Press, 1958). On Russia, the reader should consult the complex but ultimately rewarding book by Paul Dukes, *The Making of Russian Absolutism 1613–1801*, 2nd ed. (London: Longman, 1990). Although it may not quite fit the bill in this respect, Karl A. Roider, Jr.'s, study, *Austria's Eastern Question 1700–1790* (Princeton, N.J.: Princeton University Press, 1982), offers much of interest.

Among solid monographs on specific aspects of the diplomacy of eighteenth-century France, the following stand out: Rohan Butler, *Choiseul: Father and Son* (Oxford: Clarendon, 1980); Jonathan R. Dull, *The French Navy and American Independence: A Study of Arms and Diplomacy, 1774–1787* (Princeton, N.J.: Princeton University Press, 1975); Thadd Hall, *France and the Eighteenth-Century Corsican Question* (New York: New York University Press, 1971); Orville T. Murphy, *Charles Gravier, Comte de Vergennes: French Diplomacy in the Age of Revolution, 1719–1787* (Albany: State University of New York Press, 1982); and Arthur

M. Wilson, *French Foreign Policy During the Administration of Cardinal Fleury, 1726–1743* (Cambridge, Mass.: Harvard University Press, 1936).

This field, like all others in French history, has yielded important essays in scholarly revisionism. Ragnhild Hatton, for example, has reassessed the literature on Louis XIV's foreign policy in "Louis XIV et l'Europe, éléments d'une révision historiographique," *XVIIe Siècle* 123 (1979), pp. 109–35. Jeremy Black has performed a like service for students of Cardinal Fleury in "French Foreign Policy in the Age of Fleury Reassessed," *English Historical Review* 103 (1988), pp. 359–84. Aspects of Choiseul's diplomacy are carefully reconsidered in H. M. Scott, "The Importance of Bourbon Naval Reconstruction to the Strategy of Choiseul After the Seven Years' War," *International History Review* 1 (1979), pp. 17–35. Robert Rhodes Crout has reappraised Louis XVI and Vergennes in "In Search of a 'Just and Lasting Peace': The Treaty of 1783, Louis XVI, Vergennes, and the Regeneration of the Realm," ibid. 5 (1983), pp. 364–98. As a final example in this vein, readers may want to peruse T. C. W. Blanning, *The Origins of the French Revolutionary Wars* (London: Longman, 1986).

War, of course, has ever been the handmaiden of diplomacy; thus it is only a short step from a citation of works in diplomatic history to a cursory mention of studies dealing with the armed forces of ancien régime France. The historiography on the French army in this period is, predictably, immense. The reader will especially want to refer to the following: Jean-Paul Bertaud, *The Army of the French Revolution: From Citizen-Soldiers to Instrument of Power*, trans. Robert R. Palmer (Princeton, N.J.: Princeton University Press, 1988); André Corvisier, *L'Armée française de la fin du XVIIe siècle au ministère de Choiseul. Le soldat*, 2 vols. (Paris: Presses Universitaires de France, 1984); Lee Kennett, *The French Armies in the Seven Years' War: A Study in Military Organization and Administration* (Durham, N.C.: Duke University Press, 1967); Emile G. Léonard, *L'Armée et ses problèmes au XVIIIe siècle* (Paris: Plon, 1958); and Samuel F. Scott, *The Response of the Royal Army to the French Revolution* (Oxford: Oxford University Press, 1978). Although the literature upon the French navy is not as voluminous, at least three books require mention: Paul Bamford, *Forests and French Sea Power, 1660–1789* (Toronto: University of Toronto Press, 1956); E. H. Jenkins, *A History of the French Navy* (Annapolis, Md.: Naval Institute Press, 1973); and James Pritchard, *Louis XV's Navy, 1748–1762: A Study of Organization and Administration* (Kingston, Ont.: McGill-Queen's University Press, 1987).

Finally, this study has repeatedly raised the question of the resonance of French geopolitical fortunes in domestic public opinion. The reader especially interested in this subject should consult, among other sources:

Frances Acomb, *Anglophobia in France, 1763–1789* (Durham, N.C.: Duke University Press, 1950); Jacques Godechot, "Nation, Patrie, Nationalisme et Patriotisme en France au XVIIIe siècle," *Annales historiques de la Révolution française* 43 (1971), pp. 481–501; Josephine Grieder, *Anglomania in France, 1740–1789* (Geneva: Droz, 1985); Beatrice Hyslop, *French Nationalism in 1789 According to the General Cahiers* (New York: Octagon, 1968); and R. R. Palmer, "The National Idea in France Before the Revolution," *Journal of the History of Ideas* 1 (1940), pp. 95–111.

ADMINISTRATION, FINANCE, AND POLITICS

There is a rich literature on the development of absolutist institutions in the old regime. An excellent overview of the subject is furnished by Pierre Goubert, *L'Ancien Régime*, 2 vols. (Paris: Colin, 1969–73). Michel Antoine has studied the process of state building from the perspective of the king's Council in *Le Conseil du Roi sous le règne de Louis XV* (Geneva: Droz, 1970). On those crucial avatars of royal authority in provincial France known as the intendants, see Paul Ardascheff, *Les Intendants de province sous Louis XVI*, trans. Louis Jousserandot (Paris: Alcan, 1909); Richard Bonney, *Political Change in France Under Richelieu and Mazarin 1624–1661* (Oxford: Oxford University Press, 1978); Maurice Bordes, *L'Administration provinçiale et municipale en France au XVIIIe siècle* (Paris: Société d'Edition d'Enseignement Supérieur, 1972); and Vivian R. Gruder, *The Royal Provincial Intendants: A Governing Elite in Eighteenth-Century France* (Ithaca, N.Y.: Cornell University Press, 1968). For the story of municipal developments in this era, consult Bordes, "La Réforme municipale du contrôleur-général Laverdy et son application dans certaines provinces," *Revue d'histoire moderne et contemporaine* 12 (1965), pp. 241–70; and Nora Temple, "The Control and Exploitation of French Towns During the Ancien Régime," *History* 51 (1966), pp. 16–34. Of course the difficulties of forging absolutism loom especially large when one considers the process from a provincial viewpoint. William Beik has demonstrated this cogently in the case of Languedoc: *Absolutism and Society in Seventeenth-Century France: State Power and Provincial Aristocracy in Languedoc* (Cambridge: Cambridge University Press, 1985). Robert Harding has focused on the military governors in *Anatomy of a Power Elite: The Provincial Governors of Early Modern France* (New Haven, Conn.: Yale University Press, 1978). Sharon Kettering has stressed other kinds of challenges to state building on the local level in *Patrons, Brokers, and Clients in Seventeenth-Century France* (New York: Oxford University Press, 1986).

Yet it was perhaps the concept of representative governance associated with Estates General, parlements, and provincial assemblies that over the long run posed the greatest danger to absolutism's writ in France. In this area the reader might start with Elizabeth Adams, *Seventeenth-Century Attitudes Toward the French Estates General*, Ph.D. dissertation, West Virginia University, 1976. For a scholarly disagreement over the Estates of 1614–15 rich in implications for any comprehension of constitutional issues in the ancien régime, see George Rothrock, "The French Crown and the Estates General of 1614," *French Historical Studies* 1 (1960), pp. 295–318; and J. Michael Hayden, *France and the Estates General of 1614* (Cambridge: Cambridge University Press, 1974). J. Russell Major and David Parker also have had some valuable things to say about the Estates General and, more generally, constitutional evolution in Bourbon France. The former's chef d'oeuvre is *Representative Government in Early Modern France* (New Haven, Conn.: Yale University Press, 1980); the latter's major conspectus is *The Making of French Absolutism* (New York: St. Martin's, 1983). The scholarship upon the parlements is very extensive. The reader should see, among other works, A. Lloyd Moote, *The Revolt of the Judges: The Parlement of Paris and the Fronde, 1643–1652* (Princeton, N.J.: Princeton University Press, 1971); Albert N. Hamscher, *The Parlement of Paris After the Fronde, 1653–1673* (Pittsburgh: University of Pittsburgh Press, 1976); Jean Egret, *Louis XV et l'opposition parlementaire, 1715–1774* (Paris: Colin, 1974); William Doyle, "The Parlements of France and the Breakdown of the Old Regime, 1771–1788," *French Historical Studies* 6 (1970), pp. 415–58; and Bailey Stone, *The French Parlements and the Crisis of the Old Regime* (Chapel Hill: University of North Carolina Press, 1986). The ministers' experimentation with provincial assemblies in the late eighteenth century is taken up in several books, most notably Pierre Renouvin, *Les Assemblées provinciales de 1787: Origines, développements, résultats* (Paris: Picard, 1921).

Government finance is another subfield in old regime and revolutionary historiography that, although well represented in older scholarship, has especially come of age in recent years. On the bellwether subject of taxation, the reader should consult (along with the pioneering works of historians like Marcel Marion) two recent articles in particular: C. B. A. Behrens, "Nobles, Privileges, and Taxes in France at the End of the Ancien Régime," *Economic History Review*, 2nd ser., 15 (1963), pp. 451–75; and Peter Mathias and Patrick O'Brien, "Taxation in Britain and France, 1715–1810. A Comparison of the Social and Economic Incidence of Taxes Collected for the Central Governments," *Journal of European Economic History* 5 (1976), pp. 601–50. Julian Dent has discussed the government's developing financial apparatus (and its failings) in the first century of Bourbon absolutism in *Crisis in Finance: Crown, Financiers and Society in Seventeenth-Century France* (New York: St. Martin's, 1973). George T. Matthews has studied the increasingly indispensable Farmers-General of finance in *The Royal General Farms in Eighteenth-Century France* (New York: Columbia University Press, 1958). J. F. Bosher, Jean Egret, and Robert D. Harris have led the way in a reassessment of Jacques Necker's finance ministries that has shed new light on the entire subject of government finance in the twilight of the old regime. Consult, among their many books and articles, Bosher, *French Finances, 1770–1795: From Business to Bureaucracy* (Cambridge: Cambridge University Press, 1970); Egret, *Necker: Ministre de Louis XVI, 1776–1790* (Paris: Champion, 1975); and Harris, *Necker: Reform Statesman of the Ancien Régime* (Berkeley: University of California Press, 1979) and *Necker and the Revolution of 1789* (Lanham, Md.: University Press of America, 1986). Useful if somewhat technical overviews of old regime government finances are provided by Alain Guery, "Les Finances de la monarchie française sous l'ancien régime," *Annales: E.S.C.* 33 (1978), pp. 216–39; and Michel Morineau, "Budgets de l'Etat et gestion des finances royales en France au dix-huitième siècle," *Revue historique* 536 (1980), pp. 289–336. Finally, an intriguing battle has been joined in recent years on the relative wisdom of the war-financing policies of the ministers from the 1750s on. In addition to the works of Bosher, Egret, and Harris already cited, the reader should see James C. Riley, *The Seven Years War and the Old Regime in France: The Economic and Financial Toll* (Princeton, N.J.: Princeton University Press, 1987); Lucien Laugier, *Un Ministère réformateur sous Louis XV: Le Triumvirat* (Paris: La Pensée Universelle, 1975); David R. Weir, "Tontines, Public Finance, and Revolution in France and England, 1688–1789," *Journal of Economic History* 49 (1989), pp. 95–124; and (in the same journal) Eugene N. White, "Was There a Solution to the Ancien Régime's Financial Dilemma?" 49 (1989), pp. 545–68.

Politics, in the modern sense, began to develop, tentatively in the run-up to the Maupeou crisis of 1770–74 and more fully in the prerevolution of 1787–88. On the former subject, see D. C. Hudson, "The Parlementary Crisis of 1763 in France and Its Consequences," *Canadian Journal of History* 7 (1972), pp. 97–117; J. F. Bosher, "The French Crisis of 1770," *History* 57 (1972), pp. 17–30; Hudson, "In Defense of Reform: French Government Propaganda During the Maupeou Crisis," *French Historical Studies* 8 (1973), pp. 51–76; and Durand Echeverria, *The Maupeou Revolution: A Study in the History of Libertarianism, France, 1770–1774* (Baton Rouge: Louisiana State University Press, 1985). The standard treatment of the later crisis remains Jean Egret, *The French Prerevolution, 1787–1788*, trans. Wesley D. Camp (Chicago: University of Chicago Press, 1977). See also, by the same author, *La Révolution des notables:*

Mounier et les monarchiens (Paris: Colin, 1950). Vivian R. Gruder has carefully reappraised Calonne's Assembly of Notables in a number of articles. Most readily accessible are "A Mutation in Elite Political Culture: The French Notables and the Defense of Property and Participation, 1787," *Journal of Modern History* 56 (1984), pp. 598–634, and "Paths to Political Consciousness: The Assembly of Notables of 1787 and the 'Pre-Revolution' in France," *French Historical Studies* 13 (1984), pp. 323–55. Two articles notably informative and provocative on the transition from prerevolution to revolution are Michael P. Fitzsimmons, "Privilege and the Polity in France, 1786–1791," *American Historical Review* 92 (1987), pp. 269–95; and Timothy Tackett, "Nobles and Third Estate in the Revolutionary Dynamic of the National Assembly, 1789–1790," ibid. 94 (1989), pp. 271–301. Finally, readers will find an interesting analysis of the early years of the monarch of this period in Pierrette Girault de Coursac, *L'Education d'un roi. Louis XVI* (Paris: Gallimard, 1972).

SOCIAL HISTORY

Several experts in the field have authored helpful sketches of social-elite evolution during the old regime. They include Marcel Reinhard, "Elite et noblesse dans la seconde moitié du XVIIIème siècle," *Revue d'histoire moderne et contemporaine* 3 (1956), pp. 5–37; Denis Richet, "Autour des origines idéologiques lointaines de la Révolution française: Elites et despotisme," *Annales: E.S.C.* 24 (1969), pp. 1–23; William Doyle, "Was There an Aristocratic Reaction in Pre-revolutionary France?" *Past and Present* 57 (1972), pp. 97–122; Colin Lucas, "Nobles, Bourgeois, and the Origins of the French Revolution," ibid. 60 (1973), pp. 84–126; and Guy Chaussinand-Nogaret, "Aux Origines de la Révolution: Noblesse et Bourgeoisie," *Annales: E.S.C.* 30 (1975), pp. 265–77.

This book has identified venality of office as the cardinal mechanism of social mobility (and of the modernization of elite values) in old regime France. Not surprisingly, literature on the subject has flowered in recent years, supplementing the massive scholarship of Roland Mousnier and several other scholars of his generation. David D. Bien offers a general perspective on the subject in "Offices, Corps, and a System of State Credit: The Uses of Privilege Under the Ancien Régime," in Keith M. Baker, ed., *The French Revolution and the Creation of Modern Political Culture*, vol. 1: *The Political Culture of the Old Regime* (Oxford: Pergamon, 1987), pp. 89–114. So does Ralph E. Giesey in "Rules of Inheritance and Strategies of Mobility in Prerevolutionary France," *American Historical Review* 82 (1977), pp. 271–89, and "State-Building in Early Modern France: The Role of Royal Officialdom," *Journal of Modern History* 55 (1983), pp. 191–207. William Doyle documents the overall appreciation in late eighteenth-century office values in "The Price of Offices in Pre-Revolutionary France," *Historical Journal* 27 (1984), pp. 831–60. How the exercise of (venal) office in the various branches of the government served to promote mobility and the modification of elite values has been the subject of numerous studies. On the king's advisers at Versailles, see J. François Bluche, "The Social Origins of the Secretaries of State Under Louis XIV, 1661–1715," in Ragnhild Hatton, ed., *Louis XIV and Absolutism* (London: Macmillan, 1976), and "L'Origine sociale du personnel ministériel français au XVIIIe siècle," *Bulletin de la Société d'Histoire Moderne* (1957), pp. 9–13. Vivian Gruder's and G. T. Matthews' books on the intendants and Farmers-General, respectively, have already been cited. So has my own conspectus on the parlements in the twilight of the old regime. As for the army, see in particular: David D. Bien, "La Réaction aristocratique avant 1789: L'Example de l'armée," *Annales: E.S.C.* 29 (1974), pp. 23–48, 505–34; and "The Army in the French Enlightenment: Reform, Reaction, and Revolution," *Past and Present* 85 (1979), pp. 68–98. These essays update Emile G. Léonard, "La Question sociale dans l'armée française au XVIIIe siècle," *Annales: E.S.C.* 3 (1948), pp. 135–49. On the telltale case of the *secrétaires du Roi*, Bien's latest offering is "Manufacturing Nobles: The Chancelleries in France to 1789," *Journal of Modern History* 61 (1989), pp. 445–86. Gail Bossenga has concentrated on officeholding in the *bureaux des finances* in *The Politics of Privilege: Old Regime and Revolution in Lille* (Cambridge: Cambridge University Press, 1991).

The reader may also wish to follow the fortunes of *officiers* (and the emergence of a new class of *notabilité* in general) in specific communities of prerevolutionary France. Studies worthy of note in this connection include Adeline Daumard and François Furet, *Structures et relations sociales à Paris au milieu du XVIIIe siècle* (Paris: Colin, 1961); Olwen H. Hufton, *Bayeux in the Late Eighteenth Century* (Oxford: Oxford University Press, 1967); Lynn A. Hunt, *Revolution and Urban Politics in Provincial France: Troyes and Reims, 1786–1790* (Stanford, Calif.: Stanford University Press, 1978); Georges Lefebvre, "Urban Society in the Orléanais in the Late Eighteenth Century," *Past and Present* 19 (1961), pp. 46–75; and Daniel Roche, *Le Siècle des lumières en province: Académies et académiciens provinçiaux, 1680–1789* (Paris: Mouton, 1978).

The reader can also consult a legion of works on specific professions and groups in old regime society. On the pivotal calling of law, for instance, see Philip Dawson, "The *Bourgeoisie de Robe* in 1789," *French Historical Studies* 4 (1964), pp. 1–21; L. R. Berlanstein, *The Barristers of Toulouse in the Eighteenth Century* (Baltimore: Johns Hopkins University Press, 1975); Richard L. Kagan, "Law Students and Legal Careers in Eighteenth-Century France," *Past and Present* 68 (1975), pp. 38–72;

and Robert Forster, *Merchants, Landlords, Magistrates: The Depont Family in Eighteenth-Century France* (Baltimore: Johns Hopkins University Press, 1980). On the increasingly crucial interest group known as *rentiers* (i.e., stockholders), see M. Vovelle and D. Roche, "Bourgeois, Rentiers, and Property Owners: Elements for Defining a Social Category at the End of the Eighteenth Century," in J. Kaplow, ed., *New Perspectives*, pp. 25–46. On the artisanry, see (among a plethora of works) William H. Sewell, Jr., *Work and Revolution in France: The Language of Labor from the Old Regime to 1848* (Cambridge: Cambridge University Press, 1980). And on the peasantry, consult, among the most up-to-date studies, the following: Hilton L. Root, *Peasants and King in Burgundy: Agrarian Foundations of French Absolutism* (Berkeley: University of California Press, 1987); P. M. Jones, *The Peasantry in the French Revolution* (Cambridge: Cambridge University Press, 1988); and John Markoff, "Peasant Grievances and Peasant Insurrection: France in 1789," *Journal of Modern History* 62 (1990), pp. 445–76. The possibilities, in this field as in all others, are obviously endless.

IDEAS AND IDEOLOGIES

Under this rubric, an especially contentious subject today is the emergence of public opinion in the old regime. Keith M. Baker has discussed its importance in the 1750s and beyond: See "Politics and Public Opinion Under the Old Regime," in Jack Censer and Jeremy Popkin, eds., *Press and Politics in Pre-Revolutionary France* (Berkeley: University of California Press, 1987), pp. 204–46. Yet that it clearly had substantial roots in the past is the message of Joseph Klaits, *Printed Propaganda Under Louis XIV. Absolute Monarchy and Public Opinion* (Princeton, N.J.: Princeton University Press, 1976). Refer also to Thomas E. Kaiser: "Rhetoric in the Service of the King: The Abbé Dubos and the Concept of Public Judgment," *Eighteenth-Century Studies* 23 (1989–90), pp. 182–99, and "Money, Despotism, and Public Opinion in Early Eighteenth-Century France: John Law and the Debate on Royal Credit," *Journal of Modern History* 63 (1991), pp. 1–28. Yet there can be little doubt concerning the waxing importance of public opinion as the 1700s wore on. For indications of this, refer to Mona Ozouf, "L'Opinion publique," in Baker, ed., *The Political Culture of the Old Regime*, pp. 419–34; Daniel Gordon, " 'Public Opinion' and the Civilizing Process in France: The Example of Morellet," *Eighteenth-Century Studies* 22 (1989), pp. 302–28; and Sarah Maza, "Le Tribunal de la nation: Les Mémoires judiciaires et l'opinion publique à la fin de l'ancien régime," *Annales: E.S.C.* 42 (1987), pp. 73–90.

Inevitably, however, the Enlightenment – and its putative links with the Revolution – still hold center stage in this subfield of French historiography. The reader will wish to start with Daniel Mornet, *Les Origines intellectuelles de la Révolution française 1715–1787* (Paris: Colin, 1933), but then should go on to Keith M. Baker, "On the Problem of the Ideological Origins of the French Revolution," in Dominick LaCapra and Steven L. Kaplan, eds., *Modern European Intellectual History* (Ithaca, N.Y.: Cornell University Press, 1982), pp. 197–219. Robert Darnton has labored rewardingly to place the Enlightenment in a sociopolitical context and refine our notions of its revolutionary implications for Bourbon France. See, among his works, *The Business of Enlightenment: A Publishing History of the Encyclopédie 1775–1800* (Cambridge, Mass.: Harvard University Press, 1979); *The Literary Underground of the Old Regime* (Cambridge, Mass.: Harvard University Press, 1982); and *The Great Cat Massacre and Other Episodes in French Cultural History* (New York: Vintage, 1985). Jeremy Popkin has faulted Darnton for sorting the philosophes arbitrarily into factions of literary mandarins and penniless Grub Streeters in "Pamphlet Journalism at the End of the Old Regime," *Eighteenth-Century Studies* 22 (1989), pp. 351–67. Roger Barny has tackled the old controversy over Rousseau's degree of subversiveness in *Prélude idéologique à la Révolution française: Le Rousseauisme avant 1789* (Paris: Les Belles Lettres, 1985.) On the unsettling impact of both American and French brands of Enlightenment, see Durand Echeverria, *Mirage in the West: A History of the French Image of American Society to 1815* (Princeton, N.J.: Princeton University Press, 1956); and Patrice Higonnet, *Sister Republics: The Origins of French and American Republicanism* (Cambridge, Mass.: Harvard University Press, 1988). The role of women in the movement is treated in Dena Goodman, "Enlightenment Salons: The Convergence of Female and Philosophic Ambitions," *Eighteenth-Century Studies* 22 (1989), pp. 329–50.

The disputes within the Gallican church, and the possible links between ecclesiological issues and the outbreak of the Revolution, have also received scholarly attention. Consult, for example, Dale Van Kley, *The Jansenists and the Expulsion of the Jesuits from France 1757–1765* (New Haven, Conn.: Yale University Press, 1975); and *The Damiens Affair and the Unraveling of the Ancien Régime, 1750–1770* (Princeton, N.J.: Princeton University Press, 1984). Jeffrey W. Merrick has explored the destabilizing effects of these and other imbroglios in *The Desacralization of the French Monarchy in the Eighteenth Century* (Baton Rouge: Louisiana State University Press, 1990). Eighteenth-century constitutional questions have also been creditably analyzed in earlier works: Elie Carcassonne, *Montesquieu et le problème de la constitution française au XVIIIe siècle* (Paris: Presses Universitaires de France, 1927); and Pierre Grosclaude, *Malesherbes, témoin et interprète de son temps* (Paris: Fischbacher, 1961). On the specific constitutional issues of the prerevolutionary crisis, the reader is directed to Ralph W. Greenlaw, "Pamphlet Literature in France During the Period of the Aristocratic Revolt," *Journal of Modern History* 29 (1957), pp. 349–54; and Kenneth Margerison, "History, Representative Institutions, and Political Rights in the French Pre-Revolution," *French Historical Studies* 15 (1987), pp. 68–98. The *cahiers de doléances* of 1789 are the focal point for George V. Taylor, "Revolutionary and Nonrevolutionary Content in the *Cahiers* of 1789: An Interim Report," *French Historical Studies* 7 (1972), pp. 479–502; and Roger Chartier, "Cultures, Lumières, Doléances: Les Cahiers de 1789," *Revue d'histoire moderne et contemporaine* 28 (1981), pp. 68–93.

ECONOMIC AND DEMOGRAPHIC HISTORY

Here, again, the reader should begin with a perusal of classic surveys and monographs before moving on to more contemporary literature. Marc Bloch stressed the obstacles to economic growth in the old regime. See "La Lutte pour l'individualisme agraire dans la France du XVIIIe siècle," *Annales d'histoire économique et sociale* 11 (1930), pp. 329–81, 511–56; and *French Rural History: An Essay on its Basic Characteristics*, trans. Janet Sondheimer (Berkeley: University of California Press, 1966). C. E. Labrousse, on the other hand, spoke of a long-term upturn followed by a short-term recession in the eighteenth-century French economy. See *Esquisse du mouvement des prix et des revenus en France au XVIIIe siècle*, 2 vols. (Paris: Dalloz, 1933); and *La Crise de l'économie française à la fin de l'Ancien Régime et au début de la Révolution* (Paris: Presses Universitaires de France, 1944). David S. Landes criticized some aspects of Labrousse's scholarship in "The Statistical Study of French Crises," *Journal of Economic History* 10 (1950), pp. 195–211. François Crouzet found some signs of sustained growth in the old regime's economy in "Angleterre et France au XVIIIe siècle: Essai d'analyse comparée de deux croissances économiques," *Annales: E.S.C.* 21 (1966), pp. 254–91. More recently, however, Michel Morineau has reaffirmed Bloch's thesis in *Les Faux-Semblants d'un démarrage économique. Agriculture et démographie en France au XVIIIe siècle* (Paris: Colin, 1971). So has Roger Price in *The Economic Modernisation of France (1730–1880)* (London: Helm, 1975).

A number of historians have pointed up the underlying precariousness of the ancien régime economy. See, for example, Guy Lemarchand, "Economic Crises and Social Atmosphere in Urban Society Under Louis XIV," in Raymond F. Kierstead, ed., *State and Society in Seventeenth-Century France* (New York: New Viewpoints, 1975); Steven Kaplan, *Bread, Politics and Political Economy in the Reign of Louis XV*, 2 vols.

(The Hague: Martinus Nijhoff, 1976); Olwen H. Hufton, "Social Conflict and the Grain Supply in Eighteenth-Century France," *Journal of Interdisciplinary History* 14 (1983), pp. 303–31; and Louise Tilly, "Food Entitlement, Famine, and Conflict," ibid. 14 (1983), pp. 333–49. Yet George Taylor has located some areas of innovation within that traditional economy. See "The Paris Bourse on the Eve of the Revolution, 1781–1789," *American Historical Review* 67 (1962), pp. 951–77, and "Types of Capitalism in Eighteenth-Century France," *English Historical Review* 79 (1964), pp. 478–97. For some very current thoughts on the possible economic causation of the Revolution, see David R. Weir, "Les Crises économiques et les origines de la Révolution française," *Annales: E.S.C.* 46 (1991), pp. 917–47.

Finally, the reader seeking the most updated scholarly assessment of population trends in the ancien régime should consult Jacques Dupâquier, *La Population française aux XVIIe et XVIIIe siècles* (Paris: Presses Universitaires de France, 1979).

Index

261